South Africa & the World Economy
in the 1990s

D1541726

THE EDITORS

Pauline H. Baker is Associate Director of the
Congressional International Program at The Aspen Institute.
Alex Boraine is Executive Director of IDASA.
Warren Krafchik is the Economic Consultant at IDASA.

SOUTH AFRICA
and the
WORLD ECONOMY
in the 1990s

EDITED BY

Pauline H. Baker, Alex Boraine
and Warren Krafchik

DAVID PHILIP: Cape Town and Johannesburg
THE BROOKINGS INSTITUTION: Washington DC
in association with
IDASA *and* The Aspen Institute

First published 1993 in southern Africa by David Philip Publishers (Pty) Ltd, 208 Werdmuller Centre, Claremont 7700, South Africa, and in the rest of the world by The Brookings Institution, 1775 Massachusetts Avenue N.W., Washington DC, United States of America, in association with The Institute for a Democratic Alternative for South Africa and The Aspen Institute.

ISBN 0-86486-258-X (David Philip)

ISBN 0-8157-0775-4 (The Brookings Institution)

Printed in South Africa by The Rustica Press, Old Mill Road, Ndabeni, Cape Town

CIP data for this book is available upon request from the Library of Congress

D2586

Contents

Preface

The first democratic election in South Africa will be a watershed event for the many, both inside and outside the country, who have fought for an end to apartheid. Unfortunately, neither the election nor a new power structure can guarantee political stability if the stumbling blocks of poverty, inequality and violence are not addressed.

The political transition is taking place within an inhospitable economic climate. Economic growth has failed to keep pace with the rate of population increase since 1980. Unemployment has soared and poverty has increased dramatically. According to a recent Development Bank of Southern Africa report (Nkuhlu, 1993), 16,3 million South Africans are living below the Minimum Living Level. This grim story is compounded by the legacy of apartheid's resource maldistribution, which created extreme levels of racial inequality. Unless economic policies which are capable of raising living standards for the majority of the population are urgently agreed to and implemented, unsatisfied popular expectations will threaten the country's nascent democracy.

The frightening scale of violence in South Africa poses a further threat to democracy. According to the Human Rights Commission Annual Report (1992), between 1990 and 1992 political violence was responsible for 8 000 deaths and 14 600 injuries. This violence has manifested itself in, for example, the assassinations of key leaders, community massacres and frequent train and taxi commuter killings. While the causes of the violence are complex, it is clear that violence, poverty and inequality are linked. Socio-economic deprivation and intense competition over scarce resources intensify political rivalry, and deepen racial and ethnic antagonisms.

Recognising the role of economics in the current political process, The Aspen Institute and the Institute for a Democratic Alternative for South Africa (Idasa) convened an international economics conference in South Africa in April 1993. The aim of the conference was to assist discussions across party political lines on some of the country's future economic challenges, with particular emphasis on the international dimension. In an effort to enrich these discussions with comparative economic experiences, the conference brought a group of international economists, policy advisers and practitioners to meet with South African economic policy-makers. The central focus of the deliberations was South Africa's international economic relations in the 1990s. A conscious effort was made to draw on the experiences of countries such as Mexico, Chile, Argentina, South Korea and Malaysia, which faced similar challenges at comparable stages of development. This book is a product of the conference.

Economic debate in South Africa

South Africa is fortunate to have already a rich internal economic debate. At a research level, the Cosatu–Economic Trends Industrial Strategy Research Project has completed extensive micro-level research to arrive at an industrial strategy proposal. The African National Congress, through the Macro-Economic Research Group, is fleshing out its policy guidelines to produce substantive proposals supported by an econometric simulation model. The government, too, has tabled its Normative Economic Model. In addition to these efforts, numerous research projects, including the World Bank–Southern African Labour Development Research Unit poverty project, are upgrading statistical resources and planning capacity in the country.

At a political level, an economic debate has been taking place through a series of economic negotiating forums. These forums operate at national, regional and sub-regional levels, and on specific issues, such as electricity and housing. Their participants comprise a broad swathe of civil society, including business, labour, local township and civic structures, research and development institutions and government. Given the level of inclusivity in these forums, they represent a genuine opportunity to lay the foundations of a binding social contract.

Conference theme

The depth and intensity of economic deliberations in South Africa posed a serious challenge to the conference organisers. The value of the conference would be judged on its ability to complement and extend the debates currently under way; consequently, careful design of the conference would be critical to its success. In order to ensure relevance, impact and diversity of participation, the organisers consulted with a broad spectrum of South African opinion.

The most important recommendation to emerge from these discussions was that the conference should address a well-defined topic that did not replicate existing economic initiatives and that recognised the latest developments in the South African economic debate. The conference theme was therefore narrowed to South Africa's external economic relations, including trade and capital flows and interactions with international trade arrangements and financial institutions.

There were three basic reasons for this focus. First, South Africa is emerging from the economic laager at a time of dramatic global transformation. A thorough grasp of emerging international economic trends and their implications for South Africa and the region is essential for future policy-makers.

Secondly, the rate of economic growth will significantly determine South Africa's capacity to alleviate poverty and promote a more equitable distribution of wealth. Growth, in turn, is linked to export capacity, foreign investment, loans and aid. Each of these important external factors needs to be assessed, particularly in the light of the balance of payments constraints on recent economic growth and falling domestic savings.

Thirdly, there is consensus that South Africa's current economic path will have to be fundamentally restructured. The direction of the restructuring, however, is still a subject of dispute. Not everyone in South Africa accepts that a manufacturing-based outward orientation should form the core of a future economic strategy, or that the country should work together with major international financial institutions. In fact, local experts differ on the correct balance between inward and outward orientation, as well as on the pace and nature of trade liberalisation and promotion necessary to achieve international competitiveness. However, almost everyone accepts the need for equitable development. From this basis, the conference explored an issue which has become an increasingly important component of the debate on a future development path: the role of international economic relations in spurring economic growth.

Conference participants and book contributions

The conference was attended by 92 people, including 21 foreign participants, 47 South African participants and 24 observers. The foreign participants included academics, policy advisers, business people and former government officials with knowledge and experience of African, Asian and Latin American countries. South African participants were drawn from academia, the private sector, trade unions, political parties, the civil service and the Reserve Bank. The observers comprised ambassadors and other embassy officials, local and foreign journalists, and overseas representatives of the private sector and academic institutions.

This book contains a selection of papers presented in the plenary and working groups at the conference, but does not include the rapporteurs' comments. Instead the authors themselves were asked to extend their papers so as to reflect discussions that followed their conference presentations. In addition, we requested a number of the discussants in the working groups to write up their oral presentations to give a flavour of the working groups' deliberations. This accounts for the uneven length and mix of styles of the chapters in this volume. We decided to give preference to the diversity of views, rather than impose a uniformity of presentation, allowing the reader to gain a sense of the depth and breadth of the conference proceedings.

The editors would like to thank everyone who gave their time preparing inputs for the conference. Given the calibre of the local and foreign participants, the conference generated many excellent papers and discussions. Unfortunately space constraints do not allow the inclusion of all the material available. We have tried to present a selection of issues and opinions discussed at the conference. In doing so, we have had to make difficult choices. This is the essence of economics.[1]

The project was a joint venture between The Aspen Institute and the Institute for a Democratic Alternative for South Africa. The conference co-directors were Dr Pauline H. Baker, the Associate Director of the Congressional

International Program at The Aspen Institute, and Dr Alex Boraine, Executive Director of Idasa. The Principal Project Co-ordinator was Warren Krafchik, the economic consultant at Idasa. Charlotte DonVito was Project Co-ordinator at The Aspen Institute. The principal funding for the project was provided by the United States Agency for International Development. Additional support was provided by the Rockefeller Foundation, B.P. Southern Africa, Shell South Africa and Warner Lambert S.A.

Note

1. The following papers were presented at the conference but are not reproduced in this volume due to space constraints. Nelson Mandela (President, African National Congress) – 'Opening Address' (presented at the conference by Trevor Manuel); Johan Jorgen Holst (Foreign Minister, Norway) – 'Global Trends of the 1990s: Lessons from the Past and a Glimpse into the Future'; Siteke Mwale (Mwale Associates, Zambia) – 'What Are the Comparative Roles, Functions and Institutional Capacities of African Regional Organisations?'; Len van Zyl (Chief Executive Officer, South African Foreign Trade Organisation) – 'What Are the Implications for South African Trade Policy of Continued Membership of the GATT?'; Dominic Mulaisho (Governor, Bank of Zambia) – 'What Should South Africa's Relationship Be with African Regional Organisations?'; Gunter Gosmann (Executive Director, Regional Strategies Department, Siemens, Munich) – 'What Are the Implications for Developing Countries, Such as South Africa, of Changing International Patterns of Direct Investment, Including the Globalisation of Multinational Organisations?'; John Robertson (Chief Economist, First Merchant Bank, Zimbabwe) – 'What Policies Will Attract and Maximise Foreign Private Investment for Development?'; John Williamson (Senior Fellow, Institute for International Economics, Washington DC) – 'What Exchange Rate Policies Will Encourage Foreign Investment and Limit Capital Flight?'; Eliana Cardoso (Associate Professor, Fletcher School of Law and Diplomacy, Tufts University) – 'What Are the Prospects and Problems of Using Aid, International Loans and Domestic Capital to Alleviate Domestic Poverty?'; Chris L. Stals (Governor, South African Reserve Bank) – 'What Are the Prospects and Problems of Using Aid, International Loans and Domestic Capital to Alleviate Domestic Poverty?'; Francis Wilson (Director, Southern African Labour Development Research Unit, University of Cape Town) – 'Is South Africa's Goal of Economic Development Compatible with the Goal of Regional Development in Southern Africa?'; Ullrich Heilemann (Director, Reinisch-Westfalian Institute for Economic Research, Germany) – 'What Are the Implications of Competitiveness for the Labour Market in South Africa in the 1990s?'; Marcel Golding (Assistant General Secretary, National Union of Mineworkers) – 'What Are the Implications of Competitiveness for the Labour Market in South Africa in the 1990s?', and F. van Zyl Slabbert, Director of Policy and Planning, Idasa) – 'The Global Significance of a Successful Transition in South Africa'.

Introduction

WARREN KRAFCHIK

The conference on which this book is based is part of the ongoing dialogue within South Africa, and between South Africans and those abroad, on restructuring the South African economy. For this reason it would be presumptuous to attempt a complete summary of the wide-ranging conference discussions or to present a finite conclusion. More important, the contributions in this book document a vigorous debate in process and some of the visible strands of emerging agreement. It is our hope that this project has in some modest way succeeded in enriching these discussions.

The book blends two levels of analysis. One group of chapters focuses on global and regional trends with respect to capital and trade flows and international institutions and arrangements. Flowing through each of these contributions is an assessment of the negative and positive lessons for South Africa of the policy choices in other developing countries. A second group of chapters addresses the emerging policy preferences of South African economic policy-makers with regard to international economic relations. As these contributions are drawn from a variety of the key sectors in South African society, they reflect a range of views in the robust domestic economic debate.

The book is divided into four parts: the global context, issues in competitiveness, international agreements and institutions, and perspectives on regional integration.

In Part One, Robert Lawrence and Paul Krugman construct a scenario of the world economy in the 1990s. Two trends emerge from Lawrence's chapter on the major global and regional patterns of trade and foreign direct investment. The first is a dual trend towards deeper global intra-industry trade and financial integration on the one hand and greater regional trading blocs on the other. A second clear trend is towards a greater volume of world trade and a strong (probably symbiotic) relationship between open trading regimes and economic growth in the most successful economies.

Krugman's chapter on international capital markets focuses on the resurgence of major foreign capital inflows to developing countries in the 1990s. The chapter uses these flows to revisit conventional theories of the debt crisis. It also points to a number of explanatory factors including an improved external environment, symbolic effects of the Brady Plan, greater openness in domestic capital markets, and speculation.

Both Lawrence and Krugman are cautiously optimistic about the external environment facing a future South Africa. Lawrence argues that, despite increasingly fierce competition, developing countries are largely price-takers on world markets. Krugman suggests that South Africa could attract private capital flows as Mexico has done, if it achieves a political settlement before these flows dry up. South Africa, like the rest of the African continent, is presently at the margin of world capital and trade activity. If it wishes to be in a position to take advantage of new opportunities, it is essential that it reformulate those of its domestic, regional and international economic strategies. Subsequent chapters explore the debates surrounding the appropriate policy responses, on the basis of both international experience and the structure of the South African economy.

Part Two focuses on domestic economic policies and international competitiveness. In the opening contribution, Sanjaya Lall asks what will make a developing country, such as South Africa, internationally competitive in the 1990s? His central thesis is that developing country competitiveness is a product of technological capacity or the ability to obtain, implement and use imported technology. In turn, technological capacity is affected by the domestic incentive structure, factor supplies and institutional support.

Lall's approach is informed by an interpretation of East Asian industrialisation that is critical of the view that competitiveness derives from a given set of factor endowments. Instead he argues that competitiveness is created by exposure to international competition, complemented by directed efforts to build technological capacity. On the basis of this understanding he advocates selective and compatible demand and supply interventions to support industries where market imperfections and large externalities would otherwise restrict capacity formation.

The next two contributions further explore the East Asian industrialisation experience by providing an historical perspective on two sets of policy variables. Duck-woo Nam considers the successes and failures of various South Korean export promotion regimes. Daim Zainuddin concentrates, with particular reference to Malaysia, on policies designed to attract and maximise the contribution of foreign direct investment.

Both contributions confirm Lall's emphasis on the role of government in East Asia. The question for South African economic policy is therefore not how big or how small government should be, but rather, what are the conditions for effective government. On this score, both contributions are rich in detail. Together with Lall, however, each contribution cautions against attempts to replicate the East Asian success. The conditions for effective government change over time and from country to country. South Africa in the 1990s is likely to face a more protectionist, less buoyant external environment; its interventions may also be constrained by administrative capabilities and democratic pressures.

These international perspectives are complemented by four South African contributions. The first, co-authored by Avril Joffe, David Kaplan, Raphael Kaplinsky and David Lewis, presents a preliminary synthesis of a large research project into industrial strategy in South Africa. Drawing on case studies in 13 of South Africa's industrial sectors and cross-sectional studies, the chapter outlines an approach for raising productivity growth in South African manufacturing.

The authors' framework is developed within the understanding of competitiveness outlined and used by Lall. Consequently, the chapter focuses on building an industrial capability in South African manufacturing which is compatible with higher productivity activities. The authors stress the importance of promoting technological capabilities, institutional reform and new forms of work organisation, in addition to re-evaluating the incentive structure. In order to achieve productivity growth a combination of organisational reform and the active involvement of labour is required.

This broad overview is followed by an in-depth consideration of two key components of industrial strategy. Paul Hatty offers a review of current measures that comprise trade policy, and outlines a business perspective on a desired future trade regime. Hatty concentrates on some of the incentive and pricing principles which business is likely to support in economic deliberations.

Brian Kahn presents background to recent exchange rate policy, highlighting the conflicting objectives of maintaining a stable real exchange rate which is conducive to exporting, and a stable nominal exchange rate, which acts as an anchor for inflation. He argues for a bias towards a real exchange rate rule while allowing adjustments for real shocks. Chris Stals responds by offering a South African Reserve Bank perspective of recent and future exchange rate policy options.

In Part Three the focus shifts from a discussion of domestic policy variables to a consideration of South Africa's future relations with international trade arrangements and the international financial institutions.

The first two chapters, by Sheila Page and David Hartridge, deal with the current Uruguay Round of the General Agreement on Trade and Tariffs (GATT). Both authors agree that the potential for a settlement is good, and that South African reconstruction will benefit from greater certainty and the rules ensuing from that agreement. Page analyses the likely direction of a settlement in depth and quantifies possible implications for developing countries. Her analysis suggests that middle-to-high-income developing countries with a good product mix stand to benefit most from the settlement. In contrast, the benefits to South Africa will be marginal unless it shifts from its reliance on primary product exports towards manufactured and non-traditional primary exports. Irrespective of the trade direction South Africa's future economic policy-makers decide on, they will face increased pressure to conform to GATT regulations. Against this background, David Hartridge presents an insider's perspective on some of the debates surrounding South Africa's participation in GATT, focusing on the changes that may be required in domestic trade policy.

The next set of four chapters explores the future role of the World Bank and the International Monetary Fund in South Africa. John Williamson offers a broad historical overview of these two institutions, focusing on their changing roles in the world economy. Vishnu Padayachee presents a more critical perspective of this history and discusses the implications for development of the most frequently chosen policy instruments. Both authors, however, agree that, with an informed approach, South African reconstruction stands to benefit from access to the institutions' resources, especially if used as a supplement to domestic savings. Against this background, Peter Fallon presents a detailed review of the types of assistance the World Bank is able to offer, as well as the direction of development it is likely to support in South Africa. The discussion is completed with a review of the preceding contributions, prepared by Leslie Lipschitz of the International Monetary Fund.

Taken together these chapters reflect vigorous debate on issues such as the degree of flexibility inherent in World Bank and International Monetary Fund policy prescriptions. They also point to an emerging consensus. Each of the contributions recognises that South Africa must initiate and plan its own development process and that this development must stimulate an economic growth path that enables substantial redistribution. Within the bounds of macro-economic stability, such a redistributive path may be facilitated by redirection of public expenditure, socio-economic investment, training and employment intensity, and moderately paced liberalisation. This outline forms an encouraging framework within which detailed future discussions between South Africa and the World Bank and the International Monetary Fund may be based.

Part Four homes in on South Africa's regional relationships. The first three short contributions are based on the presentations of discussants at the conference. Robert Davies and Prakash Sethi set the parameters for the discussion. Davies presents a case in favour of regional integration while Sethi argues for selective project-based co-operation. Benno Ndulu provides a regional perspective on these analyses by considering the problems and opportunities for integration associated with current regional structural adjustment programmes. One of the common arguments raised in each of these chapters is that a successful Southern African community must be based on a genuine mutuality of interest, especially between the larger and the smaller members. At present the prospects for integration are complicated by the dominance of South Africa in the region, and by the legacy of inequitable relations.

Laurence Cockcroft assesses the potential for greater regional balance in a future Southern Africa. He argues that as South Africa grows, substantially greater trade and investment opportunities will develop within the region. The problem is that while South Africa is likely to increase its regional dominance of exports in manufactured goods, the counterflow will only come in the longer term, through energy and agricultural markets and through South African investment in regional mining sectors. The question thus becomes: Which regional arrangements will best enable deepening regional co-operation without destroying domestic enterprise in the economies of the neighbouring states? To this end, Gavin Maasdorp presents a critical overview of current regional institutions. He concludes that a two-tier approach is preferable where integration is built, first, on a 'core' consisting of the South African Customs Union and the Common Monetary Area countries, and second, on an expanded membership that takes in the remaining Southern African Development Community countries when they are ready.

The final contribution in the volume is an assessment of the conference highlights presented by Stephen R. Lewis, Jr. Having reviewed the diverse opinion and approaches, Lewis outlines the areas of common ground that emerged at the conference.

Contributors

Laurence Cockcroft Consultant, Oxford International Associates, London.

Robert Davies Professor and Co-Director, Centre for Southern African Studies, University of the Western Cape; Project Leader, Regional Integration Policy, Macro-Economic Research Group.

Peter Fallon Senior Economist, Southern Africa Department, World Bank.

Paul R. Hatty Consultant, Barlow Rand Mineral Resources Limited; Chairperson, Industrial Policy Committee, South African Chamber of Business.

David Hartridge Director, Group of Negotiations on Services Division, General Agreement on Trade and Tariffs.

Avril Joffe Co-Director, Industrial Strategy Project; Lecturer, Department of Sociology, University of Witwatersrand.

Brian Kahn Associate Professor, School of Economics, University of Cape Town; Project Leader, Exchange Rate Policy, Macro-Economic Research Group.

Dave Kaplan Co-Director, Industrial Strategy Project; Director, Development Policy Research Unit, University of Cape Town.

Raphael Kaplinsky Co-Director, Industrial Strategy Project; Fellow, Institute for Development Studies, University of Sussex.

Paul Krugman Professor of Economics, Massachussets Institute of Technology.

Sanjaya Lall Lecturer in Development Economics, Institute of Economics and Statistics, Oxford University.

Robert Z. Lawrence Professor of International Trade and Investment, John F. Kennedy School of Government, Harvard University.

David Lewis Co-Director, Industrial Strategy Project; Deputy-Director, Development Policy Research Unit, University of Cape Town.

Stephen R. Lewis, Jr. President, Carleton College

Leslie Lipschitz Assistant Director, African Department, International Monetary Fund.

Gavin Maasdorp Research Professor and Director, Economic Research Unit, University of Natal, Durban.

Duck-woo Nam Former Prime Minister, Republic of Korea; Chairperson, Korea Foreign Trade Association.

Benno J. Ndulu African Economic Research Consortium, Nairobi.

Vishnu Padayachee Associate Professor, Institute for Social and Economic Research, University of Durban-Westville.

Sheila Page Research Fellow, Overseas Development Institute, London.

S. Prakash Sethi Associate Director, Centre for Management, Baruch College, City University of New York.

Chris L. Stals Governor, South African Reserve Bank.

John Williamson Senior Fellow, Institute for International Economics, Washington DC.

Daim Zainuddin Former Minister of Finance, Malaysia.

Abbreviations

ADB	African Development Bank	MFA	Multi-Fibre Arrangement
ANC	African National Congress	MFN	Most Favoured Nation
ASEAN-4	Association of South-east Asian Nations	MIGA	Multilateral International Guarantee Agency
BLS(N)	Botswana, Lesotho, Swaziland (and Namibia)	MNC	Multinational Corporation
		NAFTA	North American Free Trade Area
CAP	Common Agricultural Policy	NGO	Non-Governmental Organisation
CET	Common External Tariff	NIE	Newly Industrialising Economy
CMA	Common Monetary Area	Numsa	National Union of Metalworkers of South Africa
Comesa	Common Market of Eastern and Southern Africa	OPEC	Organisation of Petroleum Exporting Countries
Cosatu	Congress of South African Trade Unions	PAC	Pan Africanist Congress
CPI	Consumer Price Index	PPI	Producer Price Index
EC	European Community	PTA	Preferential Trade Area for Eastern and Southern African States
ECA	Economic Commission for Africa		
EDI	Economic Development Institute	R&D	Research and Development
EFTA	European Free Trade Association	Sacob	South African Chamber of Business
EMA	Export Marketing Assistance		
ESW	Economic and Sector Work	SACU	Southern African Customs Union
FDI	Foreign Direct Investment	SADC	Southern African Development Community
G7	Group of Seven		
GATT	General Agreement on Trade and Tariffs	SADCC	Southern African Development Co-ordinating Conference
GEIS	General Export Incentive Scheme	SAL	Structural Adjustment Loan
GSP	Generalised System of Preferences	SAP	Structural Adjustment Programme
IBRD	International Bank for Reconstruction and Development	SARB	South African Reserve Bank
		SME	Small- and Medium-Scale Enterprise
IDA	International Development Association	TC	Technological Capabilities
IDC	Industrial Development Corporation	S&T	Science and Technology
		TFP	Total Factor Productivity
IFC	International Finance Corporation	TRIMs	Trade Related Investment Measures
IMF	International Monetary Fund		
ITD	Industrial Technology Development	TRIPs	Trade Related Intellectual Property
JIT	Just in Time	UNCTAD	UN Conference on Trade and Development
LDC	Less Developed Country	UNCTC	UN Centre on Transnational Corporations
LIBOR	London Inter-Bank Offered Rate		

PART ONE
THE GLOBAL FRAMEWORK

Trends in World Trade and Foreign Direct Investment

ROBERT Z. LAWRENCE

Trends in world trade are important for the new South Africa for two reasons: first, as indicators of what might be learned from the experiences of others and second, because South Africa's approach must be viable in the world trading environment of the 1990s. The task of this chapter therefore will be to describe some of these trends so that conclusions for South African trade policy might be drawn.

WORLD TRENDS: GLOBALISATION AND REGIONALISATION

The word most frequently used to describe trends in world trade over the past few decades is globalisation. While the extent of globalisation is sometimes exaggerated, there is no question that the world economy has become increasingly integrated. Before turning to consider the trade performance and policies of four of the world's major regions separately, I will emphasise several developments which have been shared in most regions of the world.

Over the postwar period, world export volumes have consistently grown more rapidly than output (see IMF, 1992:24). The periods in which growth has been most rapid have been those in which trade has expanded the fastest. The nations which have grown most rapidly have been those whose trade has done likewise. Conversely, the economies which have stagnated have had sluggish trade performance. The world's most dynamic economies have thus become rapidly intertwined through the expansion of trade. While there is some dispute over the chain of causation between trade and growth (and undoubtedly the links run in both directions) there is no doubting their association. (For a summary of the evidence see World Bank, 1992a:24.)

Many South Africans acknowledge that trade is important 'because it is necessary to earn foreign exchange'. However, particularly for a country whose productivity levels are far behind those in developed countries, trade (as well as other contacts with the rest of the world) is critically important as a source of know-how. Only by competing in global markets (or with open domestic mar-

Table 1.1. Commodity composition of world trade: exports, 1980–1989 (billions of dollars and percentage)

TOTAL EXPORTS (billions)

Exporting country groups	1980	1989	% change
World	2000.9	3024.1	51,14
World			
Developed market economies	1258.9	2127.7	69,01
Eastern Europe and the USSR	155.20	194.00	25,00

COMMODITY EXPORTS: RAW MATERIALS

Exporting country groups	Food 1980	1989	% change	Agricultural raw materials 1980	1989	% change	Fuels 1980	1989	% change	Ores and metals 1980	1989	% change
World	221.10	289.80	31,07	73.90	103.50	40,05	480.80	292.10	39,25	93.50	118.90	27,17
World	100%	100%		100%	100%		100%	100%		100%	100%	
Developed market economies	64.40	66.30	-0,15	61.20	66.70	8,99	18.30	27.20	48,63	67.50	66.90	-0,88
Eastern Europe and the USSR	4.40	3.80	-13,64	8.80	7.20	-18,18	8.80	17.00	93,18	5.20	5.00	-3,85
Developing countries	31.20	29.90	-4,17	30.00	26.10	-13,00	72.90	55.80	-23,46	27.30	28.10	2,93
Latin America	14.20	12.10	-14,79	4.60	4.70	2,17	9.50	9.60	1,05	10.90	12.20	11,93
Africa	4.60	2.90	-36,96	4.00	2.90	-27,50	14.90	10.50	-29,50	6.00	4.10	31,67
West Asia	1.20	1.40	16,67	1.30	0.50	-61,50	41.50	25.70	-38,07	1.20	1.80	50,00
South and East Asia	8.00	10.10	26,25	17.10	14.40	-15,74	6.30	8.40	33,33	6.40	6.60	3,12
China	2.30	2.70	17,39	2.10	2.80	33,33	0.60	1.50	150,00	1.20	1.60	33,33

COMMODITY EXPORTS: MANUFACTURED GOODS

Exporting country groups	Textiles 1980	1989	% change	Chemicals 1980	1989	% change	Machinery and transport 1980	1989	% change	Metal manufactures 1980	1989	% change	Other manufactures 1980	1989	% change	Total manufacturers 1980	1989	% change
World	96.0	186.9	94,64	140.7	264.3	87,85	513.1	1052.1	105,05	114.1	163.6	43,38	221.1	439.6	96,82	1085.0	2106.5	94,15
World	100%	100%		100%	100%		100%	100%		100%	100%		100%	100%		100%	100%	
Developed market economies	61.30	48.20	-21,37	87.10	84.30	-3,21	85.00	83.20	-2,12	85.70	76.70	-28,33	80.10	74.20	-10,50	82.25	77.85	-5,65
Eastern Europe and the USSR	5.00	2.80	-44,00	5.50	4.50	-18,18	9.00	4.70	-53,33	6.80	6.60	-39,17	5.20	3.40	-34,61	7.19	4.38	-39,08
Developing countries	33.70	49.00	45,40	7.40	11.20	51,35	6.00	12.10	101,67	7.50	16.70	219,27	14.70	22.40	60,00	10.56	17.77	68,28
Latin America	2.20	2.00	-9,09	2.00	2.30	15,00	1.00	1.30	30,00	1.60	4.30	385,30	1.70	2.10	23,53	1.44	1.89	68,75
Africa	1.20	1.60	33,33	0.60	0.90	50,00	0.10	0.10	0,0	0.20	0.60	330,15	0.50	0.40	-20,00	0.35	0.43	22,86
West Asia	1.50	3.00	100,00	1.00	1.10	10,00	0.30	0.20	-33,33	0.40	1.10	294,30	0.60	0.80	33,33	0.57	0.76	33,33
South and East Asia	23.10	34.30	48,48	2.30	5.00	117,39	3.90	9.80	151,28	4.00	8.50	204,89	9.90	16.90	70,70	6.62	12.75	92,60
China	4.80	7.50	56,25	0.80	1.20	50,00	0.10	0.40	300,00	0.60	1.20	186,77	1.20	1.60	33,33	0.88	1.44	63,64

Source: United Nations, *World Economic Survey* 1992:200 (Table A18)

kets) can countries be sure that their products are world class. It is this learning effect which helps explain why so many studies confirm that more open economies appear to grow faster, even after other inputs are taken into account.

Developed countries

Convergence and intra-industry trade

The postwar period has been marked by a convergence of income levels in developed economies. This convergence has in turn reflected a convergence in technological capabilities, capital per worker, education levels, managerial capabilities and institutional practices. The period has also been associated with a dramatic increase in trade between the developed economies. Lower trade barriers, declining transportation costs and improved communications have contributed to this trend. However, the growth of trade among countries becoming increasingly similar is surprising when viewed in terms of the traditional explanations for international trade which stress differences in technology and factor endowments. Increasingly trade between developed countries takes place along horizontal, intra-industry lines with countries simultaneously exporting and importing the same types of products. Firms that develop a product and fill a particular market niche in one country discover markets in other countries in which there are consumers with similar tastes and incomes. As Helpman and Krugman (1985) explain, these trade patterns can be understood once scale economies, product differentiation and tastes for variety are taken into account. The theory also suggests that the potential for intra–industry trade is greatest where the scope for differentiation is greatest, i.e. highly sophisticated manufactured goods such as machinery, pharmaceuticals and instruments. Indeed, as shown in Table 1.1, these are precisely the types of products in which developed country exports have increased most rapidly. Trade in manufactured goods has outpaced trade in primary commodities, and trade in the most sophisticated products has increased even more rapidly. As reported in World Bank (1992a) the share of high-tech products in world manufactured goods trade increased from 21,4% in 1973 to 28,6% in 1988.

Foreign direct investment (FDI)

Associated with the growth in manufactured goods trade has been a rise in FDI (see Table 1.2). Firms selling sophisticated products find that a significant local presence can be a prerequisite for making sales. As they move abroad, other firms providing complementary inputs and services (such as banking, management consulting) often accompany them.

The second half of the 1980s, in particular, was marked by a massive increase in FDI that was initially concentrated in the developed economies. According to the United Nations (UNCTC, 1991:4), between 1983 and 1989 the dollar value of FDI outflows grew at an annual rate of 28,9%, three times as rapidly as the 9,4% pace of world exports and 7,8% rate of world GDP.

FDI has been growing particularly rapidly in services. According to the UN (UNCTC, 1991:15), services represented about a quarter of the total world

Table 1.2. Average inflows of foreign direct investment to developing regions: 1970–79, 1980–85, 1986–90

Host region & economy	1970–79	1980–85	1986–90	1970–79	1980–85	1986–90	1970–79	1980–85	1986–90
	Billions of dollars			Share of all inflows (Percentage)			Annual growth rate (Percentage)		
All countries	22	50	150	100	100	100	16	−1	24
Developing countries	5	13	26	24	25	17	21	4	22
Latin America and the Caribbean	3	6	9	13	12	6	20	−5	17
West Asia	0.3	0.4	0.5	1	1	0.4	–	53	37
East, South, & South-east Asia	1	5	14	6	9	9	16	7	28
Oceania	0.002	0.1	0.1	0.1	0.3	0.1	28	−1	−5
Africa	1	1	3	3	3	2	22	52	6
Other	0.03	0.04	0.05	0.1	0.1	0.03	15	−8	–
Least developed countries	0.1	0.2	0.2	0.5	0.4	0.1	27	−16	116
Ten largest host countries*	1970–79		1980–89	1970–79		1980–90	1970–79		1980–90
	4		13	16		13	23		11

*1970–79 (in order of FDI received): Brazil, Mexico, Malaysia, Nigeria, Singapore, Egypt, Indonesia, Hong Kong, Iran, Uruguay. 1980–90 (in order of FDI received): Singapore, Mexico, Brazil, China, Hong Kong, Malaysia, Egypt, Argentina, Thailand, Taiwan.
Source: United Nations. (1992). *World Investment Report,* pp. 23, 317.

stock of FDI at the beginning of the 1970s and by the late 1980s the share was close to 50%. Some of this rise in services FDI can be understood as complementary to the manufacturing investment. However, there are also independent reasons for the changes. Developments in information technologies have increased global integration in many services sectors that were once isolated. Moreover, in many developed economies, a strong trend toward financial liberalisation, privatisation and deregulation has created investment opportunities in sectors such as banking, communications, utilities and transportation in which investment opportunities for foreigners were once relatively limited. While domestic liberalisation has encouraged services FDI, paradoxically the threat of protection in the US and a 'Fortress Europe' have stimulated increased investment in manufacturing.

The new competition

The combined expansion of intra-industry trade and direct foreign investment has made competition truly global. In many industries a significant production and distribution presence in each of the world's major markets has become an essential ingredient of competitive success.

Research and development have become increasingly complex and costly, and speed in bringing new products to market has become critically important. Firms (even those as large as IBM) have discovered they can no longer generate technology and growth internally. Increasingly, therefore, they look outside for key inputs, technologies and other strategic assets. Since technological capabilities have converged internationally, these activities have become international in scope. Many large firms, particularly in high-technology activities, have formed extensive transnational alliances to develop and market new products. FDI has also been used to acquire additional technological, organisational or marketing assets (Dunning, 1992). This has naturally led to a concentration of investments in the Anglo-Saxon countries in which the market for corporate control is highly developed and such acquisitions are readily made.

Primary commodities

Trade in primary commodities, by contrast with manufactured goods, performed poorly over the 1980s. This reflected developments in both prices and quantities. The decade had begun well for commodity producers. The second OPEC oil price hike of 1979 and the inflationary conditions of the early 1980s boosted raw materials prices. However, disinflation, continued protection in agriculture and slow demand growth for raw materials created a poor environment for commodity trade over the decade. According to GATT (1992) the volume of trade in manufactured goods increased by 74% over the 1980s and prices by 30%; by contrast, the volumes and unit values of agricultural products increased by 20% and 23% respectively. Trade volume in minerals was up just 10% and unit values down 20%.

The World Bank (1992a:10) expects that primary commodity prices will remain sluggish in the first half of the 1990s but show some recovery between 1994 and 2000. In real terms the prices of non-petroleum primary commodities are expected to rise by an annual average of 1,4% between 1994 and 2000. This reflects somewhat faster growth for food (projected at 1,6%), with metals and minerals (1,3%) and timber (1,0% annually) more sluggish. Real petroleum prices are projected to rise more rapidly, averaging 4,6% annually.

Developing countries

Given the increased opportunities for manufacturing trade and the stagnation in primary commodity markets, it is no wonder that developing country trade has become increasingly concentrated in manufactured trade and that the countries with the best performances have been those able to export manufactured products. Over the past 25 years, and especially in the 1980s, manufactured goods trade has become increasingly important for developing countries, particularly those in Asia and Latin America. In 1989, manufactured exports from developing countries accounted for more than half of developing country exports, compared with 27% in 1965.

Since 1965, according to the World Bank (1992a:14), the most dramatic increases in manufacturing share have come in East Asia (34% to 69%), South Asia (36% to 69%) and Latin America (from 7% to 34%). By contrast, in the Middle East and North Africa manufacturing's share increased by 5% to 15%

and in sub-Saharan Africa the export share of manufactured goods barely increased from 14% in 1965 to just 19% in 1989.

Developing countries as a whole received about a fifth of all FDI over the decade. In the first half of the 1980s, according to the United Nations, foreign investment inflows amounted to $13 billion. In the second half this doubled to $26 billion. FDI in developing countries was concentrated in Asia and to some degree Latin America, while inflows to Africa and the least developed countries remain at extremely low levels (see Table 1.2).

These trends in developing country trade and investment are more readily explained along traditional lines. Developing countries have a comparative advantage in labour-intensive products and processes. With the requisite skills and market knowledge, they naturally export labour-intensive finished products. (As indicated in Table 1.1, in 1989 they accounted for about half the world's exports of textiles but only 11,2% and 12,1% of the global exports of chemicals and machinery respectively.)

Traditionally, FDI in developing countries occurred to gain access to raw materials. Later, in countries following protectionist import-substitution policies, it was attracted by the prospects of selling behind trade barriers in a large internal market. In the 1970s, therefore, the developing countries receiving the largest foreign investment flows were Brazil ($1,3 billion annual average inflow), Mexico ($0,6 billion), Malaysia ($0,3), Nigeria ($0,3), Singapore ($0,3) and Egypt ($0,3) (UNCTNC 1992:317). Of these, only Singapore was an open, export-oriented economy. While the motive of an attractive domestic market persists, as developing countries have lowered their trade barriers, investment has increasingly been motivated towards servicing export markets (Wells, 1992). Those able to offer export platforms have become most successful in attracting FDI. Between 1980 and 1990 the list of developing economies receiving the largest annual average inflows of FDI is headed by Singapore ($2,3 billion) followed by Mexico (1,9), Brazil (1,8), China (1,7), Hong Kong (1,1) and Malaysia (1,1). Of these only Brazil has not emphasised export-oriented investment.

Liberalisation

These emerging trade and investment patterns are the response to more liberal and outward-oriented trade and investment policies. At the start of the 1980s, with a few noteworthy Asian exceptions, most developing countries had policies which were biased against exports and aimed at import substitution. However, as I will describe in greater detail below, in the mid-1980s developing nations responded both to success and to failure by moving towards liberalisation and outward orientation. In Asia, success led to external pressures on Taiwan and South Korea to liberalise; elsewhere shifts toward outward orientations were induced by debt problems, poor performance, the Asian example, the encouragement of the IMF and World Bank, and the need to attract new capital in new forms. Liberalisation of foreign investment has spread hand-in-hand with trade. According to the 1992 World Investment Report of the UN, in 1991 for example, of 82 policy changes relating to foreign investment made by 35 coun-

tries, 80 were intended to ease the process. In 70 countries privatisation programmes are offering new opportunities for FDI.

Winners and losers

Despite the shift in policies, it is clear that not all developing countries have
been able to take advantage of these shifting global trends. Between 1980 and
1990, major advances were made in the ranks of the world's top exporting
countries: Hong Kong (up from 24th to 11th), Taiwan (23 to 12), South Korea
(32 to 13), China (31 to 15), Mexico (30 to 21) and Malaysia (40 to 26). By
contrast primary commodity exporters such as Saudi Arabia (from 6 to 19) and
South Africa (16 to 30) moved down in the ranks. On a regional basis, the most
rapid increases in export values occurred in Asia (up 9,5%), Western Europe (up
7%) and North America (up 6%). By contrast the value of trade stagnated in
Eastern and Central Europe and the USSR, and declined in Africa and the
Middle East.

Regionalisation

As countries have turned toward global markets a paradoxical consequence
has been pressures toward increased regional integration. In North America out-
wardly oriented policies by America's 'natural' trading partners, Canada and
Mexico, led them to propose free trade arrangements to secure market access
and lure foreign investment with the prospect of servicing a rich regional
market. Meanwhile, US manufacturing firms were attracted by the possibilities
of escaping restrictions on investment in Canada and rationalising their operations with continental strategies which use the Mexican labour force to competitive advantage. The prospect of a North American Free Trade Area (NAFTA)
has in turn stimulated the nations of Latin America to seek free trade arrangements to compete with Mexico and to reinforce their drives to export and
attract foreign investment.

In Europe, the European Community (EC) initiative to establish a single
market was led by Eurocrats who were motivated by the goals of political union
and stimulating growth. But it was also supported by European firms who
realised that even fairly large domestic markets such as those of Germany, France
and the United Kingdom were inadequate home bases for global competition.

In Asia, likewise, the desire to hold onto global markets has stimulated
regional investment and trade. Japan, South Korea, Taiwan, Singapore and
Hong Kong have all found that the price of success was rising wages and
reduced access to markets in the United States and Europe. To retain foreign
markets, they have relocated production to nations offering cheaper labour,
better access to foreign markets and attractive conditions for production.

The emerging regional arrangements are distinctive because they involve
investment in addition to trade. While liberalisation to permit trade requires the
removal of border barriers, a relatively 'shallow' form of integration, the development of regional production systems requires deeper forms of integration of
national regulatory systems and policies; for example, eliminating differences in
national production and product standards which make regionally integrated

production costly. Investment also requires more credible and secure governance mechanisms than the GATT system has been able to provide.

There is, however, a darker side to the regional arrangements for outsiders. Even if these arrangements do not become fortresses they could harm outsiders. In both the EC and NAFTA, local firms have tried to enhance their competitive advantage by crafting rules which limit extra-regional competitors. These involve not the resurrection of higher tariffs (which are bound by GATT) but the enactment of protectionist rules of origin. There are fears that in Asia the links between firms in closely knit groups will replicate the barriers which have made foreign entry difficult in Japan and South Korea. Similarly there are concerns that Japanese foreign aid will be used to divert trade from its competitors. These regional policies are seen by some observers as heralding the imminent fragmentation of the world economy into blocs (Thurow, 1992). But this interpretation is far too simplistic.

A dramatic overt movement toward closed blocs is unlikely. The reason is straightforward: extra-bloc trade is too important for any of the current or prospective regional arrangements to sacrifice in a closed bloc arrangement. While each of the major players may benefit from regional arrangements, none can afford to ignore its extra-regional relations.

Tables 1.3 to 1.8 provide trade data for five major regions and Japan for selected years from 1973 to 1990. The tables do indicate an intensification in the share of intra-regional trade in the second half of the 1980s in the EC and South-east Asia and a shift toward increased reliance by Latin America on trade with North America over the course of the 1980s. However, it should be stressed that over longer periods there are no clear trends towards increased reliance on intra-regional trade and that increased shares of intra-regional trade do not necessarily indicate increased barriers to extra-regional trade. As Frankel (1991) has shown, for example, the increased share of intra-regional trade within East Asia is readily explained by these nations' relatively faster growth.

The importance of extra-regional trade can also be usefully measured by the ratio of total extra-regional trade exports plus imports to GNP. Extra-regional

Table 1.3. North American exports: in billions of dollars (percentages)

	1973	1980	1985	1988	1990
North America	$34 (34%)	$82 (28%)	$122 (39%)	$153 (35%)	$178 (34%)
Japan	10 (10%)	25 (8%)	27 (9%)	45 (10%)	56 (11%)
European Community	23 (23%)	70 (24%)	54 (17%)	85 (19%)	108 (21%)
EFTA	3 (3%)	9 (3%)	7 (2%)	11 (3%)	14 (3%)
Latin America	11 (11%)	42 (14%)	33 (11%)	47 (11%)	56 (11%)
SE Asia	7 (7%)	26 (9%)	27 (9%)	51 (12%)	60 (11%)
Middle East	3 (3%)	13 (5%)	10 (3%)	12 (3%)	12 (2%)
Africa	2 (2%)	7 (2%)	7 (2%)	7 (2%)	7 (1%)
Rest of world	6 (6%8)	19 (6%)	23 (7%)	26 (6%)	34 (6%)
World	99	293	310	437	525

Table 1.4. European Community exports: in billions of dollars (percentages)

	1973	1980	1985	1988	1990
North America	$20 (9%)	$44 (6%)	$72 (11%)	$96 (9%)	$108 (8%)
Japan	3 (1%)	7 (1%)	8 (1%)	20 (2%)	29 (2%)
European Community	128 (57%)	398 (56%)	352 (54%)	628 (59%)	822 (60%)
EFTA	25 (11%)	74 (11%)	64 (10%)	112 (11%)	139 (10%)
Latin America	7 (3%)	22 (3%)	14 (2%)	20 (2%)	25 (2%)
SE Asia	5 (2%)	19 (3%)	21 (3%)	39 (4%)	52 (4%)
Middle East	6 (3%)	38 (5%)	30 (5%)	31 (3%)	37 (3%)
Africa	10 (5%)	47 (6%)	31 (5%)	34 (3%)	42 (3%)
Rest of world	20 (9%)	55 (8%)	55 (9%)	83 (8%)	105 (8%)
World	224	704	647	1063	1359

Table 1.5. EFTA exports: in billions of dollars (percentages)

	1973	1980	1985	1988	1990
North America	$3 (7%)	$6 (6%)	$11 (11%)	$15 (9%)	$18 (8%)
Japan	.7 (2%)	2 (1%)	2 (2%)	4 (2%)	6 (3%)
European Community	19 (54%)	63 (56%)	58 (54%)	99 (57%)	130 (58%)
EFTA	6 (18%)	16 (15%)	15 (14%)	25 (14%)	30 (13%)
Latin America	1 (3%)	3 (3%)	2 (2%)	3 (2%)	4 (2%)
SE Asia	.8 (2%)	3 (3%)	4 (3%)	7 (4%)	10 (4%)
Middle East	.8 (2%)	5 (4%)	4 (3%)	4 (2%)	5 (2%)
Africa	.7 (2%)	4 (3%)	3 (3%)	3 (2%)	3 (1%)
Rest of world	4 (11%)	10 (9%)	11 (11%)	17 (10%)	19 (8%)
World	36	112	110	177	225

Table 1.6. Latin American exports: in billions of dollars (percentages)

	1973	1980	1985	1988	1990
North America	$11 (37%)	$42 (38%)	$50 (45%)	$55 (45%)	$69 (47%)
Japan	2 (5%)	4 (4%)	5 (4%)	6 (5%)	7 (5%)
European Community	8 (26%)	24 (22%)	21 (19%)	24 (20%)	30 (20%)
EFTA	.8 (3%)	2 (2%)	1 (1%)	2 (2%)	3 (2%)
Latin America	5 (17%)	16 (14%)	16 (13%)	16 (13%)	20 (14%)
SE Asia	.5 (2%)	1 (1%)	3 (2%)	4 (3%)	3 (2%)
Middle East	.3 (1%)	2 (2%)	2 (2%)	2 (1%)	2 (1%)
Africa	.3 (1%)	3 (2%)	3 (3%)	2 (1%)	1 (1%)
Rest of world	2 (7%)	18 (16%)	10 (9%)	11 (9%)	13 (9%)
World	30	112	111	122	148

Table 1.7. South-east Asian exports: in billions of dollars (percentages)

	1973	1980	1985	1988	1990
North America	$8 (24%)	$31 (22%)	$57 (32%)	$91 (29%)	$100 (26%)
Japan	7 (22%)	28 (20%)	30 (17%)	48 (15%)	55 (14%)
European Community	6 (18%)	23 (16%)	21 (12%)	48 (15%)	61 (16%)
EFTA	.4 (1%)	2 (1%)	3 (2%)	6 (2%)	7 (2%)
Latin America	.4 (1%)	4 (3%)	3 (2%)	5 (2%)	7 (2%)
SE Asia	7 (21%)	30 (21%)	38 (21%)	67 (21%)	98 (25%)
Middle East	.7 (2%)	7 (5%)	8 (4%)	10 (3%)	11 (3%)
Africa	.6 (2%)	4 (3%)	4 (2%)	5 (2%)	7 (2%)
Rest of world	2 (6%)	13 (9%)	14 (8%)	33 (11%)	41 (11%0
World	32	142	178	313	387

Table 1.8. Japanese exports: in billions of dollars (percentages)

	1973	1980	1985	1988	1990
North America	$11 (29%)	$34 (26%)	$71 (40%)	$97 (36%)	$98 (34%)
European Community	5 (14%)	19 (14%)	21 (12%)	47 (18%)	54 (19%)
EFTA	1 (3%)	3 (3%)	4 (2%)	9 (3%)	8 (3%)
Latin America	2 (6%)	8 (6%)	5 (3%)	6 (2%)	7 (3%)
SE Asia	9 (24%)	31 (24%)	34 (19%)	67 (25%)	83 (29%)
Middle East	2 (5%)	13 (10%)	11 (6%)	8 (3%)	9 (3%)
Africa	.9 (2%)	5 (4%)	3 (2%)	3 (1%)	3 (1%)
Rest of world	6 (16%)	17 (13%)	28 (16%)	28 (11%)	26 (9%)
World	37	130	177	265	288

Sources: Lawrence and Litan, 1990 (updated)

trade is clearly very significant to North America and to the United States in particular. Since goods output accounts for about 40% of GDP in North America, this share implies that about 25% of sales of goods in North America involve a buyer or a seller from outside the region. Table 1.9 reports these ratios for the major trading regions.

The table illustrates that while Western European extra-regional trade is far smaller than intra-regional trade, measured as a share of GDP, extra-regional trade is actually more important to Europe than to North America. In sum, the importance of extra-regional trade to nations all over the world means that no region is in a position to sever its trade ties with the rest of the world by forming closed blocs.

Even if the regions do not become protectionist, however, there are fears that those who are excluded will become increasingly marginalised. As Katseli (1992) has emphasised, nations outside the thick networks of trade and investment that have been cemented by regional policies and corporate strategies could find it increasingly difficult both to gain market access and to attract foreign investment.

Table 1.9. Regional and extra-regional trade, 1987 (billions of dollars)

	GDP (1987)	Total trade	Regional	Extra-regional	Extra-regional trade as % of total trade	Extra-regional trade as % 1987 GDP
North America	4874.0	816.9	255.6	561.3	68.7	11.5
Latin America	802.0	205.0	28.8	176.2	86.0	22.0
EEC	4308.0	1867.4	1117.2	750.2	40.2	17.4
Western Europe	4923.0	2244.1	1604.2	639.9	28.5	13.0
Eastern Europe	1020.0	494.0	274.4	219.6	44.5	21.5
Africa	384.0	138.7	6.4	132.3	95.4	34.5
Middle East	486.0	165.2	11.4	153.8	93.1	31.6
Asia	3628.0	884.8	398.8	486.0	54.9	13.4

Source: Lawrence and Litan, 1990:275 (Table 8)
Note: GDP figures from GATT *International Trade, 88-89,* vol. II, p.11. Total trade figures from GATT *International Trade, 87-88,* Table AA10.

   GATT total trade figures for Asia are the sum of South and East Asia, Japan and Australia–New Zealand–South Africa minus figures for South Africa as given by the *UN Handbook of International Trade and Development Statistics,* pp.2–3, 119, 131. South Africa then added to Africa.

UNITED STATES

In the 1950s the US dominated the world economy. In 1950 it accounted for almost half the world's output and US living standards were more than twice as high as those in Europe and six times as high as those in Japan. The ingredients in the superior US performance included the most highly educated labour force, the latest management techniques, the most modern and largest capital stock, and a large internal market. The US was the centre of global innovation and its trade was marked by a product cycle in which new products and technologies were initially introduced in the US and later diffused internationally through both trade and direct foreign investment by American firms.

   Under these circumstances US trade policy was heavily influenced by geo-political considerations. America saw a liberal global trading order and the development of its Western allies as the best means of containing Soviet expansion. US policies for most of the postwar period emphasised multilateral approaches to liberalisation. Indeed, America saw itself as a victim of the preferential arrangements which had proved so disastrous in the 1930s. Under US leadership a series of trade rounds held by the GATT brought down trade barriers.

   Significant changes in the world economy, however, have since had dramatic effects on the international economic and trading climate in the US. Perhaps most important, given the central role played by the United States in advocating freer trade, is that in many industries American firms have lost their commanding leads. This was inevitable as technology was diffused internationally. But in addition, in the 1980s, macro-economic forces – a major drop in the US national savings rate (as reflected in the budget deficit) – also played a major role in exacerbating the competitive difficulties of US-based firms. The adoption of Reaganomics, a combination of tight monetary and loose fiscal policy, sent US interest rates and the dollar soaring. The result was large trade deficits in the first half of the 1980s and a wrenching realignment of American industry as many companies found themselves priced out of world markets.

In 1980 the US current account had been balanced. Between 1980 and 1985, however, the volume of imports soared 52% while exports volumes actually fell 8,6%. Although the dollar began to decline in early 1985, the lagged effects of the strong dollar continued to increase the US current account deficit, which peaked in 1987 at $162,3 billion. With the exception of petroleum (in which lower oil prices reduced the deficit from $79,3 to $43 billion) between 1980 and 1987, US trade balances declined in every major product category including agricultural products and industrial supplies (down $36,4 billion), capital goods (down $40,4 billion), autos (down $47,3 billion) and consumer goods (down $52,7 billion). Large swings in the US trade balance occurred with all US trading partners including Europe, Canada, the developing countries and Japan.

By 1987 the dollar had returned to its 1980 levels. Operating with the customary lags of about two to three years, US trade flows responded in the expected fashion (Lawrence 1990, Krugman 1991). By 1990, reflecting the combination of a weaker dollar and a recovery in world growth, the US current account deficit had been cut to about $90 billion dollars. The US recession between 1990 and 1992 further reduced the deficit to about $60 billion in 1992.

While US trade flows in the 1980s were predictable, the surprising development took place in investment flows. Between 1980 and 1985 the stock of foreign investment in the US surged from $108,7 billion to $185 billion. By the end of 1990 it amounted to $465,9 billion.

Direct investment flows frequently reflect skills and know-how. Firms that compete abroad suffer inherent disadvantages. They are less familiar with the environment than domestic firms, and to offset these disadvantages they must have other intangible assets such as superior technology, patents or management abilities. The increase in foreign investment in the United States underscored the technological and managerial prowess achieved by firms in other developed countries. It is striking that foreign investment increased rapidly in the early 1980s – a period in which the dollar was extremely strong. Foreign firms were moving to the US even though it was a comparatively expensive location for production. They were attracted not by the low costs of US production, but instead by the inherent advantages they could enjoy from producing in the rapidly growing US market and to a lesser degree by the fear of losing markets as a result of protectionist actions.

Policy responses

As they came under increasing pressure from the strong dollar, American firms began to call increasingly for 'a level playing field'. They argued that foreign governments provided firms with more aid and protection than the US government.

The Constitution of the United States gives the Congress, and not the President of the United States, the ultimate responsibility for international trade. The result is that while the President may generally be counted on to seek a stance which reflects broad national interest, specific interests have a powerful voice through exerting congressional pressure. It was therefore no surprise that despite its free trade ideology the Reagan administration was forced to respond to these pressures by adopting the most protectionist policies since Herbert Hoover. These included so-called voluntary restraints on imports in industries such as automobiles, steel and machine tools. In addition, US law gives firms and other private sector actors (such as trade unions) private rights of action to bring anti-dumping and countervailing duty against firms who price their products unfairly in the US market. In the first half of the 1980s, these cases proliferated, particularly in response to structural problems in the world steel market.

Since the aftermath of the disastrous Smoot–Hawley tariffs of the 1930s, US administrations have mobilised US export interests with the promise of more open foreign markets to contain protectionist pressures at home (Destler, 1992). In the 1980s this strategy was exploited with a multi-track approach.

The traditional track was the multilateral route. In 1986, at Punta del Este in Uruguay, the US gave its support to a new round of negotiations at the GATT. In particular, the US strongly supported agricultural reform and the extension of GATT disciplines to new areas such as services, trade-related investment measures and intellectual property. However, from the preliminary discussions prior to the negotiations through to the present, the GATT has presented unusually large problems for reaching a conclusion. In response, the administration turned to new approaches in its efforts to open markets for US exports and investment.

The first of these approaches was a series of new regional initiatives. In 1985 the US signed a free trade agreement with Israel; in 1988 it concluded a free trade agreement with Canada; and in 1992 it completed the NAFTA which envisions free trade and investment throughout North America. In addition, President Bush announced an Enterprise for the Americas Initiative in which he invited countries in the western hemisphere either singly or in groups to enter into free trade agreements which would eventually encompass the entire western hemisphere. (The US concluded preliminary trade and investment framework agreements with most countries in Central and South America and the Caribbean.)

The NAFTA agreement has yet to pass Congress, where it faces considerable opposition from those concerned about differences between the US and Mexico in environmental, labour and health and safety standards (Lustig *et al.*, 1992). The NAFTA does, however, enjoy the overwhelming support of US business interests and has been endorsed both by organisations representing large US multinationals such as the Business Roundtable and by those representing small and medium-size firms (the US Chamber of Commerce).

The second approach to open foreign markets has involved aggressive bilateral discussions, backed up by threats of punitive tariffs (see Bhagwati and Patrick, 1990). In September 1985 the administration initiated a series of actions (under Section 301 of the US Trade Act) aimed at foreign countries which were viewed as following unfair practices. The US Congress spurred these efforts in the 1988 Trade Act by passing additional provisions to deal with closed foreign markets – the so-called Super 301 and Special 301 legislation. In 1989, action was taken under the Super 301 statute when Brazil, India and Japan were named priority countries.

A third approach focused specifically on Japan. In the mid-1980s the Market Opening Sector Specific (MOSS) talks aimed at the Japanese market in sectors such as lumber and medical equipment. In the mid-1980s, both countries concluded the Semiconductor Agreement which was aimed at increasing the share of foreign semiconductors sold in Japan. The Structural Impediments Initiative in the late 1980s focused more broadly on barriers to adjustment in both Japan and the United States.

In sum, the position of the United States in the global economic system has gradually shifted from the dominant economy to first among equals. In an era of economic difficulties, in which the collapse of communism has given geopolitical considerations lower priority, trade and investment frictions between the US and its major trading partners, particularly Japan, are likely. US policy in the Clinton administration will continue to follow the multi-track approach. It remains to be seen if these all lead in the same direction.

EUROPE

Since the mid-1970s the European economies have undergone three distinctive phases. First, a period of long stagnation – 'Europessimism' – marked by slow growth and continuously rising unemployment, then 'Europhoria', a period of strong recovery marked by the stimulus of the EC92 programme and the unification of Germany, and currently 'Eurorealism', a period since 1991 in which recession and the overreaching initiative for European Monetary Union have again cast a shadow on Europe's future.

Poor European performance in the first half of the 1980s brought home the realisation that Europe had exhausted the benefits of removing intra-European tariffs when the European Community was formed (Lawrence and Schultze, 1987). In response, the programme to create a single market for goods, services, labour and capital by 1992 – EC92 – was launched. The aim was to achieve deeper integration by eliminating the remaining barriers that impeded the creation of a single market. Among these were domestic policies such as standards, different tax rates, professional qualifications, border controls and other regulations.

The initial impact of the programme was highly successful. Even before it was fully implemented, EC92 provided European business with a stimulus – a change in regime – which required increased investment, both domestic and foreign. Jacquemin and Sapir (1991:166) note that European business restructuring has included a growing concentration on the main product lines, an extension of geographic coverage, and a multiplication of co-operative arrangements, mergers and acquisitions. Similarly, firms owned by Americans, Japanese and residents of neighbouring countries, such as Switzerland and Sweden, increased their stakes and rationalised their production and distribution networks to take advantage of the continental strategies which now became possible. Once firms expected competition would be Europe-wide, and planned their strategies accordingly, their expectations became self-fulfilling.

The EC92 programme was received by the rest of the world with some ambivalence. While Europe's trading partners looked forward to the effects of a more vibrant EC on Europe's demand for non-European products, there were also fears that Europe might become protectionist, a fortress which would divert trade and investment flows from outsiders. Japanese and other Asian exporters without retaliatory capabilities were particularly concerned that Europe might become a rampart facing east.

In addition to this deepening, represented by EC92, Europe also broadened its membership by adding new members from Southern Europe: Greece, Portugal and Spain. Firms from Northern Europe invested heavily, particularly in the Iberian Peninsula, to rationalise production by taking advantage of the opportunities of less expensive wage labour.

The impact of these events on intra-European trade is evident in the data: intra-EC exports as a share of all EC exports increased from less than 40% in 1958 to 55% in 1970. The ratio remained roughly constant until 1985 and then increased to over 60% in 1990 (Sapir, 1992).

This recent, relative intensification of intra-European trade is due mainly to developments in agricultural trade. This reflects not EC92, but rather the impact of the increasingly protectionist Common Agricultural Policy. Indeed, no such recent trend toward an increased share of intra-EC trade is evident in the trade data for processed and manufactured products. The EC countries have become increasingly integrated into both regional *and* global markets. In a sample of nine EC economies, Sapir reports that the share of domestic products in the domestic consumption of manufactured goods declined from 66,7% in 1980 to 56,1% in 1991 with intra-EC imports increasing from 19,1 to 25% of consumption and extra-EC imports rising from 14,2 to 18,9% of consumption. By contrast, in food, drink and tobacco there are trends toward a reduction in the share of extra-EC imports (Sapir, 1992:1499).

What kind of Europe?

Currently European policies reflect several tensions. One lies between those who see a single Europe as providing increased opportunities for the operation of market forces, and those who see a single market as providing an increased opportunity for establishing more cohesive and interventionist social, industrial and agricultural policies. Indeed, support for a single market has come from both European capital and European labour with aims that are sometimes not strictly compatible.

A second important tension lies between those who would seek a more intense deepening that would evolve into something like the United States of Europe, for which the Maastricht treaty represented an important step, and those who would like a more loosely knit arrangement, with greater national autonomy and a more diverse membership. Applications to join the EC have been submitted by Sweden, Finland, Austria, Turkey and Cyprus.

Europe already has an extensive network of special trading arrangements. Indeed, it is sometimes said that only the United States enjoys Most Favoured Nation treatment. Most of Europe's other trading partners enter under preferential arrangements. These include agreements with EFTA, Eastern Europe, Mediterranean, African and Caribbean nations and with other developing countries that enjoy GSP status. A broader Europe, in particular, will offer problems both for developing countries currently enjoying preferential access and for those outside. Europe faces the special challenge of absorbing trade from the East. According to Collins and Rodrik (1991), Eastern Europe and the former Soviet Union will eventually increase their share of world trade from 10% to 23% with an impact that will be felt particularly by Western Europe. Broadening will present new adjustment problems. Eastern European countries' export potential will initially be concentrated in agricultural commodities and labour-intensive products – and thus directly competitive with the products of the developing countries. With such broadening, a new group of insiders from Eastern Europe would join nations from Southern Europe who are unwilling to see their preferential position undermined by foreign competitors.

Thus far, however, Europe has not been particularly forthcoming with market access for the East European nations. In particular, Poland, Hungary and Czechoslovakia have signed association agreements with the EC. These call for free trade by 2000 with the exception of agriculture. The Eastern Europeans are given time to liberalise their markets under these treaties, but are obliged to end most of the protection of their weak industries within five years. They are also expected to change their laws to reflect EC norms. The disappointing feature of the agreements is that they include very restrictive restraints on so-called sensitive products such as textiles, iron, steel, coal and chemicals. They contain provisions on export quotas, safeguards and rules of origin which undermine their capacity to be a true cornerstone of integration between East and West. Although steel duties will be eliminated within five years, for example, the EC expects voluntary export restraint from Hungary. The general principle in these agreements is that the East European nations can freely sell to the EC only those products they are unable to produce. They are, however, severely limited when it comes to products they are likely to produce.

A third important unresolved issue concerns Europe's role in the international trading system. Are the Europeans capable of playing a global leadership role at the same time as they forge either a wider or a deeper Europe? Some point to the delays in reaching an agreement on agricultural trade in the Uruguay Round as symptomatic of the problems of dealing with a Europe which is preoccupied by internal concerns. It should of course come as no surprise that European farmers, particularly those of France, are reluctant to agree to reductions in agricultural subsidies. The striking feature of the European position, however, is the relative absence of European firms which feel sufficiently globally competitive to provide the countervailing political support for freer trade.

PACIFIC ASIA

Japan

Japan presents a major challenge to other industrial economies, particularly in high-technology products in which it has become a world leader. Japan devotes a far larger share of its GNP to civilian research and development and investment than the United States. Japanese educational institutions produce a larger share of technically trained people and Japanese firms have developed a deserved reputation for quality and reliability that is commercially very powerful. Furthermore, the Japanese government continues to guide areas of future development, conceiving visions of the future and selecting and financing national projects to bring about such visions. Inevitably this leads it to focus on areas in which other major industrial economies have also made strong competitive efforts.

Japanese export success was, until the mid-1980s, associated with a much smaller reliance on manufactured imports and foreign investment than is the case in other industrial countries. This low reliance on manufactured imports reflects a high dependence on natural resource imports, as well as a high national savings rate, which entails the need for a trade surplus. But a strong bias toward local products – stemming not from formal tariff barriers but rather from complex networks based on traditional long-term relationships between parts suppliers, manufacturers and distributors, which are extremely difficult for newcomers to penetrate – reinforces Japan's low reliance on manufactured imports (see Lawrence, 1987 and 1991).

While the Japanese economy assumed a relatively small role on the world stage, the difficulties stemming from its relatively closed market were manageable. This, however, is no longer the case. The combination of a large and powerful competitor, large bilateral trade surpluses with the EC and the US, and asymmetrical market access has created major tensions between Japan and other developed nations.

As with many other economies, the patterns of Japanese growth in the first half of the 1980s differed radically from those in the second. In the first half of the decade Japanese growth was led by exports, particularly to the United States. In the second half, however, with the appreciation of the yen, growth was driven by domestic demand. While starting from a relatively low base, Japanese imports of all types increased rapidly. Particularly striking was the growth in the volume of manufactured goods imports.

In addition to rapid import growth, the late 1980s was a period of massive Japanese FDI. Boosted by a soaring stock market and a booming domestic economy, Japanese firms sought to secure their competitive positions through foreign investment flows. These investments reflected a variety of motives, including pure portfolio reasons (in real estate for example), to retain markets in which exporters had established a significant base and were now threatened either by cost changes or by trade protection, and to acquire new technologies. The bulk of these flows were directed towards the United States and the EC, but a significant share was directed to the rest of Asia. Some of the investment in the US and the EC was trade substituting, as Japanese manufacturing firms set up assembly operations in electronics and automobiles and purchased and revamped US steel operations. Japanese production is characterised by just-in-time production techniques which require the close proximity of suppliers and assemblers. As a result, when the major auto producers invested in the US, their component suppliers were soon to follow.

Overall, Japanese imports from developing countries, particularly from Asia, increased rapidly in the late 1980s. In the electronics and machinery categories this trade reflected the imports of products from Japanese foreign affiliates. In the main, however, trade moved into Japan through other channels. Furthermore, the recession in Japan in 1992–3 has brought Japanese import growth to a halt. At the same time, Japanese exports, particularly those to Asia, have remained fairly buoyant. The result has been the re-emergence of large trade and current account surpluses, which could renew friction between Japan and its trading partners in the years to come.

Developing Pacific Asia

After the oil shock of 1973, global economic growth slowed down dramatically. Yet a group of Asian developing countries were able not only to sustain their growth, but to do so in an outward oriented fashion. In an era in which natural resources and primary commodity prices soared it was, paradoxically, these poorly endowed nations in Asia which outperformed the rest. Indeed, it appeared as though the oil shock actually spurred Newly Industrialising Economies (NIEs) like South Korea, Hong Kong, Singapore and Taiwan to emulate Japan.

The traditional view of developing countries was that of price takers who produce primary commodities. Yet the Asian dragons who had reoriented their economies toward export-led growth in the 1960s were able to penetrate foreign markets for basic commodities, particularly steel, consumer electronics and textiles.

Since the mid-1980s the NIEs have shifted in an even more outward direction: Singapore and Hong Kong are among the world's most open economies while South Korea and Taiwan have implemented policies which will reduce their average tariffs to levels quite similar to those in developed economies. In addition, other Asian economies have followed their examples with remarkable success.

Asian economies are extremely diverse in terms of per capita income, size, openness and natural resource endowment. This leads to considerable room for specialisation. Traditionally Japan has specialised in human capital and technology-intensive products; the NIEs (except Singapore) in mainly unskilled labour-intensive products; other Asians (such as Malaysia, the Philippines, Thailand and Indonesia) in natural resource-intensive products.

Over time, however, these patterns have shifted. The traditional interpretation of this dynamic pattern of Asian development is captured by the image of the flying geese with Japan as the lead goose, followed by the NIEs, and then a second group including Thailand, Malaysia, Indonesia and the Philippines. As the flock keeps advancing each goose advances along the technology spectrum.

One key issue is where do all the geese fly to? The pattern was traditionally heavily dependent on exporting to outside the region – in particular to the United States. Indeed, during the first half of the 1980s, the Asian Pacific became increasingly reliant on the US market. As the yen began to strengthen after 1985 the NIEs found even greater opportunities to export to the US. However, exchange rate alignments in Taiwan and South Korea, combined with a re-orientation of Japan away from export-led growth, created tremendous opportunities for the next-tier NIEs. These exchange rate changes, combined with labour shortages that were reinforced by US withdrawal of the NIEs' eligibility for GSP privileges, led firms to seek out new locations for production. Investors from Japan, Taiwan and Hong Kong established operations in lower-wage nations such as Thailand, Malaysia, Indonesia, mainland China and even Vietnam. Indeed, Malaysia, Thailand, Indonesia and the Philippines have actually received more FDI inflows from the NIEs and overseas Chinese than from Japan. A regionally integrated economy emerged as both large and medium-sized firms began to integrate their production regionally. Over the 1980s, therefore, as Table 1.10 drawn from Fukasaku (1992) shows, the NIEs have shifted from unskilled labour towards technology and human capital-intensive products and there is a lessening of reliance on natural resource-based production. The new NIEs have in turn moved into producing labour-intensive manufactured goods.

As resource-intensive countries, the experiences of Malaysia and Indonesia are particularly relevant to South Africa. Oil and commodity booms in the late 1970s and early 1980s led to strong currencies and exchange rates which reduced the competitiveness of the manufacturing sector. In the mid-1980s, however, commodity price declines and debt repayment pressures created external balance problems which induced changes in domestic policies. These included currency depreciations and trade and investment liberalisation aimed at non-traditional exports (manufactured goods). These reforms could not have been better timed since they coincided with the major changes in international competitiveness of Japan and the NIEs. In the mid-1980s, by welcoming foreign investment and redirecting their economies toward exports, they achieved remarkable growth. In the 1990s, growth is targeted to continue at very ambitious rates for Thailand (9% in a five-year plan from 1992 to 1996) and Malaysia (7% until 2020).

The emergence of China as a large goose over this period has been particularly striking. Special zones in the coastal regions have experienced explosive export-led growth. Chinese exports are concentrated in natural resource-based products (coal and oil) and unskilled, labour-intensive products, although increasingly an upgrading toward medium-tech products is also visible. As observed by Fukasaku (1992:21) an important complementarity has occurred with Hong Kong, in which almost 30% of all China's exports are sent to Hong Kong and then re-exported to the rest of the world.

The ASEAN-4 nations aim at a common market by eliminating or reducing tariffs and non-tariff barriers on manufactured goods within 15 years. Tariffs on

Table 1.10. Structure of manufactured exports in Pacific–Asian economies, 1979 and 1988

A. Developed countries	Japan		Australia		New Zealand	
	1979	1988	1979	1988	1979	1988
	(Million $)					
Natural resource-intensive products	2 452	3 899	1 293	3 016	275	661
Unskilled labour-intensive products	10 540	15 486	283	504	176	337
Technology intensive products	35 271	128 907	1 057	1 828	243	670
Human capital-intensive products	50 732	108 665	1 115	1 244	328	641
Above total	98 995	256 957	3 748	6 592	1 022	2 308
	(Percentage)					
Natural resource-intensive products	2	2	34	46	27	29
Unskilled labour-intensive products	11	6	8	8	17	15
Technology-intensive products	38	50	28	28	24	23
Human capital-intensive products	51	42	30	19	32	23
Above total	100	100	100	100	100	100

B. NIEs	Hong Kong		South Korea		Singapore		Taiwan	
	1979	1988	1979	1988	1979	1988	1979	1988
	(Million $)							
Natural resource-intensive prdts	99	253	790	1 205	495	1320	967	2 574
Unskilled labour-intensive prdts	6 954	13 727	6 835	23 343	1 329	3 491	7 027	23 796
Technology intensive prdts	1 103	6 482	2 160	13 443	3 223	17 863	3 534	18 518
Human capital-intensive prdts	2 579	6 214	3 540	18 720	1 533	5 556	2 309	11 003
Above total	10 735	26 676	13 325	56 711	6 580	28 230	13 837	55 891
	(Percentage)							
Natural resource-intensive prdts	1	1	6	2	8	5	7	5
Unskilled labour-intensive prdts	65	51	51	41	20	12	51	43
Technology-intensive prdts	10	24	16	24	49	6:3	26	33
Human capital-intensive prdts	24	23	27	33	23	20	17	20
Above total	100	100	100	100	100	101	100	100

C. Next-tier NIEs	Indonesia		Malaysia		Philippines		Thailand	
	1979	1988	1979	1988	1979	1988	1979	1988
	(Million $)							
Natural resource-intensive prdts	464	3 007	1 303	962	308	547	698	1 004
Unskilled labour-intensive prdts	126	1 807	332	1 617	504	1 014	635	3 950
Technology-intensive prdts	165	378	1 169	5 469	146	883	219	2 482
Human capital-intensive prdts	78	714	207	1 639	124	128	131	1 284
Above total	833	5 906	3 011	9 687	1 082	2 572	1 683	8 720
	(Percentage)							
Natural resource-intensive prdts	56	51	43	10	28	21	41	12
Unskilled labour-intensive prdts	15	31	11	17	47	39	38	45
Technology-intensive prdts	20	6	39	56	13	34	13	28
Human capital-intensive prdts	9	12	7	17	11	5	8	15
Above total	100	100	100	100	100	101	100	100

Note: Exports refer to domestic exports only, except for Singapore where re-exports are included.)
Source: Fukasaku (1992)

many goods are to be reduced to no more than 20% within 5 years and 5% by 2008.

The Asian pattern of regional specialisation could offer an important lesson for Southern Africa. It underscores the immense potential for international specialisation. It is inaccurate to think of trade as involving fully completed products. It is more accurate to appreciate that trade often reflects specialisation along vertical lines, in which particular components and processes are sourced in the most suitable location. Asia demonstrates how these opportunities exist, not simply between developed and developing countries, but even between developing countries. This suggests there may be similar potential between South Africa and its low-wage neighbours.

Australia is another economy with which South Africans often compare their own. Like South Africa, Australia has a long tradition of high domestic protection. However it has a programme of liberalisation which, according to Ross Garnaut (1991), 'will leave international trade and payments less fettered by government intervention than in any OECD country today'. The Australians plan to remove all quantitative restrictions on imports, institute a maximum tariff of 5% by 1996 (with four exceptions) and provide zero tariffs for imports from developing countries. Garnaut ascribes Australia's policy shift to the influence of the region. 'Australia's location in the western Pacific caused it to feel more quickly and more strongly the economic and political impact of the East Asian industrial dynamism' (Garnaut, 1991). This shift also reflects a change in intellectual climate. The intention is to reorient the economy towards exports of services and manufactured goods rather than producing protected manufactured products and exporting natural resource exports. The programme has shown some success, and from a low base exports of manufactured goods have grown rapidly.

. New Zealand embarked on comprehensive economic reforms in 1984. These included elimination of export subsidy schemes, phasing out of import licensing (with exceptions in textiles, clothing and footwear, which have special liberalisation plans), a phased 50% reduction in tariffs between 1986 and 1992, lifting foreign exchange controls and liberalising foreign investment. Having implemented this programme, in 1992 New Zealand announced additional plans for reducing tariffs between 1992 and 1996. Australia and New Zealand have also formed a free trade area, which established free trade in goods in July 1990, five years ahead of schedule.

LATIN AMERICA

The 1980s are known as the lost decade in Latin America. Between 1980 and 1990, according to the World Bank (1992a:12), aggregate real GDP for the continent increased at just 1,6%, a pace insufficient to prevent per capita incomes from declining at an annual rate of −0,5%. Both growth and trade performance over the 1980s have been heavily influenced by adjustment to the debt crisis. The first half of the decade was marked by depression, plummeting imports and sluggish exports; the second by recoveries, in which exports played an important role.

In response to the abrupt reversal of capital flows in the early 1980s, Latin America's trade position shifted from a deficit of $13 billion in 1980 to a $27 billion surplus two years later. This reflected a dramatic cutback in imports because of severe measures, including quantitative restrictions, foreign exchange controls and sharp real devaluations. In the second half of the decade, however, liberalisation has been the order of the day. For the decade as a whole, the volume of Latin American exports increased at an annual rate of 5,5%, which compares favourably with the 5,1% between 1965 and 1980. A noteworthy feature of this performance has been the shift towards manufactured goods, whose share in exports increased from 18% in 1980 to 39% in 1988, and away from mining products, whose share declined from 50% to 28%.

Today, almost all Latin American nations are committed to open or relatively open trading policies. This pervasive shift towards more liberal trade policies throughout the continent is a striking and remarkable change. As late as 1984, most economies in the region had closed and controlled trade regimes. Indeed, the model of state-led industrialisation and import substitution was synonymous with the region. It was Raul Prebish in the 1950s who had laid out the strategy which much of Latin America followed for almost three decades. Moreover, Latin American performance prior to 1980 provided reasonable support for the approach. Latin American growth had accelerated from an annual average of 5,2% between 1953 and 1963 to a rate of 6,4% annually between 1963 and 1973. After the first oil shock, Latin American growth had been sustained at the expense of increased indebtedness. But the combination of a global recession, high real interest rates and plunging commodity prices exposed the vulnerabilities in this approach.

Latin American trade strategies were changed, partly because this was a requirement of the adjustment loans administered by international lending institutions; partly because of the demonstration effect of the successful East Asian countries; and partly because of growing need to attract foreign capital.

Individual countries' policies have varied, but a typical package includes devaluation, relaxation of foreign exchange controls, elimination of import controls, adoption of relatively uniform tariffs and elimination of export controls, taxes and subsidies. Among countries with the most dramatic reforms are Mexico, Bolivia, Chile, Uruguay, Haiti and Venezuela. Within five years, Mexico shifted from a highly protected regime with extensive import controls to maximum tariffs of 20% and import licences applying to only 20% of imports. Bolivia in just one year implemented a complete decontrol of foreign exchange, lifted all import restrictions and imposed a uniform 20% tariff. Chile continued to move in the liberal direction it had begun to follow in the late 1970s and by 1988 its tariffs had been lowered to a maximum of 15%. In 1987, Argentina signed a trade policy Sector Adjustment Loan and reduced import licences and tariffs to an average rate of 15% and a maximum of 24% in 1990.

A series of programmes has moved Brazilian policies towards liberalisation (see Fritsch and Franco, 1991). By 1989 average tariffs were down to 35% compared with 50% two years earlier. In 1990, a new programme designed to reduce both the levels and dispersion of tariffs was introduced and quantitative barriers were replaced by tariffs. In 1992, a new schedule with a maximum of 35% to be enacted in early 1994 and bound in the GATT was introduced. In 1991, as noted by the UN, Colombia, Jamaica, Peru and Venezuela all commenced or accelerated trade reform.

These unilateral liberalisation measures have been accompanied by the assumption of greater obligations at the GATT and by numerous regional free trade initiatives. Sub-regional arrangements are flourishing: these include NAFTA; Mercosur (Argentina, Brazil, Paraguay, Uruguay) which aims at a common market for goods and services by 1994; the Andean Pact (Bolivia, Colombia and Venezuela, with Ecuador and Peru slated to join); the Central American Common Market (Costa Rica, El Salvador, Guatemala, Honduras, Nicaragua and Panama); Caricom; and a free trade area between Chile and Mexico which aims at reducing tariffs to zero by 1998. An important stimulus to these initiatives has been the invitation of the United States, under the Enterprise for the Americas Initiative, to western hemisphere nations, to enter either singly or in groups into free trade agreements with the US.

Will these initiatives reach their objectives? Sceptics point to the chequered history of similar initiatives in Latin America's past. In addition, macro-economic stability in several countries remains a major problem for such arrangements, since trade restraints and foreign exchange controls are often used to deal with balance of payments crises. Nonetheless, there is an important difference between the previous integration programmes which were motivated by the desire to implement planned import-substitution regimes on a regional level and the current initiatives in which integration is a mechanism to reinforce liberalisation programmes.

AFRICA (EXCLUDING SOUTH AFRICA)

As in the case of Latin America and Asia, since the mid-1980s African nations have also been shifting towards more liberal trade regimes. Among the liberalis-ers who have taken some measures to reduce quantitative restrictions including the allocation of foreign exchange are the Ivory Coast, Ghana, Kenya and Zaire.

In general, however, these measures have been less sustained and extensive than elsewhere. For example, the International Monetary Fund (IMF, 1992) selected a group of 36 regionally important developing countries that have embarked on trade reform programmes since 1986. Of these, 12 came from Africa. The IMF then classified their reforms according to their extent. The changes in Africa, while significant, were generally less extensive than those elsewhere. According to the IMF, major reforms in trade were taken in four countries – Gambia, Ghana, Kenya and Zaire. The reforms in the Ivory Coast were 'moderate' and only minor reforms took place in seven of the 12 (Cameroon, Malawi, Morocco, Nigeria, Tanzania, Tunisia and Zambia). By contrast, of the 16 nations from Latin America and Asia seven had major reforms, five moderate and only four reforms that were minor. Indeed, the IMF concludes on the basis of this survey that ' many countries in Africa ... have not yet opened their economies to significant foreign competition; much of the

Table 1.11. African trade in global perspective (billions of dollars)

Total exports	1980	1985	1989	89/90
World	2000.90	1933.40	3024.10	1.51
S Africa	25.68	16.523	22.22	0.87
Other Africa	94.90	59.30	56.10	0.59
Food				
World	221.10	199.20	289.80	1.31
Other Africa	10.17	7.77	8.40	0.83
Share	4.60	3.90	2.90	0.63
Ag. raw material				
World	73.90	61.20	103.50	1.40
Other Africa	2.96	2.39	3.00	1.02
Share	4.00	3.90	2.90	0.73
Fuels				
World	480.80	361.60	292.10	0.61
Other Africa	71.64	41.58	30.67	0.43
Share	14.90	11.50	10.50	0.70
Ores and metals				
World	93.50	70.60	118.90	1.27
Other Africa	5.61	3.32	4.87	0.87
Share	6.00	4.70	4.10	0.68
Primary commodities				
World	869.30	692.60	804.30	0.93
Other Africa	90.38	55.06	46.95	0.52
Share	10.40	7.95	5.84	0.56
Textiles				
World	96.00	103.20	186.90	1.95
Other Africa	1.152	1.3416	2.9904	
Share	1.20	1.30	1.60	1.33
Chemicals				
World	140.70	152.40	264.30	1.88
Other Africa	0.84	1.22	2.38	2.82
Share	0.60	0.80	0.90	1.50
Machinery and transport				
World	513.10	601.10	1052.10	2.05
Other Africa	0.51	0.60	1.05	2.05
Share	0.10	0.10	0.10	1.00
Metal manufactures				
World	114.10	104.80	163.60	1.43
Other Africa	0.23	0.31	0.98	4.30
Share	0.20	0.30	0.60	3.00
Other manufactures				
World	221.10	227.30	439.60	1.99
Other Africa	1.11	0.91	1.76	1.59
Share	0.50	0.40	0.40	0.80
Manufactured goods				
World	1085.00	1188.80	2106.50	1.94
Other Africa	3.84	4.39	9.16	2.38
Share	0.35	0.37	0.43	1.23
Primary commodity share in other Africa exports	95.23	92.85	83.69	
Manufactured goods share in other Africa exports	4.05	7.40	16.33	

Source: UN World Economic Survey 1992
Note: Other Africa excludes South Africa

reform has focused on inputs for production, and they now face the more diffi-cult task of liberalising quantitative restrictions on competing products and reducing very high tariffs' (IMF, 1992:40).

African nations have also tried to establish regional arrangements. In 1991, for example, the OAU signed a treaty establishing the African Economic Com-munity which includes a plan to begin with a stabilisation of tariff and non-tariff barriers, pass through a phase as a free trade area and eventually evolve into a customs union at the continental level 'over a period not exceeding 34 years'. Eastern and Southern African countries have discussed an 18-nation preferential trade area which would evolve into a common market.

Table 1.11 provides some data on the composition and growth of African trade over the 1980s as estimated by the United Nations.

When viewed from an aggregate perspective the picture appears grim. Indeed, between 1980 and 1989 Africa's share in world exports declined from 4,7% to 1,9%. Measured in US dollars, African exports declined from 94,9 to 59,3 billion dollars (about 40%) between 1980 and 1985 and an additional $3,2 billion (4,9%) between 1985 and 1989. This slump was heavily influenced by the fall in fuel prices, although it also reflected Africa's declining shares in exports of all major categories of raw materials. Similarly, as shown in Table 1.12, Africa has not shared in the dramatic growth in foreign investment inflows in the second half of the 1980s.

Annual average inflows to Africa expanded, but the growth was virtually confined to oil exporters, mainly Egypt and Nigeria. As noted by the UN in its 1991 World Investment Report, Africa has been marginalised: 'Despite the increasing openness towards transnational corporations in sub-Saharan Africa, deteriorating business conditions and political instability in many of these coun-tries have contributed to persistently low foreign direct investment.'

The silver lining, however, lies in Africa's manufactured goods export perfor-mance, particularly between 1985 and 1989 when the dollar value of these exports doubled (from $4,4 billion to $9,2 billion), a pace sufficient to raise Africa's global share by 23%, albeit from a minuscule 0,37% to 0,43%. The growth in manufactured goods exports coupled with the poor performance in primary commodities resulted in a rise in African exports accounted for by manufactured goods from 4% in 1980 to 16% in 1989.

In sum, Africa, outside of South Africa, has not participated fully in the global changes. In an era in which trade has depended on manufacturing and is linked to foreign investment, Africa's concentration on primary commodities has left it on the sidelines.

FUTURE POLICY TRENDS: TOWARD DEEPER INTEGRATION

The world economy has become increasingly globalised. Declining transport-ation and communications costs, the international convergence of technological capabilities, and the spread of multinational companies with global reach have all made many countries fairly close locational substitutes. In such an environment,

Table 1.12. African inflows of foreign direct investment in global perspective (billions of dollars)

	80–85 Annual average	1986	1987	1988	1989	1990	86–90 Annual average	80–85
World	49.83	78.28	132.95	158.29	195.15	183.84	149.70	3.00
Developed	37.20	64.10	107.93	128.57	165.40	152.06	123.61	3.32
Developing	12.63	14.18	25.02	29.72	29.76	31.78	26.09	2.07
S Africa	0.08	-0.05	-0.08	0.12	0.01	-0.01	0.00	-0.02
Other Africa of which	1.41	1.73	2.19	2.33	4.45	2.20	2.58	1.83
Oil exporters	1.04	1.54	1.66	1.89	3.67	1.63	2.08	1.99
Other	0.37	0.19	0.52	0.43	0.78	0.56	0.50	1.35

Source: UNCTC: *World Investment Report* 1992, pp. 311–12

relatively small differences in institutional practices and shifts in relative competitiveness can have large effects on international trade and investment flows.

Globalisation has generated at least two quite different policy responses in the trading system. For those whose politics follow logically from underlying economic trends, the answer is to harmonise national differences; if economic trends are leading to integration, then so should institutions and laws. Traditionally, international policies have emphasised 'shallow integration', i.e. the removal of border barriers and elimination of policies which intentionally discriminate against foreign products and firms. However, proponents of deep integration seek to reconcile even those practices which may inadvertently discriminate against outsiders. This, of course, implies a curtailment on national sovereignty.

The alternative response to increasing globalisation is to resist market pressures in efforts to ensure 'equitable results'. This generally involves efforts to manage trade (e.g. through quotas) and investment (e.g. through local content provisions and performance requirements). The prime example at the global level is the extensive system of managed trade in textiles in the Multi-Fibre Arrangement.

But harmonisation or management at the global level is particularly cumbersome. As a result, many of the institutional responses to globalisation have taken place at a sub-global level. In the 1980s, some of these efforts have also aimed at harmonisation, most notably the EC92 initiative and the MOSS (Market Opening Sector Specific) and SII (Structural Impediments Initiative) talks between the United States and Japan. In addition, there has been an increase in initiatives such as the NAFTA and Australia–New Zealand Closer Economic Relations Agreement, which move beyond simply removing trade barriers.

On the other hand, there have also been new, sub-global initiatives aimed at managing trade: in particular, the 'voluntary restraint arrangements' and orderly marketing agreements which have proliferated against Japanese and other Asian exporters, and the arrangements which seek quotas and regulate prices in semiconductor trade.

At the time of writing, the outlook for the Uruguay Round is cloudy. With such uncertainty about the future prospects for the Round, it is difficult, if not hazardous, to project how the world trading system is likely to evolve in the decade ahead. It is likely, however, to involve some combination of four elements: multilateralism, regionalism, managed trade and deeper integration.

Multilateralism

If the Uruguay Round succeeds, it will represent considerable progress towards removing border barriers. Nonetheless, there are reasons to be sceptical that, at least for some significant period of time, the GATT can meet the need for deep integration that globalisation requires. The GATT's scope is simply too confined and its membership too diverse and there will be pressures to deal with integration through other forums and means.

Regionalism

Accordingly, at least in the near term – a decade, if not longer – increased regional integration is inevitable. The critical question, though, is whether the regional arrangements will become 'building blocks' in a more integrated global system or 'stumbling blocks' that cause the system to fragment (Lawrence, 1991). With the noteworthy exception of agriculture, the experience of the EC in general leaves room for optimism: increased European integration was compatible with sustained progress in liberalising extra-EC trade. The extent to which each potential regional bloc continues to rely on extra-regional trade reinforces the conclusion about building blocks: none of the regions can afford to neglect their extra-regional trade links. It is also crucial to recognise the motives for current liberalisation efforts – to enhance market forces and adopt market-oriented policies – are radically different from the motives behind the block arrangements in the 1930s and the regional initiatives in Latin America in the 1960s. Overall, therefore, the regional measures are unlikely to result in trade wars, but they could pose new challenges and introduce or spread more subtle forms of protection based for example on restrictive rules of origin.

Managed trade

Management of trade through quotas and local content rules currently applies to global trade in sectors such as textiles and steel. Invariably, such arrangements grow out of the friction between the United States (or the EC) and Japan and have then diffused globally. Additional sectoral problems could increase the use of managed trade, perhaps leading to efforts to manage aggregate trade flows and balances. Continued trade friction between the United States and Japan increases the likelihood of this outcome. Under these arrangements political forces will dominate outcomes.

Deeper integration

The most ambitious direction for the world trading system would be represented by a movement beyond the GATT toward deeper global harmonisation:

'GATT-plus' or perhaps 'OECD-2000.' Patterned perhaps on the EC92 pro-gramme (excepting provisions for free labour migration) this would entail increased efforts to harmonise global rules and reconcile practices in areas such as competition policy, standards, regulatory practices and technology policies. The industrialised countries might pursue such an option immediately with condi-tional most-favoured-nation treatment accorded to developing countries seeking to join.

Which of these directions will predominate? The answer to this question has become increasingly important to developing countries that are implementing trade-led growth strategies. The success of such policies will depend critically not only on the domestic economic responses but also on a hospitable interna-tional environment. Market access for developing countries will differ depend-ing on which of these elements predominates, and countries will be affected dif-ferently. Regional location and commodity patterns of specialisation play impor-tant roles in affecting access. In particular, one distinction is between those countries falling within a region and those falling outside it. Another is between exporters of primary products and exporters of manufactured goods.

For countries with opportunities to join new regional groupings, market access will become more secure and the ability to attract foreign investment enhanced. For those currently participating in regions, preferences could be eroded. For those outside regions, however, trade and investment diversion could become a threat, particularly if the GATT is weakened or if trade wars break out between the blocs. Even if these arrangements are not closed they will enhance the competitive advantages of their members, and thus weaken the prospects for those who have been excluded. In a world in which competition to attract foreign investment is increasing, nations offering stable environments and a secure access to foreign markets will have important advantages.

A second feature is the pattern of commodity specialisation. Agricultural exporters could be particularly damaged by closed regional arrangements. They clearly have a strong interest in GATT-imposed disciplines on agricultural subsi-dies and protection. Producers of other primary commodities and minerals which are generally not subject to high tariffs are unlikely to be affected by these developments. Producers planning to export manufactured goods, particularly those seeking to attract foreign investment, will be the most heavily impacted.

Under the GATT system of shallow integration, developing countries should in principle enjoy unconditional market access. However, the newly emerging global arrangements increasingly impose conditions for access. Even in the GATT, the codes signed at the Tokyo Round (e.g. government procurement, subsidies, and anti-dumping) were only extended conditionally. Similarly, the new regional arrangements such as the NAFTA and the EC require adherence to developed country norms as a quid pro quo for entry. Managed trade tends increasingly to be used against Asian countries that are different. Anti-dumping and subsidies actions by the US, the EC and even recently Japan are levied against foreign firms that price 'unfairly' or that benefit from government sub-sidies. This shift to deeper integration imposes important constraints on the scope for independent national action.

While the environment for outward-looking policies appears tough, it should not be used as an excuse for inaction. Simply because some foreign markets may be protected, it does not follow that inward-oriented strategies are superior. Developing countries' manufactured goods exports have grown rapidly over the past two decades, despite a decline in global growth and an increase in protectionist actions.

According to the World Bank (1992a), in 1980 all developing country exports of manufactured goods met 2,4% of total consumption in the EC, North America and Japan; by 1988, this had grown to 3,1%. Even if all developing countries had the same growth as South Korea their share would still have amounted to only 3,7%.

It is a useful working hypothesis to assume, therefore, that developing countries are price takers. Ultimately success will depend on the ability to supply rather than the adequacy of demand. Nonetheless, it is clear that competition for export markets and foreign investment has become increasingly tough, and those not favoured by location need to compete even harder if they are to succeed in the current trading environment.

Concluding comments

South Africa has not participated in many of these trends. The 28% share of GDP accounted for by South African exports in 1989 was barely higher than the 26% share in 1965. Similarly, the share accounted for by manufactured goods in total exports has barely increased in an era in which primary commodity prices have on the whole been rather depressed (World Bank, 1992b). South Africa's capacity to attract foreign investment has clearly been negligible. To be sure, this failure can in part be ascribed to political factors. But the poor overall performance of the economy remains an important lesson of the costs of not following a strategy which is suited to global economic trends.

South Africa has many problems, but its most important is probably a lack of skills and know-how. Correcting this problem obviously requires improving the education system. But it also requires upgrading the skills and know-how of South African workers and entrepreneurs who have completed their formal education. The contribution made by trade in supplying foreign exchange and improving resource allocation is often acknowledged. But it is important not to overlook the role of trade and foreign investment as a source of knowledge and skills.

This chapter should end with a warning: trends are made to be changed. Think back to the early 1980s and reflect on the degree to which the patterns of global growth shifted over the course of the decade. In 1980, for example, Latin American nations appeared solid credit risks, having followed policies of state-led investment; primary commodity producers looked like winners with the second oil shock and the explosion in gold prices, the United States economy had a trade surplus while Europe was mired in 'Europessimism'. Developing countries relied increasingly on debt financing. The West continued its struggle with the Soviet Union, which loomed as a formidable adversary. In Asia, the South Korean economy was in trouble, experiencing the unwinding of an excessive strategy of export-led investment. While there are other trends which have been durable (in particular the shift toward global integration), simple extrapolation is bound to be wrong.

2

Changes in Capital Markets for Developing Countries

PAUL KRUGMAN

The big international financial surprise of the 1990s so far has been the re-emergence of large capital flows to developing countries. As recently as 1990 it was conventional wisdom, indeed virtually the unanimous opinion of businessmen and economists alike, that countries which had experienced debt servicing difficulties during the 1980s would not regain large-scale access to voluntary capital inflows for a generation. Instead, capital flows to developing countries have revived on a scale that in some cases is substantially larger than anything seen during the height of the bank lending boom in the late 1970s.

The most spectacular cases are those of Mexico and Argentina, the two countries whose inability to meet debt service in 1982 triggered the debt crisis. Figure 2.1 tells the story.

During the 1980s, the collapse first of voluntary lending and then even of the 'concerted' lending that was supposed to ease the liquidity squeeze forced both Mexico and Argentina into running small current account surpluses and hence large trade surpluses. Over the last three years, however, both nations have received so much voluntary capital inflow that they have been able to run current deficits of as much as 8% of GDP – larger than any deficits in the pre-1982 era – while still adding to their foreign reserves.

The surge in capital flows to developing countries is also notable for its novel form. In the 1970s, such flows primarily took the form of lending either to governments or to enterprises whose borrowing was backed by government guarantee. In effect, the lenders were betting on the stability and trustworthiness of governments rather than trying to make any evaluation of the returns from the particular projects they were backing. Indeed, private investors whose decisions were not shaped by government guarantees, namely the private citizens of the countries involved, were moving their capital the other way: a large fraction of the accumulation of debt in Latin America between 1973 and 1982 effectively financed capital flight rather than current account deficits. The new wave of capital inflows, by contrast, is taking place independently of government borrowing or guarantee. Mexico, in particular, is running a substantial budget surplus even as it runs record external deficits. Correspondingly, the new inflows do not take the form of bank loans. Instead, they are a mix of a limited amount

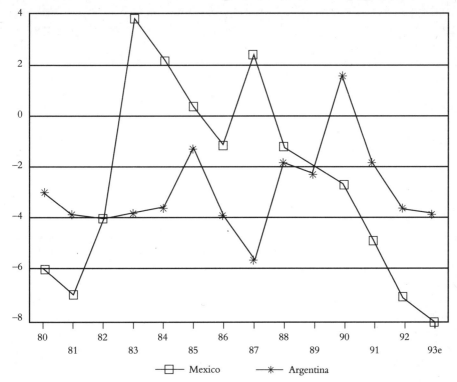

Figure 2.1. Current account balances as a percentage of GDP:
Mexico and Argentina, 1980–1993

of direct investment, a probably somewhat larger flow of money into the 'emerging' stock markets that have become the hottest financial items, and a large amount of bond purchases mediated by high-yield investment houses.

The resurgence of the developing country capital market raises several inter-related questions. First, it raises the question of how to interpret the debt crisis of the 1980s: if the very same countries that were savaged by that crisis now appear to be such good investments, why did the crisis happen in the first place? The answer to that question evidently bears strongly on a second question, which is why capital flows have in fact surged: why, and why now? Finally, there is the question of the sustainability of the current surge: will the optimistic bond buyers of today eventually look as fatuous as the optimistic bankers of the late 1970s?

For South Africa, of course, the pressing questions are not parochial. How can the country get in on the new wave of capital availability? For that matter, should it try to get involved – or would it be better off avoiding what may turn out to be a speculative bubble?

Clearly nobody can answer any of these questions with any certainty (after all, hardly anybody predicted either the onset of the debt crisis or the abrupt rehabilitation of highly indebted countries by capital markets). The purpose of this chapter is instead to offer a review of some of the arguments that bear on the questions, in the hope that by so doing we can at least have a sensible framework for discussion.

The chapter is in four parts. First, a selective review of the history of the capital market for highly indebted developing countries since 1980, focusing on the changing perceptions of market participants and policy-makers. The second part turns to the new wave of capital movement, examining several hypotheses about the reasons for that turnaround in market behaviour. Third, we question the sustainability of the investment surge – in particular, are there risks of a debt crisis repeat? A final section speculates briefly on the opportunities available to countries, like South Africa, that have not shared in the recent capital flow revival.

Making sense of the debt crisis

Although the developing country debt crisis dominated many world financial events during the 1980s, and attracted an astonishing amount of attention from both policy-makers and academics, there is still no consensus about what it was all about. Clearly there were major mistakes and misjudgments – but by whom, about what? At various times the conventional wisdom has held that the crisis was a panic among creditors, unjustified by the fundamental situation of basically solvent countries, or that banks had simply lent far more to the countries than they could repay. A recent, provocative interpretation by Dooley (1993) argues that the crisis is best seen as a prolonged standoff between banks and creditor country governments, with the debtor countries essentially passive victims.

As a way to structure our discussion of this confusing prospect, I will summarise the way that the debt crisis appeared at various points over the past dozen years.

The view in 1981

Whatever anyone may now claim, very few observers saw the debt crisis coming. As late as 1981 there was general agreement that while a few countries might be overborrowing, and policies in many countries could be criticised, international capital markets were on the whole doing pretty much the right thing.

It is worth citing several pieces of evidence, among other things to point out that bad predictions are not the exclusive province of economists or anybody else. First, we may note that the bankers were of course sanguine about the prospect. Citibank's 1981 annual report argued that sovereign debt was in general a very safe bet, and further pointed out that because most of the bank's developing country lending was at fairly short term, it could be quickly run down in the event of a change in that judgment. (Nobody seems to have thought about what would happen if everyone tried to do the same thing.) Other investors were equally relaxed. As late as April 1992, the survey of country risk managers by Institutional Investor flashed no warning lights. Mexico was actually rated above South Korea.

Economists took a more quantitative approach. Most of them – myself included – argued that since real interest rates were very low, and certainly below the growth rates of recent years, developing countries were unlikely to have any problem rolling over and servicing their debt. A major survey of the debt situation by Jeffrey Sachs in the 1981 Brookings Papers further argued that since the current account deficits of developing countries had been used in most cases to increase investment rather than consumption, there was no particular reason to regard their borrowing as risky.

It is easy to regard the optimism of 1981 as a case of mass foolishness. Certainly some foolish things were said. Given what was known at that point, however, it was not unreasonable to conclude that the debt of developing countries was not a problem. Indeed, as we will see shortly, from the perspective of 1993 the optimism of 1981 looks quite understandable.

The view from 1983

By 1983 the situation had shifted dramatically. Argentina had actually been the first country to move into debt moratorium, but that was discounted as a special circumstance connected with the aftermath of the Falklands War. With the Mexican moratorium of August 1982, however, the debt crisis was on in earnest, quickly spreading to the rest of Latin America and with a lag to other countries such as the Philippines and eventually South Africa.

What new information had become available to justify this crisis? One point, strongly emphasised by Dooley (1993), was the revelation that external debt was considerably larger than anyone had realised. In general, observers had looked either at standard statistics on medium- and long-term debt or at cumulative current account deficits to assess the extent to which debt had been growing. It turned out that even some medium- and long-term debt had escaped the reporting net, and that there had been a huge build-up of short-term debt as well. This debt accumulation had not been reflected in corresponding current account deficits because it had been matched by large-scale export of capital from many debtor countries. Indeed, Argentina managed to have a debt crisis without ever running large external deficits, and Venezuela topped that achievement by experiencing a debt crisis despite a consistent history of current account surpluses.

If the crisis led to the revelation of the unexpected size of indebtedness, it also led to a realisation of the vulnerability of debtor nations to liquidity problems. The heavy burden of short-term debt alone would have ensured such vulnerability. That burden was reinforced by the *de facto* shortening of maturities that occurs in an inflationary environment: in a world of steady 10% inflation, the annual real amortisation on a debt composed of seven-year loans is as large as that on five-year loans under stable prices. It turned out that none of the debtors was remotely capable of servicing its debt once it was unable to engage in fresh borrowing.

The most important new information, however, was not about the developing countries but about their external environment. The industrial country recession of the first half of the 1980s was much more severe than anyone expected; more important, as Figure 2.2 indicates, real interest rates rose to historically unprecedented levels and stayed there.

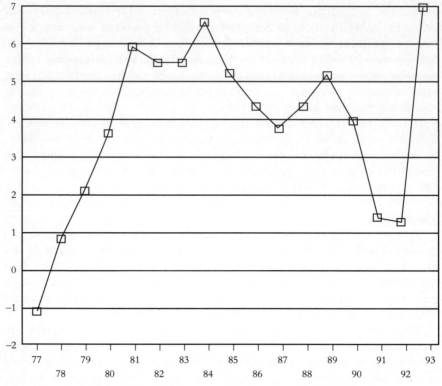

Figure 2.2. US short term interest rates, 1977–1992

In spite of these adverse developments, however, most people who thought about the debt crisis in its first two or three years regarded it as a temporary problem that was solvable without any major writedown by the banks or bailout from creditor country governments. In effect, this consensus view saw the debt crisis as the equivalent of a run on a basically solvent bank. Such a run, if unchecked, can in fact bust the bank and make the people who ran first seem prescient; but if it can be stopped it will seem in retrospect unjustified.

Why did informed opinion continue to have a favourable long-term view of developing country prospects? Essentially it was a matter of arithmetic. The debts of developing countries just did not seem that large relative to the debtor economies, and their long-term service did not seem that hard, given even a moderately pessimistic view about long-term growth.

It is still easy to reproduce the essential argument underlying these calculations (for an extended discussion, see Feldstein 1986). Imagine a debtor country whose external debt is equal to 50% of its GDP. Imagine also that the real interest rate it must pay on this debt is 5%; if we let world dollar inflation be 4%, this implies a nominal rate of 9%. Suppose finally that the economy is capable of a long-term growth rate of 3%, i.e. roughly zero per capita growth for a high-birth-rate debtor like Mexico (or South Africa).

It is easy in this example to see how the possibility of severe liquidity problems can co-exist with seemingly very favourable long-run arithmetic. The nominal interest payments on this country's debt will amount to 4,5% of GDP. Even with full rescheduling of commercial bank debt the combination of inevitably incomplete coverage of that rescheduling and some capital flight could easily force the country to run a trade surplus of 6% or more of GDP, which would impose major adjustment problems. Yet if the country retained access to capital markets it could keep the real value of its debt constant with a trade surplus of only 2,5% of GDP. With any growth in the economy this would imply a declining ratio of debt to income; with 3% growth the debt–GDP ratio could be stabilised with a trade surplus of only 1% of output. Thus, if markets had faith in the country's willingness and ability to pay, it seems as if it should have no trouble generating enough foreign exchange to service its debt.

In 1983 a number of people made more elaborate calculations more or less along these lines; the most influential published document was the study by Cline (1983), but similar studies were carried out within major institutions. These studies all concluded that the essential problem was one of getting debtor countries through several years of liquidity squeeze. In time, as creditors saw the debt ratios improve, they would resume lending to the countries and the crisis would be over. From this followed the strategy of rescheduling reinforced both by official provision of new money and by 'concerted' lending by existing creditors, a strategy essentially restated by the so-called Baker Plan of 1985.

The view from 1989

By early 1989 the guarded optimism of 1983 had come to seem almost as wrong-headed as the cheerful views of 1981. More than six years after the onset of the debt crisis, debtor countries had not regained access to credit markets. Indeed, they seemed further from such access than ever: in what was now a sizeable secondary market for debt, prices for claims on highly indebted developing countries averaged only about 30% of par.

What had gone wrong? At a mechanical level, several of the presumptions of the 1983 strategy had failed to work out. Firstly, the concerted lending strategy effectively lasted only about two years; after 1984 only trivial amounts of new money were provided from private sources. With nominal bank claims on developing countries at a standstill, real bank exposure was therefore steadily declining. Official lending meanwhile continued, the result being that official discussions increasingly focused on what was seen as a transfer of risk from private banks to taxpayers.

At the same time, and in spite of the fact that little new money had been made available, the expected decline in debt ratios had not materialised. There were two reasons for this. First, highly indebted developing countries had turned in a much worse growth performance than expected, with substantial declines in real GDP per capita. Second, valuation effects – notably the real devaluations forced by the need to run large trade surpluses – had reduced the dollar value of GDP and to some extent exports.

The arithmetic that said that the debt of the major highly-indebted developing countries should not be large enough to be a serious problem remained unchanged. After so many years of debt crisis, however, hardly anybody could accept that arithmetic anymore. And so by early 1989 a new orthodoxy had emerged, which saw a major programme of debt forgiveness as necessary to end the crisis. Loosely, the argument was that the poor growth performance of the debtor countries was the result of the burden of unpayable debt, and that a reduction in that burden would start a virtuous circle of faster growth and hence further-improved debt ratios.

It was of course widely accepted that the adjustment problems caused by the need to switch rapidly from debt-financed trade deficits to debt-servicing large trade surpluses had thrown developing countries into severe recession. The new argument, pushed initially by strong advocates of the developing nations like Jeffrey Sachs (1984), but eventually accepted much more broadly, was that the level of debt itself acted as a constraint on growth. In the form in which the argument was often cast, the realisation that capital might be taxed in an effort to pay debt acted as a disincentive to investment, and thus in turn made full payment of that debt all the less likely. This was summed up in the idea of the 'debt Laffer curve', in which increases in debt above some level actually reduced the expected present value of repayments.

The US government was initially reluctant to consider the possibility that forgiveness as opposed to simple help in financing might have to be a part of the debt strategy. In March 1989, however, Treasury Secretary Brady conceded the point and launched the so-called Brady Plan. In its initial conception this plan was extremely confused, but with considerable intellectual help from Mexican debt negotiators, 'Brady deals' eventually solidified into a more or less standard package in which creditors were offered a menu of choices, but were obliged in effect either to sell their claims at a substantial discount or to provide new money that helped purchase other creditor claims.

The interesting point about the change in debt policy in 1989 was that while it was backed up by some theoretical arguments, it was never solidly grounded in any convincing evidence that debt forgiveness was what the debtors needed. Indeed, such quantitative evidence as there was tended to point the other way. For example, efforts to estimate any relationship between the debt burden and investment, the key linkage in most stories about the disincentive effects of debt, failed to find such a link or at least to find one that was very strong. Cross-sectional estimates of the debt Laffer curve found, at best, that a few very highly indebted countries were on the reverse slope (Claessens, Diwan, Froot and Krugman, 1990). There was a clear case that any efforts to reduce debt should be carried out on a concerted basis, perhaps along the lines of the Mexican plan, in order to minimise the windfall gains to the creditors, but there was never a strong case that debt reduction itself was a very important issue.

Nonetheless, by 1989 a consensus had developed that highly indebted countries would not be able to work their way out of their debt problems, and that debt forgiveness was essential to get economic growth under way once more.

The view from 1993

As we have already noted, what actually happened in the early 1990s was exactly what was supposed to be impossible: debtor countries regained access to world capital markets, indeed on a scale that, in some cases, exceeded anything seen in the best years of bank finance.

We will turn to the possible reasons for this surge in the next part of the chapter. The important point to make now, however, is to rule out what might seem like an attractive story – that Brady deals did just what they were supposed to, reducing debt to a level which allowed growth to resume. It is possible that Brady deals did make a difference – but not because they significantly reduced the debt burden. They were simply too small to have had that effect. The reason was that the deals typically exempted significant parts of debt – applying in general only to non-trade-related bank debt, and thus leaving trade credit, bonds and official claims untouched – and that the packages that financed the deals themselves required running up more debt, this time from official sources. Mexico's package, for example, involved about 30% reductions in the value of affected debt, but once the details had added up the overall reduction was less than 10%. In turn this meant a reduction in the flow of interest payments of less than 0,5% of GDP, which one might think would hardly be enough to produce a dramatic change in the country's economic situation.

And yet there was a complete reversal of investor sentiment, beginning in Mexico's case almost immediately following its debt reduction. And we may note that those few banks that chose to provide new money rather than accept a reduction in the value of their claims were quite soon rewarded for their courage by a virtual disappearance of secondary discounts on Mexican debt.

Lessons of the debt crisis era

What can we learn from this roller-coaster experience? First, we learn that there are no last acts. In 1981 conventional wisdom held that international financial markets had done a wonderful job, allowing smooth recycling of the surpluses of OPEC nations and helping promote economic development. By the late 1980s the story had been rewritten in people's minds, with the history of Third World lending an example of the folly and stupidity of bankers and governments. Today the original view that developing countries were good markets for capital looks pretty reasonable once again, and their isolation from international capital markets between 1982 and 1990 looks like an extended and unnecessary panic on the part of creditors. Who knows how the history will be written ten years from now?

Second, we learn that the behaviour of international capital markets is based, at best, on measurable economic data. The arithmetic of debt still looked reasonably good in 1983, in spite of the adverse shifts in the world economic environment; nonetheless, voluntary lending to developing countries dried up completely. Conversely, there was very little substantive reduction in the debt burden after 1989, yet investors fairly suddenly decided that highly indebted developing countries were good bets after all. It is difficult to escape the sense that there is a strong element of psychological or herd behaviour involved. This is important as we turn to our next topic: explaining the recent surge in capital flows to developing countries.

The capital surge of the 1990s

We have ruled out as arithmetically wrong the idea that capital has started flowing to developing countries because the Brady deals lowered their debt enough to put them on higher growth paths. What then can explain the turn-around? I offer here four, not necessarily inconsistent, hypotheses. These are that the new capital flows are due to (i) a genuine and coincidental improvement in the external environment, primarily a fall in real rates of interest; (ii) the perception that the debt reductions under the Brady Plan satisfied the political need to take a pound of flesh out of creditors, and that countries would henceforth be willing to service their debts; (iii) the emergence of a shared belief on the part of both investors and developing country governments that market-oriented reforms will lead to much-improved economic performance; and (iv) a simple speculative bubble.

The external environment

We have already seen from Figure 2.2 that the early 1980s was marked by a rise in real interest rates to historically unprecedented levels. The same figure shows that the early 1990s has been marked by an equally striking move in the opposite direction. Real interest rates on short-term debt in the US are now once again barely positive, and again well below rates of growth that developing countries ought to be able to achieve even on pessimistic assumptions. (In fact, the improvement may be even greater than may appear when looking at real interest rates. A country that is unable to borrow but can reschedule the principal is strongly concerned about nominal as well as real rates, and nominal rates have fallen to levels not seen in 20 years.)

Admittedly, the low interest rates have been accompanied by a serious recession in the industrial world. For a developing country with substantial amounts of floating rate debt, however, it takes a very severe recession in the world economy to reduce foreign exchange earnings by the same amount that 3 or 4 percentage points on LIBOR reduces debt service, so for the most troubled debtors the decline in interest rates has outweighed any adverse effects from the recession.

There is therefore a case to be made that the revival of capital flows to selected countries is driven in large part simply by a dramatically improved environment.

Political implications of the Brady Plan

The Mexican debt reduction package provided very little direct relief to the economy. Within only a few months, however, the plan produced a dramatic improvement in the fiscal situation of the Mexican government, for a surprising reason: real interest rates on domestic debt, which had been set at 20% or more in order to prevent capital flight, dropped rapidly into single digits as flight capital began returning.

The suddenness of this change suggests that the debt package, modest as it was, was perceived as marking a turning point. One reason was surely that it was seen as making it possible for Mexico to put the debt issue behind it as a political matter.

Anyone who has spent time discussing policy in a highly indebted developing country is aware that the bad taste left behind by the debt crisis makes it difficult to move forward on other economic reforms until some symbolic resolution of the crisis has been made. It may be objectively true that debt service is only a modest drag on the economy, and that in any case only a fraction of debt can plausibly be considered a target for significant reduction; in practice none of the countries that are now favoured by international investors was able to achieve debt forgiveness that reduced its real obligations by as much as 1% of GDP annually. Nonetheless, as long as the general public feels that the country has been ill used by foreign banks it is difficult to move on with economic reforms until these banks have been made to swallow at least a moderately bitter pill. This is particularly the case when the economic reforms involve opening to external markets and providing a more hospitable climate for future foreign investors.

So one can suggest that the Brady Plan worked, but for an unanticipated reason: it effectively allowed governments that were essentially able and willing to service their debt to hold a show trial of their bankers, mete out visible if minor punishment, and then get on with business. International investors, understanding that the political need for revenge had now been satisfied, were then prepared to go ahead and put in their capital.

Economic reforms

One need not be a total cynic to realise that there are fashions in conventional economic wisdom. At any given time, serious people – including officials at multilateral agencies, policy-makers in developing countries and investors – tend to hold a similar set of beliefs about what sorts of policies work and how well they will work. These beliefs are often based on experience and evidence, but they typically go well beyond what the solid evidence shows. There is clearly a process of reinforcement in which important people talk to each other, and come to believe what they say with all the more conviction because they hear it from other important people.

There are historical examples of this process, which make one a little nervous about contemporary conventional wisdom. For example, in the 1950s there were very few critics of import-substituting industrialisation. Yet there was no solid evidence that it was a good strategy, and indeed it has come to have a bad name in retrospect. So how did it come to be so widely approved? Economic theorists may have provided some support, but the self-reinforcing role of conventional wisdom was surely the main reason.

What makes all this relevant is the way that a liberalising orthodoxy has become universally accepted in the last few years. Policy-makers in developing countries now agree with what the World Bank has been telling them for some time, that privatisation and open markets are the best strategy. Equally important, international investors not only think that liberalisation is a good strategy, but they expect it to produce dramatic results fairly quickly.

Because of the emergence of this policy orthodoxy, a number of developing countries have recently made dramatic changes in their trade and industrial policies. As an example, Table 2.1 illustrates the changes in Mexican trade policy in the late 1980s.

Table 2.1. Mexican trade policy

	June 1985	June 1988
Coverage of import permits	92,2	23,2
Maximum tariff	100,0	20,0
Weighted tariff	23,5	11,0

Note that the policy changes took place well before NAFTA; indeed, NAFTA may be seen as more a matter of locking in past reform than as a major new liberalisation. And the markets approve of these changes. So the process of reform has helped to open up capital markets to developing countries.

Is it a bubble?

The most cynical, and most worrisome, explanation of the surge in capital flows to developing countries is that it is essentially a speculative bubble. It is possible to argue that whatever the specific reasons why the turnaround in investor sentiment began, optimism about developing countries has been self-reinforcing. One can point to several possible mechanisms.

First, a significant fraction of the investment in developing countries has been in equities. The new popularity of so-called 'emerging markets' has led to the very large increases in price–earnings ratios shown in Table 2.2, and hence large capital gains in these markets.

Table 2.2. P/E ratios in emerging markets

	1988	1991
Argentina	11,30	38,89
Chile	4,40	17,38
Mexico	5,04	24,36
Venezuela	11,45	30,50

These capital gains have in turn made investing in such markets a hard-to-resist prospect, even if investors know intellectually that capital gains in the past do not imply similar gains in the future. We may also note that there is an obvious process of 'generalisation' going on: investors look at the large gains made in one developing country and hope to do similarly well in others. There is thus the possibility of a bubble, in which the expectation of high returns temporarily creates the fact.

A second channel through which capital flows may be self-reinforcing involves macro-economic factors. A country that becomes favoured by international investors will, by that fact alone, see a considerable improvement in its immediate situation. Foreign exchange shortages will disappear and growth will accelerate. Large capital inflows will also tend to produce a real appreciation; while this is going on, real interest rates in terms of domestic goods will appear lower than those in terms of foreign goods, and thus domestic borrowers may be willing to pay interest rates that appear very attractive compared with those abroad.

Finally, there may be a self-reinforcing mechanism that operates through perceptions about politics. Suppose that a government begins a reform programme; and that this programme encourages investors, who put large quantities of money into the country. The favourable effect of these capital inflows may then make it more likely that the reformers will be able to carry out and extend their programme, reinforcing the optimism of the investors, and so on.

All of these 'feedback mechanisms' may be seen at work in the Mexican case. The debt settlement seems to have turned the psychological tide: stock prices soon surged. Growing capital inflows allowed normal debt service to resume, which led to a resumption of economic growth and fed a large real appreciation. The economic successes in turn helped convince investors that President Salinas would be able to set an irreversible process of reform in motion.

It is worth pointing out that a case can be made that the 1990s surge represented not the emergence of a positive speculative bubble, but the bursting of a negative one. One might argue that the optimism of 1983 or even 1981, about long-term prospects for developing countries, was right after all. What happened in the 1980s was then, essentially, a panic by creditors that, by provoking a cash crunch, did exactly the reverse of what we have just seen can happen as a result of capital inflows. That is, foreign exchange shortages, recession and real depreciation created an apparently unfavourable economic performance; and the economic distress threatened to produce political radicalisation, all of which seemed to confirm investors in their initial flight. In this view, the Brady deals essentially allowed everyone to take a deep breath and see that the fundamentals were better than they appeared.

A judicious view (which may be the wrong one) would split the difference. There has surely been some exaggeration, at least in some cases, of the success of reform efforts. For example, some commentators have pronounced a 'Mexican Miracle', when so far Mexico has only managed four years of slightly positive per capita growth. Perhaps the best summing up was the terse remark of one Mexican official: 'We weren't that bad', he said, 'but we're also not that good.'

Prospects for developing country capital flows

It is possible that the growth of capital flows to developing countries will continue; essentially, the Latin American debtors will lead the way to a new era of really large-scale North–South resource transfers. For those countries that have experienced the largest inflows so far, however, it is more likely that the inflows will actually slow. At worst there could be serious problems – in effect, a repeat of the debt crisis, albeit with different details.

The main reason for expecting some slowdown is simply that even if the new capital flows are fully justified by the underlying economics, we must conclude that investors were overly optimistic during the 1980s. As a result, part of the current surge can be thought of as recovering lost ground, and that the catch-up part of the surge will at some point taper off.

More serious are concerns that the wave of foreign investment will end suddenly with adverse effects. Worries on this score fall under two headings: micro-economic and macro-economic.

Micro-economic concerns

The most worrying thing about large-scale capital movement to developing countries is that it seems to be based to an important degree on faith that economic reform policies will produce both dramatic and fairly quick results. Unfortunately, there are good reasons to doubt this.

The point is not that freeing up markets is not a good thing; it is that investors may expect too much from it. Loosely speaking, we may say that investors seem to think that liberal trade and investment policies will produce East Asian-style economic takeoffs in other parts of the world. Conventional estimates of the costs of protection in developing countries are, however, no more than a few per cent of GDP – i.e. less than half a year's growth for a South Korea or a China. It has been claimed that cross-sectional evidence shows that there are additional large 'dynamic' gains from liberal policies, but the correlation between measurable differences in, say, trade policy and economic growth is actually fairly weak (Edwards, 1992).

The dissonance between the highly optimistic views of economic reform apparently held by investors and the rather modest quantitative results that we are sure of seeing presents the risk of a sort of 'morning-after' effect. Suppose, for example, that after two or three years there is a growing sense of disillusionment with Mexico as a place to produce – that US firms complain about education levels, or infrastructure, or simply having to pay wages that are four times what they can pay Chinese workers of comparable skill – and that there is a series of well-publicised decisions by US firms to close their Mexican operations and move them to Asia. It is easy to imagine that the effect could be chilling, on capital flows not only to Mexico, but to those to the rest of the developing world as well.

The micro-economic risk could be greatly reinforced by macro-economic risks, arising from the way that reform has been accompanied in key countries by efforts to peg the exchange rate.

The macro-economic risks

The counterpart of a large capital account surplus is a large current account deficit. Policy-makers in Mexico, Argentina and elsewhere have taken pains to point out that their recent deficits are essentially a sign of strength, not weakness, that they are driven by the desire of investors to put money into their countries. Nonetheless, the sheer size of these deficits creates some real risks.

Suppose that for some reason the capital inflows to a recently attractive developing country were to dry up. Then the country would be faced with a serious adjustment problem, since the previous capital inflows will have led to substantial real appreciation, making some exports uncompetitive and fuelling an import boom. In this, a country is no different from a region within a single country: when investment declines in, say, California there is also an adjustment problem. In either case, a recession is the immediate result.

The problem is what comes next. Regions within nations cope with local recessions through a mixture of deflation and emigration. A national economy can cope solely through deflation – but this is a very expensive and prolonged process. It would be particularly agonising for countries that have only recently resumed growth after a decade of punishment during the debt crisis.

The alternative is devaluation, to eliminate the real appreciation fed by the capital inflows. This, however, runs up against other policy concerns. Many developing countries have a history of out-of-control inflation; the anti-inflation strategy of choice has involved using an exchange-rate peg as a nominal anchor. In the most dramatic example, Argentina has gone over to a full 'currency board' scheme in which the domestic currency is fully backed by dollar reserves and the parity is rigidly set at unity. Countries that have staked their reputations on fixed, or at least slowly crawling, exchange rates fear that if they abandon their pegs they will lose hard-won credibility. This unfortunately leaves them with no good policy options.

At least one observer, Rudiger Dornbusch (1993), believes that the large capital inflows into some developing countries have more to do with their exchange rate policy than with any fundamental change in global markets. He sees the process as one in which inflationary momentum creates a real appreciation, which at first draws in speculative capital; in this view the seeming transformation of the prospects of developing countries is more like the ultimately disastrous experience of 'southern cone' stabilisation in Latin America in the 1970s and early 1980s.

Even if one does not accept so pessimistic an assessment, there is an obvious scenario in which a drying up of capital inflows eventually forces countries to abandon their exchange rate targets, and in which the resulting loss of credibility leads to a bout of capital flight that greatly worsens the crash. The point is that the real appreciation in Argentina and Mexico since the late 1980s has been so large that it is difficult either to imagine that it is sustainable or to see how it can be smoothly worked off.

The reopening of international capital markets for developing countries then poses at least some possibility of a replay of something like the 1982 crisis. One can, however, offer a number of reasons why the current situation is much better – notably, the form of the recent capital inflows involves having foreign investors bear much of the risk. And it is possible that the markets are right, and that economic reform will generate such an improvement in growth performance that no big real depreciation will be necessary. There is, however, clearly a growing sense of concern.

Can/should South Africa get into the act?

This final section will be brief, and will simply allude to some familiar points about the resemblances and differences between South Africa and other developing countries.

South Africa as a potential attraction for foreign investors

In some broad respects South Africa bears considerable resemblance to Mexico, which both led the developing world into the debt crisis and has been the star performer in terms of attracting capital in the new global environment. South Africa and Mexico have approximately the same per capita income. Both are resource-rich; both have a history of relying on raw material exports and industrialising behind trade barriers (although the South African economy, with its smaller population and traditional strong trade ties with the UK, is considerably more open to trade). In at least two respects South Africa is in a better situation than Mexico. First, the burden of debt is quite small for a developing country, about 16% of GDP. Second, inflation is also fairly low for a troubled developing economy, in the low double digits.

South Africa and Mexico also share some similar problems. In both countries there is massive unemployment and underemployment. Income inequality is also very high in both countries. Finally, in both countries per capita income has fallen considerably since 1980.

In general, in sheer economic terms South Africa seems to fit the profile of the kinds of countries that have indeed been able to take advantage of changed investor sentiment to re-enter international capital markets in a major way.

The problem with the parallel is, of course, the political dimension. In Mexico and other countries that have managed to attract foreign capital, the governments were able to establish a reputation as determined reformers breaking with bad old statist policies and providing a newly hospitable environment for investment of all kinds. Although hard numbers are lacking, there is a general sense that these policies have been associated with a widening of income differentials; certainly, some once-powerful labour groups, like the workers in formerly protected industries, have suffered sharp declines in real wages (although Mexico has had considerable success in the last few years in combining its free-market tilt with a major programme of aid to the rural poor). And as argued above, the movement toward economic reform seems to have generated a virtuous circle in which capital inflows appear to validate the new policies. Obviously South Africa cannot offer an identical political scenario. The question is whether some other scenario can play the same role.

Some preconditions for attracting capital inflows

It is very difficult to offer any set of hard-and-fast rules about what is necessary for a country to attract foreign capital in the 1990s. As the history of the debt crisis makes clear, markets seem to be driven by obscure factors and a good deal of herd behaviour. Nonetheless, we can suggest several policy conditions that might help South Africa gain access to what are, at least for the time being, relatively optimistic world capital markets.

First, there is the question of property rights. It is natural that a new South African government may feel pressure to undo some of the property relations created under the old regime, breaking up large firms, possibly expropriating some assets or seeking forgiveness for some debt. The experience of debtor countries does not suggest that some repudiation of contracts is a bad thing. It does suggest that it should be got over with quickly. The long suspense over whether debt forgiveness would come, and how big it would be, was at least one reason why Mexico could not regain access to world capital markets. Once a settlement was made in 1989, even though it involved in effect a repudiation of old debt contracts covered by only a thin legal veneer, the markets concluded that the political need for a settlement had been satisfied. So the main advice here would be to decide what break-ups of existing firms, repudiation of debts, etc. are needed and get them over with quickly.

Second, countries that have regained access to capital markets have done so by demonstrating a new orientation toward the market mechanism. This need not involve a rigid commitment to *laissez-faire* economics, but in general capital has tended to flow toward countries that have been more market-oriented than previous experience had led investors to expect. If the new government in South Africa shows an unexpected willingness to allow markets to work, it would not be surprising if that willingness is rewarded by capital markets.

Finally, exchange rate policy and the related issue of capital controls are important. Mexico was able to attract capital following its 1989 Brady deal because, among other reasons (a) it had what appeared to be a highly competitive exchange rate and (b) as a result, it was able to allow investors free exit (as well as entry) from the country. It is worth noting that as of 1989, the peso was sufficiently low that Mexican wages averaged less than $260 per month; this made it seem plausible that Mexico could become a major manufacturing platform for the US market, helping provide a basis for investor confidence. (Since then the inflows of capital have themselves brought about a much stronger real peso, but that is another story.) By contrast, the South African exchange rate does not make it appear to be a very attractive place to produce; in 1991 the wage rate was more than $670 per month. Correspondingly, South Africa continues to maintain capital controls and a dual exchange rate. As long as the rand is perceived as overvalued, it will be difficult to attract capital inflows.

I would suggest, then, that South Africa will be more likely to gain access to world capital markets if it can get any restructuring of property rights behind it; if it can demonstrate that it is more market-oriented than investors now expect; and if it can offer what appears to be a competitive rand. There is no guarantee that these conditions will produce large capital inflows, but the world capital markets have recently seemed quite willing to give countries that meet these criteria the benefit of the doubt.

Some hard questions

Let me conclude with three questions that are difficult to answer but that may help focus discussion:

(i) Can South Africa put together a convincing political picture that will attract capital inflows?

(ii) Will the open capital market for developing countries last until South Africa is ready to enter it?

(iii) If the answer to (i) and (ii) is yes, should the country try to prevent over-heated capital inflows, or should it take whatever it can get?

PART TWO
INTERNATIONAL COMPETITIVENESS

3

What Will Make South Africa Internationally Competitive?

SANJAYA LALL

The issues of South African industrial competitiveness are to some extent *sui generis*. South Africa has a relatively large and diversified manufacturing sector of long standing, clearly the most advanced manufacturing sector on the African continent.[1] It is largely privately owned and responsive to market forces. It serves a reasonable-sized domestic market with concentrations of high income and sophisticated tastes. It has been open to inflows of new technologies from the developed industrial countries, and has drawn on a base of well-trained managers, engineers and technicians. It has established areas of competence in several complex activities.[2] Many of these are in heavy and technologically demanding industries that have matured behind protective barriers into international competitiveness, such as metallurgy, chemicals, paper and some industrial mining equipment. In addition, it also exports significant amounts of textiles and processed foods. In 1991 its manufactured exports amounted to $7,6 billion, up from $5,3 billion in 1988.[3]

Yet, despite these achievements, large areas of South African industry are neither competitive nor technologically dynamic. Its manufactured exports are about one-tenth of those of similar-sized East Asian Newly Industrialising Economies (NIEs) like South Korea or Taiwan (Lall, 1991). In comparison to these relative newcomers to industry, South Africa shows particular weaknesses in advanced engineering activities (especially electronics) as well as in mature, labour-intensive products like garments and footwear. Its productivity growth over the past two decades has been disappointing – about 0,5% per annum according to estimates by the NPI (1989) – far lower than recorded in East Asia.

With current changes in its economic and political situation, which require a far greater openness to world trade, South African industry today faces difficult problems of industrial competitiveness and restructuring. The roots of these problems lie in long-standing features of its political regime and industrial strategy. It started with import substitution some 70 years ago, and stayed with this orientation over time. Inward orientation was intensified during sanctions, with the result that South African industry remained relatively isolated from normal international trade and competition for longer than any relatively industrialised market economy. When South African industrial firms competed abroad, it was mainly in neighbouring, far less developed countries. The array of complex trade and other controls needed to make the economy function in the isolationist period imposed various distortions on top of the heavy weight of protected inward orientation (see Belli *et al.*, 1993).

It was not just the distorted incentive system that led to the setting up of high-cost industries and the relative lack of technological dynamism. Apartheid imposed its own costs. The base of skills and entrepreneurship remained narrow as the majority of the population was cut off from good education and access to training and capital. Inflows of foreign direct investment were sharply constrained, and with it the transfer of the most advanced new technologies and skills. Local firms did not develop a 'technology culture' that would lead them to invest in their own research and development to replace the drying up of direct investment. Sanctions meant that local firms were not exposed to the full force of international competition. The broad institutional structure needed to support the development of industrial competitiveness could not be developed.

In recent years there has been considerable liberalisation of South Africa's trade regime. Quantitative restrictions have been largely replaced by tariffs. Export incentives are greatly improved. However, the tariff structure remains complex, offering high and variable levels of protection to industrial activities (Belli *et al.*, 1993). There is currently a lively debate in South Africa on the merits and nature of further trade liberalisation. On the one hand are the multilateral organisations like the World Bank and local institutions like the Industrial Development Corporation which support rapid and sweeping liberalisation. On the other hand are a number of South African researchers who question the need for further rapid liberalisation, partly because of its macro-economic costs and partly because of doubts about the efficacy of simple free-market solutions to the problems of competitiveness and restructuring.[4]

This debate touches on many critical issues in the determination of South African competitiveness. The debate is far from resolution.[5] This chapter touches on some aspects of the question of how exposure to international competition affects the building of industrial competitiveness. It also highlights some issues on the development of industrial capabilities that the debate on incentive issues tends to neglect. Much of the past discussion lacks a good 'feel' for how industrial firms become competitive, and thus tends to oversimplify the needs of policy support in factor and product markets that do not function with the efficiency that economic theory expects.

What determines industrial competitiveness?

If one assumes that developing countries depend on using technologies imported from developed countries, and have access to the same markets for technologies and equipment, their competitiveness depends on how well they are able to access these (imperfect) markets, implement the relevant technologies and use those technologies in production. This depends, in turn, on their managerial and technological capabilities (industrial capabilities for short).[6] A great deal of research, in developed and developing countries, establishes that competitive advantages in industry arise at the firm and national levels from deliberate efforts to build industrial capabilities rather than from 'given' factor endowments (see Lall, 1990; 1992a).

The implementation of most new technologies in developing countries is likely to call for considerable learning, search and skill development within individual firms. Simply providing equipment and operating instructions, patents, designs or blueprints does not ensure that imported technology will be properly used. There are 'tacit' elements of a technology which have to be taught and learned.[7] Technological capabilities in industry are the skills – technical, managerial and institutional – that allow productive enterprises to utilise equipment and technical information efficiently. They apply to all industrial activities, though the composition and levels of skills and information needed vary by activity.

Technological capabilities (TCs) should not therefore be thought of as the ability to undertake frontier innovation, though innovative capabilities are one form of TC. They are the engineering, technical and operational skills and knowledge that allow the plant to be used at its 'best practice' level of efficiency. They are a firm-specific form of knowledge which can differ between individual enterprises, depending on their investments in TCs, the effectiveness of these investments and the institutional coherence to take advantage of the skills and information created (see Enos, 1992). Thus, in any economy there will be firms at different levels of efficiency, and any economy will differ from any other in terms of its industrial competitiveness (i.e. the proportion of 'good' to 'bad' enterprises).

The learning process for complex technologies can be long, costly and uncertain, though the duration and costs will differ by industry: given all the right conditions, easy technologies may take a few months, complex ones a decade or more.[8] This generality apart, in a new environment, with different physical conditions and fresh workers and managers, the results of adopting any new technology cannot be entirely predictable. Thus, even the achievement of static efficiency usually involves search, experimentation and interactions within firms as well as between them. In a dynamic world, with market conditions and tastes changing, technologies improving, new competitors appearing, skill needs evolving and inputs altering, the process of becoming and staying efficient is even more difficult. Any firm that is to stay competitive has to invest in constant skill development and technological effort. The nature of the effort will differ according to the nature of competition and efficiency of factor and product markets, but success will generally depend on constant investment in capability acquisition.

It is now conventional wisdom that technical inefficiency in developing countries is a more important source of low productivity and poor competitiveness than allocative inefficiency (Pack, 1988). In general, enterprises in these countries are inept at using technologies they import, and their productivity can be raised more by improving their capabilities (without adding to physical capital) than by correcting static resource allocation. It is interesting to note that the TC approach has many affinities to Liebenstein's classic concept of 'X-efficiency' (Liebenstein, 1966). However, there is an important difference, which has a bearing on the subsequent analysis.

In X-efficiency theory, there is slack in deploying technology which is assumed to have been fully mastered, and the remedy is to expose managers to stronger pressures to use capabilities than their enterprises already have experienced.[9] In developing countries this may be achieved by removing all artificial barriers to competition, just as recommended by the proponents of rapid and sweeping liberalisation. In other words, immediate incentive reform is all that is needed to ensure efficiency, and any activity that does not survive is by definition inherently inefficient. In the TC approach, in contrast, the technology may not have been mastered fully because the learning process has been distorted by wrong incentives and factor market failures. Many activities that are not fully competitive today may thus become competitive by building upon the capabilities that they have developed, by a process of 'unlearning' and 'relearning'.

This may be a slow and costly process, in which incentive reform (liberalisation) is one of several ingredients. The pace of liberalisation, moreover, has to match the capability rebuilding process and the rate at which the other elements of TC development can be supplied. The policy implications that follow are very different, spelled out later in this chapter.

What determines the pace of TC development? The decision to invest in TCs depends on the interaction of three broad sets of factors that affect the firm: the incentive framework, which provides the demand for capability development, the 'supply' factors, which include finance, skills and information, and the 'institutional system' that supports industrial activity.

Incentives

Incentives refer to the signals that arise in input or output markets, and govern the raising and allocation of resources and effort by firms, both to setting up physical capacity and to developing new skills, know-how and innovations. Incentives arise from the macro-economic (and political) environment: stability, realistic exchange and interest rates, competitive prices for labour and other inputs, and clear, predictable regulations are all conducive to high rates of investment in capacity and capability building. The provision of physical infrastructure provides a similar stimulus. These are general and widely accepted propositions, and do not need elaboration here.

The incentives that are considered particularly relevant to industrial competitiveness arise from trade and industrial strategies. There is now general agreement that outward-oriented trade strategies are more conducive to building competitive industries than protectionist, inward-oriented strategies, for several reasons. Activities geared to world markets face stronger pressures to develop competitive capabilities, and to upgrade them continuously by importing new technologies: competition provides the strongest incentive to invest in capability development. Not only is capability development faster, but the nature of capabilities developed is also different. World competition encourages capabilities that are more directed to cost reduction and product development than, as in inward orientation, to making do with available materials and stretching the life of capital equipment. In addition, world markets enable scale economies, where they exist, to be realised fully. They feed back a great deal of free valuable technical and marketing information. Exporters thus tend to be technologically alert and dynamic, and to specialise in areas to which their capabilities are best suited.

Export orientation need not, however, mean free trade or the absence of other forms of government intervention. There has been a widespread, and unfortunate, tendency in writings on trade strategy in developing countries to identify one with the other.[10] There are theoretical and empirical grounds for this tendency. In economic theory, neoclassical economics provides a powerful theoretical case for free trade. This has been taken to be supported, on the empirical plane, by the success of export-oriented economies in East Asia, perhaps the most compressed and impressive experiences of industrialisation in recent economic history. Together, theory and evidence have provided the current case for liberal trade policies, and so for the rapid and sweeping liberalisation of protected economies.

However, these links between theory, evidence and reality have not gone unquestioned. While the case for free trade has an irrefutable theoretical basis, given its assumptions, those assumptions are very stringent, and are rarely approximated in the real world. Among many other things, it assumes that technology is freely available to all countries and firms, and its absorption is costless and instantaneous. As suggested below, there are strong theoretical grounds, if market failures arising from learning costs, defective information and capital markets and externalities are taken into account, for believing that free trade does not lead to optimal resource allocation. In any case, even under its simplifying assumptions of perfect markets, the theory proves that free trade optimises static resource allocation rather than dynamic growth. As the proponents of 'new growth theories' note, under neoclassical assumptions trade liberalisation can only provide a once-and-for-all improvement in resource allocation – by itself, it cannot lead to the higher rates of growth that provide its empirical underpinnings (see Lucas, 1988). A sustained increase in the growth rate can only come from investments in human capital and technology that raise the productivity of other factors of production.

A consideration of the process of capability building in industry – the technological learning assumed away by current economic theory – provides arguments in support both of exposure to international competition and of selective interventions to promote entry into activities with difficult and lengthy learning periods (Lall, 1992; Lall *et al.*, 1992). International competition stimulates and shapes the process of capability acquisition; it provides a much stronger basis for efficient activity and the development of dynamic export activities than an environment which does not offer such competition. Once efficiency and productivity are made dependent on a continuous learning process that responds to external stimuli, the case for world competition is no longer one only of static resource allocation. Such competition can provide at least some of the human capital and technology to which the new growth theories assign a central role.

However, international competition is a double-edged sword. It can stimulate healthy capability development, but full exposure to it can prevent firms from entering activities with difficult, risky and prolonged learning (or 're-learning') requirements, when they have to face competitors that have already undergone the learning process. This is the traditional case for infant industry protection, well known to classical economists, dressed in modern garb of 'market failure' arising from pecuniary and technological externalities, dynamic and unpredictable learning sequences and risk aversion (see Jacobsson, 1993; Lall, 1992a). These are compounded by capital market failures, which should ideally be addressed at source, but in the interim may be countered by subsidising firms. As long as significant learning costs and risks exist, and firms in developing countries find that they deter entry into more difficult activities, free trade cannot optimise resource allocation over the longer term (though it can lead to the realisation of static comparative advantage). There is a case for intervention, therefore, to promote the realisation of dynamic comparative advantage. This intervention has necessarily to be selective, since technological factors dictate that the learning process differs by industry.

There are well-known dangers in selective protection. While infant industry protection can provide the 'breathing space' in which new entrants can develop their capabilities, protection can retard or distort the process of investing in ITD, especially if domestic competition is weak and the protection is granted in a widespread and indiscriminate manner. The general experience of import-substituting regimes is that highly protected enterprises never mature to competitive levels because there is little incentive to invest in the capabilities needed (see Belli *et al.*, 1984; Pack, 1988). There is evidently a need to combine the benefits of international competition with the need to foster infant activities. One way to do this may be to limit the extent and duration of the intervention. Another may be to expose firms to world competition in the form of export activity while protecting the domestic market. Yet another may be to insist on performance requirements.

So much for theoretical considerations. Empirical evidence shows that widespread selective trade interventions were used to promote highly successful industrial development in the medium-sized NIEs. So much has been written about this in recent years that the portrayal of South Korea and Taiwan as paragons of liberal strategy is accepted as false and misleading.[11] Their experience shows that export orientation can coexist with considerable protection for infant industries, as well as government interventions in directing credit, providing support technology and training, and in institution building to support the process of capability acquisition. However, unlike classic import-substituting economies, protection was limited in spread (a few activities being promoted at one time) and duration, and its deleterious effects on incentives to invest in efficiency were offset by pressures to enter export markets as soon as feasible.

Other incentives to capability development arise from internal competition, which is governed by industrial policies. There is little to add here that is not obvious: internal competition should be promoted to the extent that the realisation of scale economies permits. Where the achievement of world class competitiveness calls for very large firm (as opposed to plant) size, it may be necessary to deliberately foster large firms or groups. This was the strategy pursued by South Korea (but not by Taiwan, except by setting up public sector firms). It led to the internalisation of a number of deficient markets by the giant South

Korean conglomerates, the *chaebol,* so that they could enter the heavy, skill- and technology-intensive activities being promoted by the government.

The South Korean policy was also driven by nationalism, the clear objective being to keep the ownership of industry as far as possible in local hands. This necessitated much greater investments in indigenous research and design capabilities than if the country had chosen to depend heavily on multinational companies. The cost was an enormous concentration of economic power. The benefit was a broad and deep base of domestic technological capabilities. The deepening of technological capabilities can suffer market failures of its own. If access to ready-made foreign technologies is too easy, a culture develops in which it is very difficult for firms to invest in their own innovative capabilities (an 'infancy' case of a different sort). This is especially marked in countries like Mexico that have fairly good operational capabilities but practically no local research and development in private industry. The result is less dynamism and greater concentration on medium-technology activities than in a country like South Korea.

In sum, the correct incentive framework for technology development is given by the 'right prices', but 'getting prices right' may involve intervening in free markets when there are market failures (Stiglitz, 1989). Neither theory nor practice supports the case for completely liberal trade policies. There is no instance of a developing country mastering complex industrial activities (disregarding enclave activities by multinational firms) without protection or subsidisation to overcome the costs of learning. However, the crucial question remains whether governments are capable of making better choices than imperfect markets. Government failure haunts all discussions of industrial strategy. The problem is certainly a real one, but not as difficult as is made out. We return to this later.

Supply side factors

'Getting prices right' provides the signals for firms to respond to in developing capabilities. Their ability to respond depends on the availability of productive factors to the firms, and the ability of factor markets to respond to the signals given. If there are failures in factor markets that cannot be overcome by firms internalising those markets, the process of capability development will be deterred or distorted. If such failures exist, no amount of protection or subsidisation will help firms to become competitive. Factor market failures have to be tackled at source. One of the most important lessons of the East Asian success is that they intervened extensively in factor markets, and that the pattern of interventions was integrated into interventions in product markets. Both were geared to a common strategy, with large elements of selectivity in both sets of interventions (Lall, 1990; Lall *et al.,* 1992).

Factor markets may be considered under three headings: finance; skills; and local technological effort. These are taken briefly in turn, since each is important for analysing the South African situation.

Since the development of TCs is an investment involving time and cost, the availability of finance at the appropriate time, in appropriate amounts and at the appropriate price is an important determinant of ITD. Capital market failures can constitute a barrier to capability development, in general terms by retarding the allocation of resources to, or within, manufacturing activity, and in particular by constricting resources for technology development. Capital market failures are widespread in developing countries, and have been widely discussed (see Stiglitz, 1989). They do not need detailed analysis here. There is general agreement on the need to strengthen the human capital base of developing countries to promote the growth of TCs. In the industrial context this includes the skills imparted by the formal education and training system as well as those created by on-the-job training and experience. Even the simplest of technologies, if they are to be operated at world levels of efficiency, need a range of worker, supervisory, maintenance, quality control and adaptive skills. Advanced activities need far more, not just in a static sense, but continuously as technical change creates the need for new capabilities.

The market failures that can affect the education systems of developing countries in fulfilling this task are too well known to merit discussion here. There is also little here that is controversial. Most governments, including those in advanced industrial countries, accept the role that the state must play to support the education system. The experience of the NIEs of East Asia clearly shows how industrial success depended on the creation of human capital by extensive and continuous investments by the government (Lall, 1990). Moreover, it is not just the volume of investment in education that is important – the quality and relevance of the education provided is a vital determinant of its contribution to industrial development. This places corresponding demands on the education system.

Institutions like the World Bank readily accept the need for interventions to strengthen the human capital base: the 1991 World Development Report (World Bank, 1991) is full of praise for such 'market friendly' functional interventions in factor markets, as opposed to selective interventions in product markets. While this is all right as far as it goes, however, there are two problems with such an interpretation of the correct role of government. First, such interventions are considered 'friendly' to markets because they are functional rather than selective (they do not, in other words, attempt to promote some selected activities over others). But, as noted, theory does not exclude selectivity when certain kinds of market failure exist. Selectivity is just as market friendly as functionality.

Second, the identification of factor market interventions as being functional, and product market interventions as being selective, is too simple, even disingenuous. The creation of skills can be selective, if it is geared to supporting particular activities, while protection can be non-selective if it is offered to broad groups. As the need for high-level skills grows with industrial development, so does the need for selectivity in setting up education and training programmes. NIEs like South Korea in fact intervened very selectively in higher education to ensure an adequate supply of skills for the specific industries being targeted for future development, and industrialists formed part of the selection mechanism for human resource planning. In other words, industrial success at advanced levels requires selective interventions in factor markets to complement those in product markets.

Formal pre-employment education is only one component of the human capital creation process. The other is on-the-job training, and further formal training of employees sponsored by enterprises. However, apart from giving the on-the-job training that operational efficiency requires, most enterprises in developing countries tend to invest relatively little in upgrading the skills of their employees by providing formal courses. East Asian NIEs like South Korea and Singapore are striking exceptions, largely because of the specific interventions undertaken by their governments to promote such training. Even the on-the-job training provided by many developing country enterprises may be inadequate.

This failure to invest in training may be due to three reasons. First, enterprise managers may not be fully aware of the skill needs of the technologies they are using. Second, managers may realise that employee skills are deficient, but may not be able to remedy this effectively. They may not have access to skilled trainers in-house or in the local market, and there may be no local institutions, official or private, that offer the right level and quality of training. Finally, employers may be averse to investing in upgrading employee skills when they are unsure of being able to recoup the full benefits of their investments.

Coming now to technical effort, most of the technological activity that firms undertake to cope with production problems, cost reduction, diversification and so on is an in-house affair. However, all in-house technological effort takes place in a dense network of information flows between firms, and between firms and research and other institutions. This is the formal and information technology 'market' in which individual firms develop their own technical knowledge. This market is also prone to several forms of failure.

Most of these arise from the fact that there are several technological functions that have 'public goods' features, whose rewards are difficult to appropriate by private firms. These include the encouragement of technological activity in general (overcoming risk aversion and the 'learning to learn' barrier – Stiglitz, 1987); the development of special research skills; the setting of industrial standards and the promotion of quality awareness; the provision of metrology (industrial measurement and calibration) services; the undertaking of contract research, testing or information search for firms that lack the facilities or skills; other extension services for small enterprises; and the undertaking and co-ordination of basic (pre-commercial) research activities. The provision of these services then has to be an infrastructural service.

The need for information and technical support grows with the level of TC development, but some needs exist even at the starting levels. The weakness of the support structure is itself a symptom of the low levels of skill and TC development, but the strengthening of the structure can greatly help the technological development process. In almost every country, however, an important problem with the science and technology (S&T) infrastructure has been its lack of effective linkages with the productive sector. Most developing countries have set up networks of technology institutions, but few have been able to harness them to raise productive efficiency in industrial enterprises. This does not mean that the institutions are unnecessary for ITD. They are vital to meeting certain needs, and their utility grows with the level of industrial complexity, but policies must be designed to link them intimately to the needs of manufacturing enterprises.

Other forms of market failure in the undertaking of technological effort arise from factors noted above: externalities that are inherent in firm-level technological activity ('leakages' of information); lack of information on the benefits and means of undertaking technical effort; and risk aversion. These are obvious enough, and do not need further discussion here.

Institutions

A large variety of institutions is essential to support market and industrial development, and several have been mentioned above. The efficient allocation of resources requires a set of competent financial institutions; regulation and competition require legal institutions; skill development depends on education and training institutions; technology development calls for scientific research institutions; technology diffusion, especially to small-scale firms, calls for extension, subcontracting-promotion and other institutions; the development of export marketing requires information, design, credit, standards and quality assurance institutions; and so on. The spectacular success of the Asian NIEs was built on the back of widespread, assiduous institutional development, staffed by well-educated and motivated personnel (Wade, 1990).

The government itself is the most important 'institution' in the development process. Its ability to design and implement policies determines industrial competitiveness, and the best set of policies is not that of a 'minimalist state' which provides law, order and defence and leaves the rest to (perfectly functioning) markets.

As noted above, however, there is a serious risk of 'government failure', for several reasons (see Lall, 1992c). Governments often fail to design or implement sound policies. They lack the information on which to base industrial strategies. They are subject to special interests. They are often venal and self-seeking. These arguments all have some validity, but they can be overdone. Many of the past failures of industrial strategy have been due to the fact that governments were pursuing other objectives than competitiveness. They were not well informed about strategies pursued elsewhere. They intervened non-selectively and with no regard to the needs of promoting technological learning. The information needs of industrial strategy for a latecomer to industry are much less demanding than for advanced countries on the frontiers of technology, and the hijacking of policy by special interests is not inevitable. In any case, corruption and self-interest can undermine non-interventionist as well as interventionist regimes.

If it is possible to intervene effectively, and if there are costs to not intervening, the correct answer surely is to look for ways to help governments to improve their interventions, not to deny the need for interventions altogether. Governments improve over time, and administrative capabilities themselves can be learned. Incentive and monitoring systems can be improved to minimise the risks of corruptibility. In the final analysis, the strong need for proactive government policy to promote competitiveness should not be obfuscated in a thicket of suspicions of bureaucracy and officialdom.

In essence, therefore, the development of firm-level competitiveness in developing countries takes place in product and factor markets where imperfections abound. The efficacy of such development then depends on how well interventions, selective and functional, are used to overcome those imperfections, not on how few interventions exist. This is the opposite conclusion to that reached by much current wisdom, but it is based on the same theory and the same empirical evidence.

The current conventional wisdom on the universal superiority of free market solutions thus veers from neoclassical economics, which is perfectly amenable to interventions to overcome market failures, into neoclassical political economy, which takes as an article of faith that all interventions must be bad and all governments corrupt and inefficient (see Shapiro and Taylor, 1990). Responsible policy analysts must eschew dogma and examine in each case how well markets and governments work, and differentiate their recommendations accordingly. In some cases they may well recommend free market solutions, in others they may recommend a hefty dose of intervention.

Determinants of competitiveness in South Africa

This section applies the simple schema of competitiveness to the case of South Africa. For lack of information on my part, however, it will deal only with the trade regime, skills and technical effort. It is encouraging that a group of South African researchers is currently applying this kind of approach in general and to various individual industries.[12] The results of their work will provide the depth and data that my chapter lacks.

Incentives

The trade regime in South Africa has undergone significant changes over the 1980s. While it has moved from being practically autarkic to a much healthier pattern that allows for trade specialisation and export growth, there remain many inefficient elements. As noted earlier, quantitative restrictions on imports have been abolished on all products with the exception of agricultural goods and textiles. However, to quote Belli *et al.* (1993), 'Despite the substantial liberalisation of the trade regime in the past decade, there have been policy reversals. The financial rand, for instance, was reintroduced in 1985 and import surcharges in 1988. Moreover, some serious problems remain. First, the system is subject to excessively frequent changes. Second, the tariff structure is overly complex. Third, the dispersion of the tariff schedule is exceedingly high. Fourth, the regime is biased against exports.'

The complexity, *ad hoc* nature and unpredictability of the protective regime are clear disincentives to firms in terms of long-term investments in capability development and restructuring. Worse still, the tariff structure reflects the influence of a haphazard system that has grown up over time and has no underlying strategy of protecting infant industries during their learning period. The average tariff rate is high compared to developed countries, and around the median for developing countries. The dispersion of the tariff rates is one of the highest in the world, with strange, irrational deviations for individual products, what Belli *et al.* call the 'laser beam approach to protection' (1993: par. 25).

The weighted average of protection given to manufactures, based on duty collections, is 9,4%, with a minimum of zero and a maximum of 450%. Consumer goods have the highest protection, 17,6%, while intermediates receive 5,0% and capital goods 7,9% (Belli *et al.*, 1993: Table 6). At the narrower industrial level, the most highly protected activities are textiles, apparel and footwear: these are all mature, labour-intensive activities that are clearly not undergoing learning, and are being protected to preserve employment. The more dynamic areas of South Africa's future comparative advantage, say in electronics or equipment, receive far less protection. This confirms the suggestion that the protective structure is geared to maintaining obsolete and inefficient patterns of specialisation rather than to promoting a shift to a more dynamic pattern.

This impression is strengthened by data on effective rates of protection (ERPs). These calculations are intrinsically subject to many uncertainties, and industrial averages tend to conceal enormous and important variations. They cannot therefore be taken to show competitiveness of entire manufacturing activities in any straightforward sense. For what they are worth, they show that the average rate of effective protection for manufacturing is 30% (Belli *et al.*, 1993) with an enormous dispersion around the average. Textiles and related industries receive the highest rates of protection, and equipment the lowest (after food and beverages, which are resource-based). The pattern of protection is the reverse of what may be expected of a semi-industrial country that is trying to dynamise its comparative advantage in manufactures.

Apart from this, the protective regime has two other disadvantages. First, there is no underlying strategy or protection related to gains in industrial competitiveness. The extent or duration of protection does not seem to be used as a policy instrument. There are no performance requirements imposed on protected industries. There seems to be little conception of selectively promoting activities that may lead South Africa's future exports. Thus, the regime has many of the non-selective and non-economic aspects of protection that have bedevilled interventions in many developing countries.

Second, the balance of trade incentives remains in favour of the domestic market with much of recent export growth driven by excess capacity rather than a genuine commitment to profitable exporting (Belli *et al.*, 1992). This effectively neutralises the stimulus that export activity can provide to the upgrading of competitive capabilities. This is one of the most important handicaps of the present regime – the East Asian experience suggests that strong pressures to export provided the real engine of investments in TC development, despite protected domestic markets.

In sum, therefore, the current South African trade regime is not conducive to the development of competitive industrial capabilities. It protects industries without regard to their competitive potential, has no strategy for promoting new infant industries, and fails to offset the effects of protection by forcing firms to invest in building export markets. There is clearly a case for a restructuring of the protective regime, by lowering high levels of protection, making the system stable, removing many of the irrational elements of protection and, most important, gearing protection to the achievement of international competitiveness. This would involve much greater selectivity, based on a detailed analysis of the competitive problems of each industry, than exists at present. It would involve a proactive approach to promoting infant industries and restructuring existing industries. And it would involve a close integration between trade reform and supply side policies (on skills, technology and so on, see below).

Clearly an element of trade liberalisation would be part of the reform of the protective regime. In the medium to long term the objective should clearly be to bring down effective protection and reduce its dispersion. This is better achieved by a gradual, pre-announced programme of tariff reductions, coupled with supporting supply-side measures and a strong push into exports, than by rapid and sweeping liberalisation that exposes all industries to the same force of competition without regard to their capability development needs. Moreover, it is important to retain a strong element of selectivity to take account of different learning or relearning periods, and to promote the infant industries of the future.

Skills

Reforming the competitive regime will be ineffective in evoking a proper supply response unless the industrial sector has access to the skills it needs to operate efficiently. It is a strange lacuna in development policy discussions that none of the proposals for incentive reform makes any attempt to co-ordinate the pace of reform with attempts to meet the skill needs that are bound to arise. This is all the stranger when we think of the emphasis on skills given in discussions of competitiveness in developed countries.

Table 1. Relative enrolment rates (% of age group)

	SA	Zimbabwe	S. Korea	Taiwan
Primary				
1865	90	110	101	97
1987	—	136	96	100
Secondary				
1965	15	6	35	38
1987	—	46	94	91
Vocational, latest (% of total pop.)	—	0	2.1	2.2
Tertiary				
1965	4	0	6	7
1987	—	4	32	13
Of which: Science, Maths, Eng., latest (% of total pop.)	—	0.01	0.76	0.78

Source: Lall (1992b)

Table 3.1 shows the available data on educational enrolment rates in South Africa and some other countries. Unfortunately the South African government stopped providing enrolment data some time ago, so we can only guess at its educational base. All the evidence (see below) suggests that it is highly skewed and, as far as the black population is concerned, of rather poor quality. Zimbabwe is included as an example of a fairly advanced African country, while the NIEs are examples of what skill investments look like for such high levels of competitiveness in a diversified industrial structure.

Data on sub-Saharan Africa (excluding South Africa) more generally, reviewed in Lall (1992b), show that African countries lag substantially behind the NIEs of East Asia, both at the start of the period and at its end. The lag is particularly marked at the secondary education and vocational training level – yet these are the main sources of skill creation relevant for shopfloor efficiency. If dropout rates and quality considerations were brought in, it is likely that the Asian lead would increase further. Even larger gaps exist as far as tertiary enrolments are concerned, and the proportion of tertiary enrolments in technical subjects is tiny for Africa as compared to East Asia.

Data on firm-level training, a vital source of skill generation, are not widely available, but scattered pieces of information suggest that a similar gap exists between Africa and East Asia. Firms in East Asia invest a great deal in employee training, with significant support or pressure from governments, either by tax incentives (as in South Korea) or by contributions to training institutions (Singapore and Taiwan).

In the absence of recent data on South Africa it is impossible to make direct comparisons with other countries. While it is likely that South Africa has a better relative endowment of high-level skills than other countries in the African region, these endowments seem to lag significantly behind those in NIEs and OECD countries. To quote from a recent study on the slow growth of South African productivity:

> The lack of high level manpower is an important productivity barrier. This is illustrated by the Population Census of 1985 which shows that only 37,5% of whites had a standard 10 certificate or higher educational qualifications in that year. The figure for coloureds was 4,0%, for Asians 13,5% and for blacks a mere 2,3%. South Africa has a unique problem regarding high level manpower, because whites represent almost the total high level manpower component. The supply of equivalent black high level manpower is still very small. Of the 11 573 new apprentices registered during 1985, whites numbered 9 246 (80%) whilst only 666 (5,8%) were blacks... Another facet of the problem is the deficiency in management skills in South Africa... Although our top managers compare favourably with those of the rest of the world, various studies conducted by the NPI indicated a severe shortage in middle management. (Du Plooy, 1988:90)

This suggests that, in terms of world-level skill endowments, South Africa suffers serious deficiencies, which may hold back a major process of structural transformation if it liberalises its trade fully in the near future. These considerations are essentially of a long-term nature. The creation of skills is itself a slow, incremental process, and requires considerable effort and investment. A great deal of slack exists in most countries' industrial sectors, so that efficiency may be raised significantly with a given stock of human capital, by better management and technical practices, reallocation of employees and upgrading of physical capital. Improved employee training can add a lot of operational skills to a given work force; the use of expatriate manpower at critical points can enable a great deal of productivity improvement to occur. The closure or trimming of uneconomic activities can release some high-level technical manpower, while greater specialisation in lower-tech activities can reduce the need for human capital.

Thus, there is much that South Africa can do to increase its competitiveness without immediately improving its education structure. In the short run, many possibilities do exist for enhancing productivity and product quality, by better management, access to new equipment and technology, exposure to competition, industrial restructuring and training. All these avenues have to be fully explored. In the longer term, however, high-level skills do have to be raised to sustain productivity growth and industrial development.

Technological effort

Considerable empirical research in Asia and Latin America has established that industries or enterprises that achieved competitiveness devoted extended efforts to conscious technological learning (for references see Lall, 1992a). As activities have grown more complex, moreover, informal efforts have developed into formal R & D, which becomes necessary even to absorb and adapt imported technologies. Along with the growth of enterprise R & D, support has had to be provided by a growing technology infrastructure. This infrastructure has provided training in specialised disciplines, testing facilities, basic research and information support, standards and metrology, and linkages between 'pure' research (at universities) and industry.

It is very difficult to measure technological effort in the broad sense. The employment of technicians, engineers and scientists is one crude indicator, but the mere existence of technical skills does not ensure that they are properly deployed in generating useful knowledge: the incentive and management structure is equally important. However, the absence of such manpower can certainly constrict technological effort at source, and this may be the case in a number of African industries or enterprises. The alternative measure is formal R & D, in terms either of expenditure or of technical manpower employed in such activity. This captures only the tip of the iceberg of technological effort, and the mere existence of R & D certainly does not ensure effective technological effort. But at least roughly comparable data are available across countries.

No data on South African research and development are available from Unesco sources.[13] However, some R & D statistics are published within the country, though they are patchy and discontinuous. The most thorough study of the subject, by Scerri (1988), concludes:

> On an aggregate level the priority set on R & D in South Africa seems to
> be low. Not only is the absolute level of R & D expenditure low when

compared to that of other countries, but the trend in such expenditure is toward the development stage at the expense of basic and applied research. This is a characteristic of technologically peripheral nations.

Excessive reliance on exports of primary products as a source of foreign exchange places a severe constraint on the scope for R & D activity. The range of innovative output in the primary sector is limited and primarily cost reducing. The ability to compete on the international markets is determined by quality considerations at least as much as by price levels. (Scerri, 1988:122)

Scerri provides data on R & D in South African manufacturing, which accounts for the bulk of such expenditure in the country. Table 3.2 sets out R & D as a percentage of sales for a number of industrial subsectors in 1966 and 1983. It shows that average research propensities were low relative to NIEs or developed countries, but that some R & D took place in almost all manufacturing activities. What is perhaps more significant, however, is that the bulk of research was conducted by government laboratories and public corporations (which are concentrated in iron and steel, industrial chemicals, electrical machinery and non-electrical machinery). The private sector, which accounted for the bulk of manufacturing in other sectors, performed relatively little R & D. Scerri traces this serious deficiency to the large minimum scale of R & D needed and the high incidence of foreign ownership of South African industry, both leading to 'heavy dependence on foreign technology' (1988:114).

Such technological dependence lowers the cost and need for local technological effort, but it imposes its own cost in terms of lags, inflexibility and lack of dynamism. As Du Plooy (1988:90–1) puts it:

The practical application of new technology in South Africa is relatively slow because the lack of competition in the local as well as international markets encourages the usage of outdated processes. Additionally, there is insufficient expenditure on research and development by the private sector since many companies traditionally receive new technology from their overseas holding companies, this avenue is threatened by the disinvestment campaign and new technologies will increasingly have to be developed locally. Research is mainly conducted by government and semi-government institutions, which often tends to compartmentalisation and to hampering technology transfer.

Du Plooy's point about technological lags introduced by the disinvestment of foreign companies (and by sanctions more generally) is significant. For a country which has used FDI as the primary source of technology, any constriction of this source is bound to have been costly and disruptive. The imposition of trade sanctions did not choke off other sources of technology, but is likely to have raised the costs of technology acquisition. In the absence of a developed local technology base, the assimilation and autonomous development of new technologies are bound to have been further retarded. In sum, the impression that South African industry has large areas of obsolescence and uncompetitiveness is further strengthened by technology considerations.

Table 3.2. R & D expenditures in SA (as % of sales)

Industry	1966	1983	% by government (1983)
Electrical machinery	0,20	2,09	85
Non-electrical machinery	0,05	1,35	98
Industrial chemicals	2,49	1,16	69
Transport equip, except auto and parts	0,30	0,45	72
Non-ferrous basic metals	0,14	0,4	85
Basic ferrous metals	0,24	0,27	87
Leather	0,17	0,23	—
Non-metallic minerals	0,40	0,21	32
Textiles	0,10	0,15	87
Wood	0,21	0,15	65
Rubber	n.a.	0,11	40
Plastics	n.a.	0,11	7
Fabricated metals, except machinery	0,08	0,1	45
Chemicals, except industrial	0,11	0,1	20
Beverages and tobacco	0,03	0,09	43
Food	0,06	0,09	30
Paper	0,09	0,08	18
Motor vehicles and parts	0,02	0,06	12
Footwear	0,05	0,03	—
Printing and publishing	0,01	0,01	—

Source: Scerri, 1988:115

It was noted earlier that South Korea and Japan forced the pace of indigenous technology development by deliberately restricting inflows of direct investment, while encouraging inflows in all other forms (including 'reverse engineering' by local firms). South Africa never opted for this route to developing its technological base, despite years of relative isolation. The price of this is that in many advanced industries South Africa is not likely to be a major industrial competitor to OECD countries or even to the NIEs of East Asia.

This does not mean that it cannot exploit its advantages in neighbouring markets where it is an industrial giant. However, as these markets also open up to international competition, South Africa will find its advantages confined to technologies in which it has a genuine advantage *vis-à-vis* developed and newly industrialising countries, based on transport cost or productivity and technological advantages. The evidence suggests the following competitive outcomes in regional markets.

First, South Africa is unlikely to displace other suppliers of sophisticated, high-technology products, technologies and services in all areas where there is no strong transport advantage. If trade liberalisation proceeds in neighbouring countries, the major suppliers of sophisticated products are likely to be elsewhere, in the OECD or NIEs. South Africa is, on the other hand, itself likely to become a major importer of such products, services and technologies as it upgrades its industries. To the extent that its neighbours, with lower costs and good infrastructures and skills, can set themselves up as staging posts for assembly or service activities, they may be able to tap some of this trade with South Africa.

Second, in more standardised products, with lower levels of skill and mature technologies, South Africa is likely to be able to establish a competitive edge especially in transport-cost-intensive products. Many capital and intermediate goods fall into this broad category, and here South Africa may already have an edge, or can rapidly establish one with some upgrading of its existing technologies.

To conclude, South Africa has a long-established tradition of R & D in a variety of industries. However, the extent of this effort is relatively limited. It is difficult to assess without further investigation how innovative its industrial research efforts have been; evidently there are various areas of strength in intermediates and some capital goods. The heavy dependence on public R & D is not a very healthy sign for industrial competitiveness. Nor is the dependent attitude to foreign investments. However, there is a need for the time being to revive this potent means of technology transfer while boosting local absorptive capabilities.

Policy implications

Many of the policy implications for developing industrial competitiveness have already been noted in passing above. The chapter concludes by bringing together the general arguments and drawing out the lessons that the NIEs may have for a country like South Africa. The appropriate pace and form of trade liberalisation has already been discussed under incentives above and need not be repeated here. This section focuses on industrial policy more narrowly defined, including the use of protective devices for infant industries.

Table 3.3 sets out in summary form the main determinants of ITD, the nature of possible market failures (not those resulting from government interventions), and the range of possible policy solutions. The table does not cover all possible market failures that can affect ITD (e.g. it does not go into the promotion of inter-industry or inter-firm linkages). It is intended to provide an impression of the main issues that arise in this area, including those arising from the structural adjustment process.

As noted above, the most serious policy problems arise in the context of selective forms of intervention. These selective policies may be of several types: the creation of particular types of skill, the setting up of institutions to promote particular 'strategic' technologies, the financing of 'mission-oriented' research, the granting of infant industry protection or subsidies, the channelling of local or foreign investments into particular activities, or negotiating with and regulating international investment and technology transfers to achieve technological objectives. These are all policies that require enormous skills, information and discipline on the part of the government. They are prone to rent-seeking behav-

Table 3.3. ITD determinants, market failures and policy solutions

Determinants	Market failures	Policy remedies
Incentives:		
Macro-economic policies	Not applicable.	
Foreign competition	Full exposure to competition leads to underinvestment in ITD because of externalities, unpredictable learning, lack of understanding of ITD process, investment complementarities, information gaps, risk aversion.	Infant industry protection for difficult new activities (very selective, monitored, limited in duration, with safeguards, integrated with skills & inst. development). Phased liberalisation, taking account of relearning costs.
Domestic competition	Market power, economies of scale and scope, complementarities, need of large size to enter world markets and undertake advanced training and R&D.	Ensure competition, regulate monopoly, but create large firms where necessary to exploit scale economies in ITD and marketing.
Skills:		
Worker and supervisory	Formal educ. investments suffer from	Govt support of schooling, higher level
Technical	lumpiness, missing markets (lack of sup-	education and special training. Control
Production engineering	ply of teachers and facilities), risk,	of education quality and content.
Design and development	imperfect foresight, lack of information.	Selectivity in creation of high-level
Scientific and basic research	Quality control and curriculum content	skills, geared to industrial strategy.
Managerial, organisational,	suffer from opportunism, information	Information, incentives, subsidies for
marketing	gaps. Investments by firms in training suffer from externalities (lack of appropriateness), lack of knowledge of benefits of training, risk aversion, capital market failures.	in-firm training. Support for foreign training, import of foreign trainers.
Information and technical support:		
Knowledge of need for ITD effort	Information gaps and fragmented information markets (on sources of tech);	Information and persuasion on need for technological activity. Strengthening of
Knowledge of kind of effort to promote ITD	'learning to learn' delays; lumpiness of infrastructure facilities; public goods fea-	intellectual property rights. Provision of infrastructural services; setting up R&D
Access to information from other firms, institutions, universities, etc.	tures of some information (externalities and lack of appropriateness); skill gaps;	institutions for selected industries (and ensuring linkages to enterprises).
Standards, metrology, testing facilities	risk aversion; absence of technological intermediation. Underdeveloped inter-	Technological extension services for small firms. Information services on
Technical extension services	firm linkages, leading to poor diffusion	sources of technology. Support of co-
Contract research, design, training	of technology. Inadequate co-operative	operative R&D by industries. Some mis-
Information services on technological sources, trends	efforts by firms to enforce standards and quality.	sion-oriented R&D support. Encouragement of subcontracting and local pro-
Basic research support	Missing links with foreign research.	curement. Links with foreign R&D.
Access to technological information worldwide		
Finance for ITD:		
Availability of finance at appropriate rates and in sufficient quantity for R&D or the commercialisation of innovations	Capital market failures from asymmetric or missing information, adverse selection, moral hazard, cost of evaluation or enforcement of ITD loans; risk aversion	Creating technology financing capabilities in banks, with training, subsidies (to start with only); special financial provision for ITD efforts that link with R&D
Equity sharing finance for innovators	or over-conservative policies by financial intermediaries. Lack of relevant financial	institutes; financial instruments for SMEs; venture capital and other schemes
Special finance for small and medium enterprises	intermediation skills.	to provide special instruments for risk sharing. Targeting of sectors with exceptional technological potential.
Technology policies:		
Technology imports, FDI, promotion of local R&D , other interventions to strengthen ITD	Insufficient investment in local R&D (due to factors above). Transfer of technology suffers from international technology market imperfections, monopolistic or oligopolistic suppliers, asymmetric information.	Fiscal and other incentives for R&D; procurement of products of local innovations; information service on sources of technology; selective control of FDI and negotiation to ensure local 'know why' development. Selective support for
	Absorption of imported technology limited by passive dependence on imported technology, plus other failures above that deter ITD.	R&D projects with large potential benefits and externalities.

iour and pressure groups. They can be very costly if they are wrongly designed and implemented.

The experience of the most dynamic industrialisers in the developing world suggests that their selective interventions determined the nature and success of their industrial development, and that such interventions were well implemented. The real issue is whether the conditions under which their governments operated are replicable in South Africa. Will the future South African government have the clarity of economic objectives, information, design skills, implementation and monitoring capabilities and the political will to carry out selective policies in the way that the larger NIEs of East Asia did?

The answer must be given by others. I can only note some general points. The level of selectivity exercised by, say, the South Korean government was so detailed and pervasive that few other countries can hope to emulate it with a comparable degree of success. It also had many advantages that may be unique: the homogeneity of the population, the relatively favourable income distribution and the mobilisation of nationalist sentiment in response to an external threat. It started with a strong base of human capital, which the government was able to enhance dramatically, partly because of local traditions. It was driven by the single-minded pursuit of particular economic objectives. It had direct economic involvement at the highest political level, close government collaboration with private business, a dedicated and well-trained civil service and the ability to monitor performance and to penalise poor performers. Its design was closely influenced by the experience of neighbouring Japan, with which there were cultural similarities and technological links. It has to be seen to what extent South Africa has, or can develop, comparable advantages.

This means that the complexity and range of South Korean interventions may not be replicable in South Africa. It does not mean, however, that no selective interventions are possible. There are valuable lessons to be learned from South Korea, if they are adapted to local economic conditions and political realities. For example, the need for promotion of infant industry learning exists in South Africa as in other developing countries. However, this promotion need not be as detailed and specific as in South Korea, where the government intervened at the level of industry, product, technology and firm. More general levels of protection, at the broad subsectoral level, may be suited to countries that have limited administrative capabilities. Market forces can then be left to sort out the best enterprises and technologies.

The most useful lessons of the South Korean experience are perhaps that many of the potential costs of protection can be overcome by instituting safeguards (early entry into export markets) and integrating the incentive interventions with interventions on the supply side. Most developing countries, possibly including South Africa, have granted protection without ensuring that their enterprises had access to the new skills and information they needed to become competitive. Unlike the South Koreans, they were not truly selective in planning industrial strategy.

The correct balance of interventions and market forces cannot be determined on *a priori* grounds. Both governments and markets fail. Both can be improved with effort. There are some governments today that are capable of mounting effective selective interventions at a fairly complex level. There are many that are best confined to functional policies, or the most general levels of selectivity (say, the food processing sector in sub-Saharan African countries). The judgment ultimately has to be a pragmatic one. General statements on the virtues of markets versus governments are suspect, and may be economically harmful.

Notes

1. Manufacturing value-added in 1989 came to $20 billion, just larger than Thailand, Indonesia or Turkey, about half the size of India and under a third of South Korea (data from the World Development Report, 1992).

2. See Du Plooy (1988), McCarthy (1988), Scerri (1990) and Strydom (1987).

3. Trade Monitoring Project, Trade Monitor, No. 1, February 1993. Also see the analysis by Bell (1992).

4. See Bell (1992) and Holden (1992) for reviews of the debate.

5. For a recent presentation of opposing views see Dornbusch (1992) and Rodrik (1992a and 1992b).

6. This assumes that all countries had similar infrastructures, macro-economic management, natural resources and access to world markets. Clearly, all these may also differ significantly, but for the purposes of focusing on industrial factors within policy control, these are abstracted from here.

7. This approach draws on 'evolutionary theories' of growth developed by Nelson and Winter (1982). Also see Pack and Westphal (1986).

8. For an instructive examination of the learning periods in complex engineering industries in a successful NIE like South Korea, see Jacobsson (1993).

9. More correctly, the process of capability building is simply ignored in this literature, as in much of the conventional textbook analysis.

10. The best-known arguments linking export orientation to liberal economic policies are in the World Development Report (1987) but this is the culmination of many writings by authors like Balassa, Krueger, Little and Harberger.

11. See Amsden (1989), Lall (1990), Lall and associates (1992), Pack and Westphal (1986), Wade (1990) and Westphal (1990).

12. This is the Economic Trends Research Group's 'Industrial Strategy Project', an initial synthesis of which is presented by Joffe *et al.* in this volume.

13. Details on NIE technology expenditures are given in Lall (1990).

4

Trade Policy and International Competitiveness: The South Korean Experience

DUCK-WOO NAM

To the outside observer, the future of South Africa appears rich in opportunities, yet fraught with great risks. As South Africa is truly a unique case, no other nation's experience can offer a reliable guide or infallible model. Nevertheless, in some limited respects, I think South Africa can benefit from the experience of a Newly Industrialising Economy (NIE) like South Korea. Let me emphasise that in what follows, the basic message I want to convey is not 'Do the same as we did', but rather 'Try to avoid our mistakes'.

In simple terms, international competitiveness means producing better products for lower prices than other countries competing in the international market. However, there are many factors affecting the quality and price of goods and services produced at home, trade policy being only one. For example, wage rates relative to labour productivity, interest rates, taxes, and charges for services – such as transportation, communication, insurance, etc. – are the major cost components and as such affect the price of export products. Even cultural factors such as traditional labour–management relations, the work ethic and the level of education can have an important bearing on the quality and prices of products in a given country.

It should also be noted that better quality and lower prices do not necessarily bid fair in the foreign market under the current international trade environment. For example, Japanese automobile plants, benefiting from superior automation and younger and better-trained workers, are known to be twice as efficient as European auto plants. But Japanese auto exports are being limited by various protectionist measures on the part of importing countries – such as higher import duties (10% in Europe and 2,5% in the US), 'anti-dumping' measures, 'voluntary' restraints, and quota agreements. Thus, many diverse factors lie outside the scope of trade policy as it is usually defined, implying that trade policy alone cannot go very far in increasing a country's international competitiveness and exports.

Foreign exchange rate policy

At the domestic level, trade policy is mainly concerned with the foreign exchange rate, customs duties, and regulation of imports. To begin with the foreign exchange rate, it is often the case with developing countries that chronic inflation tends to prolong over-valuation of the domestic currency as the rapid domestic inflation is not fully offset by the depreciation of the domestic currency, with the result that exports are discouraged while imports are encouraged. South Korea was no exception in the early days, particularly in the period 1945–60. The real exchange rate, adjusted to changes in wholesale prices at home and abroad, fell to one half of its 1945–50 value by January 1960. The drastic devaluation of the foreign exchange rate in 1961 from 50 won per dollar to 130 won and the unification of multiple exchange rates marked the beginning of the all-out government effort for export promotion. At the same time, the South Korean government relaxed import controls, and subsidies were provided to exports.

Since 1960 South Korea's exchange rate has tended to depreciate, currently standing at the rate of 780 won per dollar (February 1993). The rate was adjusted periodically by the government, but the adjustment tended to lag behind rising prices at home and abroad, mainly for two reasons. First, policy-makers feared the vicious cycle of domestic inflation and depreciation since devaluation leads to increases in won currency in import prices, which in turn aggravates domestic inflation. Second, policy-makers were also worried about the effect of the increasing won value on the nation's foreign debt and its amortisation cost that must be borne by business units and the government. Caught between the public outcry for price stability and the need for export promotion, policy-makers were reluctant to take prompt action, often swayed by political expediency rather than by any economic rationale. For example, despite domestic inflation rates far in excess of world inflation rates at the time of the oil crises in 1973 and 1978, the exchange rate was held constant at 484 won to the dollar from 1975 until 1980. This partly explains why export growth rates declined after 1976 and the volume of exports fell in terms of 1979. The needed devaluation by 20% was only carried out in 1980 after a new government came to power.

In response to changing conditions at home and abroad, South Korea adopted a floating exchange rate system in which the rates, a few years ago, were to move freely in response to supply and demand changes in the money market. One of the problems arising from the adoption of the floating rate system was that the inflow of foreign short-term capital induced by much higher interest rates at home – more than 18% per annum – tended to slow the speed of depreciation of the won despite the slow growth of exports; this contributed to a marked deterioration of the nation's current account since 1990. At present, the South Korean government is trying to liberalise the nation's financial market with the expectation that such a policy will serve, *inter alia*, to enhance competition in the market, thereby lowering the interest rate and moving it closer to the international level. To be sure, the continuing influx of short-term capital from abroad may itself help reduce domestic interest rates, but, at the same time, the nation's net foreign debt may soar to an intolerable level, while the excessively slow depreciation, due to the capital inflow, may unduly retard export growth and improvement in the balance of payments.

Incidentally, it should be noted that under the current international monetary system, exchange rate fluctuations of major currencies in recent years have hardly reflected their current account positions; they have rather reflected the movement of speculative short-term capital among the major currencies. To cope with this situation the major governments undertook to intervene and manipulate exchange rates on the basis of the Plaza Accord in September 1985 or G7 agreements in later years. This, however, raises an important question: if the floating exchange rate system fails to help correct the current account imbalances among countries, what else could serve as an international adjustment mechanism? This is, I believe, a fundamental question facing the international monetary system today.

Trade policies for export promotion

Now I would like to turn to the topic of trade policies for exports and imports. In August 1964, the South Korean government undertook far-reaching economic reforms with a view to promoting exports. Exporters were given the right to import their inputs duty-free and without restriction. The principal device for assuring this privilege was a system of 'domestic letters of credit' (DLCs), which enabled exporters to receive inputs duty-free and obtain automatic access to subsidised trade credit. Moreover, some of these benefits could be passed on by the exporter to its domestic suppliers, since banks were authorised to open further DLCs on the basis of the 'master' DLC. Exporters were also provided generous wastage allowances for the importation of raw materials. These incentives were later extended to indirect exports, namely the production of domestic inputs for exports. In addition, tariff exemptions were granted to importers of machinery and equipment used to produce direct and indirect exports, and accelerated depreciation allowances were introduced. Furthermore, inputs used in export production were free of indirect taxes and exporters received a tax credit amounting to 50% of their income. Yet another export promotion measure gave credit preference to exporters in terms of availability of funds as well as the interest rate charged. On the side of imports, in 1967 the 'positive' list of admissible imports was replaced by a 'negative' list of products whose importation required government approval. This meant, in practice, further reduction of the scope of import restriction. In sum, the export regime thus established after 1964 provided, in effect, a free trade status to exporters, with some additional incentives.

The system of discriminatory policies for export promotion, however, was not without its own demerits. For example, in order to prevent the abuse of the concessional treatment for non-export purposes, the government had to set up highly complex checking systems in the area of customs duties, taxes, and bank credit, so much so that the red tape itself became a serious barrier hindering export activities, while corruption inevitably crept into the checking process. The government, aware of this situation and spurred on by public opinion, then set out to dismantle regulations and reduce the extent and scope of favoured treatment for exports – this time in the name of a freer market and less government intervention. Thus, as Professor Balassa has noted (Balassa, 1990), there emerged the interesting phenomenon of a trade policy cycle in which periods of 'restriction' alternated with periods of 'liberalisation'.

Apart from monetary incentives, the government established the South Korean Trade Promotion Corporation (KOTRA) in 1964 to promote exports and conduct market research abroad. The government also authorised the South Korea Foreign Trade Association (KFTA), a private-sector organisation, to collect 1% of the value of specified imports for use as an export promotion fund. KFTA has been active in organising trade missions to foreign countries, training employees of its member companies, disseminating trade-related information at home and abroad, and organising trade shows in its exhibition centre.

Under the trade regime outlined above, South Korea achieved phenomenal export growth during the 1960s and 1970s. Between 1962 and 1976 the annual growth rate of South Korea's exports averaged 43% as compared with a 15% growth rate of world exports in the same period. In the subsequent period of 1977–90 the average annual growth rate of exports slowed to 17%, still substantially higher than the world average of 10%. To what extent the trade policy of the South Korean government was responsible for such rapid export growth, particularly during the period 1962–76, is a difficult question because many factors other than trade policy combined to produce such a result. No doubt one of the most important factors was the very favourable world economic environment up until the middle of the 1970s. Under the postwar world order, overseas markets were generally wide open for Korean products, particularly in the United States and Europe and to a lesser degree in Japan. Foreign capital for domestic investments was readily available from both public and private sources, and technology transfer from developed countries was relatively easy.

Since the mid-1980s South Korea's trade policy has gradually changed in response to changing conditions at home and abroad. Internally, there was a growing awareness both in and out of the government that the economy had outgrown the highly interventionist role of the state and that liberalisation of the economic activities of the private sector was called for. Externally, there had been growing pressure on South Korea from the US and EC to open up its domestic market to imports of their goods and services. As of today, South Korea has largely eliminated selective treatment for exports in the area of taxation and bank credits. South Korea's average tariff rate stands at about 6%, comparable to that of developed countries.

By the end of 1992, 98% of manufactured products and 87% of agricultural and fishery products were on the government's list for automatic import approval. Yet market openings for rice, South Korea's single most important staple grain, still remain as one of the most contentious issues at home as well as in the Uruguay Round negotiations. South Korea is currently implementing a market-opening programme for the financial and service sectors based, in part, on commitments made in negotiations with the United States and the anticipated outcome of the Uruguay Round.

Industrial policy

In the area of industrial policy, the heavy industry development programme carried out in the first half of the 1970s has attracted much attention among scholars and policy-makers abroad. The scope of this highly ambitious programme included the automobile, ship-building, steel, machinery, metal, refineries and petrochemical industries. Unfortunately, in the course of implementation, the programme fell victim to the oil crises of 1973 and 1978 and the ensuing world-wide recession and inflation – a calamity entirely unforeseen by the economic planners at the time of initiation. Naturally, the programme was criticised at home and abroad as a glaring case of over-investment and misuse of resources. Collins, for example, suggested that 'the anti-export bias' in the programme in this period was largely responsible for the decline in GDP of 4,8% in 1980.

Some qualification to this observation, however, seems to be in order. To be sure, the South Korean economy suffered from over-investment and over-capacity for a considerable period with much higher costs involved than originally anticipated. Yet many South Korean policy-makers today ask themselves: would South Korea have ever had a better chance of building heavy industry if the nation had not embarked on such a programme in those days despite so many difficulties? Many of them say no, pointing to the fact that since the time of the construction of South Korea's heavy industry there has been an enormous escalation of resource costs in international markets as well as skyrocketing land prices and construction costs at home relative to the increase in product prices. The opportunity cost of the heavy industry programme in a dynamic as well as static sense is difficult to assess, yet it remains true that exports of heavy industry products have been gaining importance in South Korea's export composition in recent years. That is to say, exports of heavy industry products have been increasing at a much faster rate than traditional light industry products (textiles, footwear, electric appliances, etc.). This trend reflects South Korea's weakening comparative advantage in labour-intensive products in relation to less developed countries in South-east Asia and China, which was predicted by economic planners at the time of the initiation of the heavy industry programme in the early 1970s. Negative GDP growth in 1980 was not entirely due to the problems of heavy industry, but was also the result of the then world-wide recession combined with internal political disruption following the assassination of President Park Chung-Hee in October 1979. At any rate, it is true that South Korea had to pay a relatively high price for building its heavy industry.

Lessons from the South Korean experience

What then are the major lessons to be drawn from the South Korean experience with trade policy for countries such as South Africa that are seeking the right path to export growth? Without much knowledge of the South African situation I am not sure to what extent the South Korean experience has relevance; however, I may offer some comments in what follows.

(1) Let me once again stress that factors other than trade policy are equally or even more important in achieving a rapid growth of exports. In the South Korean experience, besides the favourable international trade environment as previously noted, there were other positive factors that can be enumerated: first,

dynamism of entrepreneurship and business acumen; second, an exceptionally high ratio (78%) of total trade (exports plus imports) to GDP, indicating a high degree of exposure to the global economy; third, free and swift labour mobility from the agricultural to the industrial sectors; and fourth, stable labour–management relations enforced by an authoritarian government. It is worth noting that this factor could not have existed in more democratic countries, where government-enforced labour discipline would not be acceptable to such an extent. It is perhaps no surprise that South Korea's export growth has slowed since 1990 in response to a worsening international trade environment and serious labour unrest following political democratisation that began in 1989.

(2) The international as well as the South Korean experience seems to indicate that maintenance of a realistic exchange rate is a key condition for maintaining international competitiveness and continuing export growth. A prompt adjustment of the exchange rate should be made in such a way that its effect on domestic prices is minimised by concurrent use of stabilising monetary policy and wage guidelines subject to the understanding and co-operation of organised labour. The adjustment may be effected either by government decree or by the free play of market forces. A free foreign exchange market is desirable for many reasons, yet it may fail to reflect the change of the nation's current account position owing to the speculative movement of short-term capital among countries. In that case, government intervention may become inevitable for a country to defend its balance-of-payments position.

(3) The World Bank (1987) views South Korea as one of the outstanding examples of an outward-oriented and liberalised economy, whereas for others it represents a convincing case for intervention. The truth of the matter, in my view, is that South Korea created an artificial free trade regime for exporters, making it a haven for importers from the protectionist regime. Yet South Korean policy was flexible enough to adjust import policies over time in response to changing conditions at home and abroad. The principal lesson to be learned from the South Korean experience is that exports can grow rapidly only under a free trade regime, whether artificial or natural.

(4) The South Korean experience seems to indicate that incentive measures for exports were useful and effective in marshalling and channelling the energy and resources of business units to export industry in the early stage of development. But as time went on policy-makers became increasingly aware that such a system of selective measures had its own drawbacks: apart from the problems of red tape and corruption attendant on selective control, the business units habitually sought government assistance and protection whenever they were in difficulty, reducing their incentive to undertake self-help efforts for managerial and technological innovation. It was far easier for the government to grant protection than it was to remove it. It took the South Korean government years before it was able to relax import restrictions, lower tariff barriers, and eliminate income tax benefits for exporters in the mid-1970s and finally reach the present stage in which most of the selective measures are gone. The lesson to be learned here is that incentive measures are useful only in the beginning stage of an ambitious export promotion programme, when business units may need to be

externally 'motivated' to push exports. In introducing selective incentive measures, therefore, the government is well advised to announce at the same time a schedule for phasing out such measures to preclude over-protection.

(5) It is difficult to draw a clear line between an import substitution industry and an export industry. The textile industry in South Korea, for example, was initially intended mainly for import substitution but grew into a major export industry in later years. What matters is the prospect for international competitiveness. Protection is almost inevitable in the early stage of new industry, because no investment can be expected to yield a profit in the first one or two years of operation, while the financial capability of private business is generally very weak in a developing country. What is crucial is whether or not the protected project will be internationally competitive in the expected time horizon without further protection. Seen from this perspective, the argument for protection of infant industry appears to have practical wisdom in its favour.

(6) I have noted that the South Korean government embarked in the early 1970s on an ambitious heavy industrial development programme which can be viewed as a case of 'strategic trade policy' − a strategy to build new industries with the purpose, among others, of pre-empting entry into the domestic market by foreign producers. There are several lessons to be drawn from South Korea's experience with heavy industry. Firstly, the time phasing of individual projects is essential to avoid simultaneous initiation of massive projects at one time, which would overburden the financial capability of both investors and the banking system, leading to inflationary financing. It would also make it difficult for individual investors to tide themselves over the period of the initial loss resulting from new investment. Second, the assessment of the long-term prospect of international competitiveness of large-scale investment should be based on the assumption that there will be no tariff protection, even if such protection exists at the time of assessment. The viability of large-scale investment projects should be determined on the basis of the comparative advantage in the cost of labour, technological advancement and managerial efficiency. I stress this because I was once appalled by a businessman telling me that he was planning to build a petrochemical plant on the assumption that the protective tariff would be maintained indefinitely at a high level. This is why tariff barriers are prone to mislead businessmen and misallocate resources. Finally, the South Korean experience seems to indicate that in the real world of uncertainty, long-term dynamic events can easily defy judgment based on a static short-term economic analysis. This has both negative and positive implications: a well-conceived policy from a short-term perspective may fail when confronted with the vagaries of time, while risk-taking by energetic and dynamic businessmen and the government may have a better chance of success in the longer term than the more passive behaviour of those who cling to conventional wisdom and the *status quo*. As the South Korean proverb states, 'A tiger cannot be caught unless one ventures into the tiger's lair.'

(7) In any event, the tide in favour of open markets and fair trade is running high in the major industrial countries today, and protectionist measures in developing countries are likely to invite retaliation from their developed partners.

Given the current international trade climate, the South Korean pattern of trade policy in the past should not be considered ideal, nor is it likely to be copied by other developing countries today. They are better advised to put greater emphasis on the indirect support of export promotion by the government through dissemination of information, education and training of workers, promotion of research and development, providing adequate public facilities including ports, transportation and communications, and, above all, adopting a sound macroeconomic policy framework in a well-functioning market system.

5

Foreign Direct Investment: Policies and Experiences of Malaysia and Other High-Growth Asian Economies

DAIM ZAINUDDIN

Over the last three decades the East Asian newly industrialising economies and, more recently, the South-east Asian economies (ASEAN-4) have recorded unprecedented economic growth and structural change.[1] A unique characteristic of the development of these high-growth Asian economies is that it appears to follow a cascading pattern of development driven by trade and foreign direct investment that takes advantage of the factor endowments and changing comparative advantage of each country. As a result, Malaysia and the other ASEAN-4 countries, especially Thailand and Indonesia, are fast emerging as second-tier NIEs. This market-led economic integration through trade, technology transfer and investment flows is one of the major underpinnings of the economic dynamism of the Pacific Basin.

The prominent role of foreign direct investment (FDI) in the region's continuing growth, especially in the late 1980s, has generated much optimism about the positive, dynamic effects of FDI. Viewed against the long-held concern over the adverse effects of FDI on the host country, such as domination by multinational companies and economic dependency, it is perhaps timely and pertinent for other developing countries to examine the Asian experience with FDI.

In this chapter I shall discuss the foreign investment policies and experiences of the high-growth Asian economies in general, and Malaysia in particular. Specifically, I shall examine the policy dimension of FDI, focusing on how developing countries can maximise the benefits of FDI and conversely reduce host country costs. A major emphasis of the discussion is that policies targeting FDI cannot be designed independently of the trade and industrial policy regime. Thus, I shall begin with an overview of the role and contribution of FDI and relate it to the development approaches and policies adopted in the various Asian economies. Following this, the countries' policies and experiences in attracting foreign private investment are examined. This is followed by a discussion of the major policy issues and an attempt to distil the policy lessons from the Asian experience. In the concluding section I will highlight the prospect for regional co-operation to promote South–South trade and investment flows.

Economic performance and foreign direct investment

Economic performance

The four NIEs (South Korea, Taiwan, Hong Kong and Singapore) and the ASEAN-4 countries (Indonesia, Malaysia, Philippines and Thailand) differ considerably from each other in size and income level, especially across the two groups. The NIEs, which are resource-poor, pursued industrialisation vigorously in the 1960s and 1970s while the resource-abundant ASEAN-4 countries took a longer time. Per capita income level in the NIEs ranges between US\$ 5 400 and US\$ 11 490 compared with US\$ 570–US\$ 2320 in the ASEAN-4 countries (Table 5.1). Economic growth as measured by gross domestic product (GDP) in the NIEs averaged 9,6% per annum during the period 1965–80 and 7,7% from 1980–90 while the ASEAN-4 countries achieved 6,9% and 4,8% in the corresponding periods. However, in recent years the growth rates of the ASEAN-4 countries have overtaken the NIEs. Between 1988 and 1991 Indonesia, Malaysia and Thailand achieved real GDP growth rates of 7,1%, 9,2% and 9,8% per annum respectively. In comparison, the GDP growth rates of South Korea, Taiwan, Hong Kong and Singapore were 7,8%, 6,6%, 3,2% and 8,0% respectively (Malaysia Ministry of Finance, 1992/3).

Table 5.1.   GDP and GDP growth rates of NIEs, ASEAN-4 countries and selected countries/region

	GNP per capita 1990	GDP (US$mil) 1965	GDP (US$mil) 1990	Average annual growth rate of GDP (percent) 1965-80	Average annual growth rate of GDP (percent) 1980-90
NIEs					
S. Korea	5 400	3 000	236 400	9,9	9,7
Taiwan[1]	6 058	2 340	55 100	9,7	na
Hong Kong	11 490	2 150	59 670	8,6	7,1
Singapore	11,160	970	34 600	10,0	6,4
ASEAN-4					
Indonesia	570	5 980	107 290	7,0	5,5
Malaysia	2 320	3 130	42 400	7,4	5,2
Philippines	730	6 010	43 860	5,7	0,9
Thailand	1 420	4 390	80 170	7,3	7,6
OECD				3,7	3,1
USA				2,7	3,4
Japan				6,4	4,1

[1]GNP per capita and GDP are 1988 figures, based upon ADB estimates.
Source: World Bank (1992b)

The high growth rate has been accompanied by rapid transformation in the structure of these economies. As shown in Table 5.2, the share of agriculture in total output in the NIEs and ASEAN-4 countries, with the exception of the

Philippines, declined sharply. Matching the agricultural decline is an increase in the share of manufacturing and other industrial subsectors.

Among the factors commonly cited for this impressive economic achievement are political stability, prudent macro-economic management and the adoption of outward-looking policies, especially the pursuit of export-based industrialisation strategies. Following severe macro-economic imbalances arising from unsustainable fiscal and budget deficits and the collapse of commodity prices in the mid-1980s, ASEAN-4 countries, particularly Malaysia and Indonesia, pursued vigorous economic liberalisation reforms. The trade and investment reforms were aimed at increasing private sector participation in the economy and attracting foreign investment to facilitate the industrialisation process.

Table 5.2. Structure of GDP in the NIEs and ASEAN-4 countries

Economies	Agric.		Manuf.		Industry		Services	
	1960	1980	1960	1980	1960	1980	1960	1980
NIEs								
Hong Kong	3	0	22	20	12	7	63	73
Singapore	4	0	12	30	6	7	79	63
S. Korea	37	10	14	31	6	13	43	46
ASEAN-4								
Indonesia	51	24	9	19	6	17	33	40
Malaysia	33	21	8	24	10	16	49	39
Philippines	26	23	20	25	8	8	46	43
Thailand	40	14	13	24	6	11	41	48

Source: ESCAP. (1991). *Industrial Restructuring in Asia and the Pacific.* United Nations: Bangkok, Thailand

The reforms have been very encouraging as evident in the economic boom in South-east Asia, especially Malaysia, which recorded an average GDP growth rate of 8% between 1988 and 1992. Private investment, especially FDI, played a catalytic role in the rapid economic growth of the ASEAN-4 countries in the late 1980s.

FDI patterns and trends

Global flows of FDI increased at an extraordinary rate in the 1980s. After the 1981–82 world recession, FDI outflows grew at a rate of 29% per annum. This is three times faster than the growth of exports and four times the growth of world output (UNCTC, 1991). Although the average annual flows to developing countries almost doubled between the periods 1980–84 and 1985–89, their share of the total flow fell from 25% to 19% (Table 5.3). Of the ten largest host developing countries that received three-quarters of the total inflows to developing countries, four were from the NIEs and ASEAN-4 countries, namely Singapore, Hong Kong, Malaysia and Thailand.

Table 5.3.   Inflows of foreign direct investment to developing countries, 1980–84, 1985–89

	Annual average inflows (US$ billion)		Percentage share	
	1980–84	1985–89	1980–84	1985–89
All countries	49,70	119,00	100,0	100,0
Developing countries	12,50	22,20	25,2	18,6
Africa	1,20	2,60	2,4	2,2
Latin America	6,10	8,30	12,3	7,0
East, South & SE Asia	4,70	10,70	9,4	9,0
Oceania	0,13	0,40	0,8	0,3
West Asia	0,37	0,40	0,8	0,3
Other	0,04	0,03	0,1	0,0

Source: UNCTC (1991)

During the second half of the 1980s about half of the inflows of FDI to developing countries went to East, South and South-east Asia. Of this amount, about half were accounted for by four countries: Singapore, Hong Kong, Malaysia and Thailand. The increase in investment flows to the Asian region is attributed to the liberalisation of foreign investment rules in countries like Malaysia and Indonesia, and to the currency realignments in Japan and the NIEs. The shift in comparative advantage resulting from rising labour costs and currency appreciation in Japan and the NIEs spurred a relocation of labour-intensive manufacturing industries to the lower-cost, labour-abundant Asian countries. Another factor was the loss of US GSP privileges for the four Asian NIEs. While cost pressures and labour shortages are forcing industries in the NIEs to relocate to South-east Asian countries, they are at the same time attracting FDI into their services and high-technology sectors. The investment pattern in the Asian region has also shifted from import-substitution to export-oriented manufacturing to serve the Western (Europe and America) markets, and increasingly the Asia–Pacific region (including Japan, NIEs and the ASEAN countries).

The result has been a rising trend of Japanese FDI to the NIEs and ASEAN-4 countries, and from the NIEs to the ASEAN-4 countries. In Singapore, Japanese FDI commitments increased threefold from S$ 135 million in 1980 to S$ 412 million in 1989 (Lim and Fong, 1991). In Taiwan, the Japanese share of cumulative foreign investment increased from 17% in the 1970s to 28% during the period 1981–88. In Malaysia, Japanese investment approvals rose from M$ 37,8 million in 1983 to M$ 632,7 million for the first half of 1989. During the same period, South Korean FDI approvals increased from M$ 1,1 billion to M$ 36,6 while Singaporean FDI rose from M$ 30,0 million to M$ 182,0 million.

With the transition of China and Indo-China countries to market economies, it is encouraging to note that outward FDI from the ASEAN-4 countries is also beginning. Malaysia in particular, facing rising labour shortage and cost pressures, has begun to encourage overseas investments and provide incentives for home-grown multinationals to expand their activities. Malaysia has become one of the largest investors in Vietnam. It has also ventured into construction, food processing, and manufacturing in China. Recently, the Malaysian government has been encouraging local MNCs to globalise, and about five Malaysian companies to date have invested or are actively exploring investment opportunities in Africa.

Impact of FDI

The impact of FDI on the high-growth Asian economies is generally positive, although its significance varies from country to country. South Korea developed rapidly without substantial FDI while countries like Malaysia and Singapore have relied heavily on it to sustain their growth. The other NIEs and ASEAN-4 countries lie between these two extremes. Evaluating the benefits and costs of FDI is fraught with difficulties. The lack of reliable data and the difficulty in measuring dynamic and long-term effects are among the major problems. There is therefore a danger of oversimplification in discussing the relationship between economic growth and FDI in the Asian economies. Pending more definitive theories and studies, this caution should be noted in considering the following observations.

An emerging consensus among analysts is that the indirect and dynamic FDI effects economists attribute to learning-by-doing, technological changes, market spillovers and competition are more important than the direct impact of FDI on employment, exports, government revenue, etc. FDI constitutes only a small portion of the gross capital formation in the Asian economies. Its impact, however, on the economy is disproportionately large due to the dynamic effects arising from a transfer of technology, managerial expertise, market access and re-invested profits.[2] These dynamic effects at the micro-level further strengthen the link between trade and investment on the one hand and structural change on the other. At the macro-level, currency realignments, changing industrial structure and shifts in comparative advantage are boosting trade and investment flows in the region. The sum effect is a market-driven process of regional economic integration.

Thus, the impact of FDI has been most noticeable in facilitating the structural transformation of the Asian economies. It is the main catalyst in transforming the primary-commodity-dependent economies of the ASEAN-4 countries into higher value-added, industry-based economies. In Malaysia the FDI-led industrialisation resulted in a manufacturing growth rate of 12% over the last two decades and boosted the sector's share of GDP from 10% in 1960 to 29% in 1992. A landmark transition in the Malaysian economy was achieved when the manufacturing sector contribution to GDP overtook the agricultural sector in 1987. By the year 2000 it is projected that manufacturing will contribute 37,2% of the GDP compared with 13,4% for agriculture (Government of Malaysia, 1991).

Although FDI may not be as significant in effecting structural transformation in the other ASEAN-4 countries as in Malaysia, its contribution is nevertheless fairly significant. Indonesia's recovery from the 1985–86 downturn followed substantial liberalisation of foreign investment and other economic policies. Its non-oil manufactured exports grew by 25,7% between 1986 and 1991 to lead the economic recovery and diversification away from petroleum, timber and other primary commodities.

Foreign investment policies and experience

As alluded to above, the thinking and rationale behind foreign investment policies have shifted over the decades. During the 1950s and 1960s FDI was not encouraged in developing countries since it was politically unpopular and its socio-economic costs were perceived to outweigh the benefits. The adverse perception was partly a consequence of the experience of colonialism, reinforced by the history of MNCs' exploitation of the developing countries' natural resources.

As described below, using Malaysia as an illustration, FDI policies are conditioned by both external and internal factors, or 'supply' and 'demand' factors respectively. The internal or demand factors have shifted in response to the changing needs and socio-political circumstances. The domestic or demand factors are also closely related to the role of government in the economy, particularly its involvement in industrial development through public enterprises. In the 1960s and 1970s, many of the NIEs and ASEAN-4 governments borrowed extensively to finance industrial development programmes and adjustment to the oil shocks. As a result, loan capital flow to the region outweighed FDI until the onset of debt crisis in the early 1980s.

Since the mid-1980s the ASEAN-4 countries have implemented various economic liberalisation reforms to invigorate the private sector, increase economic efficiency and reduce public enterprise industrial activities. The policies were designed more to promote foreign investment than to regulate them. As such, FDI policies and incentives in the Asian countries have converged as competition for FDI flows intensifies in the region. More important, many of the rapidly growing Asian economies are now engaging in two-way investment flows, i.e. inward and outward FDI, to facilitate the structural adjustment of the economy to one that is higher value-added and higher technology-based. In essence it shows a market-based policy response to changing dynamic comparative advantage among countries in the region.

Policies for maximising FDI

As noted above, policies to attract FDI vary between countries as well as between different time periods. They have evolved in response to changing economic conditions, development strategies and attitudes toward FDI. Nevertheless, there are many parallels in the policies adopted, since each country experienced broadly similar industrialisation phases. To facilitate discussion, three industrialisation phases are broadly defined. The characteristics of each phase are discussed in general for the high-growth Asian economies. Details of the underlying rationale of the policy regime and effects are described in greater detail for Malaysia, to illustrate the various forces impinging upon policy.

Import-substitution phase: Malaysia and the other ASEAN-4 countries pursued import-substitution strategies for a relatively longer period compared with the NIEs. Being better endowed in natural resources than the NIEs, the ASEAN-4 countries were able to finance the import and investment requirements from exports of primary commodities during the 1960s and 1970s when their demand and prices were relatively high. Industrial development was undertaken within a cascading structure of protection that gave most protection to finished goods and least to raw materials and primary products.

Prompted by the need to diversify its primary-commodity-based economy and to reverse the anti-industrialisation policy of the colonial era, the Malaysian government promoted new industries through import-substitution policies. To encourage new industries the Pioneer Industries Ordinance was enacted in 1958. This legislation basically granted tax holidays to 'pioneer' industries and to those which were insufficient in scale, with the duration of tax respite (up to five years) being determined by the investment size. In subsequent years the new industries needing assistance were provided with moderate tariff protection. To implement the case-by-case tariff policy the government established an independent agency (Tariff Advisory Board).

This board was later absorbed by another agency set up to promote industrial development and administer incentives. The agency, known as the Federal Industrial Development Authority (presently known as Malaysian Industrial Development Authority or MIDA), was established in 1967 within the Ministry of International Trade and Industry to promote and regulate industrial development. Since all firms are required to obtain approval from MIDA for new investment, MIDA was to serve as a one-stop agency for foreign investors as well as the implementing agency for the country's industrial policy.

Malaysia after its independence in 1957, like many of the NIEs and ASEAN countries, took a more accommodating approach towards FDI in contrast to the prevailing cautious view and preference for portfolio investments. This stance was partly necessitated by old colonial ties and partly due to the outward-looking approach adopted by the government. The colonial economy was dominated by foreign investments in mining and plantations as well as in financial and trade services. Manufacturing received scant interest as a consequence of the abundant natural resources. During this period FDI was welcome, but not promoted extensively. It was needed to provide the necessary capital, technology and managerial expertise. Hence, there were minimal exchange controls and no restrictions on repatriation of capital, dividends, royalties and technical and service fees. Most sectors were open to foreign investors.

In 1968, to speed up industrial growth and absorb the growing labour surplus, a new enactment was passed to replace the Pioneer Industries Ordinance 1958. The Investment Incentives Act 1968 widened the criteria for tax holidays to include location of industry, type of product, degree of local content and export performance. Alternatively, it grants an investment tax credit equal to 25% of the value of investment. Other fiscal incentives include accelerated depreciation allowances and duty drawbacks for imported inputs. Incentives for labour employment were subsequently included. These additional incentives, targeted at foreign investors, were enhanced considerably by trade protection given in the form of tariffs and temporary quotas to help the start-up of local production and avoid stockpiling by importers prior to the new tariff rates.

Complementing the fiscal incentives and trade protection was the establishment of industrial estates designed to attract FDI. Land and other essential infrastructural facilities, such as roads, water, power and communications, were provided in the industrial estates at a reduced cost for foreign firms to set up production easily.

Export promotion phase: Export promotion in the ASEAN-4 countries began in the early 1970s following structural problems after a decade of import-substitution policies. In Malaysia, growing unemployment and slowdown of the manufacturing sector as import substitution reached the limit of the domestic market contributed to the policy shift toward exports. In Thailand, slowing growth, worsening balance of payments deficits, stagnation of primary exports, decline in US military spending and decline in foreign investment prompted the shift in emphasis from import substitution to export-oriented manufacturing. In addition, the high degree of protection accorded to import-substituting investments resulted in inefficient, non-competitive and import-dependent industries. The trade policies also created an anti-export bias.

In the late 1960s, faced with growing unemployment problems, slow growth of the import-substitution-based manufacturing sector and small domestic market, the Malaysian government shifted to export-oriented policies. The policy shift can be traced to the promulgation of the Investment Incentives Act 1968. The Act, in addition to providing incentives to import-substitution industries, also extended benefits to export-oriented investment projects. Export-oriented industries were allowed 100% foreign ownership. Benefits included export allowance and double deduction of export promotional expenses from taxable income. Fiscal incentives offered to export-oriented industries included tax relief on capital expenditure incurred on warehousing and bulk storage installations and drawback of customs duties and exemption from import and excise duties and sales tax. Essential raw materials and intermediate goods were allowed to be imported free of any duty if suitable or price-competitive domestic substitutes were unavailable.

A major boost to the setting up of export industries was the enactment of the Free Trade Zone Act in 1971. This Act enabled the establishment of export-processing Free Trade Zones (FTZs) aimed at minimising customs formalities associated with imports of raw materials and components and exports of finished products. To extend the benefits of FTZs to local industries and disperse the location of export-oriented industries, licensed manufacturing warehouses (LMWs) or bonded factories were also provided. The availability of cheap labour was one of the major factors attracting MNCs to set up labour-intensive export-oriented industries in Malaysia. They were concentrated in the electronics and textiles sectors. These foreign-owned factories were able to absorb the growing pool of labour, especially that from the rural agricultural sector.

Economic liberalisation and industrial deepening phase: During the 1970s and up to the early 1980s loans outweighed FDI as the source of foreign capital to finance the adjustment to the oil price shocks and the industrial promotion programmes in several of the NIEs and ASEAN-4 countries. Since the onset of the debt crisis there has been a large reduction in the flow of private commercial loans. FDI showed a sharp increase after 1986. FDI inflows were particularly significant in South Korea, Thailand, Indonesia and Malaysia. The narrower opportunities for international borrowing have led to stiff competition to attract FDI. The ASEAN-4 countries were among the countries that offered more incentives to foreign investments in the light of competition from South Asia, China and Indo-China. A combination of factors and external shocks prompted the ASEAN-4 governments, particularly in Malaysia and Indonesia, to further deregulate the economy and promote development through the private sector.

In Malaysia, the economy's export-led growth was showing signs of faltering by the late 1970s. The industrial base remained fairly shallow and concentrated. To sustain the country's industrialisation momentum and deepen its industrial structure Malaysia embarked upon a second-round import substitution in heavy industries in the early 1980s. Again, FDI in the form of joint ventures between state-owned corporations and foreign investors was the mode preferred by the government. The expansion of the public sector, especially the non-financial public enterprises, strained the government budget and created unsustainable budgetary deficits. The adoption of prudent fiscal measures subsequently contributed to a severe recession in 1985–86, triggered by the collapse of world commodity prices, decline in world demand for the country's manufactured exports and a high Malaysian dollar resulting from capital inflows attributed to government external borrowings.

To stimulate the economy the government adopted a major economic liberalisation programme that sought to encourage private domestic and foreign investment, which had virtually collapsed during the recession. The economic stimulation package was contained in the Promotion of Investments Act 1986, which liberalised foreign investment rules and provided enhanced investment incentives. It provided for exemption from income and development tax for companies engaged in manufacturing new products or undertaking modernisation, expansion and/or diversification. Special tax incentives were given to small-scale companies and to those which complied with the equity restructuring under the New Economic Policy (NEP). Under the NEP foreign-owned firms were required to restructure their equity before 1990 so that 70% of the equity is held by Malaysian interests. The 1986 Act allowed flexibility in implementing this rule.

Other foreign investment rules were also relaxed. For example, companies which export more than half of their production or employ 350 or more full-time employees were allowed 100% foreign equity. Similarly, the share of foreign ownership in resource-based and import-substituting industries was allowed to exceed the 30% limit imposed previously. In addition to the easing of the equity conditions various incentives were provided under the 1986 Act. These included reinvestment allowances, deductions for local research and development and an incentive for manpower training. Other incentives were added in subsequent government budgets. In the 1988/89 budget the corporate tax rate was reduced from 40% to 35%, tax breaks were given to MNCs for setting up their regional headquarters in Malaysia, and established companies could qualify for tax-free pioneer status or investment tax allowances if they continued to invest in Malaysia.

Finally, various other schemes have been introduced to promote greater exports, enhance international competitiveness and encourage inter-industry linkages, particularly the development of supporting industries. These include industrial financing for capacity expansion and technological upgrading, export credit and refinancing schemes, human resource and skill development funds for upgrading the skills of the labour force, and technical assistance programmes to promote more rapid technological absorption by the local industries. These efforts are aimed at strengthening the country's industrial base. With a well-established MNC base in the country, such efforts can draw upon the MNCs' international resources and expertise to facilitate the process of technological upgrading and industrial skills training.

Policy issues and lessons

In shaping foreign direct investment flows to maximise their contribution to the economy, governments have some control over the demand factors, especially in creating a conducive investment climate and implementing supportive policies to promote private investment in the desired industry areas. However, unlike loan capital, the external or supply factors of FDI are conditioned by the world economic environment and the global business strategies of MNCs. Matching the demand and supply factors therefore is a continuous challenge for policy-makers. Some of the considerations in the policy decision-making process include the following:

(1) Changing determinants of FDI: As countries around the world compete for FDI it is clear that liberal policy measures are not sufficient to attract foreign investment. Political stability remains a prime concern of foreign investors. The country experiences have also shown that prudent macro-economic management as manifested in stable economic policies and outward-oriented trade and industrial policies are basic features of an attractive policy regime for FDI. For the new technology-based industries, the provision of efficient infrastructure facilities and availability of skilled manpower at a reasonable cost have become crucial factors in an MNC's decision to set up production facilities.

(2) Policy regime: Notwithstanding the above, active government support in the form of industrial policies, incentives and programmes such as industrial estates, free trade zones and investment co-ordination centres or promotion boards is needed to complete the package for attracting FDI in the present competitive international economic environment. In providing incentives it is better to remove investment disincentives such as relaxing equity conditions, reducing bureaucratic red tape and allowing market forces to work through deregulation than to provide incentives to compensate for the disincentives.

Another guideline for structuring incentives is that they should be based upon the performance of the investment projects rather than the size of capital *per se*. The performance criteria may be related to output growth, exports, employment creation, R & D expenditures, human resource development and domestic content. It is also important in policy formulation to eliminate the bias against local investors and small-scale projects. The latter is essential in promoting inter-industry linkages through small- and medium-scale industries. Recent theories have emphasised the importance of a network or strategic alliance of suppliers and buyers in determining the international competitiveness of an industry.

(3) Selectivity: In the present competitive international economic environment there is less flexibility for developing countries without the necessary human and infrastructural capital to design selective foreign investment policies aimed at particular industries. Although industrial targeting can be done for strategic industries through import-substitution policies, there is a danger of fostering a high-cost industry if government protection continues indefinitely and the said industry does not reach international competitiveness within the planned period. Since there is less flexibility in choice of FDI at the early stage of industrial development, the industries to be encouraged should best fit the country's resources profile and comparative advantage. However, for strategic industries, public enterprises may be the only choice provided public debts do not reach unsustainable proportions. In this case, governments still have the flexibility to consider privatisation once these enterprises become independent financially.

(4) Managing FDI: It is difficult to manage the transfer of technology, and marketing and managerial expertise. For economies which do not invest sufficiently in capacity-building such as human resource development, R & D, institutional innovation and infrastructural development, the ability to harness the benefits of FDI is limited. The experience of the electronics sector is perhaps illuminating in this regard. Once thought to be footloose, electronic MNCs are now seen to be taking advantage of the changing comparative advantage of each country. For instance, the semi-conductor companies which were attracted to Malaysia 20 years ago to set up labour-intensive, assembly-type operations in free trade zones have now moved up the value-added and technological ladder as labour grows scarce, skilled labour becomes available and industry demand changes. Thus R & D, automated production, design and testing are increasingly being shifted from the investing country to the host country.

On the other hand, the nature and pattern of FDI is changing as a result of rapid technological advancement, increases in international competition and changes in international trading rules. Developing countries therefore face a high degree of uncertainty in sustaining FDI inflows. It is therefore a virtue to diversify the sources of FDI and promote competition among foreign investors. Nevertheless, FDI should be viewed as a complementary source rather than the main source of a country's capital formation. Eventually, indigenous industrial capacity needs to be built to maintain a country on its long-term growth path.

Conclusion

The nature of FDI has changed considerably since the mid-1980s. The East Asian NIEs have emerged as key players as they relocated labour-intensive industries to the ASEAN-4 countries in the late 1980s and more recently to China, Vietnam and Cambodia. Outward investment from some of the

ASEAN-4 countries, particularly Thailand and Malaysia, has also increased in recent years as entrepreneurs take advantage of the investment opportunities overseas.

The trend in the new wave of FDI is toward joint ventures. Other forms of FDI, such as turnkey operations, licensing agreements, management and technical assistance contracts, franchising and international subcontracting, have become more common. This unbundling of FDI mirrors the growing sophistication of present-day industrial structures as well as the increasingly competitive international environment for trade and investment.

The views on FDI have changed considerably. It can no longer be treated solely as a financial resource. Instead, as the Asian experience has shown, FDI has become a major channel for facilitating the transfer of technology and managerial skills. It is, however, not a substitute for domestic capital formation or the building of indigenous industrial capacity. FDI has a useful complementary role in these two critical areas of development.

Another lesson is that the policy environment, encompassing macroeconomic, trade and industrial policies, plays an important role in attracting FDI. However, its importance relative to infrastructural facilities and availability of skilled manpower is decreasing as countries adopt liberal investment policies to compete for FDI.

Finally, the sustainability of FDI flows depends to a great extent on an open global trading environment. The increasing protectionist pressures in the developed countries and the emergence of trading blocs threaten to restrict trade and investment flows to excluded developing countries. In this respect, the policies aimed at facilitating regional co-operation and increasing South–South trade and investment flows should be explored.

Notes

1. The East Asian NIEs comprise South Korea, Taiwan, Hong Kong and Singapore. The four Association of South-east Asian Nations (ASEAN-4) members are Indonesia, Malaysia, Philippines and Thailand. Singapore is a member of ASEAN. Brunei, the remaining ASEAN country, is not included in the discussion because of its uniqueness as an oil-rich state.

2. FDI accounted for 7% of gross domestic capital formation in Singapore between 1975 and 1985, compared with 0,9% in Taiwan, 1% in Malaysia, and 1,4% in Thailand.

6

Meeting the Global Challenge: A Framework for Industrial Revival in South Africa

AVRIL JOFFE, DAVID KAPLAN, RAPHAEL KAPLINSKY AND DAVID LEWIS

South Africa makes the transition to democratic government in an inauspicious economic context. The decline of living standards through the 1980s has been extensively charted, and does not need detailed recapitulation in this chapter. It is sufficient to observe here that the trend rate of economic expansion over the past 12 years has been approximately 1,5% p.a., while population growth has been running at more than 2,5% annually. There are, of course, multiple causes for this fall in real per capita incomes, but it would be a mistake not to flag the central role played by declining rates of industrial accumulation. More particularly, since 'industry' includes both utilities and mining – which, with the exception of gold, have performed strongly over this period – it is in the weak growth-record of the manufacturing sector that the key to South African economic decline lies. Similarly it is almost certainly in the reinvigoration of manufacturing that a rosier economic future rests in the post-apartheid era.

These inauspicious domestic circumstances are compounded by the current global economic environment. With the exception of China and a few of the second-tier Asian and Latin American Newly Industrialising Economies (NIEs), there has been a universal downward trend in growth rates. Entry in external markets is increasingly difficult, partly because of the growth of protectionist barriers in key large economies and partly because of heightened competition. At the same time, most of the developing world (including South Africa) is being forced to open domestic markets to imports. Thus global competition increasingly impinges upon manufacturing in virtually all economies.

The challenges posed by these global developments arise not only from a heightened level of competition, but also from its changing structure. There is growing evidence from a range of economic sectors – particularly in manufacturing, but including both agriculture and services – that the basis of competitive performance has been changing (see Best 1990; Porter, 1990; and Dertouzos, 1989). In the past competition has largely been determined by price factors, but it is increasingly coming to be affected by a range of additional product-oriented factors. These include product quality, product variety and differentiation, and the speed of innovation.

In order to achieve these competitive attributes, producers are required to be increasingly flexible, with respect to both their output structures and the use of their inputs. Although a number of factors contribute to this flexibility, it is clear that the organisational components play a prominent role. This organisational restructuring involves different types of inter-firm linkages, new types of relationships between design, marketing and production specialities within firms, and flatter corporate hierarchies that permit the introduction of new forms of work organisation and that play a critical role in achieving the necessary flexibility and product-qualifying production parameters. Comparative global evidence suggests that the search for greater flexibility is also associated with rises in both capital and labour productivity; hence it also facilitates price competitive production. In these changing global circumstances the ability to compete internationally arises less from access to reservoirs of cheap labour and natural resources than from an endowment of widely spread skills.

A post-apartheid South African economy thus faces a series of critical challenges. As observed, over the past two decades the manufacturing sector has been unable to compete effectively in external markets; the recent moderate growth of manufactured exports has arisen primarily from a combination of export subsidies and the recession in the domestic market. In many sectors the ability of manufacturers to compete in the domestic market has reflected the effectiveness of import controls.

A large group of researchers – representing between 25 and 30 person years of effort – have been addressing both the threats and opportunities facing South Africa's industrial (and especially its manufacturing) sector. This project – the Industrial Strategy Project – initiated by the Congress of South African Trade Unions (Cosatu) and the Economic Trends Research Group, has, since January 1992, been investigating the competitive status of 13 of South Africa's industrial sectors, assessing not only their abilities to withstand global competition, but also their potential for meeting basic needs.[2] In addition the Industrial Strategy Project has also considered the role played by competition policy, trade policy and technology policy in South Africa's industrial evolution.

At this stage it is not possible to summarise the results of this research programme, since the detailed sectoral studies have not yet been completed. Moreover, the programme covers a wide agenda and space constraints do not permit us to consider all of this in an overview chapter. Therefore this chapter briefly reports some of our relevant findings and suggests a framework in which a policy agenda for promoting the international competitiveness of South African industry may be developed. We should emphasise that promoting competitiveness is not equivalent to an exclusive focus on exports, or even on tradeables. As we shall discuss below, it is imperative that low-income South African consumers have access to basic commodities at internationally competitive prices. For this reason the Project incorporates studies of the informal manufacturing sector, the baking industry, the provision of building materials for a mass housing campaign, and the provision of power distribution equipment for a mass electrification programme. It also explains why we accord so much significance to the production of those tradeables aimed at the low end of the market.

We begin by highlighting South African manufacturing's problem with productivity growth. In the subsequent section we review the incentive system which affects the competitiveness of South Africa's manufacturing sector, focusing on trade policy, competition policy, the structure of pricing for raw materials and energy which are utilised by the manufacturing sector, and the determinants of unit labour costs. However, we do not believe that industrial policy can be reduced to the structure of market incentives alone. Hence in the next section we discuss the major components of industrial strategy which are required to underpin an appropriate incentive structure for industry, to promote the growth of national, regional, sectoral and firm-level capabilities, and to develop the institutional infrastructure in which these capabilities can be strengthened. The chapter concludes with a brief discussion of the process by which industrial strategy can evolve in a post-apartheid South Africa. Because the analysis and write-up of this programme of enquiry is still at an early stage, the views which follow should be treated as provisional.

Productivity growth in the South African manufacturing sector

Productivity performance
Our concern with the industrialisation process lies in the ability of this sector, through its relatively high productivity, to generate the resources required to satisfy the needs of South Africa's population. Hence our concern with the determinants of productivity performance in the industrial sector. It is necessary to have a holistic perspective on productivity and we distinguish here between three inter-related elements of productive efficiency – the efficiency of factor use with respect to the transformation of inputs into outputs; the efficiency with which the determinants of competition other than those of price are met; and what might be termed 'social productivity', i.e. the efficiency with which the population's needs might be satisfied.

Factor productivities: The recent record of South African manufacturing suggests that there are reasons for considerable concern with respect to factor productivities. The three significant dimensions we address are capital productivity, labour productivity and total factor productivity (TFP). The year 1983 represents a significant turning period since, after some years of growth, both capital and labour inputs fell between 1983 and 1990; output continued to grow during this period, albeit at a significantly slower rate than during the 1970–1983 period (1,2% versus 4,2% p.a.).

The conclusions which we draw from this are that:

– Capital productivity appears to have fallen over the two decades, with the apparent rise during the recent period being due to a fall in the absolute value of capital stock rather than to a rise in the productivity of new investments.

– Labour productivity grew consistently through this period, although at a falling rate between 1972 and 1990.

– Data on total factor productivity growth are only available for the post-1972 period. For the two decades it was negative, at –1,02% p.a. (The positive TFP rate for the 1983–1990 period is a 'perverse' result in that it arises from a fall in the value of aggregate capital stock rather than from an increase in the efficiency of marginal investments.) No comparative countries – including relatively poorly performing sub-Saharan African economies – show such a sustained fall over this long time period.

These macro-economic figures provide an aggregate overview of the productivity crisis confronting the South African economy. However, calculations of this sort are not without their problems, particularly in the South African context. Nevertheless our sectoral studies confirm the fact that factor productivity growth in South Africa has been relatively slow (see below for some details).

Non-factor-based determinants of competitiveness: In an era in which competition was predominantly based upon price, productivity could usefully be measured in relation to factor productivities. But as non-price-based factors have become increasingly important, so other elements of efficiency have become relevant. These include factors such as product variety, speed of product innovation, product quality, reliability of delivery, involvement in inter-firm programmes of product development, and the ability to meet customer orders in short lead times.

Our researchers have not been able to produce systematic comparisons between the performance of South African and foreign-based competitors on these productivity indicators. However, there are indicators that South African firms' performance in these areas has been poor.

'Social productivity': 'Social productivity' is neither easy to define nor to measure. It refers to the efficiency with respect to which resources are being used to meet basic needs, and includes both distributional and other factors. Here the South African economy appears to have performed particularly poorly. The provision of basic wage goods such as housing and affordable transport is spread very unevenly through the system, and poor people and industrial workers appear to spend a disproportionate amount of their income on these inputs. Formal sector employees (that is, those in households earning more than R1 000 per month) spend between 8% and 10% of their incomes in energy; those earning less than R1 000 per month spend over 10% on energy. This is a direct consequence of the structure of energy provision in South Africa.

Not only are many basic goods and services of high cost to the final consumer, but they are also provided in a manner which makes poor use of domestic resources. Transport is oriented around the private provision of services, and the transport sector is thus geared towards the production of private cars rather than effective public transport systems. Environmental standards are low; both producers and consumers are adversely affected by much of the industrial sector's activities, as are those who live in close proximity to production.

Some determinants of slow factor productivity growth

Later in this chapter we will consider in greater depth some of the major determinants of this poor productivity growth which are amenable to policy interventions. It is helpful, however, at this stage of the discussion to flag those elements of poor factor productivity performance which arise from the structure of investment over the past two decades, and particularly during the 1980s. Three trends are relevant – the low overall rate of investment; disinvestment in labour-intensive sectors; and the choice of technique within the capital-intensive sector.

Low rates of investment: As noted, the value of real capital stock fell during the 1980s. South Africa's overall rate of investment has also fallen sharply, from over 30% of GDP during much of the 1970s to around 20% in the latter half of the 1980s. Consequently many sectors are saddled with outdated machinery and equipment. This is particularly apparent in the dimensional industries such as chemicals and textiles.

Underinvestment in labour-intensive sectors: Investment in the two most capital-intensive sectors (chemicals and basic metals) has grown from 40,4% of the total in 1972, to 59.8% in 1990. By contrast, the share of the three most labour-intensive sectors (clothing, leather and footwear, and wood and furniture) has fallen from 4% to 1,9%. It is significant that this does not represent so much a lower rate of growth of investment in these labour-intensive sectors as a decline in the absolute value of their capital stock. If chemicals and basic metals are excluded, the size of South Africa's manufacturing stock fell at an annual rate of 2,8% between 1980 and 1990.

Choice of technology in capital-intensive sectors: As we have observed, investment in the chemicals sector was driven by strategic factors. Obtaining petrol from coal is a high-cost operation. Moreover, the attempt to tap offshore deposits has proved to be extremely costly. The two strategic investments in the 1980s are estimated to have cost approximately R13–14bn in 1990 prices, equivalent to half of total investment during the 1980s.[3] The result is that South African produced petrol is viable only at around $40 per barrel (including fixed costs) and at $23 per barrel if only variable costs are included. (The current cost of oil is approximately $18/barrel.) The consequence of these strategic investments has been to severely dampen capital and total factor productivity, particularly during the 1980s.

How is this Industrial Strategy Project informed by South Africa's poor productivity performance?

As noted, we believe that the primary justification for an industrial strategy is that it provides for the productive utilisation of inputs and, in so doing, provides the wherewithal to meet the population's basic needs. This central principle underlies the analysis and the policy prescriptions discussed in the following sections. It is important, however, to make a number of qualifications to this strategic view.

To begin with, we are also not fetishising the adoption of high-tech equipment as a route to raising productivity within existing areas of economic activity. This is not to argue that there is no need for the adoption of new, productive embodied technologies, but rather to observe that there is much scope for raising productivity by changing organisational procedures within production and by affecting the relationship between firms and between the productive sector and the science and technology infrastructure. The discussion which follows in later sections amplifies this central concern of our industrial strategy.

A second caveat to this discussion on productivity concerns the role to be played by international 'measures' of productivity, as would be achieved by exposing South African firms to world competition and allowing this to determine the allocation of resources. We are mindful, here, that there is a range of basic needs which are unlikely to be adequately met if the sole goal of economic policy is to force South African enterprises to match international standards of competitiveness. But at the same time we are also aware that South Africa's economic growth rate is hampered by the weakness on the trade account. It is thus neither desirable nor practical to continue insulating domestic producers from these international competitive pressures if productivity growth is to reach the levels which are required to satisfy basic needs and to achieve sustained income growth. A more effective outward orientation of the industrial sector is thus an important component of the strategy to increase productivity growth within the industrial sector.

Thirdly, although we place considerable emphasis on the need to meet global productivity standards as a route to meeting basic needs, our sectoral studies have not been confined to the tradeable sectors alone. We have investigated the provision of electricity to the mass of the population and have considered the capacity of the building materials sector to meet the demands of providing housing and sanitation to the population. We have also devoted considerable resources to understanding the particular problems of the informal manufacturing sector. Whilst each of these areas of enquiry is relevant to the basic needs and employment objectives of industrial strategy, we also believe that they inform the challenge of increasing productivity growth. This is because each of these non-tradeable sectors provides key inputs into the consumption basket of the labour force. Increasing the efficiency with which these basic wage good inputs are provided allows for the possibility of maintaining real standards of living by reducing the cost of unit labour inputs.

Fourthly, we believe that there are two productivity gaps which have to be addressed by policy (Pack, 1993). The first is that which occurs within South African industry, between leading-edge and laggard firms. The second is the gap between leading-edge South African firms and those prospering in global markets. At this stage we have no evidence that the pattern of intra-South African dispersion is wider than that in other countries, but the high rates of market concentration which we have observed suggest that this may well be the case. Our policy proposals are designed to narrow both of these productivity gaps.

Finally, we believe that it is only through resumed productivity growth that it will be possible to meet the basic needs of South Africa's population. It is for this reason that we have not focused our primary attention on the meeting of basic needs or on distributional issues. Having said this, however, we believe that the path to resumed productivity growth lies in the restructuring of power and income distribution in a more egalitarian fashion. In many respects, therefore, we do not see a trade-off between distribution, social welfare and resumed productivity growth. It is in this respect that we believe that the industrial strategy which is sketched out below is innovative. It is one in which we identify a route to productivity growth built around the active participation of workers in both the conception and execution of production. It is a path in which productivity is assisted by the reduction of wage differentials in work, and in which unit labour costs are reduced through increasing the effective provision of basic wage goods.

It is to these issues that the discussion now turns. In thinking through the range of policies required to invigorate productivity growth in South African industry, we have been much informed by an analytical framework first proposed by the OECD (1987) and recently taken up in a critique of World Bank approaches to industrialisation.[4] This identifies three policy-relevant elements which seem to have been associated with rapid and sustained industrial growth in other countries – the incentive structure, the accumulation of human, technological and infrastructural capabilities, and the role played by supporting institutions.

We begin by considering those elements of the incentive system which affect the productivity of the industrial sector. Thereafter, in the context of widespread market failure, we address those parts of the policy agenda which are required to develop industrial capabilities in the medium and the long run, and the institutions which are thus needed.

The structure of market incentives

In this discussion of the influence of the incentive structure on South Africa's industrial performance we will consider five issues – the role of trade policy in transmitting the incentives that flow from the international economy; the pattern and intensity of competition in the domestic market; the pricing structure determining downstream industry's access to raw materials; the price paid by the industrial sector for energy; and the unit labour costs influencing the industrial sector's competitiveness.

The role of the trade policy regime

In recent years trade performance and trade policy have come to the fore in the discussion of industrial strategy, and the boundaries between trade and industrial policy have frequently been collapsed. This narrowing of the policy agenda has especially been the case in LDCs, where industrial strategy has been heavily influenced by the major multilateral aid donors. At least until recently, the World Bank and the International Monetary Fund have shared a common approach towards trade policy involving, *inter alia*, a standard approach towards the sequencing of reform. In this, the first step has been to abolish non-tariff barriers, substituting tariffs for quantitative controls. This is to be followed by a reduction in the dispersion of the trade regime and then by a fall in the overall level of protection. A key principle underlying this standard sequencing has been that external economies will flow from an outward orientation; this is seen to be positively associated with technological learning and the reaping of scale economies in production. A subsidiary principle is that an outward or neutral orientation to trade arises when the trade regime proximates most closely to a liberal trading environment.

South Africa's trade regime has a number of distinctive features, which are in sharp contrast to this idealised picture of an optimal trade policy. By comparison with 32 LDCs (for which data exist), with the exception of final consumer goods the overall level of South Africa's tariff protection is not high.[5] South Africa ranks 20 out of the 32 countries for all goods, protection of mining products only ranks at 3, whilst capital goods and intermediate goods rank 12 and 14 respectively. (These rankings are based upon the principle that 1 = least protection, and 32 = most protection.) Moreover, these figures tend to overestimate the effect of South Africa's protective environment since there is a range of exemptions and special arrangements in play. Thus when account is taken of the effective tariff take (which is not the same as the effective rate of protection), South Africa appears to be amongst the least protected of all of these 32 countries, falling to a ranking of one.

In a comparative context the distinctive feature of South Africa's protective regime is its complexity, its instability and its degree of dispersion. The economy with the most numerous set of tariff rates next to South Africa is Nepal with 87 items; South Africa has 35 *ad valorem* tariff rates, 2865 items with specific/formula/other types of rates, plus four levels of import surcharge rates. Associated with this variety of tariff regimes is a high measure of dispersion – South Africa's ranking with regard to the coefficient of dispersion is exceptionally high.

Both our own trade study and the World Bank trade study (Belli *et al.*, 1993) also highlight the relative ineffectiveness of attempts to compensate potential exporters for the high cost of domestically supplied inputs. The overall picture is one of a bias against exports, except (generally, but not always) where the General Export Incentive Scheme (GEIS) export subsidies come into play. But these export subsidies are very costly, accounting for a substantial proportion of total tariff receipts. The tariff structure also reflects a policy regime in which special pleading by individual interest groups is widely felt. It is significant here that in some cases tariffs and tariff exemptions are effectively firm-specific since the production of particular items is monopolistic. Two other problems with GEIS are that its benefits often flow to firms who would have exported anyway ('free-riding'), and that it runs against the provisions of the GATT and may therefore be unsustainable in the future.

In the light of these findings the agenda for trade policy reform set out in a recent World Bank paper provides a welcome departure from previous orthodoxy. The first suggestion is that South Africa commit itself to an outward orientation. Secondly, the Bank argues that the existing complex and unstable tariff regime should be cleaned up. This will involve a very significant reduction in the number of tariff items, as well as the abolition of the numerically small non-tariff barriers and tariff items with exceptionally high rates of protection. Thirdly, the paper proposes that an effective programme should be introduced to provide exporters with automatic access to inputs at world prices; the existing duty drawback and duty exemption schemes work poorly. In addition, it is suggested that the liberalisation of protection over intermediates should take preference since this will facilitate manufacturing exports. Thus in arguing for an elimination of anti-export bias, the Bank recognises that this can occur before moving to a more liberal tariff regime. It thus appears to have responded to criticism and to acknowledge that liberalisation may be neither a necessary nor sufficient condition for export expansion. As a final proposal, and only after these three measures have been implemented and exports have increased, the Bank suggests the transition to an across-the-board lowering of tariffs. But this liberalisation should be staged slowly to prevent the loss of potentially viable industrial capacity.

Our own research findings generally support those of the Bank and we agree with most of their proposals for trade policy reform. However, as regards the reorientation of South Africa's trade regime in the context of the objective of stimulating the growth of South African industry, we would add the following points.

– Although not explicitly stated, there is some suggestion in the revised Bank document on South Africa (and in much of the Bank's prescriptive work in other environments) that industrial policy can be reduced to this revised trade policy. Our detailed sectoral studies make it evident that whilst a reformed trade regime will undoubtedly strengthen South African manufacturing's ability to compete with external competitors, it is by no means a sufficient initiative. (We return to this theme below.)

– We are not yet convinced that exporting automatically leads to the external economies which are implicit in the Bank's approach to trade policy. This conclusion is supported by comparative evidence contained in a recent WIDER study which examined the impact of trade reform on the industrialisation of 17 countries. It found no significant link between export expansion and productivity growth.[6] Our own research has explored the link between export growth and productivity growth in a number of sectors. The results are mixed but certainly do not show unambiguous support for this assertion by the Bank.

– Whilst the ultimate objective of the Bank approach to trade policy is to harmonise tariff rates across sectors, we believe that a degree of selectivity will always be desirable. In some cases this might arise from classical concerns with infant industry (as long as mechanisms exist to force them to 'grow up' as they age). In other cases it may arise from the pursuit of dynamic comparative advantages such as those arising from technological learning and the pursuit of scale economies (Krugman, 1986). In others it might arise from the need to effect a socially sustainable retreat from a sector undergoing a rapid and terminal decline.

– The Bank document supports what has become conventional wisdom on the issue of the sequencing of trade reform, namely that trade in intermediate goods be liberalised prior to lifting protection on final consumer goods. We support this need to liberalise the importation of intermediates to facilitate exports, but will argue below for a detailed case-by-case examination of the impact of liberalising trade in selected consumer goods. Whilst mindful of the potential employment and balance of payments implications of a precipitate liberalisation of labour-intensive consumer goods, the imperative of lowering the cost of basic wage goods (and thereby cutting unit labour costs for all sectors) dictates a less programmatic approach to the crucial question of the sequencing of trade reform.

– There is strong comparative evidence that an appropriate real exchange rate is strongly correlated with high and sustained rates of both export and output growth of manufactures.[7] Although there are important issues concerning the direction of causality in this correlation, we are persuaded that South African industry needs a competitive exchange rate if exports are to grow, and since growth has been constrained by the trade account, we give this some priority. Given the limited prospects for our traditional natural-resource-based exports, this exchange rate will need to be at a level which will act as an incentive to investment in non-traditional manufactured exports.

On the basis of our sectoral evidence in which we document widespread distress exporting (due to the prolonged domestic recession), GEIS-induced exporting and exporting designed to make better use of installed capacity (which does not provide a long-term basis for export growth), we believe that the existing exchange rate is somewhat over-valued. However, at this stage we are not able to quantify the extent of this overvaluation and are commissioning more research to determine the impact of a lower real exchange rate on manufactured exports.

In addition to a lower real exchange rate, it is important that manufacturers operate with stable real exchange rates. This has been determined as being of critical importance in the experience of South Korea and other successful exporters of manufactures (Balassa and Williamson, 1987). We thus believe that an appropriate and stable real exchange rate rule should be followed as a strategic instrument of long-term export-oriented manufacturing growth (Williamson, 1993).

However, this stability is not easily achieved in the context of endogenous and exogenous real shocks to which South Africa is especially prone in the light of fluctuations in the foreign exchange price of many of its principal exports – notably with respect to gold. We are thus in agreement with the suggestion that a 'stabilisation fund' be established to insulate the real exchange rate from substantive changes in commodity prices (Williamson, 1993). But operating a stable real exchange rate rule is of course not free of problems, including the choice of currencies in the basket. In addition some flexibility will be necessary in order to deal with exogenous shocks so that a real exchange rate rule should apply within a limited 'band' rather than being completely fixed. However, exchange rate realignments would need to reflect changes in the fundamental determinants in order not to undermine the policy itself and the confidence of investors and exporters.

We note, moreover, that because different industrial sectors have different trade structures (different levels of external trade as well as different trading partners) and different trade regimes (for example, the balance between tariffs, export subsidies and quotas), the maintenance of a real exchange rate rule may result in the exchange rate facing individual sectors and firms departing significantly from the 'average' (Kahn, 1992). Where there are specific industries that are particularly affected because of their different trade regime or tariff structure, this is best corrected by specific measures directed at the affected sector.

We also note an important institutional dimension to the determination of exchange rate policy. The South African Reserve Bank has for some time been concerned with macro-economic policy and stability and appears to have favoured a nominal exchange rate rule to provide an anchor against inflation. By contrast, the Department of Trade and Industry, the Board of Trade and Industry, and the Industrial Development Corporation, whose concern is with industrial development and (theoretically) with industrial policy and trade, would presumably tend to favour a stable real exchange rate. Thus the determination and implementation of a suitable exchange rate policy will require that attention be given to these potential inter-institutional difficulties.

Competition and co-operation in the domestic market

The prevalence of collusion: Whilst the important role of competition between domestic firms in enhancing manufacturing performance is acknowledged, there is also growing recognition of the importance of inter-firm co-operation. International experience, ranging from the networks of small firms in the regions of the 'Third Italy' through to the extensive co-operation that characterises the operations of the Japanese *keiretsu,* confirms the practical importance of this insight and, as important, confirms that competition and co-operation are not mutually exclusive phenomena. In the optimal case, there is an absence of collusive activity (fixing profits or market shares) and a prevalence of those forms of co-operative behaviour which are best designed to ensure collective efficiency. In the latter case, this co-operative behaviour occurs in a competitive context, whether as a result of domestic or foreign competitive pressures or both.

The high and growing levels of concentration that characterise most major product markets in South Africa are widely acknowledged. Whilst oligopolistic market structures are suggestive of potential anti-competitive collusion, it may be reasonably argued that, in a relatively small and open economy, scale considerations and the imperatives of international competitiveness presuppose concentrated markets. But it may be even more forcefully argued that, suitably monitored, the most intensive and productive competition can flow from markets which are dominated by a small number of well-resourced firms. In support of this argument the Minister of Trade and Industry has recently asserted that SAPPI and Mondi – the oligopolies that control paper and pulp production in South Africa – 'compete the hell out of each other' (*South African Labour Bulletin*, 1993).

Our research findings do not, in general, support this assertion. On the contrary they confirm the rather more orthodox view that suggests that in South African manufacturing a highly concentrated market structure is conducive to collusive rather than competitive conduct. Collusion is difficult to establish but it is strongly held that it is reflected in price fixing arrangements and in agreements to allocate exclusive market shares. Indeed, it is our strong impression – and one that is admittedly difficult to confirm conclusively – that a disaggregation of many oligopolistic markets would in fact reveal single-firm domination of major product lines. The paper and pulp market is a clear case in point. SAPPI and Mondi – in common with oligopolies in many other markets – do produce some competing products but, equally, major pulp and paper products are the exclusive preserve of one or other of these companies. The manufacture of telecommunications equipment is another instance.

In so far as co-operative behaviour which has the effect of ensuring collective efficiency is concerned, we have observed poorly functioning inter-firm networks in South African industry. This is particularly the case in relation to small- and medium-scale enterprises (SMEs), and has a number of implications for policy towards these SMEs and for regional development, which we will address below. But a further particular characteristic of South African industry is that whereas in other national contexts it is common to find large firms competing in the domestic market but colluding in export markets, our analysis of the minerals and mineral-beneficiating sectors suggests that the obverse appears to be occurring in South Africa. That is, collusive behaviour is evident in the local market, but there is little sign of co-operation between firms in external markets.

These patterns of sub-optimal behaviour are promoted by two factors. The first is weak competition policy. Our policy recommendations will include the strengthening of the authorities responsible for regulating market structure and conduct. This should extend beyond merely enhancing the resources and punitive capacities of the competition authorities. Crucially, the aim should be a more effective integration and mediation of competition policy and industrial policy. (At present, the competition authorities and those responsible for trade and industrial policies report to different Ministers.)

The structure of ownership, characterised by pervasive conglomeration, predisposes to collusive conduct. The practice of 'conglomerate forbearance', agreement to refrain from vigorous competition in a given market for fear of retaliation in an unrelated market, is illegal but appears to be widespread. Moreover, this anti-competitive practice is promoted by ever-closer links between the corporate shareholders that dominate the South African economy. These links are apparent in the growing incidence of interlocking directorships on the boards of competing companies or, what is more common, on the boards of corporations which control companies that are active, or may otherwise be active, competitors. Our policy recommendations are not for a programmatic – and ultimately quixotic – attack on oligopolistic markets. We are persuaded that oligopolies *may* be the most effective competitors. Our concern is to ensure that policy addresses those underlying conditions that promote collusive rather than competitive conduct in oligopolistic markets.

Corporate governance: The structure of ownership embodies additional complex and important implications for the competitiveness of the manufacturing sector. Ownership in South Africa is dominated by a small number of shareholders, in particular by the Anglo American Corporation, the Rembrandt group, the Anglovaal group, and the three major life offices, the Old Mutual, Sanlam and Liberty Life. Strong ownership positions translate into unassailable control via the practice of pyramiding and cross-shareholding, and enable the six corporate groups listed here to control companies representing some 90% of the market capitalisation of the Johannesburg Stock Exchange.

A powerful convention in industrial organisation holds that the separation of ownership and control – the rise of 'managerial capitalism' – has enabled strong centralised management to wrest control from weak, diffuse stockholders. This form of corporate governance is frequently suggested as an important factor underlying the decline of British and US firms in particular. In South Africa, it has been argued, the existence of strong centralised shareholders forestalls the problems of managerial dominance that allegedly beset the US and British economies (Gerson, 1992).

Our research rather suggests that shareholder power – and its converse, managerial weakness – in South Africa is an important aspect of the manufacturing sector's problems. In particular, strategic control – over investible surpluses – lies very clearly with the powerful shareholders. Our sectoral researchers encountered the frustration experienced by senior operating executives at having their ability to reinvest their operating surpluses controlled by shareholders and portfolio managers with little working knowledge of the requirements of the wide range of manufacturing activities under their control and at the narrow financial criteria that determined their investment decisions. Shareholder control – exercised through the main conglomerate boards which are effectively responsible for the management of the portfolio of the dominant shareholder – partly explains the unusual degree of diversity of the major South African conglomerates. These are corporations constructed to minimise investor risk rather than maximise operating synergies.

This is not to suggest that the conglomerate head office (the shareholder representative) generally intervenes in the daily operations of its subsidiaries. Our sectoral researchers have, by and large, verified the claim, persistently made by conglomerate executives, of non-interference in the affairs of their operating subsidiaries. The point to emphasise, however, is not, as the conventional presentation would have it, that this represents owners allowing managers operational 'space'. Rather it represents owners that do not have the necessary competence to intervene across the diverse sectoral range represented by the conglomerates. They also do not have the incentive – their brief is to monitor the financial ratios.[8] Shareholder control is effected through control of dividend policy, rights issues, and the raising of loans. Concern with the economies that may be attained by co-operation between affiliates in areas like group export marketing, technology development and human resource development effectively lies outside the brief of a portfolio manager, whose task is to represent the interests of a powerful shareholder. South African manufacturing is thus characterised by large corporate groups, the constituent parts of which are held together by their links to a common shareholder, but co-operation between the group operating companies is effectively non-existent.

We should add that our generally negative view of the impact of strong ownership is not contradicted by the existence of some exceptionally dynamic corporate groups. However, in those cases the company tended to be managed by its founder (for example, the Altron and Trencor groups), who maintained a strong ownership stake or else, for a variety of largely historically specific reasons, is dominated by its managers (for example, the Murray and Roberts group). These groups tended to be less diversified than those referred to above, and their executives to be more engaged in the operations of their subsidiaries, particularly in promoting intra-group co-operation.

Indeed, in these dynamic corporations the head office management tended to be interventionist, to be engaged in the major operating decisions of their subsidiaries. And yet, contrary to popular wisdom, this form of engagement did not generate antagonism from the managers of the operating subsidiaries. Interviews conducted by several of our sector researchers confirmed that the operating executives in the subsidiaries of these corporate groups viewed their head office executives as partners in the process of production and growth as opposed to competitors in the process of capital allocation. For example, the hostility expressed by senior operating management in one large, highly diversified, shareholder-dominated group to their corporate head office is in marked contrast to the view of managers in one of the more dynamic, management-dominated groups. In the latter we were told of 'stainless steel strategies' and 'group export drives', whereas in the former the prevailing view was one that ranged from indifference to the regular arrival of the head office accountants, to hostility at having had their access to the capital markets cut off by the head office's control over their investment decisions. Alternatively expressed, in the dynamic groups the internal incentives operated more effectively than in those highly diversified groups dominated by powerful shareholder interests.

These market and ownership structures have a significant impact on competitive behaviour. Our micro-level evidence suggests that key pillars of a competitive manufacturing sector are severely inhibited by existing market and ownership structures. These include the ability of dominant firms in highly concentrated markets to determine the economic well-being of upstream suppliers and downstream client firms; small- and medium-scale enterprises unable to scale the barriers to entry erected by market concentration and pervasive conglomeration; and managers and workers denied the participation in strategic investment decisions that underlie the productive performance of economies as otherwise diverse as Japan and Germany.

Our recommendations will include an ensemble of measures: some designed to deconcentrate existing markets or, where this is not possible or desirable, to monitor the conduct of dominant firms; measures aimed at constraining shareholder power through, for example, the delisting of pyramids, stricter regulation of mergers and acquisitions and stricter regulations governing disclosure by boards of directors; and other provisions aimed at strengthening other corporate stakeholders – suppliers, managers, workers, consumers. We will also address measures to promote those elements of co-operative behaviour which are conducive to industrial growth in our later discussions of measures designed to support technological capabilities and those required to support the growth of small- and medium-scale firms.

The pricing of raw-materials-based inputs

Both the South Africa Chamber of Business (Sacob) and the World Bank studies of industrial policy flag the importance of providing downstream manufacturing with border-priced inputs if the industrial sector is to be able to compete globally. In considering this issue it is necessary to address the role which South Africa's resource sector plays as a potential provider of inputs for industry. South Africa's endowment of natural resources is possibly unique, especially in the sphere of minerals. We may no longer be the world's lowest-cost gold producer but there is a variety of high-value metals in which we hold a commanding position in terms both of global reserves and of production costs. In manganese, platinum, chromium, vanadium, gold and alumino-silicates South Africa possesses the largest reserves and is generally amongst the lowest-cost producers. In other mineral products we also rank highly, and in coal not only are we a low-cost producer but have the world's fourth-largest reserves. These rents are not confined to mineral resources, since in forestry products we have an approximate 25% cost advantage over world pulp prices, and in many fruit products South Africa is also advantageously placed.

There are two views concerning the potential relationship between these resource endowments and downstream beneficiation. On the one hand it could be expected that access to these resource rents should provide a springboard for the growth of dynamic comparative advantage as, indeed, may have been the case since there is some evidence that past industrial accumulation in South Africa has been financed by surplus generated in the gold sector. It might also be the case that there are positive externalities between downstream processing and the resource sector. For example, the auto industry is entering a new phase of using aluminium products which requires developments in materials science and manufacturing technology. Since the new aluminium smelter being built is likely also to require these technical skills, they may be profitably directed at examining further downstream uses of aluminium. Similarly, global experience suggests that rapid technological and product development thrives on close proximity (with firms moving from sequential to 'simultaneous engineering'), and this, too, may be seen as providing an underlying justification for the deepening of resource beneficiation in South Africa. On the other hand, there can be no presumption that these externalities exist or that they will necessarily be captured and some care is required in fashioning appropriate policies which aid simultaneously the development of downstream processing and the optimal growth of industrial productivity.

Our researchers have identified a number of characteristics of this rent-providing sector which have a bearing on the past and future industrial trajectory. We will discuss three of these briefly. First, there is widespread evidence that beneficiation has been limited, falling short of what is technically feasible and in those sectors where South African production could reasonably be expected to be cost-competitive globally. This applies to a range of metal-based sectors, including steel products, the production of stainless steel and stainless steel products, aluminium products and jewellery. It also applies to agro-sectors – South Africa currently exports enough wood-chips to justify a new paper mill, an industry in which South Africa is already internationally competitive. Ironically, in one of the few sectors where beneficiation does occur – in platinum – it appears as if this deepening of production (to produce automotive catalytic converters) is wholly dependent upon export incentives.

A second conclusion emerging from our research concerns the pricing policies being pursued by those who command these resource rents. Across the
spectrum we have identified a pricing regime which provides little incentive for
the deepening of value-added in these resource-based sectors.

Thirdly, and related to import/export-parity pricing, the rents accruing from
these natural resources are used in a variety of ways. Part of these rents accrue to
the fiscus. Some of the rents accrue to the private holders of these mineral and
agro-related resources and are reflected in corporate profitability, only a portion
of which is reinvested in industry. The final component of these rents is used to
buffer production inefficiencies so that the potential surplus is not realised and
cannot be utilised to support downstream industrial development. The precise
location of these rents varies between sectors, but our researchers confirm their
widespread presence, specifically in mineral beneficiation and pulp and paper.

Leaving aside for the moment the possibility of privileging downstream processing, at the least we believe that domestic manufacturers should obtain access
to inputs at FOB export-parity (rather than import-parity) prices. This is not
without difficulty since it is common in many countries for exports to be subsidised by high prices charged in the domestic market. However, because of
South Africa's virtually unique access to low-cost resources, we do not believe
that this method of subsidy is necessary for raw material exports from South
Africa. Additionally, we believe that it is necessary to develop capabilities in
those sectors where low-cost domestic resources are allied to market opportunities. At present the prospect of enhancing downstream beneficiation is being left
to the market, and we have not been able to detect any sign that the private sector is investing in the desired capacity-building areas. In jewellery there are also
clear possibilities for high-productivity value-added, but there is an absence of
focused technological capacity-building or of the institutions required to accu-
mulate these capabilities.

The pricing of energy inputs

We are concerned that the price of energy inputs to industry may be too
low. In terms of published industrial electricity prices, Eskom is the third cheap-
est supplier in the world. In part these low costs are based upon the prices
charged for South African coal (R37 per ton versus R87 per ton for exports)
and in part because of the siting of many power stations very close to coal
deposits. The consequence has been the emergence of energy-intensive production in South Africa. Of 20 countries for which data are available, South Africa
has the highest share of manufacturing value-added in energy-intensive sectors;
at the same time the energy elasticity of GDP has been falling significantly in the
industrialised countries and rising in South Africa.

There are three potentially damaging implications of this low energy price.
The first is with respect to the environment, where pollution related to the
burning of low-grade coal (which is compounded since these coal-fired power
stations do not 'scrub' their emissions) is a growing problem. This has both
adverse environmental and health consequences. The second problem is that
access to cheap energy may be prompting South African industry down a route

based on high and 'dirty' energy, just as technical change in the rest of the world is pushing industries towards lower-energy utilisation and cleaner technologies. Third, Eskom's large degree of excess capacity (and hence its low marginal costs of generation) has led it to become a direct investor in manufacturing, accentuating the trend towards energy-intensive production.

In terms of policy responses there are reasons to suppose that the current market price of energy understates its true economic cost. This being the case, the policy prescription may seem to be clear, viz to increase the costs of energy to users.[9] This, however, poses severe problems for an incoming government. Most of the population is not currently connected to the electricity grid (which has very significant levels of unused capacity), and even if current levels of connection were doubled, it would take 15 years before 85% of the population were connected to the grid. However, even at current levels of installation and even with existing cheap energy prices, many of the new consumers are unable to pay the costs required to finance their connection; for many low-income households, energy already consumes more than 10% of household expenditure. Thus any attempt to sustain, let alone to increase, the rate of new connections (which is probably of critical importance to a post-apartheid government) will require the continuation of cheap energy policies unless some form of cross-subsidy is introduced to allow low-income consumers access to low-price energy without promoting the excessive use of energy amongst high-income consumers and industry.

An additional area of industrial policy which needs to be addressed in relation to the energy sector concerns the ability of the energy utility to invest directly in downstream industry. This is one of the primary factors promoting the growing energy intensity of industrial production. Finally, although our studies show that there is excess capacity not only in energy generation, but also in those industries providing the inputs into energy reticulation, a substantial increase in the proportion of the population connected to the electricity grid is likely to have deleterious implications for the balance of payments. This is because of the foreign exchange cost in the white and brown goods sectors producing consumer durables. Assuming a conservative rate of connections of 200 000 per annum (the current rate), the likely foreign exchange cost will be in excess of US$ 2bn over five years. To some extent these costs could be mitigated by a programme of import substitution. But of all our sectoral studies we have found it least likely that South Africa will be able to generate competitive production in these white and brown goods industries, except possibly in the case of small domestic appliances. Even this relatively pessimistic final outcome is only likely to emerge in the context of a coherent overall strategy for this sector.

Unit labour costs

Although there are important sectoral variations (notably in the steel industry, but also in paper and plastics), wages in South Africa appear to be less than 20% of those in the USA; in many sectors they are an even smaller proportion of European and Japanese wages. This provides opportunities for the manufacturing sector. For example, BMW is considering using South Africa as the major site for its small series of automobiles, and in many component sectors it is believed that South African firms' low wage costs are a potential asset. However, even though South African wages are considerably lower than those of the industrially advanced countries, about half the level of the first-tier NIEs, and similar to those in Brazil and Mexico, they remain high by comparison with many other LDCs, particularly those in Asia. South African manufacturers also suffer from low levels of factor productivity, associated not only with the ineffective utilisation of capital equipment, but also with the inefficient use of labour. The consequence of low labour productivity is that South African firms can only compete by virtue of paying low wage rates.

At the same time, despite high nominal wages by comparison with many LDCs, the standard of living of South Africa's labour force is low and the rates of poverty (even amongst those employed in the formal sector) are much higher than would be expected from South Africa's international wage ranking. The reasons for this are principally associated with the racial structures of apartheid, for example the siting of workers' residences far from their places of work and the consequently high transport costs imposed upon workers. These related issues of wages, productivity and living standards all need addressing in an industrial strategy since even though labour is not the only factor input, it remains a significant element, particularly in the labour-intensive sectors.

We believe that both the paradox of high wages and low consumption and the low labour productivity are a direct consequence of the industrial and political legacy of apartheid. Now that apartheid is being superseded, the prospect arises of breaking away from these inherited structures. In addition to policies focused at raising labour productivity through changes in firm-level organisational practices (which we address below), there are two key wage-related areas in which corrective action can be taken to strengthen South Africa's globally competitive performance by reducing unit wage costs.

The selected liberalisation of basic wage goods: As a consequence of the formula tariff system, this has been one area in which the production of key wage goods – i.e. basic items consumed by those with low incomes – has benefited from particularly high levels of effective protection. Whilst we recognise the strong general argument for a trade liberalisation sequence that prioritises freeing up imports of intermediate goods, we believe that a case-by-case examination of the tariff structure may support the immediate liberalisation of certain consumer goods. This will have the effect of increasing the purchasing power of those on low incomes, thereby reducing pressure on wages.[10]

Those households with per capita incomes above R1 000 per month are likely to have at least one member in formal sector employment; those with less than R1 000 are likely to be benefiting from remittances or to have casual employment or to engage in sub-subsistence agriculture. Consider three basic items of household expenditure which involve tariff protection – clothing, footwear and bread (through protection of wheat). A breakdown of household consumption expenditure in urban and rural households in Natal showed that together these items comprise over 17% of expenditure. If tariffs were abolished on wheat, the likelihood is that bread prices would fall by approximately 10%.[11]

The weighted average tariff on clothing is 88% and on footwear 77%, but as observed they are proportionately higher on low-unit cost items (tariff data from Belli *et al.*, 1993). Assuming that the marketing mark-up on imports is 100%, then the impact of tariff reduction on prices is a 44% fall in clothing and a 38% fall in footwear.[12]

From these approximate figures it is possible to calculate the rough impact on household expenditures arising from the liberalisation of wheat imports and basic clothing and footwear imports on those households in our target group, i.e. those earning less than R2 500 per month. It is evident from this that if nominal incomes are maintained, then real consumption standards would increase, both for the non-working poor and for those in wage employment. For those poor households outside of formal sector employment (say, roughly those households earning less than R1 000 per month), the net effect would be a 3-4% increase in living standards. For those households in formal-sector wage employment (say between R1 000 and R2 500 per month), the increase rises to around 6%. Urban households tend to benefit proportionately more than rural households (5,2% versus 4%), which is due to the large share of clothing in their consumption baskets.

This focused programme of import liberalisation is likely to affect production costs or living standards in two respects. First, firms will be able to gain by addressing labour costs in their own operations. But secondly, it will also reduce production costs in all supplying industries and thus have a more wide-ranging impact on total firm production costs. Another important impact of this focused trade initiative is that it will also increase living standards in the poorest sections of the population that are without formal-sector employment.

There are of course a number of problems with this policy initiative, of which two stand out in importance. First, although the liberalisation of wheat and footwear imports is easily specified, the path is not so clear with respect to clothing. Which of the numerous tariff items are included in the expenditure basket of low-income earners will be a matter for detailed research. Second, there are likely to be severe transitional costs in these industries, which must be priorities in the policy agenda. However, we believe that there is some scope for expanded exports in both the footwear and clothing sectors, although firms will have to make considerable changes to their operating procedures and the government will have to provide support for this export initiative to succeed. We also believe that there is likely to be some scope for further import substitution in the high unit price segments of the domestic market in these two sectors. To the extent that these opportunities can be grasped we believe that there should be some measure of compensatory job creation in these two sectors. Though it is difficult to quantify, we also believe that there will be a general equilibrium effect arising from reducing unit wage costs throughout the economy and that this, too, will lead to employment creation, albeit in other sectors. We return to these problems of structural unemployment in the concluding section.

The social wage: The current paradox of 'high' relative wages and low real living standards arises in part from the low level of the social wage. In particular, much of the social infrastructure, which forms an important part of the consumption basket of wage earners, is inadequately developed in South Africa. Thus a coherent industrial strategy needs to address both the social and private domains of consumption. Two of our sectoral studies have explored the capacities of industrial sectors to deliver inputs of this sort. In the building materials sector, we have researched the conditions of production of two primary inputs into housing and other forms of construction – cement and bricks. We have also been able to identify alternative technologies which might increase labour absorption in the brick industry, and have addressed the pricing policies of the few firms that dominate the cement industry. With respect to electricity reticulation, we have explored the capacities to deliver electricity into the home. In both of these sectors our researchers have determined that there is significant excess capacity, so that the marginal cost of meeting these basic needs will not be excessive. We have however already indicated the dangers which increased household consumption of consumer durables (consequent upon better access to electricity) is likely to hold for the trade account.

Beyond incentives: capabilities and institutions

Undoubtedly, getting the incentive structure to operate in a transparent and rational manner is an important component of an effective industrial strategy. But, for reasons which we have already discussed, this is not an adequate response to the policy challenge posed in raising productivity growth in South Africa's industrial sector. In addition it is necessary to focus specifically on the building of capabilities, over the short, medium and long term. In overcoming the market failures which obstruct capability building, consideration will have to be given to institutional development. While the firm – broadly understood as comprising an ensemble of owners, management and labour – is the primary institution affecting industrial activity, there is a range of other institutions in the public and private sectors (as well as those which represent a combination of public and private sector inputs) that needs attention.

On the basis of our detailed studies of economic behaviour in the 13 sectors of investigation, as well as of our cross-sectoral investigations, we have identified four major areas in which we feel that policy attention should focus – building human resources for the production; strengthening small, medium and micro enterprises; the development of technological capacity; and the more effective organisation of production, work and inter-institutional linkages. In each of these cases we are concerned with a mix of incentives, capabilities and institutions which we have observed are not currently adequate for the extended growth of the industrial sector. We have also observed that these elements of industrial strategy are not being adequately addressed in the current policy debate, particularly in relation to the unwarranted concentration on the incentive structure in general and on trade policy reform in particular.

Human resources and production

The legacy of South Africa's apartheid policies in education will clearly live to haunt a post-apartheid economic policy, just as it undermines the current operations of many industrial enterprises. There have been improvements in the educational background of the labour force, with the mean years of schooling having risen from 4,9 to 7,1 years between 1970 and 1985. But despite this, as recently as 1985 fully one-quarter of the African working population and one-eighth of the coloured work force were without formal education. It is estimated that 45% of blacks cannot read or write (Fallon *et al.,* 1993). This compares very unfavourably with the NIEs and with many of the non-NIE LDCs. In recent years the political upheavals have led to an alarming disruption of this 'thin' layer of formal education, and the proportion of African school-leavers earning university entrance has fallen from 28% in 1987 to 17% in 1988, 10% in 1989 and only 8% in 1990.

In many areas of professional activity, however, South Africa performs well. For example, looking at the numbers of patents registered in the US (which is frequently used as an indicator of comparative R & D performance), South Africa outperformed South Korea (until 1988) and has consistently registered more than twice as many patents as Brazil. Nevertheless, it is evident that South Africa's professional educational endowment is very low by international standards, particularly in those areas which are relevant to industry's needs.

Vocational training is of particular relevance to the industrial sector. It was only after 1979 that vocational training was taken seriously, following the reports of the Wiehahn and the Human Sciences Research Council (HSRC) commissions. There are three different routes to this form of training. In the formal education sector the numbers receiving technical education within schools have increased significantly, from 9 507 Africans in 1984 to 25 968 in 1988; we have no sense of the quality or practical relevance of these educational programmes, though. Secondly, enrolment in technical colleges has also seen a significant increase from 36 186 (4 234 Africans) in 1975 to 76 769 (16 033 Africans) in 1990; once again, we have little sense of the extent to which this training programme meets the human resource needs of industry. Third, and most important, is the programme of training which occurs with the direct participation of the productive sector. The National Training Board was established in 1981, and there has recently been an important move away from the state provision of apprentice training to a system under the control of employers and trade unions. There are currently 9 private sector institutions with 65 satellite and mobile units, plus 31 industry training boards involved in apprentice training. Nevertheless, there has been a drop in vocational training between 1986 and 1991, as well as in attempts to re-train the unemployed.

We thus observe a relatively uneducated population, a problematic schooling system, underinvestment in relevant training at the tertiary level, and a falling level of commitment to vocational training within the productive sector. This is despite the fact that the private returns to education and training are high, particularly in secondary education and in vocational skills (where the rate is highest to skilled manual workers). It is striking, also, that the number of registered vacancies for artisans and apprentices rose from 10 972 in 1979 (a boom period in South African manufacturing) to 15 651 in 1989 (a year of recession in manufacturing). This suggests considerable market failure in the education and training systems.

The low level of past investment in human resource development, and the relatively large concentration on tertiary skills, occur despite much international evidence which shows that the rate of return to primary education is considerably higher. This particular form of maldistribution is a direct reflection of apartheid. This is widely acknowledged across the political spectrum, as is the recognition of the need to expand educational provision in the future, notwithstanding severe budgetary constraints.

However, even though South African industry will undoubtedly benefit from an enhanced commitment to human resource development, in itself this is an inadequate response to the human resource needs of industry, particularly in the context of competing globally. There are three reasons why a blanket and unfocused increase in educational investment will be an insufficient response to these challenges of industrial competitiveness; they reflect the structure of industrial relations that exists in industry, which, in turn, reflects the legacy of apartheid. First, academic studies are of limited relevance to industrial production – it is in the realm of vocational skills that industry's needs are to be met. This has implications for the balance between training for professionals and for the direct work force, as well as for the types of education and training which are provided to production workers. This is not to imply that academic skills are unimportant since clearly basic literacy and numeracy are a necessary component of vocational training. Moreover, the changing nature of work organisation requires the ability to communicate, to work in groups and to solve problems, and these skills are often enhanced by formal academic education. Nevertheless, we have concluded that a greater focus needs to be placed on vocational skills than that currently evident in the debate on human resource development.

Second, and related to the need for enhanced vocational skills, training does not only occur in the context of formal institutes of learning. It is becoming increasingly evident from comparative experience that intra–firm education, various forms of supplementary adult education and industry-wide training are a primary requirement in industrial competitiveness. These training schemes should be accredited and associated with the acquisition of formal certification. This will involve the development of a nationally integrated system of training which links different levels of the training and education system. In this way, all workers will be afforded the potential to proceed along a career path to which modules of accredited training contribute. But, particularly in the context of the trend towards continuous improvement in production, re-training has become an essential component of competitive production.

Thirdly, and most significantly, it is now widely acknowledged in the industrialised countries that in recent years there has been a significant change in the optimal organisation of work (Kaplinsky, 1992). Without going into too much detail, we can say that in previous years work was heavily segmented between skilled and unskilled workers, and consequently there was a sharp division of labour between the direct and indirect labour force. In many countries this was reflected in the structure of industrial relations – in South Africa's case in the division between white and black trade unions and their differential access to the institutions of collective bargaining. This, in turn, was bolstered by racially based legislation and structured access to apprenticeship, and hence to skilled work categories. In industry-wide collective bargaining agreements this is still reflected in a proliferation of narrowly defined job grades, particularly at the lower end of the hierarchy, and unusually large earnings differentials between the various grades. Although formally cast in terms of skill, the industrial relations system has long reflected an effective division between indirect and supervisory labour – or 'guard labour' – on the one hand, and direct, productive labour, on the other. The basis of labour productivity in apartheid lay in the proliferation of formally 'skilled', largely white, indirect workers, supervising formally 'unskilled', largely African, direct producers.

This division of labour took an extreme form in South Africa. In particular, the fact that many 'unskilled' workers had acquired and were using considerable skills on the job but were being rewarded at 'unskilled' rates generated massive resentment. This, in turn, increased the 'need' for strict, highly paid supervision, thus substantially vitiating the unit cost advantages of 'under-rewarding' skilled direct labour. It also, of course, substantially reduced the incentive for acquiring, much less deploying, enhanced skills.

However, as flexible production has begun to impose itself on the standards of global competitiveness, there has been a substantive trend towards new forms of work organisation.[13] In particular, workers are now required to perform a variety of tasks and hence multi-skilling has become widespread. Moreover, the transition to quality-at-source and cellular production has meant that the work force has been given more responsibility over the control of production. Finally, and most significantly, continuous improvement (*kaizen* in Japanese) has proved to be one of the most important routes to rapid product innovation and process improvement, and this arises directly as a consequence of the participation of the labour force.

Thus, because of these developments in work organisation, because of the need to promote more intra-firm and intra-industry training (which for many South African enterprises reflects a substantial reorientation from historic practices) and because of the need to expand the vocational component of training, the debate on South Africa's educational system is inadequately focused in relation to the development of a globally competitive industrial sector. The problem which we have identified is that the skill needs of industry cannot be met by the expansion of the educational system alone. The orientation of the business sector towards the participation and development of its labour force needs to alter fundamentally.

This is, of course, easier said than done, and it would be naive to believe that it will occur by exhortation alone. A higher level of exposure to competitive pressures (in both international and domestic markets) will help concentrate management's mind, as will a government policy more focused on vocational training. But there are, in addition, severe structural obstacles in the way of a fundamental reorientation on the part of South African managers. We have already noted the distance between those in control of the strategic direction of South African manufacturing and the shop floor, a distance that is reflected in the unusually large earnings differentials at all levels of South African industry.

We have also noted the complex interaction between skill, hierarchy and race, and it is evident that the development of new forms of work organisation is closely interwoven with the transition to a post-apartheid social and political accord.

Significantly, the unions are mindful of the shop-floor imperatives of economic restructuring. The innovative proposals submitted to employers by the National Union of Metalworkers (Numsa) reflect this. The Numsa position is complex and we cannot do justice to it here. In brief, it explicitly recognises the need to recast the operation of the incentive structure on the shop floor. It sets out to achieve this by introducing into the collective bargaining framework the concept of a nexus between wages, training, grading and work organisation that involves, *inter alia*, a reduction in the number of grades in the engineering agreement from 13 to 5 and a graduated reduction in wage differentials. This is bolstered by proposals around training and re-training and proposals aimed at achieving a more flexible bargaining system whilst upholding the importance of industry-wide centralised bargaining, particularly in a period of rapid change. The Numsa proposals also address the recognition of much shop-floor reality that is hidden behind the label of 'unskilled' [black] work.

We should not, however, underestimate the challenges that restructuring poses for established union practices. The issue raised here is one such challenge: confronting the necessity to restructure innovatively has inevitably raised questions regarding effective levels of bargaining and, in particular, enterprise bargaining. However, we take cognisance of the fragmentation that would arise from devolving industrial relations in the absence of a centralised framework. We therefore propose a multi-tiered system of collective bargaining governing national, sectoral and plant levels with appropriate frameworks set by each layer in turn. We are convinced that the structured, continuous engagement of labour in corporate decision-making as well as in economic policy formulation is fundamental to the process of industrial restructuring.

The development of human resources in this way represents an essential capability for industrial efficiency. We are persuaded that this constitutes one of the more constructive initiatives in the current policy debate, and, based upon our reading of the competitive environment, flag it as an issue of first-order importance.

Small, medium and micro enterprises

Comparative industrial performance appears to be significantly influenced by market structure. In some cases – notably South Korea, northern Germany and Japan – large firms seem to be associated with dynamic comparative advantage. Their size provides them with the opportunities to cross-subsidise new areas of activity. Large firms may also obviate co-ordination problems and benefit from the problems of internalising transaction costs. In other cases, large firms show few signs of the flexibility necessary for sustained growth and profitability. For example, in Peru large firms appear to block rather than to promote the achievement of dynamic comparative advantage (Alcorta, 1992). International experience also provides evidence of the potential offered by small and medium enterprises (SMEs). Both Taiwan and mid-Italy are examples of industrial dynamism based upon small-scale firms.

However, on deeper examination, many of the key cases traditionally invoked to support an argument for the superiority of one or other end of the firm-size spectrum are misleading. Hence, whilst advocates of small-scale enterprise frequently cite Taiwan's dramatic industrial performance in order to lend weight to their argument, a more detailed examination of that country will highlight the critical significance of some very large, usually state-owned enterprises at key points in the production chain. Similarly, whilst the importance of Japan's and Germany's large firms is acknowledged, so too must the major contribution of the exceptionally dynamic and innovative small and medium enterprises in those countries. Many of them are suppliers to the large enterprises. Thus the key issue is probably less about the intrinsic importance of a diverse array of firm sizes than about the relationship between firms.

South Africa's market structure is, as we have already observed, characterised by acutely high levels of concentration, in terms of both ownership and markets. Large producing units, which are grouped in highly diversified conglomerates and which have subsidiaries spanning the financial, mining and manufacturing sectors, are the dominant features of South Africa's industrial landscape. As might be expected, high levels of market concentration are evident in the capital-intensive sectors. But so, too, are they in the labour-intensive sectors. For example, in the shoe industry four firms account for 70% of output. Less well known but probably equally significant is the concentration of plant size. The average number of employees in South African manufacturing plants is twice as large as in the UK (which is, itself, well known for the relative absence of SMEs); in footwear and clothing, the average South African plant employs 175 and 101 respectively, whereas in Italy (the world's largest net exporter in both sectors), it was between 5 and 20 during the mid-1980s.

A second distinctive feature of South African manufacturing is the general weakness of medium-sized industries and the specific absence of high-tech, formal-sector micro enterprises. Even in the electronics sector – where international experience suggests that small, flexible firms tend to play an important role in industry development – we have observed the existence of a 'missing middle'. A large number of factors contribute to this gap, including the predatory expansion of large conglomerates (usually by acquisition), the presence at key points of many production chains of market-dominating firms responsible for the acute vulnerability of SMEs (whether as supplier, customers or competitors), and the weakness of the financial sector in meeting the specific needs of SMEs.

Policy options directed at promoting SMEs include redirecting the competition authorities away from their narrow exclusive focus on the protection of *consumers* from dominant and collusive firms, to one that considers the plight of disadvantaged *producers* competing and supplying within these market structures. In addition, the orientation of the financial sector – and, in particular, those public and quasi-public financial institutions with a specific mandate to support SMEs – requires further examination. Our work on technological capacity (see below) considers policy initiatives to assist SMEs in this regard. Finally, we are aware of the potentially productive co-operative relationships between SMEs, which have not as yet been fully exploited in the South African context.

A further characteristic of South Africa's industrial structure is the under-developed nature of the informal manufacturing sector. Our research has devoted considerable resources in trying to identify the size of this sector and the constraints to its growth. This is in part because its ability to produce cheap wage goods has a direct bearing on wage costs in industry and thus on South African industries' capacity to compete with foreign producers. But it is also because the sector has the potential to offer productive employment and because we are aware of its positive contribution in many other countries with similar per capita incomes to South Africa. The results of our research suggest that this sector is poorly developed in South Africa, in terms of numerical size and in terms of the incomes it offers to entrepreneurship. Our research shows that skill shortages, the absence of civil harmony, the absence of infrastructure and the shortage of marketing channels are all contributory factors, as is the low buying power of potential consumers.

We believe that a raft of policies is required to maximise the contribution which the micro-enterprise sector can make to industrial development in South Africa. Firstly, the current industrial structure constitutes an extremely hostile environment for informal manufacturing. Particularly significant here is the rela-tive absence of dynamic SMEs in the formal sector. For example, in the building materials industry we have found a strong tendency for the characteristically large-scale construction and civil engineering firms engaged in major property development activity to rely on inputs provided by brick and cement product suppliers of a similar scale. This case is pertinent because in brick and cement product manufacturing there is considerable technical scope for small-scale, labour-intensive production of products of adequate quality and because it is likely that a post-apartheid government will devote considerable resources to meet housing needs. For example, small-scale clamp firing of bricks (which are perfectly adequate for basic housing) is eight to ten times more labour-intensive than the large-scale plants, and a cheaper product is produced. We have no doubt that a vibrant SME component in the construction industry would pro-vide a more friendly climate for informal sector producers of building inputs. Hence, policies designed to support SMEs are likely to have a favourable impact on informal sector manufacturing.

Secondly, we recognise that the needs of informal sector manufacturing can-not be met by changes in the incentive structure alone since these small enter-prises often suffer from 'internal' difficulties and require support with respect to the development of managerial and technological capabilities. However, in our view the most effective general support to the informal sector will arise from programmes designed to meet housing, electrification, communications, trans-port and the gamut of urban and rural physical infrastructural needs. Specific institutions will be required (perhaps intensively populated by NGOs) which assist the informal sector to respond to these new market opportunities. This will require attention both to training and in technological support.

Thirdly, our researchers have found that policy specifically directed at informal sector producers – as opposed, that is, to the broad functional interventions referred to in the previous paragraph – requires a sectorally oriented approach. There is, in fact, little in common between informal sector producers of metal burglar bars on the one hand and 'houseworkers' taking orders from a clothing designer on the other. Hence, specific policy measures targeted at an aggregated 'informal sector' are likely to be ineffective.

Further, our researchers have disaggregated micro-enterprise production *within* specific sectors. Here, too, the results are instructive for policy formulation. In clothing – a growing site of informal sector production – there are three clear delineations. There are highly skilled tailors and seamstresses producing high-quality garments to order. There are groups of 'houseworkers' entering into contract with formal sector producers, designers and retailers. And there are poverty-stricken individuals producing cheap and undifferentiated pinafores for other, often equally poverty-stricken individuals. The first of these subsectors is unlikely to benefit from the attention of industrial policy. The third group is more likely to benefit from a general rise in working-class income than from small business hives and management courses. (Since we are also proposing the liberalisation of cheap textile imports, these enterprises are unlikely to be adversely affected by the liberalisation process outlined earlier.)

It is the second sector – the houseworkers – which warrants very close policy attention. This activity clearly has a direct impact on the cost structure of the formal centres of activities in the industry. Moreover, these groups of houseworkers are frequently co-ordinated by a skilled clothing worker-turned-entrepreneur earning considerably more than he or, usually, she earned in the formal sector. The houseworkers employed by this entrepreneur are generally themselves experienced clothing workers, working in appalling conditions with little security and no fringe benefits, and often earning much less than they took home from their erstwhile formal-sector employers. And, finally, this subsector is growing and, if both our own research results and international experience are anything to go by, will continue growing.

We are aware that this is a sensitive area for policy intervention. Many of the jobs in this sector reflect direct job losses in the formal sector, and much employment is 'sweated' labour. However we are not confident that this activity could or should be regulated out of existence. In particular it is our view that greater flexibility rather than lower direct costs may provide the competitive edge to micro enterprises, in which case a policy response may turn its attention to the factors inhibiting this greater flexibility in the formal sector itself. It has been suggested to us that the dominant and highly concentrated retailers are abusing their market power to demand unattainable levels of flexibility from their suppliers. A more co-operative and less adversarial relationship between these sectors may halt job attrition to the formal sector. Above all, our small sample already persuades us that a core of these micro enterprises is on the cusp of becoming effective small enterprises. Promotion is likely to bring them into this fold, swelling regulated employment; repression will drive them back into the ranks of sweated labour.

In summary, then, we observe the underdevelopment of the SME and micro-enterprise sectors as well as the absence of co-operation between these small firms and between small, medium and large firms. (We will address policies to promote co-operation in later discussion.) We are unconvinced that merely reorienting the incentive structure in a 'rational' way – that is, bringing market prices in line with economic costs – will be adequate to promote their development in a manner which is optimal for the South African economy's industrial needs. For their long-term future to be adequately addressed a programme of support will be required to actively promote this sector's development. In part this involves a focused direction of macro-economic programmes in housing and other social wage goods. But it will also require that specific attention be given to the promotion of capabilities amongst micro, small and medium-sized firms. This is often a long-term task and requires that careful attention be given to institutional design, particularly in the NGO sector.

The development of technological capabilities

It is now well established that investment in enhancing technological capabilities is subject to a complex series of market failures because investments in developing technological capacities have a variety of externalities and because the returns to such investments are subject to strong uncertainty (Dosi, 1988). It has therefore long been recognised that private investment in such activities will tend to be lower than the social optimum (Arrow, 1962). A further source of market failure arises in the acquisition of technology (and hence affects the decision to either acquire or develop capability 'in-house'). The tacit nature of technological knowledge ensures that only the seller of the technology can know its 'true value'. Furthermore, asymmetric knowledge frequently combines with a situation of imperfect markets, or even quasi-monopoly, whereby the technology seller may have considerable sway in the market.

We have found evidence of substantive market failure in the development of technological capabilities in South Africa. Whilst there are variations, particularly at the sectoral level (which are important in the design of sector-specific policies), the following features are especially significant: At the national level, investment in enhancing technological capability is currently declining. The national system of innovation is poorly integrated. At the sectoral level, there are low levels of R & D spending by comparison with many other countries. At the firm level, there is a general and widespread underinvestment in enhancing technological capabilities. There is a strong tendency to rely upon the acquisition of technology from abroad. South Africa is strong in scientific research but far weaker in technology application.

Taken together, these features are evidence of pervasive market failure. Moreover, they are strongly suggestive of the imperfections and inadequacies of the existing institutional arrangements, which are designed to complement and supplement the workings of the market. Restructuring the incentive system (for example, in the trade regime) is likely to secure gains through the sectoral re-allocations of productive factors. However, these altered incentives will not lead to the enhancement of technological capabilities (for example, those required for sustained export expansion, particularly in more demanding and discriminating product niches) unless they are complemented with a programme of support and the development of appropriate institutions.

While it is necessary to record the incidence of market failure and establish the basis for purposive state policies to correct such failure, it is at the same time critical to recognise also that a more competitive environment for South African industry will be an important factor in compelling firms to enhance their technological capabilities. There is clear evidence to the effect that in some sectors, notably electronics, the smaller firms operating in the more competitive sectors of the domestic market undertake proportionately more expenditure on R & D than do the large firms, which tend to dominate in their particular product markets (BMI, 1992). We also note that in a variety of sectors, there does seem to be an association between a more active participation in export markets and the tendency of firms to enhance their technological capacities. This is evident, *inter alia,* in the auto and auto components sector and in the telecommunications equipment industry where exports have in part arisen through firms capitalising on in-house R & D. It is significant here that two large telecommunications firms – Siemens and Alcatel – have decided to serve their sub-Saharan markets from their South African subsidiaries, and this will clearly be associated with an increase in developmental work which takes place in South Africa.[14]

The inward-oriented trade regime and high levels of market concentration have been major factors retarding technological development. It is likely that a more export-oriented trade regime and a restructured import regime will be associated with enhanced investments in technology. Once again, though, there is no automatic link between trade orientation and the development of technological capacities. Extra-market support will be required if South African industry is to invest adequately in technological development.

Thus, in addition to the above changes to the incentive structure, we would see the need for specific policy interventions designed to:

(1) reverse the current decline in overall national expenditure on R & D and, in particular, the decline in business expenditures on R & D;

(2) strengthen incentives to firms to invest in the development of in-house technological capabilities;

(3) affect the terms of technology transfer;

(4) restructure the funding and other incentives that currently affect the operations of the system of statutory science councils;

(5) encourage links between the universities and manufacturing industry;

(6) identify and acquire capacity in significant future technological developments.

We are cognisant of the importance of designing policies to enhance technological capabilities which recognise the limited capacities of government and the possibilities of governmental failure.

Organisational change in production

The application of technology to production raises productivity. Traditionally it has been customary to think of technology largely in embodied terms, as comprising physical plant and equipment. However, in recent years it has become apparent that changes in disembodied technology – 'organisational reform' – not only provide a high payback, but are a precondition for the use of the radical new technologies associated with the diffusion of the new computer-integrated manufacturing technologies (Hoffman and Kaplinsky, 1988).

The discussion of organisational reform in industry covers a wide agenda. Global comparative experience suggests that a wider organisational canvas is required, one which also allows for the development of new forms of inter-firm organisation affecting production scheduling, design and marketing (discussed above); changing relationships between white collar and blue collar workers within firms; changing relationships between subsidiaries and plants of the same firms; and changing relationships between science and technology institutions and the productive sector. It is important to note, however, that organisational change cannot be a substitute for embodied technological organisation (except in the short run), and the sustained development of technological capabilities requires the expansion of investment in science and technology.

There is little recognition of the nature and contemporary importance of organisational reform in South Africa's national policy-making arena. We have been unable to detect any signs that the Department of Trade and Industry, the Industrial Development Corporation, the Council for Scientific and Industrial Research or any other relevant national institutions have grasped the significance of new forms of inter-firm relations, new forms of work organisation or any other elements of contemporary disembodied technological change. Not surprisingly then, the structure of the incentive system is wholly oriented in favour of embodied technological change. Thus the tariff system is weighted in favour of capital goods,[15] and depreciation allowances are made available for the purchase of capital goods. No equivalent incentives exist to promote investments in new forms of production organisation, skill development or other elements of disembodied technological change.

Consequently, much of the low productivity we have observed in different sectors arises as a direct consequence of the anachronistic forms of organisation which pervade South Africa's industrial sector. These are particularly acute in the areas of intra-plant organisation (where the confluence of Taylorist forms of work organisation and racial division is a major cause of low labour productivity) and inter-firm organisation, although they are also prevalent in other important areas, such as intra-firm innovation processes and the links between individual firms and the science and technology system.

In proposing a programme to encourage the adoption of new forms of disembodied technology, we are explicitly recognising the prevalence of market failure with respect to the diffusion of these new forms of organisation. This market failure is not unique to South Africa, and a variety of countries (including the UK during the Thatcher administration) have developed policies in response. But in South Africa's case, it is likely that this market failure will be exacerbated since it is so heavily dependent upon the development of a pattern of social relations which were anathema to the system of apartheid. Nevertheless, a number of pioneering firms (some of which we describe briefly below) have shown that it is possible to make substantial progress in this regard. Consequently we believe that there is a 'productivity dividend' to be reaped in a post-apartheid era. This will arise not only from the widespread diffusion of new forms of organisation in production, but also from the likely fall in industrial action. Thus the intent of our policy proposals on promoting organisational change is to revive total factor productivity growth by increasing both labour and capital productivity.

Intra-plant organisational reform: A limited number of enterprises have begun to implement organisational reform in South Africa. Many of these are in the automobile sector, initially stimulated by Toyota's requirements for JIT (just-in-time) delivery and improved quality (Van der Riet and Hendy, 1986). For example, one large automobile plant has restructured its organisation over the past three years. This has led to a decrease in the labour force (from over 5 200 to 3 600 employees), and with no additional capital investment, output has risen by 30% in real terms. The firm is confident of a further 30% increase in labour productivity before additional investments will be required. In this case both labour productivity and capital productivity were enhanced.[16] It is significant here that these productivity savings have been associated with cost savings. For example, in the context of annual inflation rates exceeding 12%, a new model has just been introduced with an 8% reduction in nominal prices, providing the same level of unit profit to the assembler. Similarly in one of the more efficient (export-oriented) component suppliers, the move from older forms of functional layouts to cellular production has more than doubled output with less than half the labour force, and with no additional capital investment; product variety and quality were also substantially improved. Once again, these organisational changes have led to increases in both capital and labour productivity.

In response to the problems posed by the maintenance of outdated forms of production organisation in South African industry, we propose that a major policy initiative be introduced to speed up the process of organisational reform at the plant level, affecting the inter-linked phenomena of factory layout, production scheduling and work organisation. There are a number of components to this initiative. The first is a programme of awareness generation, directed not just at senior management (as now occurs through the operations of consulting companies), but also at trade unions, middle management and in the wider public domain. Secondly, we believe that the incentive system, which is currently almost exclusively oriented towards encouraging the innovation of embodied technologies, should be restructured to encourage the adoption of these new forms of intra-plant reorganisation. In part this involves the provision of specific incentives to encourage the utilisation of 'innovation consultants' (as has occurred, for example, in Germany and in the UK), but it also affects the structure of intra-firm training. Thirdly, in addition to influencing the demand for organisational changes in production, it is also necessary to affect the supply of expertise. To some extent this can be met through a programme of support for the producer services sector (sometimes called 'business services'), but this sector will also need to develop specific capabilities which will allow it to meet the needs of labour as well as those of management. Finally, at the sectoral and regional levels there are few specialised sectoral institutions which are at present capable of diffusing new forms of productive organisation. For example, although the printing industry has just opened a new sector-training institution – until recently, training was inadequately carried out through the general apprenticeship system – this does not appear to address any of the relevant work-organisation issues, including the move to multi-skilling of operatives. Nor does this Printing Institute appear to have plans to widen its remit in this way. Few other sectors possess even this modicum of sectoral focus.

Inter-firm linkages: The view that effective links between firms constitute a key source of competitive advantage is strongly supported by a diverse set of experiences. Italy's industrial districts, Japan's *keiretsu* and the relationships between Germany's industrial giants and the network of dynamic medium-scale enterprises are merely the outstanding examples. Moreover, evidence of the importance of industrial districts is not confined to the industrially advanced world, as is clear in the very rapid expansion of the Brazilian shoe industry (Schmitz, 1993).

At first glance, key features of South Africa's industrial landscape may seem to be conducive to productivity-enhancing co-operation. In particular, the preponderance of large groups of manufacturers, linked into even larger groups also active in mining and services, is suggestive of the dynamic groups of Japan and South Korea. However, as indicated earlier, our research has not uncovered the rich tapestry of commercial, technological and financial relations that characterises the Japanese groups, for example. As already indicated, the South African conglomerates are constructed by risk-diversifying investors and shareholders rather than by productivity-enhancing entrepreneurs and manufacturers. Our research on conglomeration and market structure has suggested a policy ultimately aimed at ensuring greater specialisation in South Africa's corporate groups.

Highly concentrated markets also suggest the possibility of co-operation. But, unfortunately, these possibilities are widely realised in the form of ubiquitous collusion. In key product markets the form that the collusion takes is a division of markets along segment or regional lines, thus underpinning the phenomenon of single-firm domination of these markets.

The collusive practices of oligopolists are not matched by significant evidence of co-operation between small- and medium-scale enterprises. There is, however, concrete scope for this in the shape of existing regional agglomerations. Our research has focused on three of these agglomerations (furniture, auto components and footwear) but has not found evidence of significant inter-firm co-operation. There is no discernible effort on the part of local government to exploit the potential economies implicit in these agglomerations. Local government policy with respect to industrial development is generally based on indiscriminate attempts to attract industry, without clear strategies rooted in a particular region's existing industrial profile.

The rather dense fabric of sector-based associations – which include employer and trade associations, trade unions and industrial councils – also offers potential for inter-firm co-ordination. However, these institutions tend to be narrowly focused. The role of many employer associations is dedicated to representing the industry in its dealings with government, with a major portion of activity (both historical and current) devoted to securing trade protection. Where collective bargaining is centralised, the employer associations have the added responsibility of representing the employers in their dealings with the unions. The recent thrust of union policy has been to extend collective bargaining into the sphere of broader industrial policy concerns. In key areas employers have accepted this, with the auto and auto components and the clothing and textile industries the best examples. Negotiations in this area will inevitably raise questions related to inter-firm co-operation. However, there generally is strong employer resistance to this extension of collective bargaining. Indeed, for the most part, there is a strong employer initiative across several sectors to decentralise all collective bargaining.

Finally, there is not much evidence of co-operation between these firm types. Here again the environment is not conducive to this type of co-operation. Market-dominating firms place small firms, both upstream and downstream, in a particularly dependent and vulnerable position that, if anything, encourages cut-throat competition between the dependent firms. It also encourages the dominant firm to promote this competition as a cost-cutting strategy, or to integrate vertically, thus cutting competitor firms out of their markets.

To some extent we believe that the adoption of new organisational forms in production will in itself lead to an improvement in this pattern of inter-firm relations. For example, the adoption of JIT production ultimately runs up against the need to persuade suppliers to co-ordinate production scheduling and for customers to integrate their ordering more closely with supplier production schedules. But, once again, we do not believe that merely restructuring the incentive system will promote optimal levels and types of inter-firm co-operation. We have not yet digested the detailed results of our region-focused research, but it would seem that part of the key to promoting greater and more appropriate inter-firm co-operation lies within the realm of regional industrial policy, as well as in the promotion of sectoral focus, as is beginning to occur in the tripartite groups operating in the automobile and clothing and textile sectors.

Conclusions

The underlying theme of this review of our early thinking on industrial strategy is thus the urgent need to revive productivity growth in the context of the likely opening-up of the South African economy and in the context of changing patterns of comparative advantage in global industry. The ultimate objective of industrialisation is to provide sustained, highly productive occupations for the population with due regard for distributional and environmental considerations. We do not believe that this can be achieved in South Africa through a policy agenda which reduces wages, and have attempted to map out an alternative agenda in which high productivity is associated with living wages, and involves the active participation of the labour force in production. We also believe that these objectives are best achieved through a policy agenda which concentrates on promotion rather than prohibition.

In achieving these goals we believe that production must gravitate towards higher-value activities. On the one hand this involves the search for sectors of higher value-added. To a considerable extent we believe that this can be achieved by moving up the value chain and into the downstream processing of South Africa's natural resources. But we also believe that high productivity can be attained by moving production to niches of high value-added within sectors. This, as we have suggested, may well mean that some low value-added activities should be jettisoned. But as with much of the industrial strategy agenda, this can only be achieved if adequate policies are introduced to buffer this transition.

Our review of South African manufacturing capabilities suggests that changes in the incentive system are a necessary component of overall restructuring. However, the prevalence of market failure (Lall, 1993) makes it clear that merely restructuring these incentives will be an inadequate response to the challenge. The upgrading of technological capabilities will need to be explicitly targeted and institutions will need to be developed which enable industry to cope with the new competitive challenges in the context of prevalent market failure.

Strategy is best seen as a process and not as a policy document, and it is obviously important to give careful thought to the particular framework in which an industrial strategy can evolve. Unless the key actors are involved in the identification of this strategy and are committed to its implementation, little can be expected, however intellectually sound the strategy might be, and however rigorous the research upon which it is based. This process of strategic formulation and implementation is clearly highly contextual. What might be appropriate and relevant in Japan might not suit America, and so on.

One of the particularities of the South African scene is the deep involvement of organised labour in strategic thinking at a variety of levels, including social and political domains, which are often thought to be outside the purview of labour's responsibility. This wider involvement in South Africa is fortunate since, as we have observed, contemporary efficiency is heavily premised upon participation by the labour force. It is thus inconceivable to think of an effective process of industrial strategy implementation in South Africa without at the same time identifying an arena in which Cosatu and its affiliated unions can participate. It is in everyone's interests that the union movement keep abreast of modern technological and organisational development and that it possesses the resources to educate its own labour force.

However critical the participation of organised labour may be in this process, it is clearly essential that the managers of capital should also be involved in this common challenge of confronting South Africa's economic crisis.

The lesson of international experience in this regard is that management and labour clearly have to develop a common agenda focused on industrial restructuring and continuous improvement. To a considerable extent this collaboration can take place autonomously, sometimes at the plant level, sometimes at the firm level, and sometimes at the industry level. But it is also important that the state play a key role in defining an appropriate incentive structure, in facilitating the growth of national, sectoral, regional and firm-level capabilities, and in promoting the development of an effective institutional infrastructure.

We have no illusions about the danger of state failure – current developments unfolding on an almost daily basis provide abundant warning. But even though its efforts are often currently inadequately focused to achieve industrial competitiveness, our reading of global experience is that without focused and effective support from the state, industry is unlikely to make the jump which is needed to attain and sustain a level of global competitiveness which is required for South Africa's social, political and economic progress.

The constructive roles that all three parties have to play in the formulation and implementation of industrial strategy are widely acknowledged, and in a number of sectors tripartite negotiations have already begun during the course of our research programme; this includes the textiles and garments sector, the electronics sector and the automobile sector. However, in other sectors, strategic formulation remains the sole purview of management and the state.

What is required is to identify a structured forum in which these strategic discussions can be pursued across the spectrum of industrial activity without at the same time becoming swamped in a wider agenda of class conflict. This forum will be required at the national levels as well as at the sectoral and regional levels. Here, as ever, progress requires co-operation, even between parties who are otherwise in conflict.

Notes

1. This chapter reflects the preliminary results of the Economic Trends Research Group Programme on an Industrial Strategy for a Post-Apartheid South Africa. Although it is heavily influenced by the findings of the individual research projects in this programme, the errors of interpretation and analysis are those of the authors alone.

We are grateful to the members of the Industrial Strategy Team for their detailed and helpful comments on an earlier draft, as well as to Gerry Helleiner, Sheila Page and the participants of The Aspen Institute–Idasa conference on South Africa's International Economic Relations in the 1990s.

Unless specifically referenced, all the data provided in this chapter are drawn from individual sectoral papers. These will be made available in due course under the aegis of the Industrial Strategy Project. Due to space limitations, evidencing of discussion is not included. Interested readers should refer to the relevant ISP papers. A fuller version of this chapter, with appropriate documentation can be found in Joffe *et al.* (1993).

2. The sectors are automobiles and components, building materials, chemicals, consumer durables (white and brown goods), electronics and energy reticulation, food (bread, poultry, meat and wine), garments, heavy engineering, the informal manufacturing sector, paper and pulp, mineral beneficiation, shoes and leather, and textiles.

3. This latter figure is based upon gross investment and makes no allowance for depreciation.

4. For an insightful discussion of this structure and its application to LDCs, see Lall (1990). For a discussion of the experience of the NIEs, see Lall (1993).

5. We are grateful to Petro Belli for permission to use these data.

6. 'The case studies in this volume offer very weak, if any support for the proposition that either import liberalisation or export expansion is particularly associated with overall productivity growth' (Helleiner, forthcoming:51).

7. The WIDER study of 17 industrialising countries found that: 'Characteristic of all 'successful' manufactured export and/or overall growth experiences in these countries at this time ... was an 'appropriate' real (inflation adjusted) exchange rate... 'Weak' performers all had overvalued currencies and unstable real exchange rates during the period under study...' (Helleiner, forthcoming:18).

8. Although, for a variety of reasons, large investors on the Johannesburg Stock Exchange (including institutional investors) tend to hold stock for long periods, the criteria used to assess cor-

porate performance are overwhelmingly short-term in orientation and are a strong reason for the lack of attention to long-term operational issues like inter-firm co-operation.

9. We are not suggesting that South Africa's energy prices be brought up to the level of high-cost countries but that they should reflect more closely the economic and social costs of generation and use. Given South Africa's low-cost coal this will almost certainly mean that South Africa will continue to have energy prices which are relatively low by international standards.

10. However, in so far as this removal of protection involves giving up certain segments of production, there will be restructuring costs particularly for those workers currently employed in the affected areas. A key part of this policy agenda, therefore, is to introduce a restructuring fund which will ease the problems of transition in these areas. Our policy discussion will address this issue in particular by considering the experience of other countries such as Australia, Japan, Canada and Sweden.

11. This is because wheat comprises 38% of total bread production costs and the cost of wheat production (rand per ton) in South Africa (R438) is high by international standards – viz Argentina (R195), Australia (R219), Canada (R295), US (R303) and the UK (R373). We assume that marketing costs are approximately double production costs.

12. This generously assumes that tariffs on low-wage products are equivalent to the industry weighted average, which we know is in fact not the case.

13. The relevance of these changes in the organisational structure of production is not limited to the production of high-income goods. They are generally also resource-saving and hence are also of relevance to the production of basic low-wage goods.

14. Exports of telecommunications equipment have grown rapidly in recent years and currently approach US$ 200m. This includes the sale of public call telephones to Eastern Europe and Siemens's exports to the former East Germany (following capacity shortages in their West German plants) and a major rise in exports to other parts of Africa.

15. For example, the weighted mean tariffs on consumer goods are 60%, compared to 19% for capital goods (Belli *et al.*, 1993)

16. Since the introduction of just-in-time inventory control also led to significant savings in warehousing and working capital, the increase in capital productivity is even more marked.

7

The South African Trade Policy Debate: A Business Perspective

PAUL R. HATTY

South Africa is a country where trade policy has been dictated by political considerations. This is particularly valid of external trade policy. The country has vast natural resources in both mining and agriculture; most of the growth in the economy until recently came from these sectors, particularly the mining sector. The industrial policy adopted was in support of a trade policy of reducing the economy's reliance on imports, and was furthermore consolidated in a period of self-sufficiency, in an attempt to make the country less dependent on imports, particularly in many strategic imports.

This was a period of local manufacture, at almost any cost. Meanwhile, exports were becoming more dependent on natural resources or primary goods, in a period when the characteristics of world trade were changing. South Africa's capabilities were being concentrated on the production of commodities when the consumption of these commodities in the developed countries was declining in both per capita and per unit of GDP.

The period of sanctions against South Africa has also not helped, as the sanctions were most effective against manufactured goods. Simultaneously, various new sources of primary materials have become available, increasing the pressure on prices and volumes of commodity exports.

In an attempt to counter the declining situation, and in order to bolster exports of manufactured goods, trade policy was modified by way of direct export assistance. This export assistance attempted to improve the competitiveness of manufactured goods in export markets. However, the policy was treating the symptoms, not the causes. One of the major causes of lack of competitiveness is cost structures, particularly of manufacturing sector inputs.

The basis of competitive performance is changing. While past competition has largely been determined by price factors, it is increasingly being determined by other product factors. However, this is not entirely correct where commodities are concerned. For commodities, the focus has been more and more on price factors alone. Commodities are generally marketed to common specifications, hence any additional product-orientated factors are not negotiable. Technology development and closer international specifications have meant that an increasing proportion of South Africa's commodity exports fall into this category.

While the competitiveness of commodities is related almost entirely to the cost of production and delivery, the competitiveness of manufactured goods is less so, as other product-orientated factors such as quality, technical specifications and design are becoming increasingly important. However, even with manufactured products, the basis of exports must have an underlying cost competitiveness. International competitiveness is seen as the ability to produce and deliver goods to international and domestic markets competitively against goods from other countries without direct or indirect subsidies.

Industrial competitiveness

Industrial competitiveness is related to the cost of the factors of production and delivery, and how efficiently they are utilised. Analysis has revealed that all three basic inputs into the manufacturing sector, capital, labour and intermediate inputs (materials, components, consumables, services, etc.), are at a significant cost disadvantage in this country. From the 1988 input/output tables, the make-up of the input to the manufacturing sector is:

capital	13,5%
labour	15,7%
intermediates	70,8%

All inputs to the manufacturing sector are resources. For each resource there is the price of the resource and the productive use of that resource. Internal factors to the company are those which management or staff can do something about and external factors are those that management cannot do anything about. Thus, management can improve the productive use of capital, labour or intermediates, but may not be able to do anything about the price of capital or the price of most intermediate inputs. However, there are some inputs where management cannot deal with the productive use factor. An example would be the extra capital required to finance the installation of productive machinery in South Africa compared to the situation for a competitor in another country.

The improvement in the price and productive use of all the inputs to a manufacturing industry, and hence industrial competitiveness, are not in the hands of management alone, but also the government and labour. Thus if the trade regime is to change, all parties should be involved and understand the implications, and develop an overall policy and strategy. This is presented in a position paper being prepared by the South African Chamber of Business (Sacob), which proposes a structure and process to deal with both trade policy and industrial policy, and strategies for industrial growth and development. However, this structure proposes changing the industrial environment for both broad-based and sector-specific growth and development. The final response will have to come from management itself, particularly in respect of productivity.

In the report on the modification of protection policy by the Industrial Development Corporation, it is recommended that import tariffs be lowered and that the cost of inputs to the manufacturing sector, such as interest rates and tax rates, will have to be reduced. However, this report does not connect the cost of inputs and the level of protection. The Sacob document 'A Concept for a New Industrial Policy' (Sacob, 1991a) attempts to link them and shows that the high cost of manufactured intermediates, together with capital and labour costs, is the main source of lack of competitiveness.

To quantify the competitiveness of the inputs to the manufacturing sector, the price and productive use of each of these resources were compared with those of other countries. This analysis revealed the following:

Capital: South African manufacturing industry needs 66% more capital, with a price 2,16 times that of the OECD countries, to produce the same amount of wealth. The cost of capital to produce R1 of wealth in OECD countries is 13 cents, while in South Africa it costs 56 cents.

Labour: South Africa uses 4 employees to produce the same amount of wealth as 1 employee does in Germany. These 4 employees, on average, cost 47% more than the 1 employee in Germany.

Materials: 58% of the intermediates are inputs from the manufacturing sector itself, where the average tariff protection by value of production is 20%. Thus, after taking into account transport, the cost of these inputs is estimated to be about 24% higher than the price available to manufacturers overseas.

In summary, the Sacob analysis estimates that the cost of manufacturing in South Africa is on average 15% higher than the average OECD country.

Trade policy effects on competitiveness

The areas where trade policy affects this competitiveness are not only in the cost structures, but also in the protection of the local market and its impact on competitiveness. Just as trade policy affects competitiveness, so does the commitment of management to be internally competitive. If this does not exist it also impacts negatively on the cost of production. In South Africa the price of goods seems always to move to the highest level that protection allows.

Trade policy cannot be examined in isolation, as it is not created in isolation. It is the summation of aspects of other policies, such as economic policy, political policy, foreign relations policy and industrial policy, which have an effect on the trade relationships between countries. Some of the aspects of the trade policy are due to the lack of competitiveness, either in local markets or in exports, and some aspects add to the lack of competitiveness.

Analysis of current trade policy

In the South African context, present trade policy has two dimensions, an internal dimension and an external dimension, both of which are linked and complementary to industrial policy. The internal dimension intends to regulate and direct industrial operations in such areas as competitive conditions for domestic trade, protection of consumer interests and controlling the format and formation of companies. The external dimension governs the relationship with other countries on all matters affecting trade. The current external trade policy can be identified in four categories: protection against imports, promotion of exports, exchange rate policies and trade relationships. Each will be dealt with below.

Protection against imports

Import protection may be classified under import tariffs, non-tariff barriers and import surcharges.

Import tariffs: In 1925, South Africa introduced a wide-ranging system of tariff protection to support a policy of import substitution. These tariffs were to be 'moderate and selective'. At the same time the Board of Tariffs and Trade was empowered to recommend tariff levels for specific activities. Prior to the 1970s, tariff protection tended to be moderate, primarily because after World War II import controls operated as the primary instrument of industrial protection.

During the 1980s the use of import controls diminished, such that the share of import value subject to import control declined from 77% to 23%. There has been little decline since, as a large part of the agricultural sector is still under import control. As import controls were reduced, they were offset by increasing tariffs, to limit the impact on industry. However, these did not take the form only of higher *ad valorem* tariffs, but included formula duties, which gave a higher level of protection against lower import prices. Import control is also particularly effective against dumping, as it operates on a reference price.

Technology has increased the varieties of products and their relative competitiveness, so that to carry out the policy of protection for import replacement the number of items identified in the tariff structures has been increased to over 13 600, of which over 2 600 are in clothing and textiles alone.

The average nominal protection enumerated by customs is 22%. However, weighted by import value, the average is 14% and by value of production 20%. What these aggregate estimates conceal, however, is the large variation across tariff lines in nominal and effective levels of protection. Of approximately 11 500 tariff items which have duty protection, 83% have only *ad valorem* duties and 17% have formula duties. Of the line items, 22,2% are still under import control.

Compared to most developed and developing countries, South Africa has a very complex tariff structure, with more tariff rates than any other country. The range of tariffs is the widest and the coefficient of variation (standard deviation as a percentage of the mean) of the tariff rates is the second highest of all countries. South Africa has 35 *ad valorem* rates and 2 865 lines with formula, specific or other type of duty.

This complex tariff structure has a wide dispersion. While there is a comparatively large portion of items with zero rates, there is also a high proportion with high rates. The highest rate of 1 389% applies to one product only. This item is woven polyester fabric containing less than 85% by mass of such fibres, mixed mainly or solely with cotton of a mass between 300 and 350 grams per square metre. The tariff for the same material with a mass greater than 350 grams per square metre is 29% and for the same material with a mass less than 300 grams per square metre is 10%.

The above example of the tariff structure is a result of the industrial policy of import replacement, almost at any cost, thus creating distortions in the local manufacturing industry such that competitiveness is not at any real level.

Non-tariff barriers: These have been a characteristic feature of South Africa's trade policy for a long time. They were originally intended to assist industrial development, but in recent years have been justified as strategic tools to attain self-sufficiency in the light of trade sanctions. As the world lifts sanctions the government is replacing these barriers with tariffs. Most of the remaining barriers are against agricultural goods.

Import controls are the largest area of non-trade barriers; the list of items requiring import permits has been progressively reduced in recent years, but still includes a considerable number of tariff items ranging from foodstuffs to chemicals, paper, textiles and machinery. In addition, all used goods, waste and scrap require import permits. Besides import permits, certain products require additional certification from government agencies before importation. These agreements are intended to protect the health or the general security or safety of the public.

Import surcharges: A large number of imports are subject to import surcharges at rates of 5%, 15% or 40% of the import value. Import surcharges were introduced in 1988 to compensate for balance of payments disequilibrium caused by sanctions against South Africa. Although surcharges were intended to be temporary they have remained in place despite favourable developments in the balance of payments.

The payment of import surcharges levied on certain capital goods, goods imported for manufacture of export goods, goods imported under rebate of duty, goods imported by religious groups, donations and goods included in a reciprocal trade transaction, may be waived.

Promotion of exports

There are a number of instruments used to promote exports. These are part of either export development or export assistance.

Export development: Export development is seen as the encouragement of new exporters and is carried out by mechanisms to make industry more aware of export possibilities and to explore export markets, particularly as much of industry has never examined export markets. The portion of manufacturing companies which are exporting is still very small.

The instrument used is the Export Marketing Assistance (EMA) scheme, which gives partial compensation for transportation costs and subsistence allowance for travel for primary export market research, outward-selling trade missions and inward-buying missions. The scheme also grants financial assistance to companies wishing to participate in specialised trade fairs outside the South African Customs Union area. The Department of Trade and Industry also bears the costs of participation in trade fairs, where South Africa participates officially by means of a national pavilion and the state carries the costs of transportation of exhibition and publicity material.

Export assistance: Export assistance is primarily to assist exporters with the comparatively higher cost of local production and the high cost of delivery to markets. There are four elements of the assistance programme.

Under the Customs and Excise Act exporters are eligible for customs duties drawbacks and exemption from customs duties paid or payable on imported materials used in manufacturing goods for export. Relief from customs duty can be permanent or granted on a specific transaction. Permanent relief is granted in accordance with standing provisions for drawbacks for materials used in the manufacture of specific products for export. Specific relief is granted on importation of certain materials stipulated in permits for the manufacture of specific products for export. In nearly all cases of drawbacks it is for the full duty paid upon importation of the goods. The system of drawbacks and exemptions is cumbersome and hence is not used as an instrument to acquire free access to more competitive inputs.

The General Export Incentive Scheme (GEIS), introduced in the late 1980s, is presently the major export incentive scheme. The scheme it replaced was based on added value and was rather complicated to administer and apply. GEIS was designed to help exporters offset the price disadvantage exporters face in international markets. It provides a tax-free financial incentive to exporters based on the value of the exports, the degree of processing and the local content of the exported product. The GEIS incentive is a factor of the level of beneficiation and takes into account fluctuations in the value of the rand against a basket of currencies, and applies to nearly all manufactured exports. As imported content, which has full duty paid, is regarded as local content, most exporters pay the duty on imports and take advantage of GEIS on the imported content. Imported materials for which duty drawback has been applied do not get the GEIS incentive on those inputs.

GEIS plays a key role in making exports profitable. However, because of the tremendous dispersion in nominal protection and in GEIS, the effect of policy on the different subsectors is very wide. GEIS is not related to protection on inputs or to the degree of effective protection in the domestic market. As a result, out of eight subsectors trade policy is pro-export-biased in three cases and anti-export-biased in the other five cases, with the highest anti-export bias in the most labour-intensive industry – clothing and textiles.

A number of sector-specific export incentives also exist. A special programme designed to promote the local motor vehicle industry is known as Phase VI of the Local Content Programme for the Motor Vehicle Manufacturing Industry. This programme requires a local content of 75% of the value of the final product in order for the producer to be eligible for tax relief and export incentives. The schemes also include rebates of excise duties on motor vehicles, based on the percentage of local content.

Another sector-specific export assistance programme is for the clothing and textile industry, where a duty-free import permit was granted to exporters in relation to the export value. However, this scheme had many problems and is due to cease in 1994.

Amongst the other incentives provided by the Department of Trade and Industry are insurance and financing facilities to exporters through the Credit Guarantee Insurance Corporation. The insurance covers commercial, political and transfer risks at a premium.

Furthermore, where the export of large capital projects which are repaid over a number of years is involved, the Department of Trade and Industry subsidises the interest rate to the same level as the 'consensus interest rate of the OECD countries'. Under the export development finance scheme, expansion of export manufacturing capacity may be financed at reduced rates by the Industrial Development Corporation.

Exchange rate policies

Exchange rate management is a major part of trade policy. The dominance of resources in the exports of South Africa, particularly gold, creates a problem for exchange rate management. Under a fully floating exchange rate, the relative value of gold exports would have a major influence on the value of the rand to the possible detriment of other exports. However, primarily due to the political situation and its economic consequences, the exchange rate has had to be managed at a higher level than the efficiency of manufacturing industry could support. This obviously has a major impact on the competitiveness of manufactured exports. To encourage industrial exports, the value of the rand would need to be maintained at a level to ensure this competitiveness, and this would most likely be considerably lower than the level maintained at present. Exchange rate policy has not been used as a means to achieve international competitiveness of industry.

Trade relationships

Trade relationships with regional and other trade organisations have largely been dealt with elsewhere, and hence will not be covered here.

A business perspective on a desired future trade regime

There are many factors which will play a role in the business perspective on a desired future trade regime. These factors are related to internal and external factors which will affect the competitiveness of business and its respondent ability to continue, develop and grow. These factors are internal and external to the business and internal and external to the country.

Businesses, particularly in manufacturing, respond to the industrial environment. As the environment changes, so does the business response. If the industrial environment, brought about by trade policy, encourages and supports exports, and if business identifies an opportunity to earn satisfactory returns or improve present returns, then business will export. If the trade regime does not create an environment of opportunity, then business will not export, and will move investment or development elsewhere. Thus the industrial environment created by the trade regime is critical to the response by industry.

The trade regime in the past has been one of promoting the development and growth of industry in a very broad range of industry sectors, all in an attempt to become self-sufficient and less import-dependent. The response has been one of the broadest industrial growth patterns in the world (comparable with the growth of some centrally planned economies). The trade regime of import protection has promoted and enabled the establishment and growth of many industries which are totally uncompetitive internationally and would never be able to become competitive. In addition, there has not been any high degree of specialisation such that areas of excellence have been developed which could be opened onto international markets.

When import replacement had run out of steam and become increasingly capital-intensive, the industrial environment was modified by the introduction of the export promotion and assistance schemes. The assistance schemes are seen as an incentive to accommodate the lack of industrial competitiveness. The manufacturing sector has responded by increasing the exports of manufactured goods, but this has been achieved in a period of excess capacity. So there is considerable investment in industry which is uncompetitive and needs import protection for its survival and assistance to export. What is the perspective on a future trade regime?

The business perspective is that South Africa must remain a committed member of GATT to ensure that we are able to retain world markets and that these markets are available on a most favoured nation basis. However, as was reported by the delegation which led the review of trade policy at GATT, they are expecting the full participation of South Africa, including a better offer of binding tariffs besides dealing with tariff structures, formula duties, export subsidies, import control, local content requirements and the input surcharge. When the list of requirements is reviewed, the major single item of trade policy is membership of GATT or not. If membership is the basic policy, then much of present trade policy is affected and trade liberalisation is the name of the game.

Trade liberalisation cannot be accepted without a greater degree of macro-economic stability. This is an essential prerequisite for successful trade liberalisation.

The GATT requirements are going to lead to an outward-orientated development. This would be acceptable, provided it creates a greater degree of neutrality between export production and import replacement. Business would not support a bias in either direction in general, but would support it in sectors or niches where it may be beneficial and correct to do so in support of specific development and growth strategies.

While the bindings to GATT will limit the flexibility available to tariffs, the business perspective would prefer a system of tariff reform that would set overall targets for tariff reductions, but with built-in flexibility through a system that allows some selectivity in support of specific strategies. This selectivity would be treated as an exception rather than the rule of uniformity on industrial strategy.

Once it is accepted that GATT is inevitable, with it would come the removal of import control, formula duties and specific duties. This will place considerable pressure on the implementation of an effective anti-dumping measure, as from past experience dumping can permanently damage local industry. There are many examples where dumping has wiped out local manufacturers, and this is quite likely to happen again unless effective anti-dumping measures are introduced.

The simplification of the tariff structure, including the removal of formula duties and the rationalisation of tariff rates, is a desired direction in which to move, if transparency is an objective in protection policies. The present protection policies with the complex tariff structures make it very difficult for the customs and excise department to monitor, and allow dishonest importers to find various loopholes, *inter alia,* through slight errors in descriptions of items or importing through different ports of entry.

The speed with which these changes should be introduced is almost academic, as the tariff bindings and subsequent reductions are linked to commitments made to GATT. It appears there may be some delay in the process if South Africa is given 'economy in transition' status, which can be granted for a limited period. What will be of greater importance is that the costs of inputs are reduced at the same time to give the local industry the chance to retain local markets. This is particularly important if the economy, and hence the markets, do not grow as at present, during the period of liberalisation.

There has already been some reduction in the cost of capital input in the last two years. The corporate tax rate has been lowered from 50% to 40%. While this is a good start, it will not be sufficient to get new business commitment locally in the manufacturing industry to compete with imports produced in countries where corporate tax rates are as low as 10%. In addition to the reduction in corporate tax rate there has been a reduction in the inflation rate and interest rates. The combined effect of these reductions is that the cost of capital which our industry needs to meet has been reduced from approximately 30% to about 20%. This should reduce the margins on sales needed to meet shareholder expectations, and hence the selling price of products.

The reduction in import tariffs on intermediates should make a good contribution to the lowering of the cost of the imported input and put pressure on the cost of local intermediates. This leaves the remaining area of labour. Here the problem is more complex as there is the cost of indirect and direct labour, which needs to be examined separately. The main problem is how to get more added value and hence output for the same labour cost, or reduce the labour cost for the same output. This is the area where business is going to have to review its situation very carefully, if it is to become internationally competitive. While much will have to be done regarding direct labour productivity in such areas as education and training, indirect labour productivity and labour structures will also have to be addressed.

Business has accepted that the GEIS will have to go as it does not comply with GATT, and market countries could easily introduce countervailing duties. The EMA concept not only should be retained, but should be expanded. However, what is required is not only to increase exports but even to retain present levels much more than a decrease in tariff protection. A holistic approach, consisting of appropriate macro-economic policy measures and a viable industrial development strategy, will be needed. That is why Sacob has concentrated on preparing a structure and process for an industrial development policy and strategy.

The business perspective recognises that the lowering of import tariffs and input prices is not the only factor that will make industry develop and grow in a more liberalised trade regime. It is all about productivity, and without satisfactory levels being achieved business will not be able to achieve satisfactory returns. Without these satisfactory returns, investment will go elsewhere to achieve them.

Some of the key areas of attention for attaining satisfactory productivity levels are the skills, training and education of the work force, the level of technology applied, the commitment to quality and the structure of industry itself. These are the issues which need to be clarified in industrial strategy and in any proposed industrial targeting, particularly for exports.

However, all the efforts of modifying the trade regime to comply with GATT, reducing input costs and improving productivity could come to naught if the exchange rate level is allowed to get out of hand or does not reflect manufacturing competitive ability. It is essential that the authorities take a realistic stance on the exchange rate level.

In summary, the business perspective is one of reaction to the environment. The future trade policy is going to be more controlled by the needs of compliance with GATT. If the internal cost and performance structures are not assisted in order to make manufacturing production more internationally competitive, then investment in this sector will decline and manufacturing will not help to grow the economy. On the other hand, if policy and strategies are developed correctly, the business response will be a growing and internationally competitive industrial sector, based on a number of successful niche subsectors.

8

South African Exchange Rate Policy and International Competitiveness

BRIAN KAHN

Exchange rate policy is an integral part of policy discussions relating to international competitiveness and export-led growth, as well as macro-economic concerns such as the control of inflation. Inappropriate exchange rate policies and misaligned exchange rates have been blamed for a range of economic misfortunes suffered by developing countries during the 1980s, including the decline of export industries (particularly African agriculture), capital flight and hyperinflation.

During the 1980s there have been significant shifts in the conduct of exchange rate policy in South Africa and these shifts have reflected changes in policy objectives as well as economic circumstances. Although a more market-determined approach to exchange rate determination was adopted during the 1980s, there was nevertheless Reserve Bank intervention in the market which was used to achieve these changing objectives. Apart from helping to stabilise the balance of payments in the face of frequent real shocks, these objectives included, at different times, the protection of the gold mining industry, providing a stable environment for manufacturing exporters and the use of the exchange rate as a nominal anchor for inflation.

This chapter analyses these recent developments in South Africa's exchange rate policy and highlights the conflicting nature of policy changes. It is argued that since 1988 the previous policy, which was beneficial to the gold mining industry, was superseded by a policy which emphasised exchange rate stability. However, as long as there is a difference between South Africa's inflation rate and that of its major trading partners, there will be a difference between stabilising the real and the nominal exchange rates. Under these circumstances the goals of maintaining international competitiveness and reducing inflation will conflict with each other.

This chapter outlines briefly some of the policy issues relevant to a discussion of South Africa's exchange rate policy, focusing on the difference between nominal and real exchange rate rules. This is followed by an analysis of developments in South Africa's exchange rate policy and an assessment of factors which could impact on exchange rate policy in the future.

Exchange rate policy rules

In general, exchange rate policies are directed to some proximate objectives, including external balance, internal balance and micro-economic efficiency (Collier and Joshi, 1989). Different exchange rate regimes can be operated to achieve the chosen objectives – these include fixed exchange rates (either single- or multi-currency pegs), independent floating and a variety of intermediate regimes such as an adjustable peg or crawling peg. The choice between regimes relates to the fixity or variability of the nominal exchange rate, which then impacts on the real rate.

A nominal exchange rate rule entails pegging the currency to that of its major trading partner or, more commonly, to a trade-weighted basket of currencies. Maintaining a peg with trading partners constrains domestic monetary policy to be in line with trading partner monetary policies, thereby restricting domestic demand. From the point of view of inflation control, a constant nominal exchange rate would reduce the imported inflation impact on the price index as long as the country's inflation rate is higher than that of its trading partners. If inflation is persistently higher in the domestic economy, this policy will result in an appreciation of the real exchange rate, which will impact negatively on manufactured exports.

It follows, therefore, that under conditions of inflation inertia, a fixed nominal exchange rate rule will lead to conflicts with policies aimed at maintaining international competitiveness. The proponents of a fixed exchange rate rule argue that the advantages are that the rule imposes a discipline on the monetary authorities to implement appropriate financial policies to reduce inflation. However, if this discipline is not binding, the country is likely to suffer from a decline in exports because of the real appreciation, successive balance of payments crises and devaluations, which then undermine the credibility of the system.

Even if appropriate macro-economic policies are applied, a country with an inflation rate considerably higher than that of its trading partners may find it difficult to reduce inflation significantly in a short period of time. A shortage of foreign exchange reserves and limited access to international borrowing also make the maintenance of a peg more difficult, particularly in the face of negative shocks.

Experience with floating exchange rates on the other hand has shown that the early optimism in the 1970s that such a system would result in stable real exchange rates has not materialised. Williamson (1993) has argued that floating exchange rates are extremely vulnerable to exaggerated swings, resulting in short-run volatility and long-run misalignments. It also creates uncertainty about future real exchange rates, which damages the confidence of exporters.

A real exchange rate rule of the crawling peg variety (see e.g. Williamson, 1982; 1993) maintains a constant real exchange rate by depreciating the currency in line with inflation differentials between one country and its major trading partners. Such a policy is supposed to stabilise the profitability of trading in real terms and reflects the perceived advantages to the manufacturing sector of having some information on the likely evolution of relative prices, thus avoiding production decisions based on incorrect expectations. Balassa and Williamson (1987) have shown that an important element in the success of the export-oriented growth strategies of Taiwan and South Korea was the maintenance of stable real exchange rates.

There are, however, various problems associated with the adoption of a constant real exchange rate rule. Apart from the problem of identifying the appropriate level of the real exchange rate, there are various factors that can permanently change the path of the equilibrium real exchange rate. These factors include permanent terms of trade changes, new natural resource discoveries, changes in domestic tariffs, international interest rates and changes in technology (see Edwards, 1989). A permanent change in one of these variables could change the equilibrium real exchange rate. This suggests that the rule should not be so rigid that appropriate realignments cannot be made following sustained real shocks.

The rationale for maintaining a constant real exchange rate is the relative price certainty that it imparts to manufacturing exporters. In general, countries applying such a rule target the 'effective' or trade-weighted real exchange rate (weighted average movement of the domestic currency in terms of its major trading partners). However, because structure of trade differs among industries, the exchange rate facing the individual industry or firm could differ substantially from the average. In other words, the industry-specific real exchange rate could differ substantially from the overall effective real exchange rate which the authorities target to keep constant. Estimates in Kahn (1992) show that industry-specific exchange rates vary considerably in South Africa.

Related to this is the problem of the appropriate definition and measurement of the real exchange rate. Holden (1991) has shown that different definitions of the real exchange rate can yield different patterns of competitiveness. The real exchange rate published by the Reserve Bank uses the purchasing power parity notion. Even if this is the appropriate measure, changes in the currency basket can change the real effective exchange rate measure. Thus in 1991, the Reserve Bank revised this series to reflect 1989 trade weights. Although this did not substantially change the pattern of movement, the new series shows a 4 percentage point lower rate of appreciation of the real exchange rate between mid-1988 and April 1991.

Opponents of the crawling peg system argue that it can reduce the pressures on governments to implement appropriate policies to reduce inflation. As Aghevli *et al.* have noted, 'The adoption of a real exchange rate target, which entails the pursuit of a real target with a nominal instrument, may leave a small open economy without a nominal anchor for domestic prices. Consequently, shocks to domestic inflation may acquire a permanent character and, under some circumstances, lead to hyperinflation' (Aghevli *et al.*, 1991:10).

The above suggests that real exchange rate rules can destabilise prices. However, although there are many examples of real exchange rate rules (of the crawling peg variety) that resulted in or accommodated high inflation, particularly in Latin America, the experiences of Asian countries, in particular Taiwan and South Korea, have shown that high inflation is not a necessary outcome. It would appear that part of the answer would lie in the level of wage indexation, the susceptibility of the economy to shocks and the accompanying financial policies which are used as the nominal anchor for domestic prices. It follows that a country that pursues excessively expansionary macro-economic policies will suffer adverse effects, whatever the nature of the exchange rate regime.

Exchange rate policy in South Africa

In 1979, after the publication of the interim report of the De Kock Commission, the South African Reserve Bank moved away from a policy of pegging to the dollar in favour of a form of variable dollar pegging, which resulted in greater variability of the exchange rate. In August 1983, the Reserve Bank ceased its policy of quoting the spot exchange rate and instead began to allow the rate to be more market-determined. The Reserve Bank nevertheless still maintains a direct influence on the exchange rate by intervention in the market. According to Reserve Bank estimates, it accounted for about 12,5% of gross turnover on the foreign exchange market between 1987 and 1990.

The Reserve Bank also intervenes to iron out what it believes to be excessive fluctuations in the exchange rate. Although it is often stated that Reserve Bank intervention has been purely for the limited purposes above, it is argued below that, at times, Reserve Bank policy was designed to achieve particular objectives. It should be noted, however, that the ability of the Reserve Bank to intervene effectively in the market to prevent excessive movements in the exchange rate has been constrained at times by the level of foreign exchange reserves.

The Bank's influence on the market also derives from its predominant role in the forward exchange market (see Ramos, 1991 and Van der Merwe, 1990). As the Bank engages in swap transactions in order to cover its forward operations, and given that the Bank is generally a net seller of forward exchange, these swap transactions increase the Bank's spot purchases.

Controls on capital movements are an important feature of the exchange rate policy environment. The existence of these controls, which limit a wide range of foreign exchange activities, has restricted the size and scope of the market. Capital controls were intensified in South Africa in 1961, following the events in Sharpeville (1960), which precipitated a large outflow of capital.

Controls imposed on residents prohibit most forms of portfolio or direct investment abroad. Any outward investment is subject to Reserve Bank discretion. Non-residents, on the other hand, are subject to the financial rand mechanism (originally known as the blocked rand and later the securities rand) for most categories of portfolio and direct investment. Foreign currency-denominated loans are not subject to the financial rand. This mechanism insulates the capital account of the balance of payments from movements of equity capital because sales and purchases of financial rand are transactions between non-residents. It also means that disinvestment has no direct balance of payments implications as disinvesting companies are required to repatriate their capital through the financial rand market. Interest, dividends and profits are repatriated at the commercial rand rate, and as the financial rand is always at a discount to the commercial rand the yield to non-residents is increased by the size of the discount.

In 1983 there were moves towards capital account liberalisation. Following the report of the De Kock Commission, exchange controls on non-residents were lifted, but were re-imposed in August 1985 in the wake of the debt crisis. The more cautious moves towards lifting controls on residents were also reversed at the same time.

Exchange rate movements 1979–92

The behaviour of Reserve Bank measures of the nominal and real effective exchange rates since 1979 can be seen in Figure 8.1.

(Note: An increase is an appreciation of the rand.)

Figure 8.1. Real and nominal effective exchange rates, South Africa, 1979–92

Until 1988 both measures were highly variable, responding to gold price and political shocks (see Kahn, 1992). Figure 8.2 shows that gold price movements impacted significantly on the rates, whilst the increased political unrest, the capital account liberalisation and the debt crisis of August 1985 also contributed to the precipitous decline between 1983 and 1986.

Since 1988 the high degree of variability of the rates during the earlier part of the decade has given way to greater stability, with the real exchange rate remaining relatively constant. Nevertheless, an upward trend appreciation can be observed during this period. Between 1988 and 1992 the rate had appreciated by approximately 10%. The nominal effective exchange rate on the other hand has depreciated by about 16% over the same period.

As argued in Kahn (1992) it would appear that until 1988, exchange rate policy provided protection to the gold mining industry, which was faced with a highly variable dollar gold price. This policy was characterised by a downward

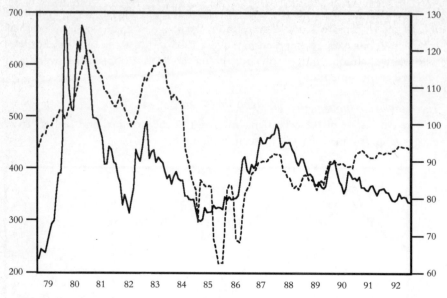

Figure 8.2. The South African real exchange rate and the dollar gold price, 1979–92

bias in that the rand was allowed to depreciate when the dollar gold price was declining, whereas appreciations were resisted during periods of gold price increases. The significant rise in the gold price in 1979 was accompanied by a relatively modest appreciation of the rand, whereas the subsequent fall in the gold price precipitated a large depreciation.

This policy had the effect of reducing the impact of a fluctuating and declining dollar gold price on the mining industry. Figure 8.3 shows that the rand gold price facing the industry exhibited a rising trend until 1988, despite markedly lower dollar prices.

Thus although the dollar gold price rose to record heights in 1979 and 1980, the rand gold price reached its peak in 1988. The result of this was to maintain a fairly constant trend real gold price between 1983 and 1988. Since 1988, however, the real rand gold price has declined by almost one-third as since then there has been a fairly constant rand gold price.

Figure 8.4 illustrates how the rand–dollar exchange rate stabilised the real rand gold price. The 'notional' exchange rate is a hypothetical exchange rate, which was constructed to show the rand–dollar exchange rate that would have been required to maintain a constant real rand gold price of R650 (the average real rand gold price between 1983 and 1988 in 1985 prices). From the figure it can be seen that for much of the period until mid-1988 the 'notional' exchange rate coincided with the actual exchange rate. This implies that the actual exchange rate was at a level to ensure a real rand gold price of R650. Divergences between the two rates until 1988 can be explained by 'other factors', i.e. real shocks that had to be adjusted to. The gold price rise of 1980 saw the reluctance of the authorities to allow the nominal exchange rate to appreci-

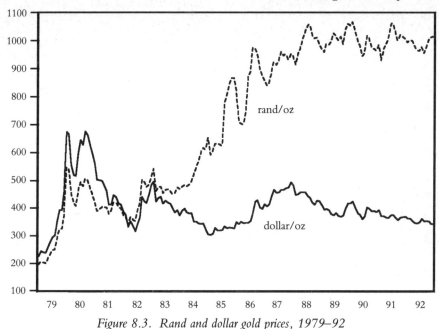

Figure 8.3. Rand and dollar gold prices, 1979–92

ate excessively. The 1985 debt crisis resulted in a collapse of the exchange rate, which then caused an effective increase in the real rand gold price.

During the middle of 1988 a divergence of the two rates emerged and widened over time. This resulted in the significant decline in the real rand gold price since that period. The figure also shows that had the exchange rate continued to move in a way that stabilised the real rand gold price, the rand–dollar exchange rate at the end of 1992 would have been significantly weaker.

During the period of real exchange rate variability, manufacturing exporters were faced with highly variable levels of international competitiveness. It also impacted on the degree of protection granted to domestic industries. According to the IDC (1990), balance of payments instability during the 1980s led to successive rounds of introduction and scrapping of import surcharges. This, coupled with a high degree of exchange rate variability, resulted in major fluctuations in effective protection. The average level of protection of just below 20%, which prevailed before 1980, in fact disappeared in some years when the rand appreciated.

Since 1988 manufacturing exporters have faced a far more stable real exchange rate, which, as noted earlier, provides a more favourable environment for this sector. It also follows from the above that at times the interests of the mining and manufacturing sectors differ with respect to exchange rate policy.

Exchange rate policy and inflation

Apart from its impact on exports, exchange rate policy (as well as the behaviour of the exchange rate) has important implications for the inflation rate. Since

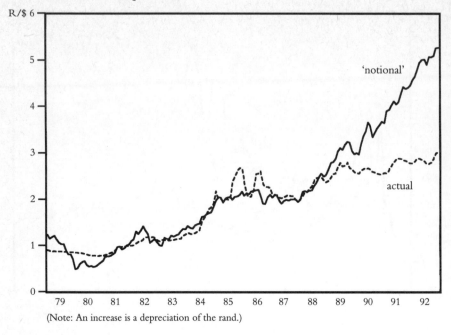

(Note: An increase is a depreciation of the rand.)

Figure 8.4. Actual and 'notional' rand–dollar exchange rates, 1979–92

Dr Stals became Reserve Bank Governor in 1989 the focus of macro-economic policy has been on the reduction of the rate of inflation. Because of the importance of imported goods in the production price index, the exchange rate plays a critical role in this respect.

South Africa's inflation rate during the 1980s can be characterised as moderate, with a high degree of inertia. As can be seen from Table 8.1, for most of the period the inflation rate hovered around the 15% level until it suddenly fell below 10% in recent months. What is of interest is the role of imported prices, which have a weighting of 19,5% in the PPI. The data show clearly the impact of the changing exchange rate regime. The precipitous decline in the value of the rand in 1984-6 had a substantial impact on the PPI, while the more stable nominal exchange rate in recent years has had a moderating influence.

Reserve Bank policy dilemmas

It can be seen that nominal exchange rate changes impact significantly on the rate of inflation and illustrate the dilemma facing the authorities in the conduct of exchange rate policy. Given the Bank's commitment to an anti-inflation stance, the preference would be for a stable nominal exchange rate. However, in the face of persistent inflation, maintaining a constant nominal rate causes the real rate to appreciate. This then puts pressure on the export sector because of declining competitiveness. At the same time the low level of reserves also restricts the Bank's ability to intervene indefinitely to prevent a depreciation.

According to the Reserve Bank, no strict rules are followed and exchange

Table 8.1. Inflation rates in South Africa (consumer and producer price index, percentage change)

	CPI	PPI	Imports[1]	Xrate[2]
1985	16,3	16,9	23,6	-32,4
1986	18,5	19,4	22,5	-15,8
1987	16,2	13,9	9,8	3,0
1988	12,9	13,1	10,9	-12,9
1989	14,7	15,2	16,3	-9,9
1990	14,4	12,0	10,1	-3,2
1991	15,3	11,4	8,3	-6,0
1992	13,9	8,3	4,2	-4,8

[1] Imported goods reflected in the producer price index.
[2] Xrate is the nominal effective exchange rate; it implies depreciation.
Source: SA Reserve Bank Quarterly Bulletins

rate movements are merely a result of market responses to macro-economic policies in general. However, it would appear that although the Reserve Bank is not following an explicit rule, and although in terms of stated objectives a stable nominal rate would be preferred, there is a concern for the real exchange rate as well. This was conceded in the 1992 Reserve Bank Governor's Annual Address, when it was stated that the Bank was able

> ...through active intervention in the foreign exchange market to pursue its objective of supporting a relatively stable real exchange rate of the rand... Through its intervention operations the Bank therefore encouraged a slight depreciation of the nominal average weighted average of the rand against a basket of currencies. Although these intervention transactions were not always in harmony in the short term with the Bank's overriding objective of a strict control over changes in the money supply, the Bank with its exchange rate policy nevertheless lends support to the notion that South African producers must remain competitive in international markets, both as exporters and as suppliers in the domestic market.

Current exchange rate policy therefore reflects the dilemma of whether to use the exchange rate as a nominal anchor for prices or for promoting exports. In any event the advantage of following a predetermined rule comes from the commitment signal that the Reserve Bank gives to the economy as a means to gain credibility for its policies. Such a commitment has not been given and the market is kept guessing as to the actual direction of exchange rate policy.

Factors affecting future policy: access to foreign capital

There are various factors that could impact on future exchange rate movements and policy. These include the possibility of real shocks (including the political situation), progress towards current account liberalisation and access to foreign capital. As argued above, the major shocks that have confronted the economy in the past have been gold price and political shocks. Over the past few years the behaviour of the dollar gold price has been far more stable and shocks of the size experienced in the early 1980s are less likely. In addition it would not appear appropriate for exchange rate policy to be directed again at stabilising the mining industry. This can be done more effectively (and more appropriately) through a commodity price stabilisation scheme. On the other hand, shocks of a political nature are likely to continue, at least through the transition, which could be relatively lengthy.

Political shocks impact on exchange rate policy primarily through their impacts on the capital account. The importance of political shocks can be seen in the effect of the 1985 debt crisis on the real exchange rate. A speedy resolution of the political situation in the country will be essential for attracting new capital as well as bringing an end to the debt standstill. However, it would appear that much reliance will have to be placed on direct investment flows or loans from international bodies such as the World Bank. As the Centre for the Study of the South African Economy at the London School of Economics has cautioned, 'the possibility of large-scale new bank lending following the resolution of the standstill is negligible since the new Basle capital adequacy requirements have made banks much more reluctant to undertake cross-border lending, particularly to non-OECD borrowers'.[1]

Increased access to foreign capital will affect not only the degree to which the Reserve Bank is able to intervene in the market but also the equilibrium level of the real exchange rate. Latin American evidence has shown that flows of capital are now more important determinants of real exchange rate movements than flows of goods and services and that capital inflows have been associated with a marked appreciation of real exchange rates in most of the countries. Attempts to avoid appreciation have caused problems for monetary and fiscal policy. This is because active intervention through the purchase of foreign exchange and the attempt to avoid domestic monetisation of these purchases results in sterilising open market operations, which then perpetuates interest rate differentials and gives rise to increased fiscal burdens (see Calvo *et al.*, 1992).

Thus, while capital inflows are generally welcomed, especially when compared to the opposite extreme of capital outflows, they often are a source of concern to the authorities because of the impact on the international competitiveness of the export sector and also because the inflows may not be sustained.

Despite the problems associated with excessive borrowing, there are nevertheless advantages in having access to foreign borrowing. The current repayment commitments have put undue pressure on the capital account of the balance of payments, which has exacerbated the current recession. Any new loans or the rescheduling of existing loans reduces the required current account surplus and therefore allows for a greater level of domestic investment. In addition, access to foreign capital helps in the maintenance of a stable real exchange rate when the economy is faced with transitory current account shocks.

Conclusion

This chapter has highlighted some of the implications of different exchange rate rules. Unlike the success stories of Taiwan and South Korea, the South

African authorities have to contend with the implications of exchange rate policy for the mining industry as well as the implications of fluctuating dollar gold prices for the real exchange rate. It has been argued that the appropriate rule for stimulating export-led growth is one that stabilises the real rate. However, given the susceptibility of the South African economy to shocks, a rigid rule is inappropriate. Adjusting the exchange rate in the face of shocks does not necessarily undermine the credibility of the rule as long as the public has the confidence that only sustained real as opposed to nominal shocks will be adjusted to through exchange rate changes that fall outside the rule.

At present, the monetary authorities in South Africa have not announced a particular exchange rate rule although Dr Stals has made the goal of the Reserve Bank 'the preservation of the internal and external value of the rand'. He has also made it clear that he 'will certainly not let the exchange rate of the rand fall simply to bale out distressed exporters'.[2] However, it would appear that at times the Reserve Bank has not been impervious to the movements of the real rate, and until the inflation rate is reduced to that of South Africa's trading partners the distinction between the real and nominal rates will be crucial and the policy dilemma will continue.

Notes

1. *LSE Quarterly Report,* February, 1993, p.15.
2. *Finance Week,* July 11-17, 1991.

9

South African Exchange Rate Policy:
A Reserve Bank Perspective

CHRIS L. STALS

The main function of the Reserve Bank is described in its mission statement, as follows: 'The South African Reserve Bank is the central bank of the Republic of South Africa. It regards as its primary goal in the South African economic system the protection of the domestic and external value of the rand. The Reserve Bank believes it is essential that South Africa has a vigorous economy based on the principles of a free market system, private initiative and effective competition. It recognises, in the performance of its duties, the need to pursue balanced economic growth.'

In other words, the Reserve Bank's task is to keep the rate of inflation as low as possible and to protect the exchange rate of the rand. When successful in creating and maintaining these stable financial conditions, the Bank would also make an important contribution to balanced economic growth. Only in an environment of overall financial stability will rational economic decisions be taken, the available but limited real resources of a country be used optimally, and maximum economic development be attained.

In order to be effective, monetary policy must be applied persistently and consistently over the medium and longer term. Monetary policy loses its effectiveness if it is used excessively as a short-term fine-tuning device. Monetary policy should therefore preferably not be applied in an anti-cyclical manner, or at times to stimulate the economy and at other times to depress it (the so-called 'stop-go' approach). Monetary policy should furthermore be guided mainly by changes in underlying financial aggregates, and not by conditions in the 'real' economy.

To fight inflation is not an easy task. In the final situation, stable domestic political and social conditions combined with sound economic policies in general are all essential ingredients of a strategy for a stable currency. The Reserve Bank's main contribution in combating price rises is to control money supply. Money is created mainly through credit extension by banking institutions, and the central bank committed to a market economy will normally influence the money supply only indirectly through its interest rate policy. To the extent that bank credit extension is driven by demand, the cost of credit – interest rates – becomes an important causal factor for changes in the money supply.

In restricting the growth in money supply within predetermined guidelines, the Reserve Bank therefore uses its discount rate as the main instrument for the implementation of monetary policy, and normally follows and endorses market trends by adjusting its bank rate upwards or downwards to reflect changes in underlying demand and supply conditions. At times the Bank may also lead the market in setting the trend in interest rates. Behind every decision to change the bank rate is the obligation to keep the rate of increase in the money supply as far as possible always in line with the predetermined guidelines so that the ultimate objective of price stability can be obtained.

Once the Bank has decided on an appropriate and acceptable range for the rate of increase in the money supply, it cannot also decide on the level of interest rates and/or on an acceptable exchange rate as independent policy objectives. The Reserve Bank, as part of its broad monetary policy, accordingly does not pursue an independent exchange rate target as an anchor for its overall objective of financial stability. Given its targets for money supply growth, it rather prefers to rely on market forces, within the framework of the existing exchange controls and tariff protection, to determine the level of the exchange rate. Efforts by the authorities to fix the exchange rate artificially at a different level would probably upset the equilibrium established by market forces between the rate of increase in the money supply, the level of interest rates and the exchange rate of the rand.

However, the Reserve Bank does of course not determine its money supply guidelines for a specific year in isolation, but has to take all economic conditions and developments into consideration. In practice, some leeway and room for discretion usually remain. The monetary approach towards the complex goal of overall financial stability as indicated by an acceptable growth rate of money supply, a relatively stable exchange rate of the rand and positive real rates of interest should therefore not be inconsistent.

Over the short term there may at times appear to be a conflict in the objective of attaining both a stable domestic and a stable external value of the rand. For example, an outflow of capital could lead to a depreciation in the exchange rate of the rand, causing a rise in domestic prices. The depreciation of the currency together with a decline in the money supply (caused by the outflow of capital) will, however, over the medium to longer term lead to changes in the relative prices of tradeable goods and therefore in the pattern of external trade, which will eventually support a more stable exchange rate of the rand. Over the long term, movements in the domestic and external values of the currency should therefore be in tandem. In fighting inflation, the Reserve Bank therefore at the same time, and with the same instruments, also protects the external value of the rand over the medium to longer term.

In view of these broad macro-economic objectives of monetary policy, the exchange rate and other financial variables are not manipulated by the Reserve Bank in the interests of certain groups and sectors of the economy. The Bank has never deliberately manipulated the exchange rate of the rand to assist the gold mining or for that matter any other industry in the South African economy. As a result of the relative (but declining) importance of gold exports in the country's balance of payments, sharp changes in the gold price have inevitably in the past had a significant effect on the exchange rate of the rand. Although the Reserve Bank could at times counter the influence of a temporary sharp rise in the gold price by purchasing dollars in the domestic foreign exchange market, its foreign exchange holdings were usually too small to enable it to offset the depreciating effect on the rand of a declining gold price. A sharp decrease in the gold price and a concomitant decline in the foreign exchange proceeds from gold sales therefore often caused the exchange rate of the rand to depreciate. The resulting higher rand price per ounce of gold produced and received by the mines under these circumstances was therefore normally brought about by changes in the underlying supply and demand conditions in the foreign exchange market, and not by deliberate exchange rate policies.

Although the Reserve Bank has no predetermined targets for the exchange rate of the rand, the Bank does regard it as its proper function to smooth out unduly large short-term fluctuations in the exchange rate, especially if these fluctuations are of a temporary and reversible nature. As a short-term measure, and as long as it does not foil the money supply objectives, the Reserve Bank often counteracts undesirable upward or downward pressure on the exchange rate by buying or selling dollars against rand in the domestic foreign exchange market.

Being the organisation responsible for the marketing of South Africa's gold production and in order to fulfil its function of intervention, the Bank stays in contact with the market at all times. Transactions in the foreign exchange market are therefore normally conducted every day on the Reserve Bank's own initiative, but the net effect of these transactions may be negligible. In smoothing out these shorter-term fluctuations in the exchange market, the Bank stays aware of the effect that these transactions may have on its operations in the domestic money market. At times the Reserve Bank's intervention in the foreign exchange market is actually aimed at effecting liquidity in the money market and not so much at smoothing out exchange rate changes.

In accordance with the principle that the exchange rate of the rand should in the long run reflect underlying supply and demand conditions in the market, the Reserve Bank avoids active management of the exchange rate level. Intervention is therefore applied within the rules recommended by the Commission of Inquiry into the Monetary System and Monetary Policy (the De Kock Commission) so that it does not counteract or offset the effects of changes in the authorities' own domestic monetary policies on the exchange rate; exacerbate exchange rate movements that would have resulted from the free operation of market forces; or reverse the direction of change in the exchange rate that would have resulted from the free operation of market forces, i.e. cause a rise in the exchange rate to be converted into a decline or vice versa.

PART THREE
INTERNATIONAL ARRANGEMENTS AND INSTITUTIONS

10

GATT and Its Impact on Developing Countries
SHEILA PAGE

Developing countries have seen four remarkable cycles of change in trade policy in the last two decades. These have affected the role of international rules, the possibility of a special place within the rules for developing countries, the relative protectionism of developed and developing countries, and, intensifying all of these effects, the growing emphasis on their participation in international trade negotiations. During most of the last seven years these processes have been unusually open, because of the Uruguay Round of trade negotiations which began in 1986 and was extended to the end of 1993.

The developing countries in GATT

GATT came into operation in 1948, as part of the post-World War II attempt both to bring greater order into international relations and to find collective ways of improving economic welfare. The essence of GATT has therefore always been its rules and procedures: the most basic commitment is not to liberalise trade, but to maintain equal treatment of trading partners, 'most favoured nation' (MFN) treatment for all fellow members, and to avoid disruptive changes in policies affecting trade, symbolised in the 'binding' of tariffs, a commitment not to raise tariffs above the level notified to GATT without agreement and compensation.

In international – as in national – economic systems, decision-makers, perhaps even more in the private than in the public sector, see strong advantages in reducing uncertainty by means of agreed rules with formal procedures for enforcing them and non-arbitrary methods of changing them. This is especially true for participants who are too poor to take major risks and too economically weak to exploit a more unregulated system. But a rule-based international system inevitably implies constraints on tariff and other trade barriers and on domestic policies and policy instruments which have potential effects on trade. In the past, freedom to set external policies has been regarded as being as essential as the right to use domestic ones by most countries which have developed successfully. This includes the present industrial countries, those usually classified as the newly industrialising economies (the NIEs of Asia), and the large import-substituting developing countries like India or Brazil. The absence of any international regulatory system until 1948, and the limited scope of GATT in its early years, meant that past generations of developing countries did not have to give up control over trade policies during their periods of structural transformation. The choice of countries like Mexico and Venezuela not to become GATT members until the late 1980s indicates that some saw even the pre-Uruguay Round system as too restrictive.

The terms of this trade-off between rules and policy freedom were sharply altered in the 1970s and 1980s with the revival of unilateral protection, through non-tariff barriers, on the part of industrial countries, particularly in commodities like textiles and clothing and steel, in which they were losing advantage to newer producers. At the same time, the systems under agreed derogations from GATT, in agriculture and textiles and clothing, became more unpredictable through modifications in the types of pricing and greater flexibility in altering the number of goods controlled, which gave increasing freedom to importers to change the rules.

The Uruguay Round was seen as the opportunity not merely to return to the existing rules, but to greatly increase their coverage, to goods like textiles and clothing and agricultural products, which had been allowed to move outside the GATT system, and to 'new areas': services, intellectual property, and some trade-related investment measures. It was also to provide more transparent and perhaps more rigorous methods of enforcing the rules. *De facto,* because of the simultaneous changes happening in the former centrally planned economies in both Europe and Asia, there would be a further, geographical extension as the membership of GATT increased.

Concessions and preferences

The only agreed exception to non-discriminatory treatment, introduced (in 1971) by amendment to the original agreement, was for developing countries: these may receive special preferences (for example, the Generalised System of Preferences, GSP) or may introduce 'exceptional' import controls. In practice, developing countries were allowed further special treatment, through indefinite postponement of their obligation to bind tariffs, and a reduced likelihood that any trading arrangements which they made with developed countries or among themselves would be questioned as violating MFN rules. But GSP preferences were not contractual or 'bound', and could be removed at discretion, not by negotiation. Developing countries were also among the major sufferers from the derogations for agriculture and textiles and clothing.

Outside GATT, the benefits of special treatment have been eroding. Pressure from the lending and aid-giving agencies to reduce their trade barriers, and the variance among products within them, have effectively imposed more constraints on developing countries' trade policy than even normal GATT rules. Further, the reductions have taken place in the absence of reciprocal agreements with their trading partners. Combined with their own shift away from choosing to use protection-based trade policies, this has reduced the advantages which they perceive from special treatment. Within GATT, outside the Uruguay Round, there has also been erosion. New developing country members (or returning ones, like China) have not been allowed as extensive exemption from tariff binding or removal of non-tariff barriers as the long-standing members, and the more successful developing countries have come under increasing pressure to give up the right to impose exceptional controls for balance of payments reasons.

The Uruguay Round has reinforced this. The NIEs are expected to participate fully in, for example, the tariff-cutting negotiations, and in all the negotiating groups developing countries have been expected to 'participate' by making their own offers of concessions. Some of the 'new area' subjects were directed very strongly at them (intellectual property, for example, in response to pirating copies), and in others the proposals offer only time-limited special treatment (services, perhaps agriculture). Both the advantages of 'special' treatment and their own interest in it may therefore have been greatly reduced.

Relative protection

Traditionally, and in much of the initial pressure exerted by industrial countries for 'full participation' by developing countries in the Uruguay Round, developing countries have been seen as the more protectionist, and both the relative positions of industrial and developing countries up to the early 1970s and the history of policy changes in the present industrial countries broadly supported such a generalisation. But the last two decades have seen a reversal. In the 1970s the developed countries started extending, reintroducing and inventing non-tariff barriers to trade. Since the 1950s these had been regarded as contrary to GATT principles (if not invariably to the letter of the rules) and they had in fact been avoided, except in a limited range of activities. Even in these it was accepted that such intervention was an undesirable relic, perhaps needed until a sector or group (like agriculture and farmers) could fully adapt to international trade. In the 1970s they began to be used as an almost normal response to loss of competitiveness, while by the 1980s the reversal had gone further, with the EC and the US even seeming at times to be turning away from the principle that multilateral agreements were basically a beneficial activity.

On tariffs, the Tokyo Round (the last negotiating round before Uruguay) of 1973–9 brought a smaller proportional and absolute reduction in tariffs than its predecessors (not too surprising as the average level had already been brought down substantially) and a clear growth in discrimination against the goods most important to developing countries, especially those most competitive with industrial countries' own products (manufactures).

In contrast, developing countries were moving from recognition, during the 1970s, that import substitution, usually behind tariff and non-tariff barriers, was not the only and not a complete path to development, and began to acknowledge, in the 1980s, an absolute commitment to opening their economies to imports and putting their emphasis on exports. As indicated above, this was partly because of outside pressure, but also because the NIEs now offered an alternative example. In the second half of the 1980s, in stark contrast to the retreat from multilateralism of the industrial countries, this led logically to growing faith and participation in multilateral negotiations.

Although the Uruguay Round appeared to begin in traditional fashion, at the initiative of an industrial country with the developing countries insisting on the writing in of special treatment and resisting the extension to new areas, by the mid-term review (1988) and scheduled end (1990) they were actively pressing for a settlement and working with different industrial country allies. It is the three industrial blocs which appear to have lost interest and to be willing now to see no agreement emerge.

Importance of developing countries to trade policy

Uruguay was the first of the eight rounds since the formation of the GATT to attract substantial interest in participation by the developing countries, both as targets for the negotiating objectives of the industrial countries and, as the Round progressed, as active participants with interests of their own. In all the major 'negotiating groups' demands were made both by and on the developing countries. This had to some extent been anticipated: the Round was opened in Uruguay. But their own interest grew during the Round, both with their increased awareness of how the various proposals could benefit them and with their belief that they needed and deserved improved access in exchange for their own falling trade barriers.

The greater emphasis placed by the industrial countries on developing country participation was inevitable given developing countries' rapidly growing share in world trade and in the traditional subjects of GATT rounds. Developing countries' share in total trade had increased from 21% in 1973, the beginning of the Tokyo Round, to 26% by 1986 when the Uruguay Round opened. They are now a significant market for most industrial countries, and access to their markets and regulation of their trade policies have therefore become important objectives. In an increasing number of products they are also competitors: over the same period their share of total trade in manufactures doubled to 15%, and the agricultural surpluses of the US and the EC brought industrial countries into competition with the traditional developing country exporters of food.

On the other side, the rise in manufactures within developing countries' trade, to more than 50% of their exports by 1986, brought more of their trade into GATT-regulated sectors. The new areas included some of their other major exports, notably agriculture and services, and also types of policy which many considered central to the process of development: the role of domestic subsidies, the transfer of technical innovations, and foreign investment.

Developing countries were no longer willing to see a major part of their exports – textiles and clothing – treated as a derogation from the GATT. As noted above, their acceptance of growing discipline on their trade policies had reduced the cost of accepting GATT rules while their exposure to the unilateral measures of the industrial countries had increased their benefit from the enforcement of such rules.

All these forces brought a clear increase in their role, up to December 1990, the original deadline. Since the breakdown then, the decision on whether there will be an outcome, and what it will be, has moved into the hands of the two largest participants.[1]

Importance of trade policy to developing countries

The developing countries also had what may be considered a policy-approach reason for taking a stronger interest in the trade negotiations of the 1980s. The emphasis which appeared from the late 1970s on the importance of exports as a force for development and of industrial transformation implies that obstacles to their exports are seen not just as barriers to static efficiency gains or extra costs, but as constraints on dynamic change and industrialisation. If it is argued that trading, rather than industrialisation itself or other changes which can be induced by appropriate domestic policy, brings more rapid growth and more appropriate structural changes, then there is clearly a greater urgency to removing any external constraints on this process. Those analyses of the success of the NIEs of the 1970s which assigned central importance to export-orientated growth thus also contributed to the next generation's greater concern about protection by the industrial countries.

This new-style dependency theory was reinforced by the emphasis throughout the Round on the great gains to be obtained from a settlement (especially notable in every report by the international financial agencies). Although all refused to quantify it, this has contributed to a view that a settlement would bring substantial world income gains, with a large share accruing to developing countries and a corresponding loss if the Round fails.[2]

It is appropriate to examine these expectations in detail and also to look at the current probability of a successful outcome. Some scepticism is in order because trade effects are usually quite diverse on particular commodities or in specified markets. But it must be remembered that a sectoral approach risks underemphasising three other positive effects because they are not susceptible to such analysis.

There is an effect on national income from the removal or reduction of trade barriers and the consequent increase in efficiency, incomes and, if this leads to more investment, growth. This effect has been the most emphasised in macroeconomic writings on the Round (and is conventionally seen as the most important result of the liberalisation of world trade which occurred in the 1950s and 1960s, partly through the GATT rounds then). It is also, however, the least measurable because it depends on altering the methods and location of present production and therefore on changing the trading patterns on which the calculations are based. It also depends on the policy responses of governments and industrialists in all countries. It is likely to be most important for the products, and therefore countries, which appear to be least affected by direct reforms. The products which will respond to income rises are manufactures (and services), not the stagnant or declining industries which have attracted most protection.

The second and third effects have already been mentioned: the return to rules, and therefore reduction of uncertainty, and the return to a multilateral system, and therefore greater willingness to participate in it and accept its disciplines on the part of those outside the oligarchy.

The Uruguay Round

The negotiations

Tariffs were, on average, below 10% before the Uruguay Round started. Although peaks remained for individual products they no longer constituted a sufficient agenda to attract either industrial or developing countries. For this reason, and also because of the growth of new types of protection and growing dissatisfaction with the exclusion of whole areas from international control, a much broader agenda was set out. This posed severe practical problems (as well as the political ones in reaching any settlement) because the traditional method was to strike bargains between the principal exporters and importers of individual products and then combine these to reach an aggregate settlement with net gains for all.[3] Quantifying settlements in the new areas and finding equivalent concessions have been difficult.[4] The growing numbers of countries joining and participating actively increased the complexity of striking deals even in traditional areas. The initial timetable made no allowance for the greater complexity. Fifteen negotiating groups were established with the objective of reaching frameworks of agreement in each before striking a final bargain across all groups. When the negotiations broke down, and then continued through 1991, 1992 and 1993, they were consolidated into seven groups: Market Access, Agriculture, Textiles and Clothing, Services, Rule-making, TRIPs, and Institutions.

The Round has already had some identifiable outcomes, and the pattern of a final settlement of the others is set; it is the size of some settlements and the conditions for exemptions or details of periods of adjustment which are the ostensible obstacles to agreement. These are obviously not minor, but nor are the achievements. Inclusion of the 'new areas' was itself subject to dissent at the inaugural meeting; they are now accepted, at least in framework, as negotiable and part of the GATT system. As part of the negotiation and quantification process, data on services, non-tariff barriers and trade regimes are greatly improved, and permanent procedures have been established to raise their quality. These include both new national procedures, backed by the international statistical services, and the new GATT system of reporting on each country's policy regime. Under these regular 'Trade Review' missions, with published reports, each country is reviewed (at two-, four-, or six-year intervals). While not condemning restrictive actions, the reports place all trade policy measures before the GATT Council. This also gives full information and opportunity to challenge to trading partners. The first report on South Africa is due to be published in 1993.

Combined, all the new sources of information since 1986 have transformed the transparency of international trade and its regulation. GATT and UNCTAD have started to publish data on non-trade barriers (which they had only started to collect at the end of the 1970s). The negotiations in the services group revealed much about how these markets actually operated, and GATT now includes services data in its annual review of trade. New information and agreed definitions have also emerged from the TRIMs and TRIPs groups.

The initial success of developing countries in influencing the outcomes of some groups appears to have produced a greater willingness to use other GATT mechanisms, e.g. appeals to the dispute settlement procedures, and (perhaps a less happy outcome) also to use traditional bilateral trade policy tools like anti-dumping procedures. The confidence in trade policy may also help explain the recent revival of the fashion for regional trading groups among developing countries.

The reforms which are now planned for the European Community's Common Agricultural Policy remove the major obstacle to a settlement on agriculture. The size and nature of cuts in agricultural subsidies came within sight of settlement with the November 1992 negotiations between the US and the EC. The size of tariff cuts and whether they should be concentrated on the lowest (because they are unnecessary nuisances) or the peaks (because they are most distorting) are traditional GATT issues, with all sides taking their traditional positions, and traditional formulas are available to solve them. The scope of a services settlement is technically more difficult, but as it was the US which placed services on the agenda and the US which now wishes more exemptions it is unlikely that any other country would break up the Round solely on this issue. A renegotiation of the Multi-Fibre Arrangement (MFA) must take place, within or outside GATT.

The questions are when and whether there will be a settlement. The Round failed to meet its original deadline of 1990 for several reasons. It was ambitious in terms of the number of issues to be negotiated and of participants. Other issues distracted international negotiators: the Single European Market, the Gulf War and, most recently, the North American Free Trade Agreement. The Round lost momentum, from missing one deadline after another. The delays led to further delay by allowing those dissatisfied with the subjects which had been agreed to to lobby and those who had not followed the agreements during the negotiations time to find objections.

If there was a clear determination to achieve a settlement, the basis for one exists, but by June 1993 this was not evident. There was still a greater than 50% probability that some settlement would emerge, out of concern for not being seen to fail. But negotiations might simply carry on, producing individual, perhaps 'provisional' settlements, and gradually merging into a new procedure of continuing trade discussions, rather than finite rounds. Many expected this to follow even a successful Uruguay Round because the growth in the size, complexity and length of negotiations would make future rounds impractical.

The details[5]

The tariff deductions proposed are about a third for all goods. Reductions would be greater for tariffs which are now above 30%. The structure of relative tariffs for each country would not be changed. Industrial countries' preferences for less processed goods would therefore remain, and would continue to discourage processing in the country of origin. At present the EC, for example, has tariffs on raw materials which are on average close to 0%; on semi-processed goods of about 4%; on finished goods, almost 7%. This encourages diversification into new primary products, rather than greater processing or industrialisation. The effective reductions in all tariffs would also be much less for exports by the developing countries which benefit from GSP (the Generalised System of Preferences), as they would not directly affect the tariffs offered under this, most of which are already below the proposed new levels. Developing countries with GSP therefore would gain nothing, and would in fact lose because their margin of preference would be reduced or removed. On the other hand, tariffs imposed by developing countries (particularly the more advanced) would be reduced by the same formulas. As they do not offer GSP these reductions would have a larger effect on their own average tariff structure and would cover all exports to them.

The remaining quantitative restrictions on tropical products (mainly beverages) would be removed (these are not serious), but although tariffs would be reduced, again tariff escalation on processed products would not be altered. As it is mainly the EC which has maintained tariffs on these goods (in order to offer free entry as a preference to the associated African, Caribbean, and Pacific – ACP – countries), the effect will be small losses for the ACP in the EC market because of diversion to non-ACP countries, with small offsetting gains to others. This will affect coffee and plants and flowers.

The proposed settlement on temperate agriculture (one of the major sticking points of the negotiations) would reduce subsidised exports by the industrial countries and therefore raise world prices and the quantities which could be exported by the rest of the world. These effects would benefit actual and potential developing country producers of grains and meat (and also the efficient developed country exporters). In both tropical and temperate, the major developing country gainers would be non-ACP primary product exporters, in practice mainly Latin America (possibly plus Asian rice producers if Japan and South Korea open their markets). Many African countries are importers of temperate products, and most exporters already have, as ACP countries, duty-free access to their major market, the EC. For Africa, the increased cost of imports will outweigh small gains on exports.

The proposed settlement would end the current system of tight country-to-country and product-specific quotas on textile and clothing trade under the Multi-Fibre Arrangement.[6] This, with its predecessor schemes, dates from 1961. The settlement would decrease quotas in three stages, removing them entirely after ten years, while simultaneously removing an increased proportion of goods from the quota system at each stage. It is structured to be loaded heavily to the end of the period, and some countries appear to have increased controls in the last two years to increase the effective period of no significant effect. Tariffs are and would remain among the highest, and are biased against more processed goods (clothing higher than fabric, and fabric higher than fibres). It will be of most benefit to countries with large supplies of low-cost labour and, among these, those with their own supplies of the raw materials; in other words, to the traditional Asian suppliers. After 30 years of detailed and constantly changing intervention in this trade, it is difficult to know which countries would gain in a different trading regime. The calculations reported simply applied a range of existing estimates of the increase in total trade uniformly across present suppliers.

Table 10.1. Summary of quantifiable effects of the Uruguay Round

		PERCENTAGE OF TOTAL EXPORTS										PERCENTAGE OF GDP	
	Tropical products	Temperate agricultural[1]			Textiles and clothing[2]			Tariffs	NIE tariffs	Pref/ 50%[3]	High/ 100%[4]	Low/ 25%[5]	Pref/ 50%	WB est. Macro.
		Pre-ferred	High	Low	25%	50%	100%							
All developing countries	0.0	0.0	0.2	-0.0	1.4	2.9	5.7	0.1	-0.2	2.8	5.8	1.3	0.4	0.4
Africa	-0.1	-0.2	0.0	-0.3	0.8	1.5	3.1	-0.7	0	0.5	2.3	-0.3	0.2	0.2
America	0.2	0.3	0.8	0.1	0.5	0.9	1.8	0.1	0	1.5	2.9	0.9	0.3	0.4
Total Asia, including Oceania	0.0	-0.0	0.1	-0.1	1.8	3.6	7.1	0.2	-0.3	3.5	7.1	1.6	0.5	0.5
South Asia	0.2	-0.3	0.3	-0.5	2.3	4.7	9.3	0.9	0	5.5	10.7	2.8	0.5	0.5
ASEAN	0.0	0.0	0.2	-0.0	0.4	0.8	1.6	0.2	1	2.1	3.0	1.6	0.5	0.5
NIEs	0.0	-0.0	0.0	-0.0	1.3	2.5	5.0	0.2	-0.7	2.0	4.5	0.8	0.5	0.5
ACP	-0.2	-0.0	0.4	-0.2	0.0	0.0	0.0	-1.1	0	-1.3	-0.9	-1.5		

[1] For explanation of 'preferred', 'high' and 'low', see Source.

[2] % are different assumptions of total changes in products now constrained.

[3] 'Preferred temperate', 50% textiles and clothing.

[4] 'High' temperate; 100% textiles and clothing.

[5] 'Low' temperate, 25% textiles and clothing.

Source: Adapted from Sheila Page, Michael Davenport and Adrian Hewitt, *The GATT Uruguay Round: Effects on Developing Countries*. London: Overseas Development Institute, 1991. The assumptions and calculations are explained fully there. Last column: World Bank, *World Development Report. 1991.*

The results of these assumptions are shown in Table 10.1, in terms of percentage of total exports. The signs, orders of magnitude and ranking of different type of exporter can probably be accepted, even with considerable uncertainty about the values. The only sectors in which there are potentially large gains are temperate agriculture and textiles and clothing. In the former, the gains for some areas are offset by losses for importers and for those which lose preference, so that most of the net gains for all developing countries appear to come from textiles and clothing where, as emphasised above, the distribution of gains is uncertain. The effects are not large: 3% of the value of exports, with most accruing to Asia and Latin America.

As for temperate agriculture and textiles and clothing, strong and co-ordinated intervention by the developing countries made the likely settlement one which would go well beyond most expectations at the beginning of the Round, and thus the gains would offer a convincing vindication of the decision of countries to participate actively.

Services offer a different lesson. The principal result of the massive expansion of data and understanding of services trade has been recognition on the part of the US that the advantages of greater competition to it were seriously overestimated, and on the part of the developing countries that they would find significant advantages. They have low labour costs and new, more modern structures: air, shipping and construction services are only the most obvious examples. The US, like the EC, has therefore become unenthusiastic about the potential gains from multilateral negotiations on all services while the developing countries want more services included.

The exchange of offers and demands for specific liberalisation is part of the unfinished business, as is the definition of an equivalent of binding: of setting limits on when countries can increase existing restrictions. The question of how to provide for any labour mobility that may be required, a crucial issue for some of the services of most interest to developing countries, also remains open.

As services are a high share of exports for many developing countries (they are estimated to be about 15% of their total exports, and under-recording is likely), and tend to be labour-intensive, any liberalisation should be favourable. As even a 10% rise could add 1,5% to total exports, gains here could add very significantly to a total outcome. The shares are largest and most concentrated in controlled services like transport and finance for the Asian countries. The typical Latin American services (notably tourism) are probably more income-elastic, so potentially more important, but they already face few controls. Africa has much lower values.

Under favourable conditions, the fact that developing countries in the future will face freer access than previous generations could compensate for their need to accept international regulation of their own services at an early point in their development. A discriminatory settlement which freed labour mobility at the professional level before or by more than the intermediate or unskilled level would limit their benefit and distort the gains in favour of the developed countries, but it is difficult to see how this could entirely offset the benefits. They will have to open their markets as well, but more slowly.

A settlement would attempt to bring greater regulation and transparency in subsidies and other non-tariff instruments affecting trade and less use of bilateral interventions; a more ambitious result would actually reduce their use. It is not possible to identify direct effects, but reaching agreement and making procedures more transparent should encourage trade and provide fewer opportunities to discriminate against weaker trading partners.

A particularly important issue has been the use of anti-dumping cases against low-cost imports by the US and the EC. Japan and the NIEs brought complaints about this to the Round, alleging a systemic bias in the procedures used. In the 1980s both the US and the EC greatly increased their use, and for each about 40% were directed at developing countries. For the US the majority were against the four Asian NIEs, Hong Kong, Taiwan, South Korea and Singapore, and the Latin American NIEs, in particular Brazil and Mexico. China was the only other large-scale target. The EC actions concentrated on a more limited number from the same group: Brazil, South Korea, Taiwan and China. In terms of products there has been a trend away from chemicals and steel and towards high-technology sectors, in particular consumer electronics. The Round proposals would regulate which export and domestic prices were used, what duty could be imposed and over what period. Any successful regulation would tend to benefit all developing countries (in so far as these compete on cost), but particularly the NIEs. For this and for MFA reform there is a possibility of loss by countries which have been used as substitute suppliers.

Copyright, patent and other intellectual property and technology issues (TRIPs) have not traditionally been seen as trade (or even 'trade-related') issues. They were brought into the Uruguay Round ostensibly because exporting counterfeit goods ranging from software to clothing was seen as a growing problem in trade with some South-east Asian countries, and the US in particular wanted to be able to enforce restrictions on this, using GATT mechanisms rather than the apparently ineffectual ones of local courts. The passage from importing (and, where possible, stealing) technology to exporting it (and regulating its use) is one all the present industrial countries have been through. Requiring countries to pay for it earlier than normal could impose extra costs of development.

Perhaps the more important aspect of TRIPs as a GATT issue is that it is a considerable extension of the scope of the GATT and of what domestic policies are considered internationally negotiable. By providing for certain 'standards' for protecting intellectual property (IP) rights, it goes well beyond simply requiring non-discriminatory (national) treatment, the more traditional rule. This is a precedent that could encourage those who want to move in this direction for services.

Trade-related investment measures (TRIMs) have receded greatly in the discussion. There are proposals for restrictions in the draft agreement, but they have received little attention, and the general move to encouraging foreign investment in all countries, developed and developing, is likely to have more effect in practice.

The fading of TRIMs and the likelihood that there will be no significant

Table 10.2. Summary of unquantifiable effects of the Uruguay Round

	Any settlement: confidence	Information effects	Reduced control on policy	Services¹	Controls on subsidies	Controls on anti-dumping	TRIPs	Effects on investment
Developing countries	+	+	?-	+	?	+	–	+
Asia	+	+	?	+	?	+	–	+
ASEAN	+	+	?	+	?	+	–	+
NIEs	+	+	?	+	?	L+	–	+
America	+	+	?-	+	?	?	–	+
Africa	?	+	?-	+S	?	?	–	+
ACP	?	+	?-	?	?	?	?	+

Notes: ? direction unknown; – negative; L larger than average for developing; S smaller than average for developing.
¹ If services exports rise by 10%, this would add 1,5 points to the total in Table 10.1 giving Preferred 4.3; High 7.3; Low 2.8.

innovation on labour movement in the services negotiations mean that there are unlikely to be large direct effects on capital or labour mobility. Any reduction in the possibilities of arbitrary intervention on trade and direct benefits found for individual sectors could increase total investment, and the developing countries could gain proportionately or slightly more if discrimination against their products is reduced. As investment tends to be anticipatory, any effects could even come before the long, end-loaded agricultural and textiles and clothing settlements. Table 10.2 summarises the direction of the effects implied by this discussion without attempting to quantify them.

The effects of the proposed settlement

Although present shares in trade in the heavily regulated sectors like temperate agriculture and textiles and clothing may underestimate the potential for developing country exports if there is a major reduction in protection, the numbers in Table 10.1, even if they were doubled, do not indicate major effects, and the short-term effects will be even smaller. The major liberalisations expected are in textiles and clothing and in agriculture: although there may be significant immediate adjustment effects these are sectors with relatively low income elasticity. The large gains with potential dynamic effects in previous GATT rounds have been in manufactures and have accrued to the major exporters. It would be wrong to extrapolate the size of their effects on the world economy to the present Round.

The conceptual difficulties of calculating the broader effects of this Round on national income have made the major international sources of forecasts and policy simulations cautious. They have not attempted estimation within their normal macro-economic exercises. The World Bank, for example, in 1991 offered a simulation in which the differences from its 'base' included a Uruguay Round settlement, but also larger tariff reductions and complete liberalisation from controls of all sectors, including agriculture and services, and, in addition, reduction in systemic financial risk, a fall of 2 percentage points for real interest rates, lower oil prices and lower risks in the Middle East and higher productivity in industrial and developing countries through changes in domestic policies. Even all this combined added only 1,1 points to industrial country growth and 1,6 to developing countries. Of this the actual gains from trade liberalisation were very small, varying from a maximum of 0,5 points for Asia to 0,2 for Africa. Clearly it is possible to increase these to any arbitrarily large number by including estimates for confidence effects from reduction in uncertainty etc.

The principal unquantifiable gains in Table 10.2 also go to the most advanced. They have suffered most from interventions in trade and they tend to have the income–elastic goods which will benefit most from any confidence effects. Because they are already advanced they also risk less from possible losses by accepting controls on their own policy interventions at a relatively early stage of development.

Taken together, all developing countries show a positive result. This is not surprising as many of the new sectors included are those in which barriers against their trade have been much higher than against that of industrial countries, or those in which the developing countries are important suppliers. In contrast, many of the gains from opening markets for more advanced products exported by the industrial countries had already been achieved in the previous 35 years of negotiations. It was fortunate, if somewhat surprising, for developing countries in 1986 that one advanced country still thought it saw enough to gain in two sectors, agriculture and services, to inaugurate a new Round, and it is not entirely surprising that such a limited developed country interest should now have faded to the point of putting the Round at risk.

This does not imply that the GATT system as it stands is not useful to the developed countries, or that it would be at risk if this Round never ends. It is because previous rounds have achieved and secured, through binding treaties, gains from trade creation in their exports that they now have less to gain from extending or strengthening the GATT system.

The gains to developing countries are entirely because of the gains from abolishing the MFA. Asia therefore gains most, and Africa gains least and in some cases may risk loss from loss of preference margin or from too early acceptance of policy constraints. It is the middle- and higher-income developing countries which benefit from trade liberalisation. This is consistent with the reasons given for increased developing country interest and participation in this Round, many of which stem from higher demand or development. Exporters still concentrating on primary products that face few constraints and low income elasticities have little to gain from the sectoral or the income effects. These results support the conventional view that trade concessions cannot be the principal means of assisting the development of countries that do not yet have the product mix to take advantage of them. One caveat must be entered to this picture: within each category it is the least processed which gains most (because of continuing tariff escalation). Although the gains to existing exporters of manufactures are greater, the direct deterrents to move into this position are not removed. This limits the influence of other countries' trade policy on the process of development.

South Africa's position

South Africa is rather more heavily weighted to primary exports, and within this to non-tariff-paying ones, than the other sub-Saharan African countries, and therefore is likely to gain even less than other African countries. The four principal goods which it exports – gold, coal, platinum and diamonds – pay no or negligible tariffs. If the clothing sector can be made competitive, abolition of the MFA would remove any potential risk of restriction, but it seems unlikely that South African exports face any threat of restriction with or without MFA.

For South Africa, the principal gains on offer from the trading system would come from acquiring GSP status. These would probably pre-empt most of, if not all, the potential gains from a GATT settlement. The total gains from GSP status would also be limited by the small proportion of exports actually facing any tariff. Even if the top 35–40 of its exports are taken, only about a third would gain from any change in external tariffs, and clearly the net effect from these minor exports on the economy as a whole would be small. The individual products would of course benefit. Promising exports like new fruits and flowers would see particularly large gains from GSP status. But for South Africa, as for other developing countries, the value of GSP status would be reduced by any major reductions in normal tariffs in the Uruguay Round and weakened by the failure to tackle tariff escalation.

As a developing country South Africa would have a presumptive claim to GSP status. As this is given as a concession, not negotiated, by each industrial country (or group) it would not have it as of right, but it does not seem unreasonable for it to expect it. A recent precedent is that some of the Eastern European countries were offered it as an initial response to their return to normal trade.

As it becomes a more active trader, South Africa will face pressure, whether classed as developing or developed country, to lower and rationalise its own tariff and import control structure. In the past it could have expected less pressure as a developing country, but both within GATT and in other international negotiations there is now less sympathy for demands for preferential rather than reciprocal arrangements for developing countries. South Africa appears to be moving to reduce and simplify import restrictions on its own policy initiatives. Like other developing countries it will face even greater external pressure from the World Bank than from GATT, so this is probably not a significant additional effect from GATT.

For South Africa, as for other developing countries, especially those in a weak trading position, the principal favourable effect from the GATT Round would probably be the benefit from reimposition on the international system of certainty and rules at a time when it is moving back into international trade. The effects of any reduction in tariffs or barriers could be positive, but only when it has altered its export structure greatly in the direction of manufactures and some unconventional primary goods.

The limited effects of the Uruguay Round on all less-developed countries and on primary exporters and South Africa in particular indicate the risks of depending on external policies to give the impulse to development. Altering these can remove specific constraints or costs, but they are not a substitute for a country's own policies to achieve structural change.

Notes

1. This reversal of a multilateral approach to trade negotiations was perhaps reinforced by the more general attempt to return to an oligarchic approach to international relations, symbolised in the establishment of purely power-based, unregulated groups like the G7.

2. This may be seen in the tradition of their (over?-) emphasis on the efficacy and benefits of co-ordinated international action. This may be particularly inappropriate in trade where major welfare gains can accrue to unilateral action.

3. All GATT negotiations embody a mercantilist approach to trade, offering reductions in trade barriers as a 'concession' rather than viewing them as a gain to those making them. This is then, under the MFN rule, extended to all other members.

4. In theory, quantifying the value of tariff reductions is also extremely complex, but the practice of previous rounds has been to ignore this and to concentrate on simple measures of the size of the reduction and the present volume of trade. The negotiators in other areas need to find similar acceptable rules of thumb.

5. The discussion and calculations in this section are based on a fuller analysis in Sheila Page, Michael Davenport and Adrian Hewitt, *The GATT Uruguay Round: Effects on Developing Countries*.

London: Overseas Development Institute, 1991. I am grateful to ODI for permission to use this material.

6. This must, in any case, be substantially modified because all importing countries other than the US and the EC have stated their intention of withdrawing from it, and the Single European Market will de facto mean the end of individual country quotas at sub-Community level. The current agreement should have expired in July 1991 and has been repeatedly extended to await a GATT settlement.

11

Implications of the Uruguay Round and the New GATT for South African Trade Policy

DAVID HARTRIDGE

The future implications of South Africa's GATT membership depend essentially on two things: the orientation of South Africa's economic and trade policies and what becomes of the GATT itself. At almost any other time in the past 40 years it would have been unnecessary to add this second consideration; it has been possible to take the GATT system pretty much for granted as a stable element in the world economic system, contributing a great deal to the growth of international trade but itself changing only very slowly. It can no longer be taken for granted. By the end of 1993, most likely, the Uruguay Round will either have succeeded or be seen to have failed. If it succeeds, the importance and the nature of the GATT will change more profoundly than at any time in its history; if it fails, the GATT and the multilateral trading system will face a crisis of confidence. But it would still be there, and would be more necessary than ever in the mood of recrimination and discrimination that would follow failure of the Round.

The implications of failure for the world economy, and especially for countries like South Africa which are outside major trading blocs and are trying to restructure their economies, are so serious that I still find it very difficult to believe that the great economic powers, which rightly insisted on launching this Round in the face of strong opposition and have invested so much effort in it, will now allow it to fail, when a massive achievement is within their grasp and the rest of the world is willing them to succeed. If we assume rationality in government we have to talk about the implications for South Africa of successful conclusion of the Round – of membership of an enlarged and transformed GATT system.

So where does the Round stand now and why would its success be a massive achievement? It has dragged on for so long, hopes of successful conclusion have been deferred so often and there are so many forecasts of its imminent collapse that it may sound odd for me to claim that by any past standards this has been a highly successful negotiation. But that is the fact. When this Round was launched at Punta del Este in 1986, nobody who was there would have forecast results on the scale of the draft Final Act which was tabled in December 1991. It contains 28 legal texts, 24 of which could be adopted now, as they stand; there have been demands for changes in some of them, but in my view further negotiation is unlikely to improve them – indeed, is more likely to do harm. The negotiation of these texts is a major achievement in itself.

In the last decade there has been no other great multilateral economic negotiation involving developed and developing countries which has produced comparable results – indeed, I can think of no other example of international cooperation on this scale. It compares pretty well with the incoherence of the G7 process, for example.

Certainly in 1986, given the background of the two-year struggle to persuade developing countries that the Round would not damage their interests, nobody would have forecast that six years later, developing countries having become the strongest advocates of early and successful conclusion, the whole enterprise would be threatened by the inability of the US and the European Community to agree on a small number of problems which are certainly difficult but were entirely foreseeable from the outset.

What has been achieved in the negotiations has to be seen in the light of the original objectives, of which there were five (five in my view at least – others may classify them differently). The first was further expansion of access to markets, by cutting tariffs and abolishing non-tariff barriers. As far as non-tariff barriers are concerned the negotiations have produced three new agreements, on rules of origin, pre-shipment inspection and import licensing procedures – unspectacular but useful progress in removing some of the unnecessary frictions which raise costs and impede trade flows. The tariff negotiations are not yet finished. This was an area in which expectations at the outset were not high, because the scope for further liberalisation was thought to be limited; as a result of earlier rounds, average industrial tariffs in the developed world had been reduced to not much more than 5% and the remaining hard core of peak tariffs on sensitive products seemed unlikely to be reduced very far. Nevertheless, for some time it has been clear that the US and the Community are aiming for a very big package of market-opening measures, in both goods and services, in which tariff peaks would be cut substantially and duties in some important sectors would be cut to zero. This would be an important boost to business confidence. Tariff cuts may not be the most vital element of a modern Round, but they are its most visible product, and are important in building the necessary coalition of industrial support for freer trade.

The second major objective of the Round was to restore the integrity of the GATT legal system, which was badly undermined by the growth of unilateralism and protectionism which followed the recession of the early 1980s. This is fundamental. The main issue in this Round is whether the trade system of the future is to be rule-based or power-based – predictable or anarchic. Many countries agreed to the launching of the Round not so much because they expected immediate benefits to their trade as because they wanted to reverse the collapse of respect for the rules whose most obvious symptom was the proliferation of 'voluntary export restraints', 'orderly marketing agreements' and other illegal market-sharing deals among the great powers. Here the Round has been an undoubted success. The draft Final Act contains 16 new agreements which interpret or amend the Articles of the GATT, and will greatly strengthen the rules governing international trade. These agreements vary a lot in importance, and since they are negotiated texts some of them contain imperfections; but in total they represent the biggest overhaul of the GATT since its creation and a major improvement on the rules and practices they will replace. It is impossible to describe them all, but, to take one example because it is relevant to the concerns I have just mentioned, the agreement on safeguards requires the elimination, within four years, of all existing 'grey area' measures, such as voluntary export restraints (with the quaint proviso that each contracting party is allowed to maintain one such deal – otherwise illegal – until the end of 1999, which happens to be the terminal date of the EC–Japan agreement on Japanese car exports to the Community). The agreements on subsidies and countervail, and on dumping, will bring stronger disciplines to areas of trade policy which have given rise to a great deal of distortion, abuse and conflict in the past. Being negotiated agreements, they do not please everybody; the agreement on dumping, for example, has been attacked both by some US industries which would like dumping findings made easier and by US exporters who want them made more difficult. Other agreements among the 16 under this heading cover the rules governing free-trade areas and customs unions, the activities of state trading enterprises, and protective measures taken for balance-of-payments reasons.

Third, textiles and clothing and agricultural trade, whose long exclusion from GATT disciplines has denied so many countries benefits they were entitled to expect from their GATT membership, will be brought within the system, and market access in both sectors will be improved. These sectors are critical for so many countries – probably a majority of the active membership of GATT – that no Uruguay Round package could be acceptable without satisfactory results in agriculture and textiles. The speed of liberalisation will not be dramatic in either case: the multi-fibre arrangement under which the textile and clothing exports of developing countries have been controlled is to be phased out over ten years, with most of the quota elimination probably taking place towards the end of that period; in agriculture, according to the agreement negotiated between the US and the Community in Washington last October, tariffs are to be reduced by 36% on average over six years, domestic support by 20% and the quantity of subsidised exports by 21%. The Blair House agreement was denounced by the former French government and is still under dispute, but it seems most unlikely that the figures could change much in either direction – the US can accept no less and the Community (or France) will concede no more. During 1992, when the entire negotiation was hostage to the US–Community deadlock on agriculture, it was sometimes asked whether agriculture could not be left aside while the other agreements were implemented. This is not possible; there is no reason why countries like Argentina and Australia should give up their leverage in areas like services and intellectual property so long as world agricultural markets continue to be grossly distorted by the agricultural policies of the Community and the USA, and the same is true for India and Pakistan in relation to textiles.

Fourth, the GATT system will be extended to cover trade in services and the protection of intellectual property rights. The inclusion of these subjects was the highest priority of the US in launching this Round, and it came to be shared in full measure by the Community, Japan and other industrialised countries. It is well known that many developing countries were extremely reluctant to enter negotiations on services, where they felt at a comparative disadvantage, or on intellectual property and investment measures, which they saw as a threat to their sovereign control over industrial policy. It is a measure of the commitment of developing countries in this Round, and of the remarkable liberalisation of economic policy in so many of them, that major agreements are at hand in services and intellectual property and a useful, though modest, agreement has been reached on investment measures. The agreement on intellectual property is extraordinary – certainly the most comprehensive and important multilateral agreement on the subject negotiated in this century. It is in fact the best proof of the effectiveness of the apparently illogical technique of multilateral trade negotiation – the reason why it makes sense to negotiate twenty-odd difficult subjects simultaneously. Outside this context the TRIPs agreement would have been inconceivable because there would have been no offsetting benefits, as in textiles and agriculture, to compensate countries which have made concessions in the TRIPs negotiations. The agreement on services is potentially even more important; it will provide the first international framework for the regulation and liberalisation of trade in the fastest-growing sector of international business.

The draft agreement on investment measures, the third of the new subjects, is more modest. It simply reaffirms, clarifies and strengthens existing GATT law by explicitly prohibiting investment measures which breach the national treatment obligation, such as local content requirements, or which involve quantitative restrictions, such as trade balancing requirements. But the agreement has teeth: all such measures will have to be notified and phased out.

Finally, the structure, and to some extent the nature of the GATT as an institution, will be changed and strengthened. The system for the resolution of disputes between governments will become more like a true judicial system: the ability of the losing party in a dispute to hold up the adoption of a decision by the GATT Council will be removed, though it will retain the right of appeal to an appeals board, whose decision will be final. There will be a single, unified dispute-settlement system covering the GATT and all agreements negotiated under it, the services agreement and TRIPs. This will create the possibility of retaliation in one sector, such as intellectual property, for failure to implement a panel decision in another, such as textiles. (But we should not exaggerate the likelihood of retaliation; there has only been one case of retaliation authorised by the Council in GATT's history.)

The draft Final Act also provides for the replacement of the GATT institution by a new Multilateral Trade Organisation which would service all of these agreements and would have, unlike the GATT, a secure legal basis, though its executive powers would be much the same. However, at the end of 1992 the US made it known that they have difficulties with the concept of a new organisation. This probably has to be seen as an issue still under negotiation.

It is well known that work is unfinished on three major subjects – agriculture, the tariff negotiations and trade in services. As I have said, it is also well known that the former French government denounced the agreement reached at Blair House last autumn; the position taken up within the Community on this point by the new government in Paris will be crucial. It is astonishing that agriculture should still be a major threat to the Round and to the future of the trading system, since the two great powers share the same basic need to reform their agricultural support policies, and there is nothing on the table that has not been foreseeable for the last six years and more. The tariff negotiations have been held up by the lack of progress in agriculture, since many countries will make no firm tariff commitment until they are confident of the outcome in agriculture, but this poses no threat; the remaining work, essentially a process of bilateral negotiations, can certainly be finished before the end of the year. The remaining work in services is also very largely a matter of bilateral negotiations, as countries table their schedules of initial commitments – that is, commitments to improve or guarantee access to specific service markets – and try to negotiate improvements in the offers tabled by others. In this case, time pressure may be more acute.

Any changes in the existing texts of subjects other than these three must be kept to an absolute minimum, given the clear danger of unravelling the whole package. At the end of last year there seemed to be a widely shared understanding of this danger, and it would be seriously disturbing if any significant number of the existing agreements were now to be reopened. Further negotiation is not likely to improve them and some, such as the agreements on dumping and textiles, are extremely sensitive politically. There will in any case be so little time available for negotiation between the granting of the US negotiating authority and the deadline of 15 December, that overloading the agenda could in itself destroy the Round.

The change of government in the US inevitably created a new uncertainty, and it is therefore encouraging that President Clinton has made it clear that he will ask Congress for the new negotiating authority he needs to conclude the Round. It is also good news that the US and the Community intend to finish the Round by the end of this year; we need an absolute deadline, and in my view there is nothing outstanding that could not be settled in three months' hard work, given adequate progress during the summer in resolving the issues which still separate the US, the Community and Japan. The fate of the Round, and of the GATT system, is in the hands of these three great trading powers. Nobody else has the power, or the slightest desire, to prevent a successful conclusion – and I believe that even Japan, despite its well-known difficulty in accepting the replacement of its ban on rice imports by tariffs, could not contemplate allowing that issue to saddle it with responsibility for failure of the Round.

South Africa, of course, has been a supporter of the Round, and an active participant, from the beginning. In the tariff negotiations it has offered reductions on about 40% of all tariff lines, reducing the average tariff on manufactures to less than 14% and bringing the number of bound tariff lines to just over 50% of the total, as compared with under 20% now. South Africa has already carried out tariff cuts on a number of tropical products and has also made a preliminary offer of initial commitments in services. South Africa will not be an obstacle to completion. In fact, it is in the position of many other countries which are undergoing profound political and economic adjustments. During the Round more than 40 countries, most of them developing countries, have liberalised their trade regimes and reformed their economic structures, accepting all the stresses that entails, in the hope of better access to export markets and a more secure trading environment. Such countries have taken at their word those who preached the virtues of competition and market disciplines. Politically as well as economically, it would be a serious mistake if their hopes were betrayed.

What would the success of the Round imply for South Africa in terms of changes in its own policies? The short answer is that all of its results will have to be accepted and implemented by all contracting parties. The previous (Tokyo) Round resulted in a two-speed GATT: the majority of the contracting parties have never accepted the Codes which were its most important outcome. This time there will be no question of accepting some of the results and rejecting others. All countries wanting to participate in the system – which effectively means wanting to remain in or enter the GATT – will have to accept all of the agreements negotiated in the Round and will have to table a schedule of initial commitments in services.

This means, for example, that South Africa, which did not join the Tokyo Round Codes on Subsidies and Anti-Dumping Measures, will have to comply with the Uruguay Round agreements on these subjects. As I understand it, policy on subsidies is already moving in that direction, since the General Export Incentive Scheme is due to be phased out in 1995, and depreciation allowances for export-oriented investments will not be renewed after September 1993. In the agricultural sector also, these pressures to reduce subsidy levels and allow food prices to move towards competitive international levels will help South Africa to reduce the cost of food to the consumer and of subsidies to the taxpayer.

The new South African anti-dumping and countervailing law, introduced in 1992, will also need to be adapted to the new agreements, although South Africa has never used anti-dumping duties on a big scale. The definition of injurious dumping in particular may need to be reviewed, since it could be argued that the law makes it too easy to prove dumping. In any case it will come under close scrutiny, like the dumping legislation of all other member countries. Moreover, the 'formula duties' which apply to about a fifth of the tariff and have a similar function to dumping duties in that they are designed to counter disruptive competition will presumably have to be converted into either normal anti-dumping or countervailing duties consistent with the relevant agreement or eliminated.

In the same way South Africa will become a party to all the other agreements in the Uruguay Round – on rules of origin, pre-shipment inspection, investment measures, services, intellectual property and so on. I have already mentioned that measures affecting inward investment which involve local content requirements or any form of quantitative restriction will have to be notified and eliminated. This applies not just to mandatory requirements of the kind which, as I understand it, are applied in the motor industry, but also to those tied to the grant of some advantage – for example, the achievement of a given level of local content as a condition for the receipt of a subsidy. The agreement on intellectual property will require high levels of protection of all kinds of intellectual property, including, among other things, strict enforcement of laws to prevent commercial counterfeiting of trademarks and copyright piracy. However, this should present no special problems, since South Africa's law in this area is already highly developed. Stronger protection of appellations of origin, which the agreement requires, should in fact benefit South African producers of wine and other high-quality agricultural products. The only exceptions to the general rule that all contracting parties must implement all agreements are the Agreements on Government Procurement, Civil Aircraft, Dairy Products and Meat, which will remain open to accession by those countries wishing to accept them.

One important consequence of the Uruguay Round will therefore be to restore the unity of the GATT system: with rather limited exceptions, mainly relating to developing countries, the same rules will apply to all member countries.

I know that there is a debate going on at present among trade economists in South Africa on the desirability of claiming developing country status in GATT, so it may be of interest to examine some of these exceptions. But I should begin by saying something about the way in which developing country status is accorded or recognised in GATT; it is not necessarily a simple matter. The criteria for developing country status in the GATT have never been clearly defined, by contrast with the category of least-developed countries, where the GATT recognises and follows the list established by the United Nations. Governments have unilaterally declared themselves developing countries, and in general, other contracting parties have accepted these self-definitions. Such a declaration by a post-apartheid South Africa would probably be accepted by its GATT partners. It is clear that South Africa has many of the characteristics of a developing economy, with its heavy dependence on exports of primary products and imports of capital goods, uneven distribution of income and high levels of unemployment. The major effort to restructure the economy which is now going on and the movement towards a more democratic political system should also help to ensure a sympathetic reception for claims to preferential treatment. However, some sectors of the South African economy are highly competitive. It also has a first-rate infrastructure and strong financial and educational institutions. There might therefore be some debate in Geneva about a decision by South Africa to reclassify itself as a developing country. There has been disagreement in the past as to whether South Africa, when consulting in the Balance-of-Payments Committee, should do so under Article XII, as a developed country, or under Article XVIII, as a developing country. (The most important difference here is that in the case of a developed country there is a basic assumption that balance-of-payments problems are a short-term phenomenon and there is pressure to liberalise or remove trade restrictions necessitated by them as quickly as possible; in the case of developing countries it is accepted that there may be 'structural' or long-term balance-of-payments problems, and this has been held to justify long-term reliance on trade restrictions – sometimes for many years. In recent years there has been less willingness on the part of developed countries to accept such long-term restrictions as being consistent with Article XVIII or in the interests of the country applying them.) The same question may arise again in July, when South Africa has agreed to consult the Committee on the import surcharge. The Committee's request for consultations on the surcharge, which was introduced as long ago as 1985, is itself an indication of closer interest in South African trade policy. The draft agreement on the GATT balance-of-payments provisions which was negotiated in the Round will tighten the procedures in some respects, for both developed and developing countries. The main differences are procedural rather than substantive: for developing countries consultations normally take place every two years instead of every year, and the Committee may agree to simplified consultations with developing countries which are liberalising their trade regimes.

In general there are signs of an increasingly critical or demanding attitude on the part of developed countries: in this Round for the first time they have insisted that developing countries should make a substantial contribution to the tariff negotiations, in the form of tariff reductions and bindings; and the European Community has announced that it will not treat Hong Kong, Singapore and South Korea as developing countries in its implementation of the results of the Round.

There is also more doubt than at any time in the past about the value of the 'special and differential' treatment which has been accorded to developing countries. By failing to liberalise their tariff structures in earlier GATT rounds and because in other ways they have shielded themselves from the stimulus of competition, many developing countries in the past cut themselves off from the main benefits of GATT membership – which are not just better access to foreign markets but, even more, the effects of competition and stable trade policies on the efficiency of their own economy. They have also made it easier for the developed world to justify discrimination against them, as in the textiles sector. This has been recognised by many developing countries during the 1980s: it is striking that many developing and East European countries – and others like Australia and New Zealand – have liberalised unilaterally during the Uruguay Round. The recent experience of many countries in South-east Asia and Latin America shows that trade liberalisation, if combined with sensible macroeconomic policies, leads to a stronger and more competitive economy. In this respect South Africa has been, until recently, something of an exception to the general trend towards liberalisation. Policies directed towards import substitution and self-sufficiency, aggravated by resource problems due to apartheid and sanctions, have shielded local industry from necessary competition and perpetuated a high-cost production structure. As always, such distortions make a crisis of the inevitable adjustment – the more severe the longer the distortions persist. South Africa's economy has many highly competitive sectors, but also many which have been heavily protected. If the future prosperity of the economy depends on the ability to export to world markets, these sectors too will have to become internationally competitive, and the only way to do that is to compete. It would not necessarily be in the country's best interests if recognition as a developing country encouraged it to go on shielding the manufacturing sector from the facts of life.

This being said, the most important elements of special treatment for developing countries in the draft Final Act are of two kinds: first, time-limited derogations or longer transition periods for implementing the new obligations, and second, more favourable thresholds in certain areas (such as lower rates of tariff and subsidy reduction in agriculture). One example of an extended transition period which might be of particular interest in South Africa is found in the draft agreement on Investment Measures. This requires local content requirements, which I understand are applied to foreign investments in some sectors of South African industry, to be eliminated within two years by developed countries but within five years by developing countries. This period may be extended upon request, if there is a consensus to do so. In the same way, the TRIPs agreement grants developing countries five years instead of one in which to bring their law into conformity with the new obligations, the agreement on subsidies provides them with eight years in which to phase out export subsidies, and the agriculture text would enable them to implement their reduction commitments over ten years, as compared with six years for developed countries. The safeguards agreement would permit developing countries to maintain safeguard measures for up to two years beyond the general maximum period of eight years.

Some of the draft agreements provide greater flexibility for developing countries in the substantive rules themselves, not merely in the timing of their application. I have mentioned that the agriculture agreement would permit lower rates of tariff and subsidy reduction for developing countries, provided that they amount to not less than two-thirds of the reductions required of developed countries. There are certain other elements of special flexibility for developing countries in the agriculture text. Developing countries with small market shares will also be accorded some shelter against countervailing and safeguard measures and meaningful improvements in market access for textiles and clothing. Several agreements require special attention to be given to the needs of developing countries whenever action is taken, and four call for the provision of technical assistance to them.

Notwithstanding all this, the fact remains that the new GATT will be a far more unified system, in which disparities between the obligations of developed and developing countries will be less significant.

I ought not to talk as if the implementation of the Uruguay Round will create hindrances in the making of South African trade policy. Market disciplines are not an imposition or a cost. Even when trade sanctions were in full application the major economic problems of South Africa were not problems of access to export markets but internal – the heavy concentration of subsidies and export incentives on capital-intensive industries, the relatively small size and high costs of the protected manufacturing sector, and the high level of unemployment. The government is already acting to correct some of these structural distortions by moving towards more market-oriented policies; it is right to do so and would be right whatever the outcome of the Uruguay Round, but there is no doubt that open and predictable world markets would greatly ease the strains that always accompany major restructuring.

It should also be stressed that a stable trade and tariff policy is badly needed by business for domestic reasons. A tariff increase intended to protect one industry is always a tax on the inputs needed by another. When these changes are frequent and unpredictable, as they have been at some periods in South Africa's recent history, they make long-term planning impossible. At present, less than one-fifth of South Africa's tariffs are bound in GATT, and the tariff structure, with about 12 600 tariff lines, is very complex. When you take into account the formula duties which in many sectors have replaced import controls and now apply to nearly a third of the tariff, and add to that the import surcharge which can add up to 40% to the cost of individual imports, the burden of tariff protection, in terms of uncertainty and import costs, is very high. As a former civil servant of a national government, I can say that one of the greatest benefits of GATT membership is that ministers tempted by a foolish or self-destructive trade measure can sometimes be told that a GATT obligation makes it impossible. Tariff bindings, which are GATT obligations, perform the same function when industry lobbies come looking for protection in the form of a tax on some other industry's inputs.

The way forward for South Africa's economy is clearly through reintegration with the world economy, from which it has been isolated by sanctions and by its own policies of import substitution. The GATT is the only legal framework within which that integration can be secured. South Africa's current move towards liberalisation of tariffs and import controls will strengthen its position in the GATT and increase the benefits it derives from GATT membership. It is easy to foresee the time when South Africa will play an important role in the GATT as a powerful and influential voice for the interests of Africa, helping to make policy rather than merely living with the consequences of decisions made by others.

12

The Impact of the Bretton Woods Institutions on the Prospects for Development

JOHN WILLIAMSON

We live in an age of hope, not least because of the extraordinary political developments in South Africa. The last time the world experienced a similar surge of hope was in the closing days of World War II, as the Allies (as they still were) laid plans for postwar institutions capable of preventing a repetition of the disasters of the 1930s. My subject is the impact of two of those institutions, the International Monetary Fund (IMF) and the World Bank, on the prospects for achieving economic development.

Both the IMF and the World Bank were created at a conference held at Bretton Woods (New Hampshire) in July 1944. The IMF, or Fund, was supposed to supervise the international monetary system and supplement the supply of international liquidity. The World Bank was supposed to provide a supply of long-term loans to replace the international capital market which had collapsed in the 1930s, and whose revival was not anticipated by the postwar planners.

The chapter starts by sketching the evolution of the 'Bretton Woods twins'. It proceeds to discuss the conditionality associated with borrowing from them and concludes by brief reflections on the possibility of South Africa undertaking such borrowing.

Evolution

After an early period of postwar reconstruction in which the IMF was marginalised by the Marshall Plan, the Fund came into its own in the late 1950s and functioned more or less as intended until the United States closed the gold window in 1971. At that point the IMF largely lost its systemic role, which was in due course – after a rather unsuccessful attempt to get by with *laissez-faire* macro-economic policies – picked up by the Group of Seven. Instead of being the centre of the international monetary system the IMF has become the adviser of and lender to non-industrial countries with macro-economic problems (no industrial country has borrowed from the Fund since 1977 and none seems likely to do so in the future).

This lending is subject to conditionality, i.e. to a set of conditions. This is not at all how Keynes had planned that the Fund would operate or how most countries thought they had agreed at Bretton Woods that it would operate, which was for countries to have the *right* to make quite sizeable unconditional draw-ings. However, the United States insisted that Fund lending would be condi-tional, and since in the 1950s they were almost the world's only creditor, they were in a position to get their way. The principle of conditionality, unlike the practice (to which I return in the next section), has long ago become uncontro-versial. Indeed, not only is IMF conditionality now essential in order to borrow from the Fund, but it is also a key requirement for rescheduling debt.

The official name for the World Bank is the International Bank for Recon-struction and Development, and in its early years its activities were focused primarily on reconstruction rather than development. It was only in the second half of the 1950s, as postwar reconstruction was being completed, that the Bank's loans to developing countries came to exceed those to developed coun-tries. Another sign of its re-orientation toward an exclusive focus on develop-ment was the creation of an agency within the World Bank group to give soft loans to low-income countries: the International Development Association (IDA) was created in 1960.

Another dimension of the Bank's evolution concerns the types of projects that its loans have been used to finance. It started off with an overwhelming emphasis on financing infrastructure projects, primarily in transport and power, but developed a profound concern with social issues (basic needs and income distribution) under Robert McNamara's presidency in the 1970s, resulting in loans to a much wider array of projects in fields like agriculture, education, health and population control. The conservative ascendancy in most of the major industrial countries in the 1980s was reflected in an enhanced emphasis on private sector development, and hence with increased influence for the International Finance Corporation (the World Bank group's instrument for lending to the private sector), as well as with the emergence of structural adjust-ment lending in reaction to the recession at the beginning of the decade. In the last few years the Bank has, at last, begun paying serious attention to environ-mental issues, as well as to enhancing the role of women in development. In each case these innovations were introduced in addition to, rather than in place of, the previous priorities. The most important change in the Bank's position arose not from its own actions, however, but from the fact that the initial sup-position that had motivated its creation was in due course confounded by events. The international capital market that had collapsed in the 1930s and been assumed dead and buried at the time of Bretton Woods sprang back to life as the postwar boom unfolded. Direct investment emerged in the 1950s, the Eurodollar market developed in the 1960s, recycling was the buzzword of the 1970s and globalisation of capital markets occurred in the 1980s. By the 1990s the flow of lending by the multilateral development banks, including the World Bank, is just a small part of the vast diversified pool of finance potentially avail-able to a country that wants to tap the international capital market in order to supplement its domestic savings.

The Bank's creation of structural adjustment loans (SALs) in the early 1980s led it into forms of conditionality somewhat similar to those of the Fund. Since conditionality is the area in which conflicts between the Bretton Woods twins

and their developing country members are most acute, it is worth more extensive discussion.

Conditionality

The Fund's conditionality is typically short-term and macro-economic in
nature and oriented toward reducing inflation and improving the balance of
payments so as to provide the basis for a resumption of growth. The IMF is generally called in where a country runs into acute payments problems, since it is in
that circumstance that a country needs the borrowing facilities that the Fund has
at its disposal. Controls and restrictions may suppress a payments deficit, but the
distortions they introduce make this a most undesirable policy weapon, which is
for this reason resisted by the Fund. Supply-side measures may be able to help in
the longer term, but it is unrealistic to think that they can normally address a
crisis situation. Hence the short-run solutions to a payments problem are limited
to some combination of devaluation and deflation, which is almost always what
the IMF prescribes. That is not a result of the institution's dogmatism, as critics
seem to assume, but of the fact that similar afflictions demand similar remedies.
There should of course be variation in the combination and dosage to reflect
differing circumstances (and it is my impression that there is indeed variety at
this level of detail).

Figure 12.1 shows a stylised (but empirically based) representation of a typical
adjustment programme drawn from a recent study by Michael Bruno (1993).

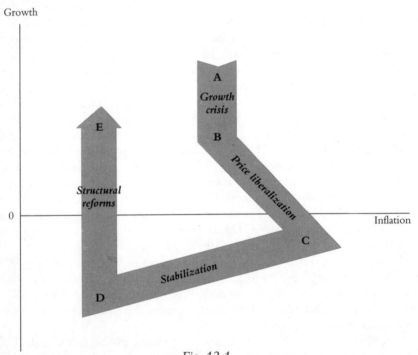

Fig. 12.1.
Stylised representation of crisis, adjustment and reform in Eastern Europe

The country is initially growing reasonably fast, with an acceptable inflation rate, at point A. It then runs into a payments crisis, perhaps because of an adverse foreign shock or perhaps because of an attempt to grow faster than its supply side is capable of sustaining. The first reaction is to cut imports by controls or deflation: growth falls to point B without doing much for the balance of payments (perhaps because by now capital is fleeing). The IMF is called in and prescribes its standard remedies of deflation and devaluation, the initial impact of which is to make things worse rather than better as inflation rises and growth falls (point C). But if the country persists it will eventually succeed in stabilising (point D), thus permitting revival and a return to growth (point E).

The Bank's policy prescriptions are less standardised than those of the Fund, but there are nonetheless some fairly strong regularities. It too preaches macroeconomic discipline (fiscal rectitude and monetary discipline), but most of its work focuses on micro-economics and the supply side. It describes the policies it advocates as 'market-friendly', meaning that one should seek to use markets rather than suppress them, while recognising a potential role for state action in supporting markets rather than assuming automatically that markets work better the less the government is involved. (Financial liberalisation provides a nice example: much evidence now shows that the efficiency of investment is indeed enhanced if the credit market is liberalised to the point where credit is rationed by price rather than by personal acquaintance or arbitrary administrative fiat, but such liberalisation is likely to be a disaster if the state simply withdraws without ensuring the presence of strong prudential supervision.) The Bank is also a strong advocate of outward-oriented policies rather than of import substitution, and supports trade liberalisation programmes designed to further the switch from the latter to the former.

The policies of competitive exchange rates, macro-economic discipline, market friendliness and outward orientation prescribed by Fund and Bank are in my view exactly what any government with a decent concern for the long-run welfare of its citizens should itself be seeking to promote. But everyone knows that countries fear the 'harsh conditionality' that is 'imposed' on them by the Bretton Woods twins. How can we explain the paradox that there is such resentment at being lent money to do what is in one's own interest? Let me suggest three reasons.

(1) Quite often the resentment against the 'harsh conditionality' of the Fund (in particular) is a case of blaming the messenger who brings bad news. And, as Figure 12.1 demonstrates, the initial impact of an IMF programme is typically to make things worse rather than better. Obviously this provides an opportunity to unscrupulous politicians to cast the IMF as a scapegoat (a role that in fact the Fund more or less accepted until Michel Camdessus became Managing Director).

(2) Some governments do not share the agenda of the Bretton Woods institutions, but still hanker after policies that are populist, inward-oriented, statist or dirigiste. It is difficult for Fund and Bank to work harmoniously with governments that have such different visions of what constitutes good economic policy. I suspect that in these circumstances the Fund and Bank feel (though

they obviously cannot be expected to say so out loud) that the most useful thing they can realistically hope to be able to do is to get the government somewhat off the back of its subjects. Naturally such a government will feel that it is having conditionality imposed upon it.

(3) However, I do not believe that all the resentment against the Bretton Woods institutions can be explained in terms of simply too many anecdotes of governments and individual public servants who share the vision of good economic policy with the Washington institutions but who end up with bitter stories about the way that they were treated. There is no accepted explanation of this phenomenon, but I would advance two somewhat speculative hypotheses. One is that too many of the employees in these two institutions are recruited straight out of graduate school and do not have the professional experience that would serve to temper the arrogance that it is easy to acquire in an elite environment. The other is that professional advancement is rarely furthered by following the ideal (but usually fictional) process for designing a programme, where the government draws up its own programme and the Fund or Bank comes in and endorses it with minimal change. It is all too easy to believe that a mission leader who can boast of having cut the government's planned budget deficit by an extra 5% of GDP will get ahead faster than one who simply says that he endorsed everything the government was proposing.

Even if my hypotheses are correct in identifying two of the warts of the Bretton Woods institutions, they should not blind us to the fact that those institutions are fundamentally allies to be exploited rather than enemies to be fought.

Prospects for South African borrowing

Let me conclude by saying a few words about the wisdom and likelihood of South Africa borrowing from the Fund and Bank. I offer you three propositions for consideration.

The first is that you should not count on the IMF as a source of finance. It may be necessary to get an IMF programme in order to qualify for debt rescheduling, but apart from the Enhanced Structural Adjustment Facility (which South Africa cannot draw on because its per capita income is too high), IMF money is available only to meet emergencies and not to promote development. Policy should be designed to try to avoid the type of emergency that would justify resorting to the IMF.

The second proposition concerns the possibility that South Africa might be ineligible to borrow from the Bank on account of a relatively high per capita income (Padayachee, 1992). It is true that per capita income is much too high for South Africa to be eligible to borrow from the Bank's soft-loan window (IDA), but so far as the Bank itself is concerned it seems that such fears are groundless. The Bank has a number of other member countries with comparable or higher per capita incomes – in Eastern Europe, South Korea or Venezuela, for example – that are currently borrowing from it.

The third proposition is to caution against expecting too much from the Bretton Woods institutions, or indeed from the international capital market in general. Foreign savings can be of critical importance in helping a country to emerge from a crisis situation, and in moderation they can be a useful regular supplement to domestic savings, which can allow development to progress somewhat faster than would otherwise be possible. But excessive foreign borrowing may well have caused more grief over the years than the good that has been done by prudent foreign borrowing, and unfortunately experience suggests that countries cannot rely on the international capital market to limit their lending to what is prudent. A developing country should, accordingly, plan to be largely self-reliant in terms of savings, tapping foreign funds only to allow a marginal increase in investment rather than to carry the main burden.

13

Development Implications for South Africa of Using IMF and World Bank Loans and Resources[1]

VISHNU PADAYACHEE

The question of financing the reconstruction of the South African economy remains one of the central concerns for those involved in the debate about economic policies for a post-apartheid era. Although differences exist regarding the relative contributions of domestic and foreign sources of financing this reconstruction, few believe that South Africa will be able, or should attempt, to manage this reconstruction without recourse to some foreign sources of funds – whether from private international banks or multilateral lending agencies such as the International Monetary Fund (IMF) and the World Bank.[2]

Both the IMF and the World Bank are well known for imposing conditions on some of their loans and credits. These conditions have tended to have a negative impact on some segments of society and on a country's overall growth and development strategy. The question of whether South Africa can obtain such financial assistance without surrendering control over key aspects of its development strategy and economic policies becomes crucial. This chapter attempts to examine this issue. It begins with an overview of the origins and development philosophies of these international financial institutions. This is followed by a summary of the nature and character of apartheid South Africa's relationship with these agencies since World War II. An evaluation of South Africa's own strengths and bargaining position *vis-à-vis* the Fund and the Bank is then undertaken, and this is followed by a brief discussion of Bank and Fund activity in South Africa since February 1990. The final section attempts to come to some conclusion, in the light of the preceding analysis, about the kind of approach post–apartheid South Africa would be advised to adopt in relation to the IMF and the World Bank.

The origins and development philosophy of the IMF and the World Bank

The IMF and the World Bank are the two key public financial institutions in the world economy. Both organisations were planned as specialised agencies within the United Nations system at the UN Monetary and Financial Conference at Bretton Woods in 1944.

The International Monetary Fund

The IMF's primary aim is to facilitate the growth of world trade, which it regards as crucial to the generation and maintenance of high levels of employment and income in member countries. The major instrument through which the Fund attempts to achieve this objective is loans to members who experience short-term balance of payments difficulties.

Despite its long history it was only in the 1970s, upon the demise of the dollar-exchange system established at Bretton Woods, that the IMF came to the forefront of public attention. As the postwar mode of regulating the world economy collapsed, problems of accumulation overtook both developed and developing countries, and many countries faced with rising costs for energy imports and falling prices for their commodity exports were forced to turn to the IMF for financial assistance. In many instances this assistance was provided after a stabilisation programme satisfactory to the IMF was agreed upon. Such a programme often dramatically altered the national economic priorities and strategies of borrowing countries.

The influence and weight of the IMF derives not from the fact that it lends much, but because the granting of its pilot loans to a developing country is the key that can open the door to the private international bank loans and bilateral aid-grants that most developing countries need to stay afloat. That seal of approval, as it were, is in general given to countries prepared to accept changes in their economic policy which the IMF demands. As borrowing reaches the higher levels of credit tranches, so conditionality (the policy changes the Fund demands as a precondition for lending) increases (see Padayachee and Goldin, 1992).

The Fund's criteria for granting this approval invariably include a fairly uniform set of market-oriented prescriptions: opposition to most forms of state intervention such as import controls, as well as to exchange and price control and to consumer subsidies. Significantly the Fund is usually not opposed to wage control. The Fund also favours a reduction in domestic demand and especially in government spending, and an increase in exports (usually through currency devaluation). Its focus invariably lies in adjusting economic policy to maintain external balances, rather than promoting national development, and it has tended to view external imbalances as being a temporary condition, rather than a manifestation of a deeper structural problem.

Despite unhappiness with IMF prescriptions (and the occasional attempt to challenge them),[3] many developing countries have had little choice, given their integration into networks of world trade and investment and the limited, virtually non-existent sources of alternative credit, but to retain a relationship with the IMF. However, while most borrowing countries have little choice but to go along with IMF conditions, the benefits of such associations are dubious, to say the least. It is far from clear that the Fund's objectives have been facilitated by its method of operation – in particular the austerity programme that is the usual precondition for loans or access to private loans. On the contrary, as Knuper observes,

> mass unemployment, pauperization and inflation are frequently the
> consequences of such austerity programmes. Moreover, there has so far
> been no indication that these negative consequences are merely the trade-

off for a long-term economic recovery: not one of the countries included in the IMF programmes can be cited as proof for the postulate that employment levels and real incomes rise following a preceding phase of 'purging' austerity. (Knuper, 1983:43)

IMF financial assistance therefore is hardly renowned for its success – except (as some would argue) if one views this from the perspective of Western interests and those national states who use the IMF adjustment programmes as a justification for rationalisation, cutting social programmes, pushing down wage rates and similar anti-working-class austerity measures. This point must not be lost sight of. At the level of domestic politics it is often convenient to make the IMF the scapegoat for austerity. As Lipietz notes, 'everyone – including the left – admits in private that the irresponsibility of ... local leaders [sometimes makes] austerity inevitable' (Lipietz, 1987:176).

The IMF has not been entirely successful in adjusting to the very changed circumstances of the post-1970 international economy. Buira (1983:117) has argued that the IMF entered the 1980s 'equipped with a set of intellectual techniques and practices intended for and inherited from the very different international economic environment of the Bretton Woods system'. This is most apparent in the areas of exchange rate co-ordination, the control of international bank lending, balance of payments adjustment and the adequacy of its lending.[4]

Thus, for example, the Fund has not been able to achieve symmetry between members with deficits and those with surpluses, nor between developing and developed countries, and in general its influence over the policies of the major industrialised countries is non-existent.

Some have argued that the Fund has in recent years attempted to respond to past criticisms. In a recent briefing paper the Overseas Development Institute (ODI) points out that it has 'become somewhat more sensitive to the potential social harmfulness of its programmes ... it has found ways of providing soft, medium term finance to low income members...'[5] The ODI nevertheless continues by observing that 'High failure rates and a paucity of "success stories" leave particular questions about the Fund's ability to operate successfully in African and other low income countries' (ODI, 1983).

The World Bank

The World Bank began its formal operations in June 1946 and made its first loans (all to Western European countries) in 1947. Unlike the IMF, which mainly provides short-term balance of payments assistance, the purpose of the Bank is to provide longer-term multilateral development aid for particular projects, some of which are made on a commercial basis. Despite popular belief in some quarters, the Bank has generally proven to be a tougher, harder lender than many commercial lending institutions.[6]

The Bank actually is made up of a group of banks, including the bank itself (now usually referred to as the IBRD), the International Finance Corporation (IFC) and the International Development Agency (IDA). The World Bank is governed in much the same way as the IMF and is dominated by the most powerful industrialised countries, particularly the USA.

The overall economic philosophy of the Bank is not dissimilar to the market-oriented approach of the IMF. Robert Ayres has referred to this ideology as that of 'neo-liberalism'. The principal objective of this approach is economic growth, and one major route to this growth is through export expansion and diversification and trade liberalisation. Other supporting ingredients of this approach include monetary and fiscal restraint, removing obstacles to the free operation of market forces, a sound currency, external economic equilibrium and a favourable investment climate. 'Deviations from any of these elements constitute deviations from prevalent Bank norms and are likely to be the subject of [a] country dialogue between the Bank and the deviating country' (Ayres, 1983:74). The anti-poverty, basic needs and redistributional emphasis of the McNamara years posed only a minor challenge to this prevalent ideology.

In the late 1970s the World Bank regarded its role increasingly as being only supportive and reinforcing of the lending activities of the private international banks, which dominated global lending from the early 1970s to around 1982.

One of the clearest and most disturbing recent developments in the Bank's operations has been a shift from individual project finance to programme and sector lending. The first of this new type of lending is referred to as 'structural adjustment loans' (SALs). The Bank has always attached conditions to its loans, but these used to relate directly to the projects that were being funded. By the 1980s the Bank sought to secure leverage over a far wider range of economic policies as a precondition for its phased disbursements to borrowers. The Bank uses this power to force borrowers to adopt policies which would bring into play the 'magic of the markets' (Pratt, 1983:65). These loans are also generally only secured if the potential borrower agrees to sign a stand-by loan with the IMF, in terms of which the country's policies are additionally 'supervised' by the Fund.

The Bank's structural adjustment loans were recently complemented by a second policy-based loan, the so-called sector adjustment loans (SECALs) which concentrate on specific sectors of the economy. A steel sector loan may not necessarily (if so chosen by the borrower) be directed at investments in the steel industry at all. It may be used to bolster a sinking currency, pay foreign debt or allow the private sector to pay for imports. The Bank may, however, insist as a precondition that the government sell its nationalised steel mills to the private sector – it would in that sense be a steel sector loan. These two programmes grew rapidly in the 1980s and by the end of the decade accounted for 36% of all Bank lending. (Cypher, 1989).

As the late 1980s approached, Western agencies, including the World Bank, have also come to place political preconditions for loans and credits. Foreign finance is in some cases being provided only if borrowing countries also embark on, and set up, Western-style multi-party democratic forms of government.

Although the costs associated with World Bank loans have therefore increased in all these ways, many developing countries still find it necessary to use them, as alternative sources of finance dried up following the global debt crisis and as the demand for external assistance increased dramatically after 1989.

In general, like IMF loans, World Bank financial assistance is not noted for its successes. A recent internal Bank report observed that some one-third of World Bank projects of all kinds are a 'complete failure'. The report went on to note that because Bank success is measured by the number of projects, not enough attention is paid to the effectiveness of loans in promoting development. This odd measure of success has led the Bank to allow some countries to flout conditions or renegotiate conditionality rather than act in a way which could terminate the project – the need to keep up the number of on-going projects being crucial.[7]

The *Financial Times* of London (13 August 1990) has observed that there are growing doubts that the Bank's 'model patients' are in fact going to recover. After more than seven years of external assistance running at an annual rate of about $500m, Ghana, for example, is still a long way from passing the test: can growth be sustained without substantial aid? While acknowledging the 'success' of the Ghana structural adjustment programme to date, Loxley casts doubts on the sustainability and replicability of the Ghana model. And he argues that Ghana's 'success' may have as much to do with other structural features of the economy, including conditions of world commodity markets, extent of capital inflows, climatic factors, etc., as on the World Bank programme itself.

While retaining its fundamental support for market-oriented solutions the Bank appears, in the wake of recent developments in Eastern Europe and in reaction to the crisis in certain regions (sub-Saharan Africa, for example), to have shifted back marginally towards an approach to development that appears to acknowledge the benefits of some interventionist policies and some direct role for the state and state-owned enterprises (though not in goods-producing and non-infrastructural sectors). It appears to have accepted that adjustments in areas such as exchange rate policy and other key prices should be more carefully managed in regard to timing, pace and scope in order to avoid disruptions, and to have recognised the negative impact of some of its prescriptions on certain segments of society.

Its 1989 report on sub-Saharan Africa sets out a 'range of proposals aimed at empowering ordinary people, and especially women, to take greater responsibility for improving their lives' and stresses a human-centred development strategy in which the social costs of economic adjustment should be recognised and measures taken to alleviate such costs. It has been argued, however, even within Bank circles that the Bank's response to this recognition has been to create a 'safety-net addendum' rather than a fundamental restructuring of the integral elements of its programmes.[8]

Its support for democratic reform and 'good governance' as necessary conditions for effective development is welcome. However, the Bank has 'perfected the art of bureaucratic impenetrability' and 'it does not seem unreasonable to suggest that a more open and accountable style of decision-making is just as likely to lead to better policies emerging from the Bank as from African governments' (Parfitt, 1993:102).

The Bank's 1990 report on Poverty is also replete with interventionist, even redistributionist rhetoric. This report observes that it is possible 'to shift public spending in favour of the poor'; acknowledges that large-scale land redistribution 'has sometimes been successful' (in Japan and South Korea); supports the argument for 'public spending for agricultural research and for dissemination of new technologies in small-scale production'; and notes that in many countries 'government subsidies to develop and improve low-return farming activities may be the only way to reduce poverty in these regions' (*Finance Week,* 11–17 October, 1990).

Preliminary reports on a Bank study of the 'Asian miracle' economies of Japan, South Korea, Taiwan, Hong Kong and Singapore suggest optimistically that a new paradigm for development may be on the Bank's drawing board for the 1990s. One of the authors of the study is quoted as saying that 'the economic policy arsenal has many more weapons than we suspected' and the Bank's senior economist for East Asia comments that the lesson from the Asian experience is that 'you need a government guiding hand; you cannot just abdicate development to the private sector'.[9]

Most progressive commentators argue that these changes at the Bank are minimal and that the essence of the Bank's structural adjustment programmes remains firmly in place. As Parfitt suggests, however, progressive forces should utilise these spaces created by the Bank's concessions in order to 'try to move aid donors such as the World Bank in the direction of a development strategy based on a process of economic diversification in which the necessary role of the state is acknowledged and supported' (Parfitt, 1993:106).

The IMF and World Bank in postwar South Africa

The International Monetary Fund

Since 1980 the IMF has classified South Africa as a 'non-oil, developing country'. Within this category South Africa is placed in a sub-group of 10 countries classified as 'major exporters of manufactures'. South Africa's share of IMF purchases and drawings, as compared to other countries in this sub-group, amounted to 10,16% of all purchases and drawings between 1947 and 1985. It has in that time drawn more from the Fund than Greece, Malaysia, Israel and Portugal, but not more than Brazil and Argentina (both of whose debt problems led to large borrowings since 1983), South Korea and Yugoslavia.

South Africa received its first loan from the IMF in 1957/58. Like the UK's standbys of 1957 and 1958 these arrangements were agreed to without conditionality or phased disbursals, which even in those early formative years of IMF lending were being imposed on other borrowers, most notably the Latin Americans (Gisselquist, 1981). This example typifies the rather cosy relationship which characterised SA–IMF dealings throughout most of the postwar period.

The IMF provided South Africa with credits of SDR 91,2m in 1975, SDR 390m in 1976 and SDR 162m in 1977. These mid-1970s borrowings were, according to South African and IMF sources, in support of the South African government programme to strengthen the country's balance of payments position.[10] In 1981, with the gold price declining sharply and imports surging, South Africa once again ran up a deficit on the current account of the balance of payments in the order of a massive $4380m. By mid-1982 South

Africa approached the IMF for a standby loan of $1,1 billion.[11] In this period IMF support for South Africa, I would argue, rested upon the strategic and economic role which South Africa had over decades come to play within Southern Africa and in the world economy. As long as the apartheid state retained its capacity to perform this historically important role, the IMF sloughed off criticisms of its support for what came increasingly to be seen as a morally reprehensible political regime. This capacity in turn rested on the maintenance of political stability in South Africa and on an economic performance sufficiently robust to ensure the profitability of foreign investment and to minimise the probability of revolutionary change in South and Southern Africa arising out of the ashes of a collapsing economic order.

The role of any particular country within the world economic system is not immutable, however, and the growing fear of political upheaval and economic degeneration in South Africa which set in from about 1976, but which escalated after the early 1980s, forced a reassessment by Western industrialised countries of their policy of continued unconditional support for the apartheid state.

Though by the end of 1982 South Africa's status and borrowing rights at the IMF remained secure, this 'special relationship' did not survive intact for much longer. A 1983 US law (the Gramm Amendment) requires that the US Executive Director at the IMF oppose loans to South Africa unless the Secretary of the Treasury certifies in person before the US Senate and House Banking Committees that the loan would 'reduce the distortions caused by apartheid'.[12]

The World Bank

South Africa is a founder member of the World Bank. The first World Bank mission visited South Africa in 1949–50 in order to undertake a survey of the economy and of investment opportunities.[13]

The country received large project loans from the World Bank in the 1950s and early 1960s (Ovenden and Cole, 1989). In 1951, for example, the Bank loaned $20m to the South African Railways and $30m to Eskom, in line with its emphasis at that time on public utility investments as a precondition for growth. These loans in the early 1950s were precursors of nearly 200 million dollars of World Bank loans during the decade, with more in the 1960s. Over the period 1946 to June 1967 South Africa received 11 loans totalling $241,8m from the IBRD. Seven of these loans were in support of the development of South Africa's transportation system and the remaining four were to Eskom for improvements and extensions to the electricity grid and network.

South Africa's loans from the bank far outstripped those received by any other African country in the period 1946–67. Only Nigeria came even close to matching the level of Bank support to South Africa. In fact the total value of South African loans compares favourably with those of Western European industrialised countries such as France and the Netherlands (Legassick, 1974).

The country has not qualified for some time for a loan from the Bank's concessionary IDA facility. In fact South Africa is now classified as a Part I country by the IDA, i.e. as a developed country, and therefore subscribes capital but cannot borrow from this facility.[14] This classification is made on the basis of

South Africa's per capita GNP (US\$ 2878 in 1990), which is higher than the cut-off guidelines set out by the Bank (US\$ 520 in 1989). South Africa has not received any project loans since the mid-1960s either, although the reasons for this are not entirely clear. A recent *Financial Times* report (25 May 1993) states that the 'World Bank stopped lending to South Africa when international sanctions were imposed against Pretoria's apartheid regime'. But when or where this decision was taken is not indicated.

Post-apartheid South Africa and the IMF and World Bank

Development strategy

The scope and nature of the IMF's and World Bank's involvement in post-apartheid South Africa will depend on a variety of external and internal factors: the state of and changes in the global political economy, South Africa's development strategy and the underlying strength of its macro-economic fundamentals, its ability to develop without running into serious and persistent balance of payments problems, its dependence upon external borrowing, its capacity to monitor and control its foreign debt, and so on.

The following discussion concentrates on the internal factors and in particular on the key aspect of post-apartheid South Africa's development strategy. I would argue that the development strategy of a post-apartheid South Africa should be based on a politically stable, unitary state playing a leading role (within a mixed economy approach) in addressing the long-term and structural problems of all South Africa's peoples, including the rural and urban poor and the working class. South Africa should attempt to maintain a national-centred orientation to development, yet one which is keenly attuned to regional and global realities, markets and opportunities, especially in the area of expanding selected manufactured exports.[15]

Such a strategy must include an emphasis on redistribution programmes to meet basic needs, and state intervention to restructure and diversify production and redirect flows of investment towards labour-intensive industries, and social and physical infrastructural investments in urban and rural areas.[16] Essential policy instruments for realising this strategy would include increasing state involvement in certain strategic and productive sectors (electricity, steel, housing), reduction in state spending on the military and on elements of the non-productive public sector, anti-trust and mergers policy, land reform, fiscal reform (e.g. abolishing VAT on basic foodstuffs) and appropriate industrial and trade policy aimed at protecting and promoting some domestic industry while also seeking to expand manufacturing production and exports in selected sectors.[17] The support of business, trade unions and other organs of civil society for such a strategy will be crucial. The growing consensus on the need for redistribution among most sectors within the economy bodes well for the eventual consolidation of such support.

The financing of the economic reconstruction should be principally based on domestic savings. Bell, for example, has argued that 'some estimates of our need for foreign capital to achieve high rates of growth are ... gross exaggerations', adding that 'rapidly growing economies have in fact depended relatively little on foreign capital, compared to domestic savings' (Bell, 1990). Although critical research has still to be focused on the question of the level and potential level of domestic savings, it would appear that such savings may not be as low as some believe. In a recent preliminary statistical study into savings, growth and redistribution, Neva Seidman Makgetla found that 'the central problem remains the translation of savings into investment, rather than low savings *per se*' (Makgetla, 1993). The task of a post-apartheid state would be to reduce existing leakages and to unlock these savings and channel them into appropriate employment-creating development projects and to introduce other schemes for raising the level of domestic savings.

The Fund's insistence on the need for financial discipline in the economic policy of post-apartheid South Africa is undisputed. It is important to understand the need for financial discipline and macro-economic balance and to accept that there will probably have to be 'painful adjustments in the structure of production' in order to achieve growth and to maintain a healthy balance of payments. As Loxley points out, 'programmes designed by governments themselves, which avoid the encroachment on national sovereignty implicit in programmes drawn up and imposed by the international institutions, cannot succeed if they fail to address the economic imbalances upon which Fund/Bank programmes focus, and if they do not map out a coherent longer-term alternative development strategy' (Loxley, 1990:26).

A post-apartheid South Africa will not be as vulnerable in dealing with the IMF and the World Bank as some other developing countries, especially those elsewhere in Africa, many of which entered into Fund and Bank programmes from a fundamentally weaker position (declining real incomes, mounting debts, low savings and investment ratios, a deteriorating physical and financial infrastructure, mounting current account deficits, declining agricultural output per capita, and less well-developed human resource expertise). South Africa has begun to experience some of these problems in recent years. However, it still possesses some significant advantages.

South Africa's bargaining position: advantages and problems

Firstly, although it has been reduced to a cliché of late and although recent changes in the global economy and in the state of the domestic economy have affected the situation, South Africa is not a typical 'Third World' country. The inherent and developed strengths of the economy are impressive, despite their racially based provision and distribution. These include its well-endowed natural resource base; its relatively strong productive base; its physical infrastructure (transport, electricity, etc.); its long-standing and (until recently) impeccable relationship with the IMF, World Bank and private bankers; and its advanced financial, banking, legal and communications network.

A second advantage relates to the country's present foreign debt situation. In 1985 foreign banks withdrew their roll-over facilities to the apartheid state. Since then there has been a dramatically reduced flow of new loan capital to South Africa. From the introduction of the first debt standstill agreement at the end of 1985 to the end of 1989 South Africa's foreign debt declined by $3,1 billion or by 13%. The country's debt to export ratio declined from 128% to 79% in this time, putting South Africa among developing countries with some of the lowest relative foreign debt burdens in the world. An IMF report listed only four developing countries with a lower foreign debt ratio. The others were all newly industrialising East and South-east Asian economies.[18]

These factors have led to a situation in which a post-apartheid state will have a relatively favourable foreign debt situation. The situation may be improved further if a democratic government succeeds in persuading international creditors to write off some portion of this 'apartheid debt'. This is a very advantageous position to be in, in negotiating the terms of foreign loans, including those from the World Bank group. However, this favourable situation should not tempt a democratic government to rush into foreign borrowing, just because some of it may be offered on easier terms than has been the case for more debt-ridden countries.

A third (potential) advantage lies in the 'Southern African' factor. A post-apartheid South Africa can play a crucial role in a mutually beneficial reconstruction and development programme for Southern Africa as a whole. As Rob Davies has argued, 'if a genuinely democratic and non-racial order were to emerge in South Africa, a possibility of [SADCC] co-operating with South Africa in the achievement of [common] goals would be opened up' (Davies, 1990:38).

A democratic government, working co-operatively with other countries in the region, can legitimately use this factor to its advantage in bargaining over the terms of foreign capital flows, especially in relation to the World Bank. Non-exploitative cross-border projects would be one way in which World Bank (and other) loans could be attracted to the benefit of all the residents of Southern Africa. With the increasing trend towards the regionalisation of 'global' economic relations, the democratic state, with the support of its neighbours, could press to secure a seat on the executive board of the IMF and World Bank, from which base it could begin to play a more influential role in shaping Fund and Bank policies and programmes for the benefit of regional economic development.

The IMF and World Bank have traditionally little or no interest in programmes of regional integration or co-operation (Isaksen, 1993). Therefore, the mechanisms for achieving this level of co-operation in the region would have to be thought through carefully, given that the international financial institutions deal with nation states on a bilateral basis.

A fourth advantage that a post-apartheid South Africa would have is its sophisticated cadre of skilled and experienced negotiators who are to be found in both the unions and the progressive political organisations. The experience gained in tough labour–capital negotiations since the early 1970s, and successes such as the labour–capital–state accord over amendments to the Labour Relations Act and current negotiations in the National Economic Forum, will be invaluable in dealing with the international financial institutions in a post-apartheid era. Trade unionists have also built up close ties with fellow unionists in other countries (including some in Africa), and these relationships should be developed and extended to include joint negotiations with the Fund and the Bank in certain areas. The existence of a core of progressive economists and social scientists who have over many years built up a close research-based relationship with the democratic movement will also be an important advantage in negotiations with the Bank and the Fund.

The Bank has recently made a commitment to involve more locals in the design and implementation of local Bank projects, and (in the words of Bank vice-president for Africa, Edward Jaycox) to encourage a 'sense of responsibility and ownership for projects and programmes by asking governments to tell us what they want, to design projects and programmes [that] are useful and then to come to us'. He also noted that at the 'root of development failure in Africa is a lack of human expertise and institutional effectiveness'.[19] A post-apartheid government will have an important advantage in these areas and will be able to turn to its local human resource expertise to help it in negotiations with the Bank and in assisting it with the design and implementation of Bank programmes, provided the Bank keeps to this latest commitment.

A fifth advantage for South Africa arises out of the enormous pressure that has been building up both within and outside the Bank about its role and lack of success in recent years, especially in sub-Saharan Africa. This has created uncertainties and divisions within the Bank, and now may be the time to exploit these differences (Stoneman, 1993). There are indications of some rethinking within the Bank about its approach to development in general and debates about the nature of its involvement in a democratic South Africa. Given its relative advantages South Africa appears to have been latched upon in some quarters as a possible success story in this part of the continent.[20]

But what are the prospects of significantly new foreign capital flows to South Africa from these and other sources? There is much speculation that a post-apartheid South Africa could expect a resumption of foreign capital inflows because of moral and political considerations – some form of 'Marshall Aid' programme for the reconstruction of the economy after apartheid, in much the same way that Western Europe was assisted in the wake of Nazi Germany's devastation of that region.

In its report on South Africa the IMF has observed that there has been 'considerable dismantling of the effective system of apartheid' and called for concerted action to 'raise the economy's access to domestic and foreign sources of savings'.[21] It was also reported that the World Bank affiliate, the IFC, was considering various schemes to finance black business ventures in South Africa.[22] All indications suggest that the World Bank is keen to resume a lending relationship with South Africa.

Nelson Mandela has recently called for Western support for South Africa's reclassification as a developing country.[23] He had hoped that the World Bank could be persuaded to take into account South Africa's racially skewed distribution of income in a way which would qualify it for (relatively cheaper) IDA Bank loans. However, while pledging some US$ 1m worth of development projects aimed at improving housing, health and education 'for South Africa's poor blacks', once a non-racial transitional government is in place, World Bank vice-president for Africa, Edward Jaycox, recently ruled out concessionary loans on the grounds of the country's 'relative wealth'.[24]

US Secretary of State Warren Christopher has announced that the Clinton administration has urged the 'World Bank and the parties in South Africa to begin planning now the projects that will lead to economic growth'. He expressed the hope that 'US business would be in the vanguard of investment in South Africa'.[25]

Despite these developments, it is important to warn against raising expectations about foreign capital inflows too high. For one thing, we must absorb the lesson learnt by other developing countries that foreign capital inflows are not unambiguous blessings and are not costless. Competition for global funds has also intensified. In this context no country should simply bank on foreign financial support, however morally strong its case may be.

South Africa's objective should be to finance as much of its economic reconstruction from domestic sources as possible. However, if judiciously used there is little doubt that appropriate forms of external finance can make an important contribution to growth.

World Bank and IMF activity in South Africa since February 1990

In order to arrive at some understanding of the extent to which these ideas and assessments about a possible South African development strategy, its bargaining position and the potential for foreign capital inflows coincide with or deviate from Bank and Fund thinking, it is necessary to look at the policy and discussion documents which the IMF and World Bank have drawn up on South Africa in the last few years. No attempt is made here to analyse these reports in detail. I shall do no more than make some general observations on Bank and Fund activity since 1990 and comment briefly on the reports that have been prepared in relation to the specific issues which have just been posed.

While the Bank has had little to do with South Africa since about 1967, the Fund has maintained a regular presence in this country through the 1970s and 1980s and has held annual consultations with the Department of Finance and the Reserve Bank. Since early 1990, however, the pace and regularity of IMF and World Bank visits has intensified and the nature and content of their work here has changed. One observer has noted that 'even by World Bank standards' the Bank's presence represents 'an unusually large research effort' and that, 'given their resources and access, [the Bank] will gather large amounts of material and arrive at potentially important, if not necessarily correct, conclusions.'[26] Both institutions have held consultations with a wide variety of interest groups, including labour and opposition political organisations, and both have produced major documents and reports, including (in some cases) recommendations for future economic policy.[27]

The first general point that needs to be made is that despite various newspaper reports to the contrary it would appear that no new funding or balance of payments support is being contemplated at the moment. At a meeting with UN agencies in May 1992 (at which the issue of socio-economic assistance to South

Africa was debated) these international agencies, including the World Bank, were informed by Cosatu and the ANC that there would be problems should formal agreements be reached and lending relations be resumed before, at the very least, an interim government is in place.[28] As Goldin correctly warns,

> The signing of a formal agreement with these institutions will have a direct impact and would bind a future government to policies agreed by its predecessor. For this reason there may well be an argument for delaying signature until a democratically elected government is in power, allowing it to control the full range of economic policies and enter into agreements which accord with its development priorities. (Goldin, 1992:24)

A second general point is to warn against the danger of accepting in an unquestioning way the comparative cases to which the Bank refers as exemplifying the success of its market-led approach to development. The Bank's early documents frequently made (positive) references to the Malaysian experience. An informed academic commentator on Malaysia has contested

> the Bank's representation of Malaysia as exemplifying a market-led strategy of growth and redistribution – if anything, Malaysia represents a case of heavy state intervention in key sectors. More generally, the Bank is making (neo-)liberal use of 'comparative models' as rhetorical devices that are invoked in an *ad hoc,* selective, and decontextualised fashion to legitimate particular policy positions. (Hart, 1992)

Thirdly, some significance should be attached to the fact that the Fund and the Bank have consulted fairly widely on their South Africa visits, with the ANC and Cosatu as well. It would appear that the Bank's and the Fund's view of entering discussions with trade unions has elsewhere, in general, been shaped by a view of unions 'as narrow self-interested bodies opposed to any policy formulation that conflicts with established interests'. The World Bank team which first visited South Africa in 1991 were, according to one observer, 'struck by the "national" orientation of the union movement' and appeared persuaded that 'these are powerful institutions who should be structurally engaged in the process of policy formulation'.[29] This kind of attitude can only facilitate the Bank's exposure to alternative development thinking, values and strategies as they set about rebuilding their relationship with this country.

We turn now to the IMF report 'Economic Policies for a New South Africa'. This study focused on the growth and redistribution policies needed in the new South Africa and looked at issues such as the poverty profile of the country, sources of savings, the composition of government expenditure, and the scope for more liberal trade and payment systems within the context of an outward-looking strategy. The report was well received by sections of business, as reflected in comments in the business sections of the daily and weekly press, and by the Reserve Bank, which has expressed the view that the report 'says all the right things'.[30]

In stressing the importance of fiscal discipline and the need to maintain macro-economic balance, the recommendations are not dissimilar to the ANC's interim economic policies. However it would appear that this is seen in the context of the usual IMF formula, rather than (like the ANC's ideas) within the context of a different developmental strategy. As Tjonneland observes, 'the basic message emerging from the IMF recommendation may be summed up as growth first and redistribution later' (1992:61). In their view economic growth will

> trickle down to the poor through employment growth and through an increase in government revenue, permitting greater social spending. The main problem with this prescription is that it underestimates the wide-spread distribution of poverty and lack of skills which limits access to formal employment. The result will be that while some may benefit marginally from economic growth resulting from the IMF recommendations, this will not be sufficient to change current income patterns and inequalities. (Tjonneland, 1992:61–2)

Finn Tarp commends the Fund for its efforts, but argues that the policies it proposes to address South Africa's problems are 'not very helpful'. He questions the Fund's premise that a contraction of public sector expenditure is a precondition for greater private savings and investment;[31] and criticises the Fund's analysis of the constraints on tax revenue for being too static, arguing that it takes no account of the impact of future growth on tax revenue. Overall he argues that

> It is, in fact, quite obvious that a re-orientation of fiscal spending priorities will be needed in South Africa … but one is left speculating whether the IMF would be prepared to impose conditionalities to ensure this takes place in reality… Fiscal moderation may well be advisable…, but rigid adherence to a standard IMF model to reach this conclusion is not the most convincing analytical route to follow given the complexity of the situation in South Africa.[32]

One of the most critical reviews of the IMF report is made by Patrick Bond. Bond charges that the report says 'nothing about the redistribution of investment away from the overtraded luxury consumer goods sector', ignores expanding budget options outside of taxation, and over-emphasises export orientation. In summary he argues that 'South Africa seems set to fall into that notorious IMF economic quicksand: blanket prescriptions for different diseases'.[33]

The IMF model is also criticised for its statistical limitations. Charles Meth argues that '…the IMF model for the economy cannot stand rigorous inspection… One reason is the Fund's uncritical reliance on government data. The IMF report is as unreliable as the poor data upon which it's based…'[34] While this may be true for now, we should not dismiss the potential which exists for the Fund and the Bank to use their huge resources and international experience to build up a statistical data base, information and analysis for the South African economy, which could be to the benefit of all.

The World Bank decided to concentrate its resources in the first year of its South African programme on four areas: macro-economic policy, employment prospects and their related implications, industrial policy with a special emphasis on employment generation, and public expenditure alternatives. Within this framework, which considers a wider set of social and economic development issues than the Fund's report, the Bank has produced a remarkably large number of working papers on South Africa already, including one on South African manufacturing and employment, another entitled an 'Economic Work Program on South Africa', and a series of preliminary papers and notes on education, small- and medium-scale black business development, agriculture and the rural economy, and electrification. Let us look at some of these earlier papers first.

The Bank's initial assessment of policy options to shift the economy in a way that 'is both poverty-reducing and sustainable' and addresses current inequities[35] represents a curious mix of the usual prescriptions and some interesting new ideas, even though these remain within the broader ambit of recent Bank thinking. The Bank's warning about increasing the size of the fiscal deficit, about the need to maintain good fiscal management in order to ensure macro-economic stability, etc., is well taken. Among the more familiar views it offers are opposition to an expansionary role for the state, especially in regard to fiscal instruments to stimulate demand, an outward-orientated strategy of development and a preference for maintaining 'an appropriately depreciated real exchange rate' in order to stimulate private investment and the expansion of non-gold exports.

The Bank clearly opposes nationalisation as a way to diversify the ownership of the means of production, suggesting instead that we look at the Malaysian experience of maintaining support for the role of the private sector, 'whilst using action in the capital market, essentially via a mutual fund, to expand ownership amongst the disadvantaged Malay population'.[36] It would be useful to learn from those who know more about this experiment, to what extent this was classic capital market action and what role the state played in retaining control over the transfer and management of these funds.

On a more encouraging note the Bank appears to favour the use of special employment programmes in the short to medium term as a means of generating additional employment, especially in areas where there exists labour surpluses. It calls for 'great priority' to be attached to improving the skills of disadvantaged groups and argues (although it notes that research needs to occur to clarify this further) that '...there continues to exist significant potential in the upmarket segments of labour demanding activities ... [and that] policy initiatives may be an important source of encouragement for South Africa's private sector to invest in the acquisition of competitive capability in labour – rather that capital-intensive sub-sectors of industry.'[37]

At the presentation of the Old Mutual–Nedcor scenario to the World Bank, Bank researchers criticised the scenario for its narrow focus on exports, suggesting an approach to industrial policy which focuses on the domestic market.[38]

Two further World Bank discussion papers, one on the macro-economy and the other on trade, were published in March 1993 (Fallon *et al.*, 1993 and Belli *et al.*, 1993). The Bank's framework in these papers remains located within a market-oriented 'growth with redistribution' approach, using the language and rhetoric of its more recently articulated and more sophisticated positions. I would therefore stop short of labelling them 'departures' from the Bank's development thinking.[39] Nevertheless, they do contain some interesting, and potentially progressive, proposals.

(1) The Bank advances the view that a judicious and targeted public sector investment related to infrastructural development to benefit the poor would be an important element of a growth strategy. The view expressed that such public sector investment may also stimulate private sector investment (crowding-in) is also notable. However, the Bank's warning that such investment should not put budgetary targets at risk by raising recurrent government expenditure seems to ignore inevitable interactions between capital and current expenditure, especially in education, health and related types of social spending.

(2) The Bank suggests that import liberalisation needs to occur gradually, that policies such as Export Processing Zones and the General Export Incentive Scheme may not offer the most productive ways of promoting exports, and that the system of import duties needs to be administered more efficiently and made more transparent.

(3) The Bank recommends the promotion of small-scale black agriculture and land reform. This is again a significant point, although it is not clear which land is being referred to. Will black farmers have to be resettled on more productive land as a precondition for success?

Other interesting recommendations relate to (a) skills upgrading for all levels of workers (although the moratorium on worker action suggested as a quid pro quo is rather naive in present circumstances) and (b) the maintenance for some period in the transition of exchange controls and the financial rand.

The papers fail to offer a view on other important issues such as industrial concentration, the informal sector, education and human resource development. It should also be remembered that the papers remain 'discussion papers' which do not yet have the status of 'policy'.

Despite these limitations and qualifications, and the need always to avoid over-optimism in assessing Bank and Fund proposals, the World Bank's views as expressed in these latest papers suggest that (at least in some areas) useful debate could be entered into between it and a democratic state which is committed to the kind of developmental strategy outlined earlier in this chapter. One may argue that the papers offer a more useful basis for a discussion of development in a post-apartheid era than those put forward by the current state (such as in its Normative Economic Model) or most sections of South African business.

Assessment and conclusion

The world economy has become highly interdependent in recent decades. Recent changes in the global economy have made the pursuance of strategies for disengagement and autarkic national development, so popular in the 1960s, virtually impossible today. For South Africa, with its historically open economy (exports and imports together make up over 50% of GDP), such strategies become even less feasible.

As Stuart Corbridge has pointed out, however, this integration of the capitalist world economy across national boundaries has not entirely rendered impossible the pursuance of economic strategies which are oriented towards national, domestic ends. He argues that nation states can still to some extent 'mould and change' events and that recent changes in the world economy have opened up opportunities for, as well as set limits or constraints on, national development. There is no need to slip into a politics of disengagement and despair (Corbridge, 1988).

It is, however, necessary to continue to point clearly and repeatedly to the dangers and costs of external financial assistance from the World Bank and others, in order that South Africans are not lulled into adopting too casual and lackadaisical an approach to these institutions; and because the experience of other developing countries, in Africa and elsewhere, has pointed to the real dangers of not having a coherent approach to such external borrowing.[40]

I would argue against a democratic South Africa 'disengaging' from the world economy and breaking with the IMF and the World Bank, despite recent calls from such notable economists of Third World countries as Samir Amin for 'delinking, turning the economy inward to ensure that the democratisation process is thoroughgoing and not just cosmetic'.[41] If by this Amin means that the principal aim of our development strategy should be a nationally oriented one and not *primarily* an outward-looking one (the 'dream of global competitiveness') and that attention should be directed at improving external economic relations of a South–South variety, then I would be in total agreement. His point about the need for the gradual restructuring of productive industry 'to achieve changes associated with the redistribution of income' is entirely correct.

But if Amin means that South Africa must spurn all and any possibilities for utilising financial assistance from the Fund, the Bank or other sources in industrialised countries or ignore the potential to selectively diversify exports beyond the existing primary product base, then I would be less enthusiastic about his proposal. Are these really mutually exclusive options within the context of a development strategy implemented and monitored by a strong unitary state, appropriately incorporating wider social forces?

Amin's warning about the dangers of turning the economy outward is an important one for us to reflect upon, but it would be useful if he would clarify his usage of the term 'delinking'. Clearly the middle-path option I am suggesting is less precise, more murky and in need of very careful analysis, but I would argue (for the reasons I have already advanced) that it is in this terrain, regrettably, that we have to fight in order to achieve the objectives which Amin correctly identifies.

The essence of the approach suggested here, therefore, is to make the case for a 'critical engagement' with the Fund and the Bank, as much for political necessity as for economic reasons. Such an approach should be based on a clearly articulated and implementable alternative development strategy, and on a credible macro-economic analysis and framework. It would have to balance demand management with fundamental economic restructuring. It would be national-oriented and directed at addressing and correcting the structural inequalities and imbalances in productive capacity that are the legacy of South Africa's postwar growth model. It would have to be cognisant of the need to protect external macro-balances in order to minimise the need for IMF assistance.

Mass-based support for such a strategy, accompanied by the development of an awareness of the need for, and capacity to mount, non-violent resistance to any 'unwarranted' Fund and Bank programmes, would have to form an important supporting strand of our overall approach.

We must persuade the Bank to give serious attention to the state of the economic crisis which confronts us now and to the underlying structural causes of the crisis. If we do have to turn to the Bank for financial assistance we need to convince them to direct appropriately designed loans (term structure, interest rate) into certain crucial areas of the economy, such as skills development, education, health and housing (which were heavily neglected in the apartheid years), and other major projects which are growth-oriented and labour-absorptive, without imposing too onerous repayment terms or conditionality. In borrowing from the Bank, or from any other foreign source for that matter, we should try to ensure that we do not commit ourselves to massive short-term repayments well before these investments begin to show some positive returns. The failure to co-ordinate and synchronise debt repayment schedules with schedules of estimated returns and (possibly) foreign exchange earnings from investments for all categories of foreign borrowing has often led countries into very dangerous waters.[42]

The global political economy, in this the last decade of the twentieth century, is in a highly volatile and uncertain state. Under these circumstances access to IMF credits and special facilities will also be crucial.[43] The use of such IMF facilities should be seen as a temporary solution necessitated by exceptional circumstances; other longer-term strategies and policies aimed at protecting the balance of payments will be required.

World Bank economists have estimated that South Africa's GDP could be raised by as much as 5% with a level of investment only just sufficient to maintain existing levels of capital stock. If foreign finance can be secured in adequate amounts and on reasonable terms, a faster development path could be financed through a judicious use and careful monitoring of such external financial support. However, the finance needed for South African economic reconstruction should, wherever possible, be generated principally from domestic sources.

Notes

1. A fuller treatment of many of the issues raised in this paper is to be found in V. Padayachee (1992). An abbreviated version of some of these arguments also appears in *Beyond Apartheid: Discussion Papers on a Democratic Development in South Africa*. Centre for Development Research, Copenhagen, 1992, pp. 247-79.

2. Ben Turok, *Weekly Mail* 9-15 November 1992, appears to be an exception. Although I am fully in agreement with the essence of his arguments about the dangers of IMF and World Bank intervention, I am not convinced that his recommendation that a post-apartheid state should not use any foreign funds is correct or entirely realistic in contemporary global conditions.

3. See for example Brazil's decision to suspend interest payments in 1987.

4. These issues are discussed more fully in V. Padayachee (1987). 'South Africa's International Financial Relations, 1970-1987: History, Crisis and Transformation.' Unpublished PhD Thesis, University of Natal, Durban, Chapter 2.

5. The reference here is to the Fund's Extended Structural Adjustment Programme (ESAF), its so-called 'soft-window' loans which expire in November 1993.

6. See Eugene Rotberg, *The World Bank: A Financial Appraisal,* World Bank Report, Washington DC.

7. See Special Report, February 1993.

8. BBC Special Report, February 1993, referring to a recent internal World Bank Report.

9. Prowse, M. (1993). 'In Search of the Secret of Asia's Economic Miracle', *Business Day,* 30 April.

10. *IMF Survey,* 15 November 1976.

11. *Center for International Policy Newsletter,* 1983. The controversy over IMF loans to South Africa in the mid-1970s and again in 1982 is not examined here. For this see Padayachee (1992).

12. For a fuller treatment of the reasons underlying the break in SA–IMF relations, see Padayachee (1992).

13. Annual Reports of the IBRD, 1949/50 and 1950/51.

14. *Business Day,* 24 September 1990.

15. The emphasis on expanding regional and international market opportunities inherent in this approach should dispel any notion that the strategy amounts to, or would lead to, autarky.

16.. This chapter cannot examine such alternative development strategies in detail. For this, see for example Gelb, S. (1990). 'Democratising Economic Growth: Alternative Growth Models for the Future', in *Transformation,* 12; as well as other articles and comments in this same issue.

17.. These ideas have much in common with the ECA's alternative development strategy as set out in its strategy document, 'African Alternatives to Structural Adjustment Programmes: A Framework for Transformation and Recovery'. Concern about the ECA's plans centre around its rather ambitious nature. Parfitt notes that it 'makes extensive demands of a group of states that are mostly weak and disorganised' (Parfitt, 1993:105). However, a democratic South Africa is likely to be better placed in these respects than many other African countries.

18.. South African Reserve Bank. (1990). *Annual Economic Report,* p.34.

19.. 'Africa: World Bank Pledges More Local Involvement in Projects', *IPS E-Mail,* 21 May 1993.

20. Internal memorandum to Economic Trends members, following a presentation of the Old Mutual–Nedcor scenario to the World Bank, 1991.

21. IMF Staff Report on South Africa, 1990, p.12.

22. *Business Day,* 31 October 1990.

23. *Business Day,* 10 May 1993. The value of reclassification needs to be assessed carefully, as various counter-arguments in support of the retention of the present status (with some specific concessions) could also be made.

24. *Financial Times,* 25 May 1993.

25. *Financial Times,* 24 May 1993.

26. Internal memorandum to Economic Trends members, 1991.

27. See e.g. the IMF's 'Economics Policies for a New South Africa', January 1992; and numerous working papers of the Bank, including 'Economic Work Program on South Africa', and 'How can South Africa Manufacturing Efficiently Create Employment? An Analysis of the Impact on Trade and Industrial Policy', by Brian Levy, January 1992, among others.

28. United Nations Conference on Socio-Economic Problems in South Africa, Windhoek, May 1992.

29. Internal memorandum to Economic Trends members, 1991.

30. Tarp (1993:46)

31. His argument is that the link between savings and investment is more complex than assumed by the Fund, 'in particular considering the dramatic reconstruction process that will have to take place in South Africa' (1993:47).

32. Tarp (1993:47)

33. Bond, P. (1992). *Work in Progress,* 81, pp.28–9.

34. Meth, C. (1992). *Work in Progress,* 81, April.

35. 'Economic Work Program on South Africa' undated, p.1. Henceforth abbreviated EWP.

36. EWP, p.5.

37. EWP, p.11.

38. Internal memorandum to Economic Trends members, 1991.

39. The views expressed here on these Bank papers have benefited from discussions with local and international economists who participated in the workshops of the ANC's Macro-economic Research Group (MERG) in Johannesburg between 13 and 23 April 1993. Opinion among the group differed sharply on the question of the extent to which Bank thinking as set out in these two papers represents a 'departure' from its usual policy advice.

40. See, among the arguments against heavy reliance on the World Bank and IMF, Ben Turok's article in the *Weekly Mail*, 9–15 November 1990.

41. *Work in Progress*, 11 February 1993.

42. In the late 1970s and early 1980s the South African Reserve Bank lost control over these sorts of calculations with disastrous consequences. It is important to get these 'little things' right.

43. The IMF has, for example, just approved the creation of a new facility, called the Systemic Transformation Facility (STF), to help member countries facing balance of payments difficulties arising from severe disruptions of their traditional trade and payments arrangements owing to a shift from significant reliance on trading at non-market prices to multilateral, market-based trade (*IMF Survey*, 3 May 1993).

14

The Implications for South Africa of Using World Bank Facilities

PETER R. FALLON[1]

The most important role that the World Bank can play in South Africa is to assist in reviving economic growth along a path that permits a substantial degree of redistribution. South Africa's economic problems are very serious – negative per capita growth, widespread and rising unemployment, and an extremely uneven income distribution that is made less tolerable by major disparities in access to publicly provided services and facilities. The Bank is prepared to work closely with future governments and offer its full range of facilities in an attempt to address these problems.

After a political settlement is reached it is certain that a new government will wish to reverse the economic stagnation that has dominated recent years and to redirect the economy towards a new, more labour-demanding growth path. Although some short-term economic gains will be realised as the economy pulls out of the present recession there can be little doubt that, to achieve positive ongoing per capita growth, resources will need to be channelled more rapidly than at present towards domestic investment.

Where will these additional resources come from? While some additional investment might be financed through new domestic savings, the past experience of the South African economy would suggest that, once the recession lifts and the growth process starts to gather momentum, it will become necessary to obtain additional finance from abroad. Otherwise, balance-of-payments problems are likely to force the authorities to choke off the recovery through restrictive fiscal and monetary measures. Since 1985 South Africa has been a net repayer of its foreign debt as new foreign finance has been quite limited in the presence of financial sanctions and largely confined to short-term borrowing and trade credits. This situation may soon change substantially.

An internationally recognised political settlement would undoubtedly bring in its wake access to a number of sources of foreign support, both multilateral and bilateral. The World Bank fits very prominently into this picture. As I argue further below, the Bank should not be seen purely in terms of its role as a source of foreign development finance, but also as a more general facility that can be used as support for the development process. In fact, with the help of local institutions, the Bank has already been very active in non-lending activities in South Africa.

Functions of the World Bank

The World Bank group is a family of institutions consisting of the International Bank for Reconstruction and Development (IBRD), the International Development Association (IDA), the International Finance Corporation (IFC) and the Multilateral International Guarantee Agency (MIGA). The IBRD and IDA are administered as a common institution generally known as the World Bank or more succinctly as 'the Bank'. The central aim of the Bank is to serve as a channel of resources from developed to poorer countries to promote economic and social development. As outlined below, it does this through lending and by providing policy advice and technical assistance. This contrasts with the *raison d'être* of the Bank's neighbour, the International Monetary Fund (IMF), which oversees the international monetary system and helps member countries overcome short-term balance-of-payments problems. All Bank loans, whether IBRD or IDA, are made either to governments or to other domestic institutions with a government guarantee on the debt service. Such institutions include parastatals, domestic development banks and commercial banks within the recipient country. In contrast, the IFC specialises entirely in promoting the development of the private sector in developing countries through equity investments and loans. The MIGA was established quite recently in 1988. Its purpose is to insure foreign investors against non-commercial risk and to provide governments of developing countries with both advice on how to improve their domestic investment climate and technical services. My discussion below centres upon the narrow definition of the Bank, i.e. IDA and IBRD.

The range and scope of Bank activities directed towards client countries has expanded considerably over the years and may be broken down into four broad categories: lending and portfolio management; economic and sector work (ESW); co-ordination and other country support; research and training.

Lending and portfolio supervision

The Bank is at present the largest specialised development-lending institution in the world. Its 'hard-loan' agency, the IBRD, had lent in total over US$ 218 billion by end June 1992, at which time over US$ 100 billion of its assets took the form of unrepaid loans. IDA, the Bank's soft-loan facility, is somewhat smaller, but has still managed to lend over US$ 71 billion since its inception in 1960. IDA lending is available only to the poorest countries – currently those with per capita incomes of US$ 765 or less,[2] while other less-developed countries are eligible only for IBRD. IDA loans (or credits in Bank terminology) carry a grace period of 10 years and a final maturity of between 35 and 40 years. They are interest-free, although the borrower does incur a service charge of 0,75%. IBRD lending is on harder terms – a grace period of 3 to 5 years, a repayment period of 15 to 20 years and an annual interest rate (currently 7,4%) usually at about 1 percentage point below London Interbank Rate (LIBOR). IBRD loans are nevertheless at significantly lower interest rates than commercial alternatives and have a typically much longer repayment period. Both types of lending are thus concessional in the sense that the borrower receives more competitive terms than from commercial financial sources, but IDA is much more concessional than IBRD.[3]

There are very broadly two[4] different types of Bank loans: lending for projects and specific activities within sectors (investment lending) and policy-based lending (adjustment lending). The Bank started off solely as a project-lending institution, and this remained the case until the late 1970s when adjustment lending was introduced. A common feature of all forms of Bank lending is that loans must be guaranteed by the government of the recipient country.

Investment lending still accounts for about three-quarters of all funds disbursed by the Bank. Usually, the borrower is a parastatal or a government that seeks finance for either a clearly defined project – in World Bank parlance, a specific investment loan – or for sectoral activities such as an overhaul of much of the educational system – a sector investment and maintenance loan. The choice whether to use a project or a sector investment loan[5] depends very much on which is easier to package and whether a local agency exists in the country in question that has the capacity to administer a sector loan. Typically, investment loans[6] are disbursed against pre-identified capital and recurrent expenditures. Conditionalities take the form of counterpart actions. For example, if the Bank were financing the construction of new classroom space, then the loan agreement might contain conditions requiring that more schoolteachers be trained or that the administration of the educational system be strengthened.

The Bank never covers the full cost of a project through its lending, as it aims to encourage financial support from other sources. The balance of the cost is met by the borrower and through finance by other institutions where available. The Bank has in fact become increasingly active over the years in assisting its clients to find sources of co-finance for its projects. Such co-finance often takes the form of grants supplied by one or more bilateral donors, and projects in the poorer developing countries are increasingly financed in this manner. The Bank can also, however, enter into co-financing agreements with non-concessional financial sources such as export credit agencies and commercial banks, and partially guarantee the private finance.

About one-quarter of Bank lending is for adjustment. This quick-disbursing type of lending – normally two lump-sum payments or tranches within one or two years – can be for macro-economic structural adjustment, adjustment within an individual sector or urgent rehabilitation of key infrastructure. Adjustment loans are disbursed, not against pre-defined expenditures as with investment lending, but against related imports. The Bank introduced adjustment lending in 1980 following the second oil-price shock amidst concerns regarding the severe macro-economic problems facing many developing countries. Structural adjustment lending helps countries to tackle such problems as rising inflation and existing or projected balance-of-payments problems and aims to move them towards a new, sustainable and poverty-reducing growth path. Typical adjustment programmes involve reallocating and, if necessary, reducing public expenditure, opening up the economy to external and domestic competition, freeing prices to allow them to reflect economic values, improving government delivery of infrastructure and social services, and developing, as needed, other institutions required in a well-functioning market economy. Structural adjustment programmes are usually conducted alongside an IMF-supported stabilisation programme.

The task of preparing investment operations is the responsibility of the borrower – Bank staff only assist in preparation of investment loans. However, through the various preparatory stages of the project cycle – i.e. identification, preparation, appraisal – the Bank must satisfy itself that the project is both feasible and socially worth while and that sufficient administrative capacity exists in terms of qualified individuals and institutions to support implementation. The borrower is the implementing agency, not the Bank, although loans are monitored by Bank staff.

Economic and sector work (ESW)

A large chunk of the Bank's staff-time goes into the provision of analysis and policy advice to client countries. This point is often insufficiently appreciated by those unfamiliar with Bank operations. As its name implies, economic and sector work in a given country consists of studies both on the economy in general and on specific sectors, e.g. industry, energy, agriculture, etc. In addition, however, there are numerous studies that cut across different areas, public expenditure reviews being perhaps the clearest example. The main purpose of ESW is always to give advice to the client, although the analytical findings may be used to inform lending operations.

Co-ordination and other country support

The Bank also exerts considerable effort to assist its clients to obtain much-needed foreign finance from other sources. The Bank's role in co-ordinating donor aid to the poorer less-developed countries through its chairmanship and organisation of the various consultative group meetings in Paris provides the clearest example. Assistance in obtaining non-concessional finance may also be provided in certain cases, and the Bank has on a number of occasions helped improve the terms of existing debt in highly indebted countries.

Research and training

The Bank has long believed in the importance of strengthening institutional capacity within its client countries. The Economic Development Institute (EDI) has since the mid-1950s tried to assist this process by providing a range of courses attended by government officials and others involved closely in development matters in these countries. These courses have covered a wide range of areas including techniques of project appraisal, public sector administration and macro-economic policy. For many years, the Bank has also had an active research programme oriented towards development-related policy issues. Much of this research is of a comparative nature although many research projects involve detailed analysis of specialised topics within individual countries.

World Bank–South Africa relations

The Bank is not in a lending position with regard to South Africa at the present time, and this position will only change when there is sufficiently broad-based support within the country for lending to resume, backed by a consensus among the Bank's shareholders.[7] South Africa is of course a founder member of the Bank and did receive IBRD support between 1953 and 1966. However, given growing international pressure, the Bank's management announced in late 1967[8] that no more loans would be considered – a decision that has remained in force right up to the present day. From 1967 to 1990 there was relatively little contact between South Africa and the Bank although South Africa has remained a full member and has contributed to IDA replenishments.

Following encouraging political developments in 1990 we explored the possibility of conducting a small programme of ESW in South Africa with the aim of repositioning ourselves for an eventual resumption of lending. The government agreed that we would be free to consult with all groups within the country and we have conducted business on this basis ever since. South Africa was transferred to the Africa region within the Bank at the beginning of 1991 and the first missions visited the country in April of that year.

The aim of our ESW programme is to advise on how South Africa might move onto a higher growth path that is associated with a substantial degree of ongoing redistribution. In this context we have conducted two economic missions and numerous others in a wide range of areas, including agriculture, trade policy, small- and medium-scale industry, education, health and the urban sector. Although for the most part we have relied on published information, we have helped initiate the collection of new data on the poorest sections of the population through a poverty assessment exercise conducted by local universities. As we cannot prepare formal World Bank reports under present circumstances we have disseminated the output from these activities through other means. So far we have released three informal working papers on aspects of the economic work, with others soon to follow, while a draft policy document was discussed recently with the government, the ANC, Cosatu and a number of other groups. We expect soon to release several further papers relating to our sectoral work. In addition we have held workshops in collaboration with local institutions on policy issues relevant to South Africa. There have been two workshops on education and one on land reform. Given the success of these efforts, more workshops are in the pipeline.

The nearest that the Bank has come to formal activities in South Africa has been through the efforts of the EDI. Courses on relevant economic topics have been arranged in co-operation with local universities and were attended by ANC nominees. Very recently the EDI also successfully conducted a course in local government management with a wider range of attendees.

Some implications of World Bank lending

Perhaps the first implication is that as Bank finance will be only mildly concessional, future governments should be sure that projects are worth while before approaching the Bank for finance. As the per capita income of South Africa is around US$ 2500 per year it will certainly be treated as an IBRD-only country. Although prospective loans will be carefully scrutinised it is not the business of Bank staff to set policy priorities – only the government can do this.

However, it must be remembered that, bilateral aid apart, IBRD loans are a significantly cheaper source of foreign finance than that available from commercial sources. As it is likely that South Africa may need to seek external finance in the future, IBRD borrowing may be a convenient and cost-effective route for some purposes.

We believe that a resumption of Bank–IMF financial support will have a significant catalytic effect upon the willingness of other external financial sources to lend to South Africa. Much, I suspect, will depend upon the credibility of the policy framework adopted by the new government and upon foreign banks' assessment of the stability of the future South Africa. Certainly, the position adopted by the Bank and the IMF will weigh in some measure with potential foreign creditors, but it remains to be seen whether this will prove to be a significant factor in the light of other considerations. As noted above, the Bank does possess facilities to generate a direct catalytic effect by combining its lending with that of other commercial sources. However, no plans are on the table to trigger these facilities in the near future.

The areas in which South Africa may wish to borrow remain unclear, and even if such areas were identified sufficient detail is unavailable regarding possible projects. What I can do, however, is to indicate some of the main policy directions that the Bank is likely to suggest to South Africa through its policy advice.

In the area of fiscal policy the Bank is likely to support the restructuring of government expenditure within the limits of a sustainable fiscal deficit. There are really two points here. First, the fiscal deficit has reached runaway proportions in the last year or so, and the Bank supports the effort indicated in the recent budget to bring this down in a phased manner. It must be remembered, however, that South Africa is currently in the throes of a deep recession and that an unusually high deficit may be appropriate as a temporary measure while this situation persists. Second, as both a redistributive measure and a measure necessary to engender the social stability required by sustained economic growth, the recent rapid growth in real recurrent expenditure experienced over the last decade needs to be curtailed and capital expenditure given more emphasis in future. Massive investments are needed in those urban areas in which much of the disadvantaged majority of the population lives, while increased capital expenditure is also badly needed in education and health. The recent report released by the government (CEAS, 1993) also reflects a similar view of the need and direction of budget restructuring.

It should be emphasised that such expenditures would be directed very differently from the public expenditure of the past. A significant source of the slowdown in economic growth observed during the 1970s arose from a reallocation of the country's capital stock towards highly capital-intensive parastatal activities. Today South Africa has excess capacity in electricity generation and in much of its transport system. It is unlikely that the Bank will recommend major investments in these areas in the short-to-medium-term future.

The Bank is likely to give considerable emphasis to human capital formation in its policy advice. When taken as a whole, the South African labour force is relatively unskilled and uneducated for a country at this stage of economic development. This is both a potential impediment to a growth revival in the economy and, given huge disparities in skill levels across racial groups, a major source of inequality. The evidence from our research so far is that more rapid improvement in the skills and job status of black workers would be compatible with higher economic growth, reduced unemployment and narrower racial wage differentials (see Fallon, 1992). While improved education for the disadvantaged is both socially necessary and an essential part of any process of skills acquisition, emphasis should also be given to upgrading the skills of the existing work force. It is encouraging to see that increased training is a central part of the strategy envisaged by some leading South African trade unions.

The Bank will also probably advise that the South African economy moves onto a more export-oriented growth path. One conclusion of our ongoing research in this area is that this could be encouraged by a systematic overhaul of South Africa's system of trade protection. At present this system is overly complex and discourages exports by ensuring that production for the home market is more profitable than production for overseas. This would entail the introduction of new policy devices such as a transparent and easily managed duty drawback scheme, a widespread simplification of the protection system, and a gradual reduction in tariff levels. Given widespread unemployment in South Africa, it would seem unwise to move to a 'big bang' reduction in tariffs at the present time.

The Bank is likely to put much emphasis on additional policies that would increase the rate of employment creation. For this reason agriculture is likely to receive more attention than one would expect on the basis of its 6% or so of GDP. The Bank may also be sympathetic to well-thought-out measures to encourage small-to-medium-scale industries and the adoption of more labour-intensive practices in the formal sector.

Above all, however, in every policy area, the Bank will encourage future governments to first choose their approach and then to maintain consistency and transparency when it comes to policy implementation. This will be essential to ensure that hoped-for responses emerge from economic agents and that a level playing field emerges.

Notes

1. The views expressed in this chapter are those of the author and not necessarily those of the World Bank.

2. Under formal guidelines, countries with per capita incomes of less than US$ 1 235 are eligible for IDA. However, US$ 765 is the cut-off used in practice. Some countries may borrow on IDA terms for social sector projects and on IBRD terms for other sectors. Zimbabwe (GNP per capita = US$ 610) is an existing example.

3. There is also a major difference in the way in which the IBRD and IDA are financed. The IBRD obtains most of its funds by selling bonds on the capital markets of the industrial countries. In contrast, IDSA is funded through donations made by governments.

4. The Bank actually distinguishes 11 distinct instruments at the present time. To save space and unnecessary detail the discussion avoids some of the finer distinctions.

5. In addition to the 'specific' and 'sector investment and maintenance' loans discussed here, there are also special forms of investment lending such as 'financial intermediary' and 'technical assistance' loans.

6. Investment loans may, however, have mid-term or special reviews that examine whether conditions of disbursement for special project components have been satisfied.

7. The Bank's shareholders include the great majority of the world's governments.

8. For a discussion of the Bank's decision see: Mason, Edward S. and Asher, Robert E. (1973). *The World Bank since Bretton Woods*. The Brookings Institution: Washington DC.

15

Review of the Debate on the Prospective Roles of the IMF and World Bank in South Africa

LESLIE LIPSCHITZ[1]

In my role as a discussant I have been asked to do four things: to comment briefly on each of the preceding contributions by John Williamson, Peter Fallon and Vishnu Padayachee and, time permitting, to offer some thoughts on the role of the IMF in South Africa. I have little to say on two of the three chapters and shall be very brief; on the Padayachee chapter I shall have somewhat more to say; and I hope the topic of the role of the IMF – both current and prospective – can be covered in the form of questions and answers in the subsequent discussion.[2]

John Williamson's chapter is characteristically lucid and a delight to read. A part of its charm derives from bold simplification – eliminating the shades of grey. I agree with much of the paper, but I want to take issue with three contentions that seemed to me to stretch simplification into caricature.

First, the assertion that the IMF has lost its systematic role and is now nothing more than an adviser of and lender to non-industrial countries is, I think, untenable. Certainly the managing director and most of the staff of the Fund would not recognise this description.[3] Only about a third of professional time at the Fund is spent working on programmes with developing countries. A great deal of energy is devoted to bilateral surveillance of the industrial countries, the World Economic Outlook and other multilateral surveillance exercises that focus on systematic issues in the international monetary system and feed into the deliberations of the Interim Committee, the Group of Seven (G7) and the other principal forums on these issues. The managing director of the IMF frequently attends the meetings of the G7, and the latest communiqué of the Interim Committee, issued at the end of April, stated that finance ministers intended to 'strengthen our collaboration with the Fund as the central international monetary institution'.

Second, the view that the Fund almost always prescribes deflation and devaluation was more true of the old Fund – when John was on the staff – than of the Fund today. Certainly, a balance of payments crisis requires either a reduction in demand or an increase in output, and policies to reduce demand usually work more quickly. But Fund-supported programmes – especially those of longer duration – have focused more and more on output-enhancing policies –

that is, correcting relative price distortions and removing structural barriers to growth.

Finally, one cannot but chuckle at the impish depiction of an IMF mission chief as a callow youth straight out of graduate school with little experience of the real world and a professional incentive for forcing the government into a tougher policy stance. But the humour is purchased at the price of serious distortion. The average IMF mission chief in Africa is over 50 with more than 20 years' experience (in a wide variety of countries) in the Fund and, usually, additional experience in a national government or the private sector. Indeed it is more often the case that our interlocutors in national governments, especially new governments, are young and relatively inexperienced. The most successful IMF programmes that I have been close to (South Korea, Thailand, Czechoslovakia and, more recently, the Czech Republic) have been those in which the authorities have come to the Fund early with an adjustment programme – sometimes significantly more rigorous than that eventually incorporated into the IMF arrangement – that merited financial support. As much as its financial resources, these countries have sought to draw on the Fund's experience – its institutional memory – to compare their situation with analogous circumstances in other countries at other times.

Peter Fallon's chapter is an honest commercial for the Bank; I endorse it without reserve. It seems to me that there is already broad appreciation in South Africa of the work that the Bank has done in identifying and analysing microeconomic and structural policy issues. The cautionary note sounded by Ben Turok and other critics is so obvious as to be almost trivial: of course borrowing should not be premature – that is, the specific projects should be carefully analysed and should be properly integrated into the government's own development strategy – and, of course, the evaluation of any investment project should be cognisant of its macro-economic implications – given macro-economic constraints, choosing project A often means, in practice, deciding against project B. But these are obvious quibbles. The role of the Bank, in both analysis and the provision of financial resources, will be invaluable to South Africa.

In Vishnu Padayachee's chapter, despite its criticism of the international financial institutions, I found a fair amount with which I could agree. For example, the view attributed to others but, I think, endorsed in the paper, that growth will have to rely chiefly on domestic savings rather than external resources to finance investment is quite correct (I shall have more to say on this later). Second, Mr Padayachee's cautionary note on financial discipline – that is, the importance of containing macro-economic imbalances throughout the transformation – could well have been written by an IMF mission. You certainly will not find any disagreement in the Fund.

And third, the position that I think is implicit in the paper, that South Africa should work out a coherent economic policy on its own, that the government should identify the problems and determine a strategy for their solution before approaching the Bank or the Fund for financial support, is also dead right. This does not mean that the international financial institutions should not be consulted in the formulation of economic policies; indeed, it makes sense to draw on whatever sources of wisdom are available. Nor does it mean that the Fund will necessarily support any programme drawn up by the government; we are charged by our shareholders to use our resources prudently and will evaluate programmes carefully before offering financial support. But it is essential that any macro-economic programme supported by the Fund be well rooted in the government's own views and command a broad enough acceptance within South Africa to be implemented with commitment.

But there is one aspect of Mr Padayachee's chapter that seemed to me symptomatic of the problem in much of the discussion on this topic in South Africa at present. This is a preference for the general over the specific and a certain philosophical abstraction from the concrete economic circumstances of South Africa. Let me be more specific.

The way that the authorities can best make use of the Fund is to start by identifying the principal macro-economic problems, analysing them and proposing solutions. The Fund can then serve as a sounding board on the proposed policies, a useful sounding board because it can bring a huge amount of institutional experience, culled from the history of about 170 member countries, to bear on the issues under discussion. If the problems involve temporary balance of payments financing, and agreement is reached on the feasibility of the programme and its consistency with the objectives of external financial viability, stability and growth, then it is worth pursuing the question of Fund financial support. If not, neither participant is any the poorer for the discussion.

In this light, let me sketch briefly the contribution that I would have preferred to see from Mr Padayachee. It would have started off by spelling out the major macro-economic problems.

In the short run South Africa is mired in a prolonged recession with a level of unemployment that is politically untenable. The consensus projections for 1993 envisage anaemic domestic demand with the only positive impulses coming from net exports and the inventory cycle. *What policies can be adopted to nurture any positive cyclical influences without weakening growth potential over the medium term?*

Second, there is an external debt problem that has to be resolved before the end of the year. That means negotiations are currently under way and, clearly, South Africa's options are constrained by recent developments in risk premiums on loans from abroad and in reserves. *What are the feasible options on external debt?*

Third, there is an intertemporal fiscal constraint that will limit the scope of action of government in the future; by the end of the fiscal year government domestic debt will have risen from about 33% of GDP in 1990 to about 45% of GDP; in addition there is a large stock of debt guaranteed by the government, a substantially under-funded government pension scheme and other contingent liabilities that will have to be met by any new government. *How restrictive is this intertemporal constraint, to what extent will current policies exacerbate the problem, and what can be done to help ease it?*

Fourth, there is a longer-run problem of potential macro-economic imbalance. In 1992 private domestic savings, equivalent to about 20,5% of GDP, financed a general government deficit of 6% and an external current account surplus of 1,5%, leaving only about 13% of GDP to finance private investment.

An investment ratio this low is barely enough to cover depreciation and maintain the capital stock, let alone to spark growth. To get the private investment ratio up to 20–23% of GDP will require an additional 7–10% points of savings. Foreign sources cannot provide anything like this much; sustaining a higher rate of investment and growth will depend, therefore, on mobilising domestic savings and reducing the extent to which these savings are appropriated by government consumption. Unless these issues are addressed, any incipient recovery of private investment is likely to be crowded out by government or to weaken the external position. While some external financing would be normal, I agree with Ben Turok, Vishnu Padayachee and others that South Africa should be careful to avoid the debt trap that has ensnared so many countries in Africa. *What stance of macro-economic policies will help to ease the savings constraint on investment and growth over the medium term without stifling any prospective recovery in the short term? By what criteria should the government judge how much foreign borrowing is advisable and what form it should take?*

This, of course, is not an exhaustive list of relevant issues, but it would have been a useful starting point for a paper on South Africa and the Fund. The paper might then have gone on to examine the various options on each of the questions posed, the need for balance of payments financing and the basis for IMF financial support. In most respects the paper is easier to write for the Fund than for the World Bank. Any prospective role for the IMF is much simpler than that of the Bank. The IMF is concerned chiefly about the broad macro-economic framework: the setting of policies that, while facilitating recovery and growth, avoid the traps of accelerating inflation and an unreasonable external debt burden. On this there is already an apparent consensus. It will be much more difficult, time-consuming and, I suppose, politically divisive to sort out the details of various prospective Bank-supported projects.

For both institutions, however, the situation in South Africa is extraordinarily complicated. Macro-economic policy – the province of the Fund – will have to be formulated in the context of a pressing need to tackle the unemployment problem and redress the inequities of the apartheid economy; without progress on these fronts there is unlikely to be an enduring commitment to any package of policies. Micro-economic policies will have to establish economic structures conducive to the growth of output and employment and to determine the priorities among a host of competing social needs.

Notes

1. The views in this chapter are those of the author and should not be construed as representing the position of the International Monetary Fund.

2. For a detailed description of the functions and facilities of the IMF see 'Supplement on the IMF', *IMF Survey*, September 1992.

3. Like John Williamson, I am afraid I shall slip into Washington jargon from time to time by referring to the IMF as 'the Fund' and the World Bank as 'the Bank'.

PART FOUR
PERSPECTIVES ON REGIONAL INTEGRATION

16

The Case for Economic Integration in Southern Africa

ROBERT DAVIES

A fundamental policy question that will confront a post-apartheid Southern Africa is whether a regional economic programme should aim at promoting integration or confine itself to a less ambitious adjustment of a series of sectoral relations combined with functional co-operation in various sectors.

A few years ago there appeared to be widespread support across the political spectrum throughout the Southern African region that the future lay in the direction of integration. Members of the present South African government and business sector appeared to agree with the OAU, SADC, the PTA, the World Bank and a host of other organisations that a regional programme should have as its objective the creation of a Southern African common market or economic community.

Signs of some retreat from this apparent consensus on the part of the South African state and corporate officials have, however, more recently emerged. The Governor of the Reserve Bank, Chris Stals, for example, spoke out in a 1992 *Financial Times* newspaper interview against 'vast new common markets in Africa' on the grounds that 'there's too great a divergence between the stages of development of the various countries, making it impossible to integrate the economies and placing a huge burden on the more advanced nations' (*Financial Times,* 17 November 1992).

By contrast regional organisations have strengthened their commitment and advanced their preparations for an integration project which they hope a democratic South Africa will eventually join. The PTA has adopted a programme aimed at transforming the preferential area into a common market (PTA, 1992). SADC has adopted a treaty whose fundamental aim is to advance a development integration programme in the region (SADC, 1992).

Identifying the options available in this critical area of future international economic relations requires 'unpacking' several issues. First, it is necessary to distinguish the concept of economic integration from two other concepts with which it is often used interchangeably – co-operation and co-ordination.

Integration, in fact, refers to a process in which the economies of individual states are merged (in whole or in part) into a distinct entity – a regional economy. Economic co-operation, on the other hand, is a much more open-ended concept referring to a range of situations in which individual states act together for mutual benefit. Co-ordination refers to cases where policies, strategies or regulations are harmonised to bring them into line with those of partners, again in situations where this is seen to be of mutual benefit. Co-operation or co-ordination may or may not be undertaken with the aim of promoting economic integration.

Two considerations would appear to be particularly relevant in considering the options in this regard. First, there is the reality that all countries in the region confront the objective necessity to restructure their economies in the face of a changing global economy, and in particular to reduce their dependence on primary product exports, by becoming more significant exporters of manufactured goods. Second, there are the asymmetries in international economic relations. Not only are there acute disparities in the global distribution of wealth and economic power, but there are increasing signs that unless the countries of the South become more significant players in the world economy, international economic relations might be restructured to the benefit of the developed North at the expense of the underdeveloped South. It has been argued that, under these circumstances, a more integrated regional economy would benefit all the countries and peoples of Southern Africa in at least the following ways:

(i) by allowing certain economies of scale which will facilitate restructuring at a higher level of productivity;

(ii) by creating a climate conducive to raising levels of investment and encouraging investment in new forms of production;

(iii) by helping to create the kind of competitive environment likely to facilitate innovation;

(iv) by encouraging a rationalisation of investments in infrastructure and creating economies of scale which make infrastructural projects more economically viable;

(v) by helping to strengthen the bargaining position of the countries of the region in an asymmetrical world;

(vi) by promoting the freer movement of human resources, and thereby increasing output and productivity;

(vii) by helping to create an environment conducive to non-violent forms of conflict resolution and the creation of a non-militaristic security order in Southern Africa (SADCC, 1992).

There is no doubt that increasing involvement in regional trade, construction and infrastructural projects, as well as greater access to regional resources and infrastructure and co-operation in various sectors, could all be of great significance to efforts to promote growth and development in a democratic South Africa. More than that, the overall regional ambience will be of considerable significance for a democratic South Africa. A region characterised by relative growth and stability will have very different implications from one plagued by stagnation and crisis.

A more integrated regional economy, which made cross-border investments and projects supplying goods to the markets of several countries feasible, would greatly facilitate a regionally orientated minerals beneficiation industrial strategy.

A more integrated region could also have considerable trade-creating effects. There is already a significant overlap between products currently manufactured and exported by South Africa and imports of SADC/PTA countries. A more integrated region, in which the South African market was also opened up to other countries, could facilitate a significant re-organisation of production and trade patterns, in which not only would South African goods compete with goods imported from outside the region, but a range of producers and industries would begin to find niches in a broader regional market. Component manufacture, with enterprises in several parts of the region producing a part of final products, destined for export as well as the regional market would also be possible.

Under these circumstances the options for promoting the kind of closer regional economic relationships now almost universally held to be potentially advantageous to all parties cannot be seen in terms of a polarised choice between co-operation and integration. The real issue, rather, is to identify that combination of co-operation, co-ordination and integration, realistic and feasible under prevailing conditions, which can best advance the goals of contributing to growth and development.

A fundamental consideration for the development of any such programme would need to recognise what the African Development Bank study has called the 'variable geometry' of the region (ADB, 1992). The level of integration and existing patterns of relations vary between individual countries and groups of countries in the region. An arrangement appropriate, at least initially, to one particular sub-group of countries may not be appropriate to others. This would imply that the integrative component of any regional programme should be premised on a recognition that different arrangements may have to apply among particular subsets of countries for a time, while aiming at the progressive harmonisation of these at an increasingly higher level of integration across the region as a whole.

Weighing against all of the above considerations is the fact that integration schemes and projects, particularly in regions of the South, are notorious as graveyards of failed expectations. None of the existing programmes in the Southern African region can be described as an unqualified success. More precisely, the programmes of SADC, the PTA and SACU all have areas of relative success, that need to be built on in the future, but all are at the same time beset by deep-seated problems. It will not therefore be a case of a democratic South Africa simply buying into an ongoing programme, in the way that a new member joins the European Community, for example. Rather, it will be a case of working together with its partners to devise and develop an appropriate, viable programme. This will require reflecting seriously on the reasons for the failure of previous integration initiatives, including problems of polarisation and the need to develop effective 'political will' or commitment on the part of member countries. Several of the earlier generation of integration programmes, including the East African Community and the Federation of Rhodesia and Nyasaland, can be identified as having failed, in part at least, because the benefits were seen to be flowing disproportionately to the stronger and most powerful members.

The acute potential for polarisation in a regional programme involving South Africa and current SADC or PTA member countries cannot be ignored. Not only is there a great unevenness in the sizes and degrees of development of the economies of individual countries in the region but existing relations are characterised by structured imbalances and inequities. Under these circumstances, a *laissez-faire* approach towards promoting integration could well reproduce or even exacerbate tendencies toward polarisation already evident. Thus a democratic South Africa should expect its prospective partners in a regional programme to push for specific measures to promote a more balanced pattern of regional development. Both SADC and PTA documents envisage such measures (SADC, 1992; PTA, 1992).

A regional integration programme could, however, also founder if it becomes merely a mechanism for weaker partners to place ever-increasing demands on the stronger. A perception that South Africa's involvement in such a programme will lead to just that appears partly to underlie the negative sentiments of the Reserve Bank Governor cited above.

All of this leads to the conclusion that the principle of mutual benefit, long defended by regional organisations, must underpin a regional programme. Only if all partners see concrete benefits from participating in such a programme is it likely to draw the practical support necessary to sustain it.

This last point is closely linked to the question of commitment or 'political will'. Successful integration programmes have invariably been driven by a high level of continuing commitment on the part of co-operating partners. They have worked because co-operating partners have identified clear benefits from participation, or in some cases seen serious disadvantages from not being involved. Many of the large number of failed integration schemes, on the other hand, have been characterised by a low level of real commitment or political will. This has often been manifest in the signature of paper agreements, which are ignored or flouted in practice.

A viable integration programme thus needs to consolidate statements of intent or treaties adopted at summit meetings into a commitment that is both deeper, in the sense that it embraces a series of concrete actions in various sectors and areas, and wider, in the sense that it embraces a broader range of social forces and potential actors. Only if there emerges a popular constituency in favour of the goals of integration can the programme be expected to develop real momentum.

17

A Cautionary Note on the Prospect of Regional Economic Integration in Southern Africa

S. PRAKASH SETHI

The desirability and 'inevitability' of eventual total economic integration in Southern Africa has almost become an item of faith among large segments of the political and intellectual elites of that region. It is reflexively chanted as a 'mantra' by means of which the region's economic woes would be ameliorated and the prospects of socio-political stability vastly improved. I have argued that the case for economic integration on the model of the European Community, or something approaching it, is based on faulty economic logic; on an erroneous understanding of experiences of contemporary attempts at regional economic integration in other parts of the world; a misinterpretation of intra-regional and inter-regional trade data; and unrealistic assumptions about the prospects for political co-operation among the region's nations. Finally, it depends on the implausible belief that a democratic non-racial South Africa would have the means and the will to meet the capital and growth needs of its neighbours while sacrificing its domestic concerns.[1]

While there is no question that any growth initiative for that region must involve significant levels of co-operation among the region's nations, with South Africa playing an important role, it does not substantiate the case for total or even substantial regional integration. Instead, an uncritical predilection for regional economic integration would most likely burden the economy of the region with high transaction costs, impose an inefficient and time-consuming overlay of bureaucracy, retard technology transfer, decrease consumer welfare through reduced competition, and worsen the terms of trade between the region and the outside world to the detriment of the region's nations with, perhaps, the sole exception of South Africa.

The most ambitious plans envisage the creation of a Common Market for Eastern and Southern Africa (Comesa) by the year 2000. It was spurred by the EC's progress toward building a Common Market by 1993, which 'galvanised PTA's ambition' to achieve that goal. It was also considered desirable because PTA had already put in place all the necessary implementation mechanisms.[2] Lest we forget, EC took more than 30 years to reach its present state and its initial objective was a very modest one, i.e. a common steel and coal policy to reduce excess capacity among the participating countries. Even now it is having problems in creating an integrated market despite decades of experience, a high level of industrialisation, a greater degree of mutuality of interest than in the case of Southern Africa, and the availability of a large cadre of skilled professional managers. The Southern African region on the other hand is having considerable difficulty in managing intra-regional disputes even among the more mundane existing institutions, which are beset by problems of overlapping jurisdictions. Nor have they demonstrated by any reasonable criterion their positive impact on the economy of the region, given its current dire economic straits and mismanaged national economies.

An important factor to note is that regional economic integration is neither a necessary nor a sufficient condition for economic growth. With the sole exception of the European Community, most other attempts at regional economic integration either have been stillborn or have failed to achieve their declared objective. This has been especially so in the case of economic blocs involving developing countries dependent on trade in agriculture or extractive industries. Even the EC, despite all its promise, has failed to deliver above-level growth rates or insulate the region from the vagaries of economic cycles, unemployment or technological stagnation. Conversely, the four tigers of Asia, i.e. Hong Kong, Singapore, South Korea and Taiwan, have consistently delivered double-digit growth rates while competing vigorously with each other. Further evidence can be seen in the case of China, the Philippines, Thailand and Malaysia, which have succeeded in attracting massive private foreign capital and generating domestic savings to fuel explosive economic growth.

Regional economic integration for Southern Africa is being advocated for all the wrong reasons. Although there is tremendous trade between South Africa and other countries of the region, its patterns are highly skewed and do not justify the case for regional economic integration.[3] South Africa dominates the region in producing and exporting manufactured goods. However, it is an inefficient producer. Thus by building tariff walls around the region, the already poor consumers in other countries would be subsidising South Africa. Imports to South Africa are concentrated in primary, mostly agricultural, goods, competition for which among the region's nations is not likely to be lessened, and thus the terms of trade would consistently favour South Africa, unless South Africa was willing to institute a common agricultural policy along the lines of the European Community and guarantee 'above market' prices to the farmers of the region. This is highly unlikely given South Africa's own budgetary crisis, development needs and excessive inflation.[4] Furthermore, in view of South Africa's highly developed infrastructure, most foreign investors are likely to select that country as their first choice for establishing plants. Thus South Africa would have no incentive to restrict growth within its own borders in order to nurture infant industries in the rest of the region except where they are 'branch plants' or support the industrialisation needs of South Africa. This is not a pernicious argument. It is based on both solid economic grounds and historical evidence of relations among countries with unequal bargaining power, resource dependency and varying levels of existing economic development.

For regional economic integration to succeed, the stronger nations of the region must be willing to export capital and transfer resources to the weaker nations to equalise levels of development, wages, social support networks and employment opportunities. Otherwise a massive migration of labour will disrupt historically established social and cultural arrangements and thereby create political instability. Witness the reluctance of the EC in allowing newly independent countries of Eastern Europe to come into the Community's fold. Even Germany, the richest of the EC members, is reeling under the staggering cost of providing investment capital and social welfare benefits to the former East Germany. It is estimated that the five East European countries, i.e. Bulgaria, Czechoslovakia, Hungary, Poland and Romania, would have received an annual transfer of over 13 billion emus in 1990 had they been full members of the Community and eligible for its subsidies under various development funds and common agricultural policy. Moreover, their agricultural and low-wage products would have caused tremendous strain and political unrest in the economies of the developed countries of the region facing slow growth and relatively high levels of unemployment.[5] Would South Africa have the resources to transfer to the rest of the region, given its own massive needs of capital for economic growth and building social infrastructure? Would it guarantee the region stable prices for agricultural products and pay for excess produce so as to stabilise farm incomes in those countries? Even the most optimistic among the supporters of regional economic integration would be hard pressed to answer in the affirmative.

The best course of action for the region lies not in the integration of the economies of the region, but in creating project-based strategic alliances where major capital-intensive industrial projects and physical infrastructure are collectively developed, organised and managed, on the basis of considerations of scale economies of production, uniform product standards, a large tariff-free internal market, and political guarantees of non-intervention on the part of national governments. These projects would have to be justified by productive efficiencies and distributive fairness. Projects that by their very nature are best developed on a regional basis, e.g. common highway and railroad or air transport systems, power generation and river water management, would be operated by professional management under common regional political oversight and with investment capital raised in private markets and subject to the criteria of commercial feasibility. This would avoid the dual problem of building white elephants and political obstruction. A similar logic would apply to the establishment of large region-wide industrial plants, e.g. automobile, steel, machine tools, telecommunications. Through a careful structuring of political governance and private management, the locus of decision-making could be so established as to diffuse domination by any one country in all aspects of industrial and infrastructural development. At the same time a judicious location of different industries in different parts of the region would create core competencies in those countries and accelerate industrial development and economic growth through a multiplier effect. Above all, the process would minimise the inevitability of internecine political rivalry, which has in the past aborted, and would most likely in the future abort, any realistic growth prospects for the region and condemn its millions to an abject state of poverty.

Notes

1. The arguments against Southern African regional economic integration presented in this brief chapter have been elaborated by the author in two articles which the interested reader may want to review. These are: S. Prakash Sethi. (1991). 'Prospects and Problems of Two-way Exchange in the Economic Arena between Post-Apartheid South Africa and the Rest of Africa', Paper presented at a Conference on the Challenges of Post-Apartheid South Africa, Windhoek, Namibia, 8–10 September. Sponsored by the Africa Leadership Forum, P O Box 2286, Abeokuta, Ogun State, Nigeria; New York Office, 871 United Nations Plaza, New York NY 10017; and S. Prakash Sethi and Bharat B. Bhalla, 'Strategic Economic Alliances: An Approach to Integrating the Economy of Post-Apartheid South Africa into Sub-Saharan Africa', *Development Southern Africa,* Vol. 9, No. 3, August 1992, pp. 331–345.

2. Siteke G. Mwale. (1993). 'What are the Comparative Roles, Functions and Institutional Capacities of African Regional Organisations (ADB, PTA and SADC)?', Paper presented at the Conference on South Africa's International Economic Relations in the 1990s, sponsored by Aspen–Idasa, Mabula Lodge, South Africa, 27–30 April.

3. See the presentations of L. Cockcroft, Gavin Maasdorp and D. C. Mulaisho at the Aspen–Idasa conference.

4. This argument is supported, albeit indirectly, in the presentation of Professor Francis Wilson at the Aspen–Idasa conference.

5. 'Will More Be Merrier? What Are the Costs or Benefits of an Enlarged European Community?', *The Economist,* 17 October 1992.

18

Regional Co-operation in Southern Africa: A Comment[1]

BENNO J. NDULU

My comment will address some of the major challenges to regional co-operation, as well as the implications for this effort of the changing regional economic environment.

1. *First, what lessons do experiences from past and present economic co-operation efforts in the region provide to future undertakings?*

(i) Unless the gains and losses from integration are evenly distributed among potential partners or a workable transfer mechanism is instituted whereby net gainers compensate net losers, it is difficult to sustain an integration arrangement. These gains and losses stem from two critical concerns. The first is the strong belief that industrialisation holds the key to achieving the modernisation of the economy and provides the dynamic for growth and development. Invariably all economies in Southern Africa have embraced this belief, as exemplified by the pervasive import-substitution strategies adopted. Indeed one of the key factors behind the break-up of the East African Community was the failure to implement an agreed allocation of industries across the partner countries so as to avoid polarisation of industrial development and minimise the possible loss of industrial activity by the weaker partners. The current negotiations within SACU are also informed by this.

Second is the concern for loss of revenue in cases where partners have to agree on compensation for loss of revenue related to preferential tariff reduction. This is particularly serious in situations of severe budgetary constraints such as those faced by a large number of countries in Eastern and Southern Africa, and where serious trade imbalances exist.

(ii) Severe trade imbalances among partners in the absence of a common or convertible local currencies has led to severe constraints on payment mechanisms. In spite of the setting up of a Clearing House for PTA, serious problems continue to exist in the settlement of payments because the net trade balances have to be settled in hard currencies earned through trading with outsiders. Unless such imbalances are corrected through specific arrangements, the potential for expanding trade amongst the partners is restricted. The foreign exchange constraints faced by a large number of economies in East and Southern Africa exacerbate this problem.

The above observations point to a fundamental concern in the consideration of regional co-operation arrangements. A framework of sustained growth for all participating members is fundamental for sustaining co-operation in the long term. Polarisation of growth in general and of the dynamic sectors for growth in particular undermines the basis for a long-term relationship and leads to unsustainable trade imbalances.

2. *What are the implications for integration of the changing economic environment and policies in the concerned countries?*

The key changes here are related to the ongoing structural adjustment programmes and institutional reforms in each of the countries.

Unilateral trade liberalisation: Almost all countries pursuing SAPs have taken on board non-preferential tariff reductions (rates and categories) and the dismantling of quantitative restrictions on external trade. While this offers an opportunity to harmonise tariff systems more quickly and reduce barriers to trade, it reduces the need for preferential arrangements and the use of a common external tariff to promote regional integration. The rationale for adopting regional import substitution (protectionism) strategies is weakened, and partners will invariably have to face stiffer competition from the rest of the world.

Increased external orientation of the economy and diversification of the export basket: In an effort to increase the external orientation of the economy and reduce reliance on primary exports, a large number of the countries have adopted strategies to diversify their export basket. Exports of manufactures and other non-traditional exports are receiving more attention. Should these enter into the basket of goods traded within the region they are likely to meet the strongest protective resistance as the current tariff structures (including those of South Africa) are heavily loaded against them. And yet this kind of trade is likely to promote intra-industry trade, offering a stronger basis for balanced trade.

Privatisation of public enterprises and investment promotion: Large sales of public enterprises are imminent in the adjusting countries as governments reduce their involvement in the productive sphere. These are simultaneously complemented by new investment codes that offer incentives to private investors. On a positive note, this offers possibilities for increased capital mobility within the region to take advantage of the relative differences in returns and opens opportunities for intra-firm trade across countries. With reduced constraints to repatriation of profits, this could turn out to be an area of active involvement for businesses. Concerns of capital flight are, however, likely to be raised, particularly in the South African case, in view of the large investible resource requirements for a post-apartheid programme of reconstruction.

Financial liberalisation: Financial reforms being pursued in adjusting countries aim at the liberalisation of the banking sector and the broadening of the range of financial instruments to mobilise domestic as well as external resources for development. This again provides opportunities for trade in services, particularly in view of the large differences in skills, experience and financial capabilities within the region. Capital mobility may again be promoted through this route.

3. *What role will private businesses play in determining the integration and co-operation arrangements in the region?*

The experience of the 1980s for SADC and PTA countries has been that business organisations have played a passive role in the design and implementation of economic co-operation arrangements in spite of the fact that ultimately these are the principal agents of co-operation. Consultations were mainly inter-governmental, focusing on the broad rules of the game as well as sectoral programmes.

More recently, however, business organisations have started to play a more active role in influencing co-operation arrangements. The Forum for the Restoration of the East African Community, PTA, Association of Chambers of Commerce and Industries, and the SADC Business Councils (with a secretariat in Gaborone) are some of the avenues towards this more active role. There is a need to encourage this form of participation in strengthening the various institutional arrangements for co-operation.

Notes

1. Editor's note: The scope of the author's comments is limited by the fact that this chapter was originally intended as a comment on the papers by Gavin Maasdorp, which is included later in this volume, and Dominic Mulaisho, who was unable to attend the conference.

19

Is South Africa's Goal of Economic Development Compatible with the Goal of Regional Development in Southern Africa?

LAURENCE COCKCROFT

The development of economic communities on a regional basis in sub-Saharan Africa has remained a chimera since most countries achieved independence in the early 1960s. With the exception of the two francophone communities (UDEAC and CEAO)[1] the tendency has been to dissolve those economic communities which were in place (such as the East African Community and the Central African Federation) rather than deepen them. Although recent years have seen important attempts to reverse this process – Economic Community for West African States (ECOWAS), Preferential Trade Agreement (PTA), Southern African Development Community (SADC) and the African Economic Community – none of the newer regional initiatives has developed the institutional depth which characterised the East African Community (EAC) and the Central African Federation (CAF), or continues to characterise the Southern African Customs Union (SACU) and the Common Monetary Area (CMA).

Many national leaderships in sub-Saharan Africa now openly regret this lack of substantive progress, and in response to a variety of factors are nominally placing a renewed emphasis on deepening the existing institutional structures. Those who have been associated with the failed initiatives of earlier years tend to regret the lack of progress: in 1991 Julius Nyerere described Tanzania's role in dismembering the EAC as 'my greatest mistake'. The strategic pressure exerted by the OAU in association with the African Development Bank for the further development of existing and potential regional communities reflects this sense of opportunities lost. This pressure is of course also a response to the birth and development of a series of major economic communities in the world as a whole, and a sense that Africa cannot be left out.

There is little doubt that, at the national level, some of this support is nominal, and in fact major disagreements on economic policy and shared institutions are constantly undermining real progress. More important, there are significant well-informed voices in economic thinking in national governments, particularly those who have participated in past failed initiatives, who question whether the economic costs of fostering such communities are outweighed by the gains. However, the momentum for the further evolution of regional economic communities is now so strong that it is very unlikely to be reversed in the medium term. A majority-ruled South Africa will find itself confronted with a continuation of those choices in regional economic policy from which it has never escaped – of the colonial vision of 'Cape to Cairo', the apartheid-era vision of a 'constellation of states' or the probable post-apartheid vision of solidarity with the former 'front-line states'. The real question is whether it is in the interests of South Africa to foster a deepened economic community within Southern Africa, or should its strategy be to provide nominal support but withhold real commitment?

Conditions for economic growth in South Africa

There appears to be a degree of consensus emerging over South Africa's future economic strategy, which seemed extremely unlikely as recently as two years ago. The key ingredients of this consensus will be summarised below, before their implications for 'regional development' are examined in more detail.

The poor growth record of South Africa in the 1980s may be attributed to several key factors: a relatively depressed international minerals market, manufacturing and agricultural sectors which were highly protected and therefore relatively high-cost, immense budgetary pressures (not least military) which constantly forced up government expenditure as a percentage of GDP, and a highly structured social system which imposed a wide variety of constraints on economic growth.

A 1991 report commissioned by the South African Chamber of Commerce (Sacob, 1991a) analysed the problems of the manufacturing sector very effectively. It found that the price of capital was higher than in the OECD countries, but capital–labour ratios were twice as high as in the newly industrialising economies of Asia (NIEs). Manufacturing labour costs, defined as gross earnings per hour, were found to be as much as half of those of the US, but twice the level of the NIEs and on an upward trend. With the exception of electricity the costs of all intermediate inputs were higher than those prevailing on world markets. This is largely a function of tariff policy: for 22 subsectors of industry which account for 30% of value-added, the average rate of protection was over 50%.

Various forms of economic 'liberalisation' have been adopted as the most appropriate approaches to containing and reducing these cost levels. In relation to the manufacturing sector there has been a general acceptance that some reduction in tariff levels is essential. The Industrial Development Corporation report released in 1991 called for a series of systematic cuts in tariffs and additional duties to a composite rate of 30% on consumer goods and 15% on all other products, assuming a stable exchange rate. Whilst there were and are important voices of dissent on the scale of such tariff reductions, the need to lower the cost of imported capital and intermediate goods is widely accepted.

In the agricultural sector a strong 'liberalisation' policy has been adopted since 1988: farm gate subsidies to the crop marketing boards have been drastically curtailed, which in turn has led to a sharp fall in real farm gate prices of basic cereals. As a result there has been a major shift towards higher value crops (notably horticulture and more intensive forms of livestock production), generating substantial increases in export revenue.

The objective of the tariff reduction strategy is to enable South Africa to produce and export manufactured goods and agricultural products more competitively on international markets, including those of the region. The objective of cost containment is as valid for the mining sector as for the manufacturing sector, although South Africa's technological lead in aspects of mining may continue to give it an international edge. Ironically, the overall high cost structure of the economy may be an argument against 'beneficiation' of minerals before they are exported. Overall, the current liberalisation strategy assumes that realising the potential to export more competitively will raise levels of investment from both domestic and international sources. To what extent will these objectives be furthered by the pursuit of regional integration?

Conditions for regional economic growth

The key justification for closer economic integration in the Southern African region beyond the SACU states must be that it will lead to higher levels of sustainable economic growth than individual countries could attain without further integration. The problems in fostering such integration in the region are well known.

Perhaps the dominant underlying problem is the fact that all the countries of the region remain primarily exporters of commodities and importers of manufactured goods. Commodities account for 88% of the exports of the 15 larger member countries of the PTA, which are mainly channelled to markets outside Africa, and primarily to those of the OECD. Manufactured goods accounted for 86% of imports of the PTA in 1989. In the case of South Africa itself, commodities – nearly all in the form of minerals – accounted for 66% of exports in 1989. On the other hand, between both the 17 member states of the PTA and the 10 member states of the SADC, inter-country trade is only 5–6% of total trade; imports into South Africa from rest of Africa in 1989 (US$ 360m) were only 2,0% of total imports.[2] Trade creation between states with these underlying characteristics is conspicuously difficult.

Within this broad framework the comparative strengths of national manufacturing sectors differ considerably, with Kenya and Zimbabwe having a much higher potential to export manufactured goods than the other countries of the region. Thus, in 1989, 18% of Kenya's exports and 16% of Zimbabwe's exports went to other PTA countries of the region; an additional 10% of Zimbabwe's exports went to South Africa. The integration of South Africa itself into a regional economic community would reinforce this imbalance since, for instance, South Africa's manufacturing sector is over five times larger than that of the SADC as a whole. Although there is significant complementarity between the manufacturing sectors of Zimbabwe and South Africa, and scope for an expansion of trade in manufactures between them, the broader contemporary picture is one of lack of complementarity between economies.

However, although this characterises the current situation the underlying potential is rather different. As demographic pressures build up, and as an increasing proportion of the population is in the urban sector, the demand for marketed cereal products will increase by a factor of at least 2,5.[3] It will almost certainly not be possible for those countries with a high population pressure on land resources (Zimbabwe, Malawi and particularly South Africa) to meet this demand from their own agriculture. This creates a very good opportunity for other national suppliers within the region to meet the demand. Further, development of the regional market, and particularly that of South Africa, is very unlikely to be matched by similar opportunities elsewhere on the international market, where various forms of agricultural protectionism are likely to continue to apply.

A comparable situation exists in relation to power supplies. South Africa's existing resources for generating electricity are either limited (hydro) or high-cost (coal-based). As the country's demand for energy grows, the most cost-effective source for these supplies will be the hydro resources of the region. Again, these are not resources which could be marketed elsewhere since transmission costs would be too high.

Thus, whilst at present there are only limited complementarities between economies, the conditions will exist for increased complementarity as the economy of South Africa itself grows. Further, proximity to South Africa gives the region opportunities to market its natural resources which it could not achieve elsewhere. In this sense, *ceteris paribus,* regional integration has the potential to foster a higher level of economic growth than countries would achieve without it.

Is there conflict for South Africa in its regional and international strategies?

This summary of key issues to be tackled in establishing a Southern African economic community serves to highlight the fact that for South Africa there will be costs as well as benefits. South Africa will be expected to be the main source not only of investment capital, but also of 'compensation finance' to the community's weaker members, and possibly to be the main financier of a regional trade finance facility. Several states of the region, through the structural adjustment process, have lowered their external tariffs to levels below those typical for South Africa. As a result, within the framework of a joint economic community, South Africa might well find itself under pressure to reduce its external tariffs to a lower level than its own priorities justified. South Africa would certainly be under pressure to allow continuous immigration of labour from the region.

In contrast, given the economic problems listed above, South Africa might give priority to increasing the share of its manufacturing output which is exported (currently about 10%) and augment as rapidly as possible its share of world trade in manufactures. Evidence from the Asian NIEs and, for instance, Mexico would suggest that this is most efficiently achieved by rigorously adapting export strategy to the demands of OECD markets rather than to those of the regional 'hinterland'. Basic elements of any such strategy are the need to constantly update investment in manufacturing capacity, achieve systematic increases in the productivity of labour, and closely monitor and adjust to changes in demand on international markets. The fastest-growing or most appropriate 'niches' in OECD markets – such as textiles and electronics – may not be those which are characteristic of the structure of demand in the region. Production runs for products geared to world markets are likely to be longer than those geared to regional markets.

Finally, there is the question of the relative purchasing power of different markets. Whatever payments mechanism might be devised within a Southern African economic community, it will certainly not offset the basic balance of trade deficit between the states of the region and South Africa, currently about US$ 1 billion.[4] Consequently the capacity of the region to pay for imports from South Africa will always be limited, whereas sales to OECD markets will be in hard currency and will place less of a risk on South Africa's export credit facilities.

These constitute important arguments in assessing the degree of commitment which South Africa can sensibly make to the region in the 1990s. However, there are major counter-arguments which offset these. They may be summarised as follows:

– The region is a significant importer of intermediate and capital goods manufactured in South Africa.

– South Africa has good and potentially excellent physical access to the markets of the region.

– Institutional arrangements could be developed to give South Africa modest preferential access *vis-à-vis* suppliers from the rest of the world to the regional market.

– By the year 2000 it is very likely that South Africa will have an energy deficit which could most efficiently be met from hydro-power generated within the region (notably the Zambezi and Congo rivers).

– Whilst South Africa's mining industry is a competitor on global markets, it has a comparative advantage as an investor, supplier of technology and marketing agent within the region.

The strength of these points will be examined in turn.

Interface between RSA exports and regional imports

An analysis commissioned by the African Development Bank[5] which compares PTA and South African trade statistics indicates that there is a good 'fit' between the profile of PTA imports and the profile of South Africa's exports. The analysis indicates that in 1989 there were 55 categories of traded goods (measured to 3 SITC digits) for which PTA imports from all countries and South African exports to all countries exceeded US$ 5m, and in 21 cases exceeded US$ 2m. In fact, the value of South Africa's total exports of manufactured goods to all countries was about US$ 3,7 billion in that year.[6] This suggests that there is a firm basis on which to expand exports to the region since of the PTA's total imports of US$ 15 billion in 1989, only about US$ 1,2 billion were from South Africa.

Further, South Africa itself is a significant importer of agricultural and other commodities which are produced in the PTA, to a total value of US$ 1,3 billion in 1989. At present only about US$ 316m of this is sourced in the PTA, although PTA exports to the rest of the world of the same products total US$ 2,9 billion. Given some elasticity of supply, it should not be difficult for the PTA to increase its production for export of some of these commodities – notably fish, coffee and tea, tobacco and textile fibres.

The potential trade interface between South Africa and the PTA, or SADC, is therefore substantial and could certainly be increased. In the case of South Africa's manufactured exports this need not be at the expense of trade with the rest of the world, although there would be some conflict with manufactured exports from Zimbabwe and Kenya on the PTA market. The combined total exports of these two countries to the PTA market are currently about US$ 60m and it is likely that South Africa would win at least a third of this business. On the other hand, Kenya could expect to achieve improved access for its commodity exports and some food products to South Africa (which Zimbabwe already has under its trade agreement with South Africa).

Transport and market access

The existing transport infrastructure was largely developed during the colonial era when there was fairly free trade within the region and a free flow of goods, for example from South Africa to Maputo for transshipment elsewhere. As a result of the period of destabilisation and civil war in, particularly, Angola and Mozambique, and of maintenance problems elsewhere, this infrastructure is now in need of substantial reinvestment. Average utilisation rates of rolling stock in the region are about 60% compared to 80–85% in South Africa itself.

However, given such investment the system potentially gives South Africa excellent access to the regional market. In fact Spoornet, the subsidiary of Transnet, typically has over 5 000 trucks outside South Africa operating on the regional network as far north as Lubumbashi and Dar es Salaam. Even under present conditions the average turnaround time from Richards Bay in South Africa to Lubumbashi is a not excessive 22 days.

The action required to develop the railways system as a better-integrated network should be well within the capacity of a regional economic community, particularly given the existing knowledge and capacity within Spoornet. On this basis South Africa should be able to achieve efficient access to the markets of the region.

Potential preference system

The further expansion of South Africa's manufactured exports to the region would involve South Africa increasing market share at the expense of suppliers from the OECD and the Asian NIEs. As noted above, current levels of production costs may make this a difficult task unless South Africa has a degree of preference over the rest of the world.

A central issue in the level of preference which South Africa might expect to achieve is not only the percentage tariff reductions which might be negotiated, but also the level of external tariff to which they relate. The PTA is committed to eliminating all tariffs on goods traded between members by the year 2000 and in principle to abolishing the 'Common List' which has so far restricted the items to which its tariff cuts apply. By 1995, 50% of the scheduled cuts are to be achieved; to date, cuts of 30% are due (having been scheduled in three instalments) and have for the most part been implemented, but not yet by all member states. However, the significance of these reductions depends on the level of external tariff to which they are applied.

In the case of Zambia, Tanzania and Zimbabwe, tariffs are already relatively low (mainly under 30%) and are falling further in line with policy changes adopted under their structural adjustment programmes. Comparable downward pressures are at work on tariffs in other countries of the region. If the member states of a Southern African community adopted a common external tariff, it is likely to be set at a level much lower than the level of external tariffs which prevailed up to the late 1980s, and so the degree of preference afforded to all member states – including South Africa – will be modest. Nonetheless South Africa's current cost structure suggests that the degree of preference which a regional community could offer would be an important ingredient in expanding its total manufactured exports.

Any such realignment would have to subsume South Africa's current trade agreements with Zimbabwe, Malawi and Mozambique, each of which gives South Africa modest tariff concessions in the three markets (but less than the 30% cuts now applicable within the PTA) and in return grants a range of preferences in the South African market (which in the case of Zimbabwe averages between 25% and 30%).

Financing exports

The major constraint on the expansion of South Africa's exports to the region is not the level of tariffs, but the ability of potential importers to pay. At present over half the cost of imports to several countries of the region (such as Tanzania and Mozambique) is met by bilateral and multilateral financial aid; in nearly every country of the region aid is a critical source of finance for imports. For the most part, South Africa has not been eligible to bid on contracts related to these imports, whether they relate to projects or finance balance-of-payments-type assistance (and so facilitate the import of a range of goods). This is both because about 34% of bilateral aid is restricted to the donor countries' own suppliers,[7] and because bidding for multilateral contracts has excluded South Africa (either at the request of the importing country or as a procurement rule of the agency).

The lifting of such restrictions is now a necessary condition for the expansion of South Africa's exports within the region. The opportunities for additional exports to be financed by increases in South Africa's own export credit facilities are very limited. However, given the formal ending of sanctions, South Africa would have access to bidding on multilateral contracts; in relation to bilateral contracts it would be reasonable to seek to negotiate an arrangement whereby suppliers from within the region were eligible to bid as well as suppliers from a donor's own country. Elements of this approach already exist in relation to IDA-financed contracts.

There have been exhaustive analyses of the role of 'clearing house' arrangements within a Southern African regional community, designed to enable member states to finance imports in their own currencies by striking a balance between imports and exports with other member states. The existing PTA Clearing House has been successful in financing about 60% of trade within the PTA, worth a total of about UAPTA 45m,[8] and is likely to succeed in raising this further. However, the fact that the other members of a regional community would inevitably run a substantial trade deficit with South Africa substantially limits the value of the clearing house approach to financing trade within the region. Ultimately net deficits in trade would have to be financed by payments in foreign exchange, as they are now within the PTA. For this reason a further expansion of South Africa's exports to the region is likely to have to be financed by aid flows.

Economic interdependence

Amongst the several unanswered questions about the long-term future of the South African economy, those of future sources of basic foodstuffs and of energy supplies remain crucial. Although South Africa has been a regular exporter of cereals, and particular maize, to the region over the last 20 years the recent liberalisation of the cereals market has tended to reverse that pattern, as farmers in South Africa have tended to concentrate resources in the higher-value horticultural and livestock sectors. Thus the maize crop from 1989/90–1991/2 was nearly 20% less than the 1980/1–1982/3 crop.[9] The drought in the 1992/3 marketing year was a separate phenomenon, but has tended to reinforce this trend.

The significance of this trend in the overall production of cereals is in its relation to long-term demand projections, taking into account both national population growth rates and urbanisation. Current growth rates suggest a total population of approximately 65m by 2025, of which about 50m are likely to be in the urban sector.[10] It is very unlikely that South Africa's agricultural sector could meet this level of increased demand without a very heavy and expensive dependence on irrigation. Obviously some part of the incremental demand will be imported from world markets, but a significant and possibly major part could usefully be sourced from production in the region (from areas such as central and northern Zambia, southern Tanzania and northern Mozambique).

The question of potential interdependence in energy supplies is even more pressing in strategic terms. South Africa's electricity supply company, Eskom, estimates that by the end of this decade South Africa will have absorbed all of its installed generating capacity, and that annual increments of 1 000–1 500 MW will be needed. The hydro-power resources of the region (particularly the Zambezi and Congo rivers) are the key to providing such incremental supplies. Each 1 000 MW of installed capacity is likely to have a value to the region of US$ 100m: thus over a period of 10 years total installed capacity of 10 000 MW could generate an income of US$ 1 billion. Whilst this will be costly to South Africa, it represents a cheaper and more environmentally appropriate source of energy than the coal-fired and nuclear stations which are the prime alternative. It also provides a most appropriate means of offsetting South Africa's trade surplus in manufactured goods.

Mining investment within the region

South Africa's mining companies have been muted players and investors in the region in recent years. Nationalisation, civil war, unattractive tax regimes and sanctions have all contributed to this position, although most of the large mining houses have continued to play a quiet role as suppliers of technology, manpower and equipment. The combination of the recent adoption of policies favourable to direct foreign investment by many governments in the region, and of a positive attitude to South Africa, has begun to re-open investment opportunities that appeared long dead.

There is no doubt that the expertise held within South Africa's mining industry could be of further benefit to the region, both in opening up new opportunities and in increasing the efficiency of existing operations. South African mining houses are participants in the global minerals industry and are active investors in countries as far apart as Bolivia and Russia. However, the Southern African region – other factors being equal – represents an area which competitors from other parts of the world are likely to find less attractive and in which South African companies have a comparative advantage. A stable and functioning regional economic community could therefore provide a valuable outlet for additional investment of South Africa's mining expertise, technology and capital.

Creating a mutuality of interest between South Africa and the region

The above arguments suggest that active participation in a Southern African economic community would be in South Africa's long-term self-interest, and that in the long run this would be a superior strategy to one which focused entirely on growth based on maximising exports to OECD markets. Obviously the two approaches are not incompatible, but South Africa's commitment to a regional community will certainly involve costs which need to be recognised, as well as the benefits noted above.

What are the specific conditions in which such a community is likely to develop on a sound and sustainable basis? First principles and practical experience confirm that there has to be a genuine mutuality of interest, particularly between the smaller members and the largest. This mutuality of interest has to be perceived from the start rather than from a potential vantage point 10 or 15 years away. The dilemma in Southern Africa is that the strategic advantages for the states other than South Africa are primarily in the opportunities for selling energy, agricultural produce and acquiring on-going investment in the mining sector. These will materialise in a substantive form only over the long term. In the short term the primary advantage will appear to be to South Africa for the sale of its manufactured products.

A mutuality of interests in the region must therefore be based on phasing in the benefits to South Africa and the other member states of a community at roughly the same time. An equilibrium of interests would not occur for at least ten years, or more or less at the point when South Africa's demand for increased energy and food supplies cannot be met from domestic resources. This suggests that whilst the institutional arrangements for a community should be established in the short run they should be based on giving South Africa a graduated preference in regional markets, at the same time as South Africa extends full preference to other community members. This could be achieved by member states offering to South Africa a 50% reduction in the tariff applicable between themselves in return for tariff-free access to South Africa. This would be most efficiently achieved if the community could adopt a common external tariff (CET). As discussed above, without such an arrangement the value of tariff reductions is unequal, and at present cuts in South Africa's relatively high external tariffs would be worth more than cuts made by countries with lower tariffs. Whether such an arrangement is made in the context of a CET or not, the initial 50% preference awarded to South Africa would be phased into a 100% preference over time as the potential advantages of the community to other member states come closer to realisation.

To what extent is a reformulation of one or other of the existing institutional structures – PTA, SADC and SACU – compatible with this approach? As their protagonists have noted in many analyses, each of these institutions has strengths which suggest that they are the ideal vehicle. The PTA embraces 17 countries, including more northerly markets (Kenya and Ethiopia) which could be of considerable value to South Africa. It has always been perceived as an organisation devoted to the promotion of a common market. SADC is a more homogeneous region which has been knit together by investment capital, labour flows and various forms of institutional integration. SACU is already a genuine economic community in which economic resources move freely, with the exception of restraints on labour migration.

The weakness of the PTA is that it is too diverse, and although it has maintained credibility over the last ten years its achievements in ensuring that tariff cuts actually happen are modest. It has grave difficulties in reconciling the interests of some of its members, such as Ruanda and Kenya, and includes states in which major or minor civil wars are taking place. The weakness of SADC is that it owes its inception to a condition which has ceased to exist – the international isolation of South Africa, although at least one of its members also continues to be ravaged by civil war. Its adoption of a new charter in August 1992 sets new directions for the organisation, including the adoption of a major role in trade policy and the setting of tariffs. The weakness of SACU is that it consists of one whale and four minnows,[11] and has been held together in the past mainly by the muscular strength of the whale. Whatever the merits of SACU, there are weaknesses in building on a construct which has only been held together by *realpolitik*.

The merits and demerits of each of these institutions is a large topic which cannot be adequately discussed here. However, on balance it appears that the case for working with the SADC group of countries is the strongest of the options. However, since SACU members currently have tariff-free access to each other's markets it is very unlikely that they would wish to move a step back from this status, particularly if some variant of the current revenue-sharing formulae is retained. The SACU nucleus could be expanded over time as the reciprocal nature of the benefits of the free-trade area become clear, although it would not be feasible to extend the current revenue-sharing formulae to other states.

Notes

1. Union Douanière et Economique de l'Afrique Centrale, and Communaute Economique de l'Afrique de l'Ouest.

2. Figures released by government to *Finansies en Tegniek,* October 1991. These are informally estimated by the South African Foreign Trade Organisation to be an underestimate by about 30% since this volume of additional trade is not captured by the official statistics. However, this adjustment raises the total to only US$ 358m.

3. The 1989 total population of the 12 countries of the region (Angola, Botswana, Kenya, Lesotho, Madagascar, Malawi, Mozambique, Namibia, South Africa, Tanzania, Zambia and Zimbabwe) was 150m. World Bank projections indicate that this will be 370m by 2025, of which 190m will be urban, and of this urban population 50m will be in South Africa (World Bank, 1991). Demand for cereals and particularly maize is projected to keep roughly in line with population growth.

4. *Finansies en Tegniek,* October 1991.

5. To be published in 1993; the author of this paper was responsible for the trade and agricultural sections of the African Development Bank report.

6. The data are from the South African Foreign Trade Organisation. The figure excludes minerals and processed minerals, as is consistent with UN statistical practice.

7. US$ 17m out of a total US$ 52m of bilateral aid in 1990, Source: OECD. (1992). *Development Co-operation 1992.* OECD: Paris.

8. One UAPTA is equivalent to an SDR.

9. 9,16 mt compared with 11,0 mt of the aggregate of white and yellow maize. Dates refer to marketing, not production, years. Source: Maize Board.

10. See note 3 above.

11. Botswana, Namibia, Lesotho and Swaziland.

20

The Advantages and Disadvantages of Current Regional Institutions for Integration

GAVIN MAASDORP

'Integration' in economic literature refers to trade integration among countries. There are four stages of true trade integration, starting with a free trade area and progressing through a customs union and a common market to an economic union. A free trade area could be preceded by an agreement on preferential tariffs while an economic union could, in theory, develop further into a full political union. In Southern Africa the institutional framework for economic integration in broad terms consists of four organisations. This chapter describes them briefly and examines their present position. It then discusses South Africa's possible future economic role in the region and the institutional implications of that role.

Existing institutions

The Southern African Customs Union (SACU)[1]

The first customs union in what is present-day South Africa was established in 1889, and by 1895 it had grown to cover the entire area of what are today South Africa, Botswana, Lesotho and Swaziland. The administration of German South West Africa (present-day Namibia) passed to South Africa in 1915. Thus, the five countries have a long, unbroken experience of being together in a common customs area. The present SACU Agreement was negotiated in 1969, and Namibia became a formal member in 1990 after attaining independence.

The SACU is the only institution in the region which meets the textbook definition of economic integration. It provides for the duty-free movement of goods and services between member countries and also for a common external tariff against the rest of the world, but also goes beyond a pure customs union in that it includes excise duties as well. The revenue-sharing formula contains a compensation factor of 42% for BLSN.[2] The amounts so calculated are then amended by a stabilisation factor aimed at guaranteeing to each BLSN country a rate of revenue of between 17 and 23%.[3] The Customs Union Commission meets annually, but the SACU has no office or staff: it is handled by government departments in each member country while the common revenue pool is managed by the South African Reserve Bank.

In 1981 BLS requested that the SACU Agreement be renegotiated. For various reasons talks about renegotiating are still continuing, and the parties have differing views as to the appropriate emphasis and role of the SACU.

South Africa argues that the emphasis should be on its development enhancing role rather than on revenue-sharing. One view in Pretoria – at least from the Department of Trade and Industry – is that South Africa is no longer receiving a sufficient share of the receipts because of an overly generous revenue-sharing formula and that it can no longer afford such an arrangement (Naudé, 1992). In 1969/70 BLS received 3,9% of the common pool and South Africa 96,1%. By 1990/91 the BLS share had increased to 17,1% and, with a further 8,3% going to the now independent Namibia, Pretoria's share had fallen to 74,6%.[4]

This view has some validity in that the Agreement did not allow for the possibility that SACU tariffs might be reduced in terms of the GATT requirements for the liberalisation of trade and also to make exports from the region more competitive. By reducing tariffs South Africa has been penalised for doing the right thing by a formula and stabilisation factor which, by guaranteeing a minimum rate of revenue to BLSN, were valid only if duties were not reduced.

Two other factors serve to reduce South Africa's share of total revenue. The first is the inclusion in the revenue-sharing formula of excise duties. The purpose of such duties is to raise revenue for a government. Excisable goods produced in the customs union are overwhelmingly South African, and these duties contribute on average over 60% of the common pool. This led McCarthy to argue that 'South Africa's fiscal problems could be eased immensely if excise revenue was excluded' (McCarthy, 1986:127). That certainly would be the case, but he conceded, and both the Margo Commission (RSA, 1987) and the White Paper (RSA, 1988) accepted, that practical problems of administering such a system, requiring as it would stricter border controls, made it essential to retain excise duties in the formula. BLSN also argue that the inclusion of excise duties is justified because their consumption of these goods contributes to South African economic growth and employment. Moreover, there is some dispute as to double-counting in the formula in South Africa's favour with regard to the treatment of inputs imported into the Customs Union which are used in the production of excisable goods.

The second factor is that there is an asymmetry in the formula in favour of BLSN: it includes BLSN imports from South Africa, but not vice versa. Although South Africa's imports from partner countries are relatively small in relation to its total imports, their inclusion would increase the denominator in the formula and thus decrease the share payable to BLSN. This led Colclough and McCarthy (1980:78) to state that the formula 'considerably augments' the share of these countries at the expense of South Africa.

But the Department's view also has its shortcomings. First, it excludes the transfers made out of the common pool to the TBVC states from its calculations, but these areas are not formal members of the SACU and the transfers are a purely domestic arrangement. In 1990/91 these transfers accounted for 19,8% of the common pool, reducing Pretoria's official share of 74,6% to 54,8%.

However, as far as BLSN (quite correctly) are concerned, Pretoria's share is 74,6%. Second, it does not consider the fact that BLSN provide a market for 25% of South Africa's manufactured exports and 10% of its total exports by value, and that a substantial number of jobs are attributable to the SACU. McFarland's estimate was 300 000 (McFarland, 1983:266 and 273) although his methodology might be questioned. Third, it is remarkably insensitive to calls (and indeed timetables) for greater integration in Africa (including, let it be said, calls from the Ministry of Foreign Affairs in Pretoria), even if the timetables are unrealistic. Fourth, it ignores the fact that, in integration arrangements, some mechanism often will be necessary to compensate poorer countries because of the unequal benefits of economic development. In the European Community, for instance, more than one-quarter of the budget goes to redistribute wealth from the richer to the poorer countries by means of the so-called structural funds.

BLSN are indeed concerned about the effect of any changes in the revenue-sharing formula on their government revenue. But they are also concerned about the two-year time lag in revenue payments, and have pressed for its elimination. At the 1969 negotiations BLS did not allow for a rapid increase in their imports as their economies grew, and therefore they are stuck with a formula which allows a two-year lag in cash flows and which is consequently unfair to them. Other aspects of concern to BLSN are the inadequate provision in the Agreement for them to protect infant industries, the weakness in the treatment of dumping, and inadequate machinery for consultation.

The protracted nature of the negotiations has led to individual member countries undertaking their own independent evaluations of the SACU. The problem with such studies[5] is that they tend to be static and hence ignore the dynamic aspects and unconventional benefits of integration. But the mere existence of these studies, together with some public statements by South African officials, has led to a sense of uncertainty about the future of the SACU. However, the SACU could be renegotiated in a way which satisfies the major problems of its members. If any country were to quit, the message it would send to the rest of the region (and also Africa) about the possibility of future economic integration certainly would be a very negative one.

The Common Monetary Area (CMA)[6]

Monetary integration forms part of the highest stage of economic integration, namely an economic union. The SACU is largely paralleled by the CMA, and thus Southern Africa has a higher degree of economic integration than is suggested merely by the Customs Union.

The CMA's origins are roughly similar to those of the SACU, but monetary integration was only formalised in 1974 when South Africa, Lesotho and Swaziland signed an agreement establishing the Rand Monetary Area. Botswana had used South African currency ever since its economy became monetised, but opted out of the talks in 1974 and introduced its own independent monetary system in 1976. The 1974 Agreement was superseded by the Trilateral Monetary Agreement of 1986 establishing the CMA. This Agreement has now given way to the Multilateral Monetary Agreement of 1992, in terms of which Namibia has become a formal member of the CMA. The Multilateral Monetary Agreement is accompanied by bilateral agreements between South Africa and each of its partners.

The three smaller countries each have their own currency, which at present is at par with the rand although this is not essential. Common exchange controls apply; the CMA retains the free movement of funds among member countries, and Swaziland, Lesotho and Namibia have access to the South African capital market. As with the SACU there is no permanent staff, but a commission meets to discuss progress and common problems.

The CMA is the most invisible of the organisations, receiving relatively little attention in the literature. Swaziland, despite close monitoring, continues to maintain its exchange-rate parity with the rand while Namibia has now decided to introduce its own currency within the CMA, but is still to make a decision on its long-term membership. A recent study (Stuart, 1992) examining the position of Swaziland and Lesotho in the CMA concluded that they would benefit from closer monetary integration with South Africa.

Southern African Development Community (SADC)

This organisation came into being as the Southern African Development Co-ordination Conference (SADCC) in 1980 with nine members – Angola, Botswana, Lesotho, Malawi, Mozambique, Swaziland, Tanzania, Zambia and Zimbabwe. In 1990 Namibia became the tenth member. The organisation was the product of the front-line states, which were concerned at the extent of the region's dependence on South Africa in particular and the rest of the world in general. A reduction of this dependence became the principal goal, which was to be achieved through the co-ordination of regional development. The Secretariat is located in Gaborone, but each country is responsible for handling a sectoral portfolio. Priority was given to transport and communications, and later to food, security and energy. In 1992 SADCC became SADC, and the emphasis shifted to trade integration, thereby cutting across the aims of the PTA. The new structures required for this transformation have not yet been finalised.

For most of the 1980s the verdict on SADCC was generally positive, but was heavily influenced by the politics of destabilisation: SADCC was seen as a bulwark against apartheid both by donors and by politico-economic commentators. It is only since the late 1980s that more critical voices have been heard, and a growing view today is that the organisation has achieved only meagre results.[7] Donors have pulled back: they are tired of the political platitudes and critical of the bureaucracy, and are looking for more purposeful direction, greater attention to the needs of the private sector and a commitment from member countries to implement the organisation's agreed policies. SADC might have raised more foreign funding for the region than individual countries acting separately could have done, and it might have increased regional consciousness, but this has not prevented the souring of trade relations between Zimbabwe and Botswana. SADC has been tardy in recognising the role of the business sector in economic development, and its decision to concentrate on trade integration has been interpreted as being a move of desperation by an organisation fighting for its survival between post-apartheid South Africa and the PTA.[8]

The Preferential Trade Area for Eastern and Southern African States (PTA)

In contrast to SADC's political origins, the PTA was nurtured by international civil servants of the United Nations Economic Commission for Africa. A long time in gestation, the PTA commenced operating in 1983. With Namibia's accession to membership in January 1993 it now has 19 members covering a geographic area from Lesotho in the south to the Sudan in the north, Mauritius in the east and Angola in the west. Of the SADC countries only Botswana is not a member. The Secretariat is in Lusaka, and there is a Clearing House in Harare and a Trade and Development Bank in Bujumbura.

As its name implies, the PTA offers preferential trading arrangements among member countries: a list of approved products has been published on which tariffs are to be progressively reduced with the aim of the PTA becoming a regional common market. In terms of the Abuja Declaration of 1991 the target dates are 2014 for the establishment of regional customs unions and 2020 for an Africa-wide common market, with an African Economic Community, i.e. an economic and monetary union, planned for 2034. However, in January 1993 the PTA approved the establishment of a Common Market of Eastern and Southern Africa (Comesa) by 2000, thus accelerating the Abuja goals.

Although the PTA continues to expand its membership, six member countries – Sudan, Djibouti, Ethiopia, Somalia, Mozambique and Angola – do not have the economic capacity to play any role in the Clearing House. Some other countries do not have the political will to implement PTA protocols on trade and transport. The result is that intra-PTA trade has hardly changed as a proportion (about 5%) of the total foreign trade of member countries. Nevertheless, the PTA is perceived as an organisation which has implemented some practical steps towards facilitating intra-regional trade. Donors are concerned about its relationships with SADC, and the subscriptions of certain member countries are in arrears. As a consequence, the PTA is reported to be facing a financial crisis.

Attitudes of donors and firms

The donor community and the business sector in Southern Africa are increasingly concerned (and indeed perplexed) at the growing duplication of activities by the PTA and SADC. There is a widespread feeling that Southern Africa cannot afford to have both these organisations and that the institutional framework for regional co-operation and integration should be rationalised. According to business spokesmen the image of these two organisations in member countries has never been lower.

The image of the four existing institutions among firms may be further gauged from a survey conducted among firms engaged in cross-border trade in six SADC countries in 1992. The results showed that 85% of firms in the sample felt that the CMA had been useful to them in their business; 73% responded likewise in the case of the SACU as against 47% for the PTA and 24% for SADCC.[10] (Not too much should be read into the results as far as the old

SADCC is concerned: since it had not been orientated towards trade, it cannot have been expected to impinge much on the practical day-to-day activities of the firms concerned in the sample.) The SACU and CMA were held in such high standing because they made business transactions so much easier by eliminating or at least substantially reducing the 'hassle factor' in cross-border trade.

South Africa's role in the region

South Africa is the economic giant of Southern Africa. In 1989, for example, it accounted for 76,7% of the total GNP of the region while its per capita income was almost eight times that of SADC as a whole. South Africa's main links with the region lie in trade, transport and employment.

On the trade side,[11] about one-eighth of South Africa's foreign trade by value is with SADC countries while over 30% of its manufactured exports by value go to these countries. These figures exclude unrecorded trade flows, which are substantial, especially across the border with Zimbabwe. The foreign trade of BLSN is heavily orientated towards South Africa (especially on the import side) while South Africa is a major trading partner of Zimbabwe and Malawi. Its trade with other SADC countries is growing as political obstacles disappear. Of total SADC foreign trade in 1984, 25% was with South Africa. This percentage has almost certainly increased since then.

South Africa's transport network continues to provide a critical service to landlocked SADC countries, including those north of the Limpopo. This has been well illustrated in the transport of food supplies under international drought relief assistance programmes in the last year.

Official figures on migrant labour in South Africa are no longer kept, but employment on the mines, despite falling, still offers an important outlet to Lesotho, Mozambique, Swaziland and Botswana. Growing in importance, however, are the flows of skilled and semi-skilled individuals from Southern Africa (and indeed other parts of Africa too) to South Africa as that country's previously tight immigration controls fall into disarray. No figures are available in respect of these flows, but they are resulting in a serious brain drain for some countries.

It is often mentioned today that South Africa could act as a springboard for foreign investment into the region. The reasoning is that many companies think in terms of a regional market and then choose their location, and that South Africa will be that location from whence funds as well as goods and services will be channelled to other countries. A number of multinational corporations have stated their intention of supplying the rest of the region from South Africa but, because of an unfavourable investment climate, little foreign direct investment has found its way into the region in recent years. Nonetheless, a prosperous South Africa could well have a spillover effect on the region in much the same way as Japan has had in South-east Asia.

Another role for South Africa is as a co-operating partner or client in infrastructural projects and sectoral development, e.g. in the development of sub-continental water and electricity schemes or in tourism and agriculture. Other constructive roles lie in technological co-operation and human resource development.

What is South Africa looking for in its relations with Southern Africa? The business sector is seeking new markets, sources of supply and investment opportunities. Its image in neighbouring countries, however, is that of a predator, but this could be changed if South African firms were to stress the mutually beneficial nature of business ventures. The government – or at least a future government – might emphasise the development of more equitable economic relations with its neighbours, especially in resource development, but some critics argue that any future government will be so preoccupied with the country's own overwhelming internal challenges that it will show little interest in the region. ANC officials have intimated that post-apartheid South Africa cannot be expected to be a source of investment for the region, i.e. presumably outside the CMA.

Institutional implications

Both SADC and the PTA have indicated that the new South Africa would be accepted into their ranks. The South African government and the business sector have indicated their interest, and have called for 'common markets' and other schemes which appear not to have been thought through thoroughly. The question is, What could SADC and the PTA offer South Africa, and what could South Africa offer them as a partner?

SADC has the institutional framework for sectoral co-operation, but it has hardly been effective. South Africa has participated effectively in some regional organisations, e.g. in the railways, without its being a member of SADC. It could bring a new sense of purpose as well as its organisational abilities into SADC. The PTA is a putative trade integration arrangement – at least it is engaged in the reduction of tariffs on a preferential basis – but has for the reasons stated above faced difficulties of its own. Again, South African membership might be a spur to greater efficiency and more rapid progress.

A regional economic bloc (built on trade integration or sectoral co-operation) might be important for improving Southern Africa's image in the rest of the world, especially in the investor community. However, the fact remains that the SACU and CMA taken together offer an advanced form of economic integration hardly matched elsewhere in the world. This is often overlooked. These two organisations are the most successful in the trade and monetary integration spheres in Africa: they are the envy of the region and are far in advance of anything the PTA and SADC have to offer. There is a growing consensus – manifested in recent reports on Southern Africa[12] – that the SACU and CMA represent a core around which economic integration in the wider region needs to be built. There probably is scope for deepening the present SACU and CMA arrangements into a common market or economic union, but widening them to include additional countries might not be an immediate prospect because of the wide disparities in inflation rates, lack of currency convertibility and so on.

Although BLSN represent a major market for South Africa there is no doubt that the prospects for expanding its markets lie in the rest of the region. The other side of the coin, however, is that some South African industries, e.g. sugar, clothing and textiles, may find it difficult to compete in a new regional trade arrangement. Trade integration will need to be carefully examined for this reason, and the PTA timetable for a regional common market is simply wishful thinking. A common market involves, over and above the elements of a customs union, the free movement of capital and labour. Southern Africa outside the SACU is far from ready for this advanced form of integration: it cannot yet implement the preferential trade protocols.

In contrast, sectoral co-operation should be easier to achieve. The advantage of sectoral co-operation is that it can spread the benefits more rapidly; e.g. if a Southern African power grid were to be established, countries north of the Limpopo would be the major beneficiaries of revenue flows.

SADC and the PTA have agreed to set up a joint ministerial committee to study ways of harmonising their activities. Nevertheless, there is a growing view that either these two organisations will have to merge or the PTA will have to split into an eastern and a southern component, with SADC then assuming PTA-type functions.[13] The five SACU countries and the remaining six SADC countries could perhaps then enter into an agreement something like that of the EC and EFTA and establish a Southern African Economic Area.[14] SACU–CMA would represent the trade and monetary integration core and would agree on preferential tariffs with the other countries whilst engaging in close sectoral co-operation; each of these countries could then join the core as and when it felt ready. This might be preferable to grandiose integration proposals complete with timetables which overlook the complexities of promoting closer trade and monetary links in a region of wide economic disparities.

Notes

1. This section draws on previous work by the author, *inter alia,* G. Maasdorp (1982). 'The Southern African Customs Union – An Assessment', *Journal of Contemporary African Studies,* 2(1); and 'Trade' in G. Maasdorp and A. Whiteside (eds.), *Rethinking Economic Co-operation in Southern Africa: Trade and Investment.* Konrad Adenauer Foundation, Johannesburg.

2. The acronym for Botswana, Lesotho, Swaziland and Namibia. Prior to Namibian accession in 1990, the acronym was BLS.

3. See Hudson (1981) for an explanation of the operation of the formula.

4. Maasdorp, 'Trade', p.43.

5. See, for example, J. C. Leith. (1992). 'The Static Welfare Economics of a Small Developing Country's Membership in a Customs Union: Botswana in the Southern African Customs Union', *World Development,* 20(7).

6. This section draws on G. Maasdorp (1991). 'Monetary Policy in the Southern African Region', in *Regional Economic Integration and National Development.* Konrad Adenauer Stiftung/ Southern Africa Foundation for Economic Research, Harare.

7. *Business Africa,* 16–28 February 1993, p.5.

8. Ibid.

9. Maasdorp, 'Trade', p.25.

10. Ibid, p.36.

11. See ibid, pp.14–16.

12. The reports of the Southern Africa Foundation for Economic Research project (see Maasdorp, 'Trade', pp.46–51) and the African Development Bank project (see *Africa Analysis,* No.167, 5 March 1993, p.6).

13. See the references in note 12 and also Hawkins, A. (1993). 'The Golden Triangle', *Southern African Economist,* 6(2), March 1993, p.44.

14. See Maasdorp, 'Trade', pp.46–51.

21

Conclusion: Conference Highlights
STEPHEN R. LEWIS, JR.

The very wide diversity of opinions, political commitments and backgrounds of the participants has, quite literally, assured the success of this conference. Our colleagues ranged from senior officials of the current government to the African National Congress, the Inkatha Freedom Party, the Pan Africanist Congress, the South African Communist Party, several trade unions, the largest mining and financial groups in South Africa, major European and American multinational companies, as well as academics, researchers and opinion leaders from South Africa and abroad, and former government officials from several continents. On the face of it, it would seem unlikely that there would be much agreement. But the world should note that the extent of consensus on many fundamental points was widespread, and remarkable. This was definitely a highlight of the conference.

The opening evening's remarks by Nelson Mandela, delivered to us by Trevor Manuel, began our discussions with a reminder. While our task is to look ahead, he said, 'it would be foolhardy to ignore the anger of the present, because it is so deeply rooted in the past history of denial'. So, one of our challenges was to recognise the history of economic discrimination and deprivation in South Africa.

There is another challenge facing South Africa in the disastrous state of its economy, however. In a speech circulated to conference participants, Professor Wiseman Nkuhlu, Executive Director of the Independent Development Trust, catalogued the economy's ills: per capita income has declined by about 15% in the past decade; more than half the labour force are underemployed or unemployed, and the numbers are growing rapidly in all groups; income distribution is extremely unequal among racial groups and between rural and urban areas; productivity of investment has been declining for many years; the import protection system is grossly inefficient; domestic saving has fallen from 25% to 18%, and investment from 24% to 16% of GDP in the past several years; capital formation in both the public and the private sectors has been in low-productivity activities; government expenditures have risen faster than both GDP and taxes; the balance of payments is 'plagued by structural difficulties' and stunts economic expansion. Ending his summary, Professor Nkuhlu notes 'these few, rather technical thoughts illustrate the depth of the mess we have got ourselves into'.

It was remarkable to me that there was an extremely widespread consensus first that this description of the economy was accurate, and second that it pointed to many of the needed reforms. Countries that have been forced into 'structural adjustment programmes' have often thought they could go on with the policies they had been following, when in fact they could *not* do so. South Africa, through a broad consensus of disparate players present at the conference, knows there must be some fundamental changes in policy. That consensus was a definite highlight.

We heard from Robert Lawrence and Paul Krugman, among others, of the opportunities in world trade and world capital markets, though they also cautioned us about the volatility of the environment and of investor sentiments. In the capital markets, today's darlings can be tomorrow's dogs, and vice versa. The fact that developing country exports of manufactures to the OECD countries constitute only 3% of the OECD manufacturing imports illustrates something of the potential for South Africa. Similarly, within Southern Africa, with an end to the past practices of destabilisation, and with growing trade liberalisation throughout sub-Saharan Africa, the potential for South African exports to Africa is, I think, quite remarkable, whether or not there is progress in the expanding regional groupings – SACU, PTA or SADC.

The information on the potential for exports, even with the caveat of uncertainty about future world trends, was of critical importance for two reasons. First, the many studies cited by Robert Lawrence and others make clear the strong relationships between export growth and income growth. Second, there was a strong, and quite widespread, consensus among participants across the spectrum that South Africa's growth should be export-oriented. There was a clear recognition that export growth leads to significant opportunities for rising incomes and output; that export production leads to learning opportunities and new technologies; that the discipline of the export market can help in the improvement of productivity at the firm and industry level; and that rapid export growth means overall output, and investment can grow rapidly without being constrained by concerns about the balance of payments. This consensus, too, was a conference highlight; it emphasises that there would be broad support for a major element in a new government's economic strategy.

Important differences existed in some of the details – and they are important details – about how fast, and how far, and by what means to reduce the present levels of protection (which guard inefficiencies costly to the entire country). I think those differences will be worked out, however, given the broad support for the basic objectives of rapid growth and of export orientation.

Another major highlight was a fairly broad (though not universal) consensus that the exchange rate of the rand should be seen as a strategic instrument of long-term economic growth, not just a means of bringing external payments into adjustment. The importance of the relationships among the exchange rate, wage rates and productivity of labour was emphasised by several speakers, including former prime minister Nam of South Korea. There was very widespread appreciation of that importance within the conference. Again, there are many important associated issues to be discussed, analysed and settled. But I can assure all of you that a consensus of a diverse group of citizens which recognises the importance of those wage–exchange rate–productivity relationships for economic development – and particularly for the employment growth that is so critical in achieving greater social and economic justice – is a significant highlight of this conference. In many countries, including the United States, the importance of these somewhat technical-sounding matters would simply not be appreciated, much less be the subject of broad consensus.

Investment is obviously a critically important issue, and the substantial decline in investment over the past decade is extremely serious. In observations from several country-oriented papers, as well as from representatives of the private sector, it was made clear that domestic investment, financed by domestic saving, is a key to development. Foreign investment – whether direct foreign investment, official multilateral or bilateral assistance, private-sector portfolio investment or bank lending – can be an important supplement, but it can never carry the bulk of the job in South Africa's capital formation. This view clearly received widespread support as well.

There was considerable discussion of the role of the World Bank and the IMF during the week. Benno Ndulu noted that these institutions, while providing relatively modest amounts of capital themselves, served as important 'gatekeepers' for other lenders and private investors, providing a 'Good Housekeeping Seal of Approval' in international markets.

Investors, both foreign and domestic, are concerned about stability and reasonable certainty in the climate for business and the policy under which they will operate. Indeed, Mr Mandela's remarks talked of the need for South Africa to have 'a will for stability and certainty'. In a new South Africa it is obviously important that this be achieved by a democratic government and society. Too often in Africa and other parts of the developing world despots and repressive regimes have used the argument of 'assuring stability for economic development' as an excuse for denying basic rights. Indeed, I heard a Nigerian political scientist remark at a conference several years ago that so widespread had been this rationalisation of repression in the name of 'stability' that it was as if a banner had been hung across Africa from Dakar to Dar es Salaam, reading 'Silence: development is occurring'.

In our discussions of policy this week, there was a curious and conspicuous lack of attention to fiscal issues. This left Dr Chris Stals of the Reserve Bank with too few instruments at hand to deal with the economy's macro-economic problems. Obviously, the fiscal policies of a democratic government will be of critical importance in maintaining the macro-economic balances that, again, with a very broad consensus, the participants felt would be important. In fact, Mr Mandela's remarks explicitly spoke of 'the need to maintain the macro-economic balances'.

There was, appropriately, some discussion of how best to handle 'shocks' to the economy. South Africa has had, and will have, such shocks, at the very least due to fluctuations in gold and other commodity prices. The uncertainties, and the volatility, of markets were illustrated dramatically in parts of Paul Krugman's paper. I think John Williamson's very useful suggestion that a new government develop some type of stabilisation policy to isolate the economy from major gold-price fluctuations would be helpful. It is a virtual certainty that if the authorities had handled the commodity boom of 1978–80 differently, South Africa would have experienced a very different economic history in the past decade.

One conclusion I have reached after watching countries, companies and universities deal with fluctuating fortunes is that the way to *get* out of trouble is to *stay* out of trouble. The time to deal with the problem of the commodity bust is during the preceding commodity boom. This is a variant on advice from my first-year calculus teacher, who used to ask us: 'If you don't have time to do it right, where will you find time to do it over?'

A lot of attention was given to the types of government intervention in the economy. Duck-woo Nam, Sanjaya Lall and others gave us very useful discussions of the types of intervention that have been successful in other countries, particularly those in East and South-east Asia. There was appropriate caution that South Korea's extraordinary success is not easily replicable, depending, as it did, on a large number of special factors, most of which are not present in South Africa and are unlikely to be in the foreseeable future, such as a highly educated and skilled labour force. But, again, there was a broad consensus: intervention is needed. The 'magic of the market' will not achieve society's goals by itself, especially in South Africa's historical circumstances. I was reminded of the remark of a former colleague, Samuel Bowles, that the 'invisible hand' can become the 'invisible fist', especially for those without the skills to play the game.

I think one can caricature the anti-intervention view popular in some quarters, but not very well represented this week, as a paraphrase of the Hippocratic Oath: 'above all else, don't intervene'. My own preference, which seemed to be echoed in the work reported by the Economic Trends group, would be for a version which reads: 'when intervening, above all else promote, don't protect'.

Perhaps the central issue in South Africa is how to achieve improved real wages for those already employed and, perhaps more important, how to achieve rapid growth in jobs for those now unemployed. How can South Africa turn the details of the critical policy discussion – on the wage rate–exchange rate–productivity–import protection issues – into a positive sum game, a win–win situation, rather than a zero-sum, win–lose proposition?

I was most encouraged by the reports of the growing business–labour–government tripartite approach to these issues – at the level of firms, industries and, perhaps most important, at the economy-wide level. The tough decisions necessary will best be made if there is open discussion, participation and widespread understanding throughout the country. These seem to me the best way to find win–win solutions. That, too, is a highlight for me.

This leads to my final point – not one that came up explicitly, but one that lurked in the background: the policy-making process and the role of technicians, in this case economists, and of the political leaders. And I am thinking of something more than President Harry Truman's plea for a one-armed economist who would not say 'on the one hand, but then on the other hand'.

When I hear economists and economic advisers say that the government won't do what the economists think is 'right' because of what they call 'political constraints', I know the policy process has failed. Economists must understand political realities and objectives, and political leaders must come to understand the overall constraints on choices and the opportunities of different alternatives. Both need to work with each other to achieve that objective.

Good policy, sustainable policy, comes out of a process of discussion and debate, testing options against what is possible. Even the detailed objectives of policy will change as options are explored and constraints probed. I cannot urge strongly enough, based on 30 years of working with and in governments of developing countries, that the policy conversation that seems to be taking place in South Africa be continued, practised, improved, and expanded into a new government.

On the opening night Nelson Mandela closed by telling us 'there is a compelling urgency to reach agreement on an economic vision' for South Africa. I think the degree of consensus expressed by South African participants at this conference on many critically important issues is a remarkable milestone on the road to achieving that vision for a democratic South Africa. It has been a privilege and a pleasure to be an observer, and even a small participant, in this critical process.

Bibliography

ADB. (1992). 'Integration Strategy for Southern Africa', draft of chapter 16, African Development Bank (forthcoming).

Aghevli, B., Khan, M. and Montiel, P. (1991). 'Exchange Rate Policy in Developing Countries: Some Analytical Issues', *International Monetary Fund Occasional Paper,* No. 78.

Alcorta, L. (1992). Finance Capital in Peru. Unpublished D. Phil. Dissertation, University of Sussex: Brighton.

Amsden, A. (1989). *Asia's Next Giant: South Korea and Late Industrialization.* Oxford University Press: New York.

Arrow, Kenneth. (1962). 'The Economic Implications of Learning by Doing', *Review of Economic Studies,* June.

Ayres, Robert. (1983). *Banking on the Poor.* MIT Press: Cambridge (Mass.).

Balassa, B. and Williamson, J. (1987). *Adjusting to Success: Balance of Payments Policy in the East Asian NIE's.* Institute for International Economics: Washington.

Balassa, B. (1990). 'Korea's Development Strategy', in Kwon, Jene K. (ed), *Korean Economic Development,* New York: Greenwood Press.

Bell, M., Ross-Larson, B. and Westphal, L. E. (1989). 'Assessing the Performance of Infant Industries', *Journal of Development Economics,* 16(1), pp. 101–128.

Bell, T. (1990). 'The Prospects for Industrialisation in a New South Africa'. Inaugural lecture delivered at Rhodes University, 17 October.

Bell, T. (1992). 'Should South Africa Further Liberalize Its Foreign Trade?', *ET Working Paper,* No. 16. Economic Trends Research Group: University of Cape Town.

Belli, P., Finger, M. and Ballivan, A. (1993). 'South Africa: Review of Trade Policy Issues', *World Bank Informal Discussion Papers on Aspects of the Economy of South Africa,* Paper No. 4. The World Bank: Washington DC.

Best, M. (1990). *The New Competition.* Polity Press: Oxford.

Bhagwati, Jagdish and Patrick, Hugh (eds.). (1990). *Aggressive Unilateralism: America's 301 Trade Policy and the World Trading System.* University of Michigan Press: Ann Arbor.

BMI. (1992). *Innovation and R&D: Efforts in the Local Electronics Sector.* Prepared by Alan Paul for Business and Marketing Intelligence (BMI), January.

Bruno, Michael. (1993). 'Inflation and Growth in Recent History and Policy: Applications of an Integrated Approach'. Paper presented to the conference celebrating the fiftieth anniversary of the Princeton Essays in International Finance, Princeton University, April 15–16. To be published in Peter Kenen (ed.), *Understanding Interdependence: The Macro-economics of the Open Economy.* Princeton University Press: Princeton (forthcoming).

Buira, A. (1983). 'IMF Financial Programs and Conditionality', *Journal of Development Economics,* Vol. 12(1/2), February/April.

Calvo, G. A., Leiderman, L. and Reinhart, C. (1992). 'Capital Inflows and Real Exchange Rate Appreciation in Latin America: the Role of External Factors'. IMF mimeo.

CEAS. (1993). *The Restructuring of the South African Economy: A Normative Model Approach.* Central Economic Advisory Services: Pretoria.

Claessens, S., Diwan, I., Froot, K., and Krugman, P. (1990). *Market Based Debt Reduction for Developing Countries.* World Bank: Washington DC.

Cline, William. (1983). *International Debt and the Stability of the World Economy.* Institute for International Economics: Washington DC.

Colclough, C. and McCarthy, S. (1980). *The Political Economy of Botswana.* Oxford University Press: Oxford.

Collier, P. and Joshi, V. (1989). 'Exchange Rate Policy in Developing Countries', *Oxford Review of Economic Policy,* Vol. 5(3).

Collins, Susan M. and Rodrik, Dani. (1991). *Eastern Europe and the Soviet Union in the World Economy.* Institute for International Economics: Washington DC.

Corbridge, S. (1988). 'The Asymmetry of Interdependence: The United States and the Geopolitics of International Financial Relations', in *Studies in Comparative International Development,* Vol. XXIII (1), Spring.

Cusumano M. A. (1985). *The Japanese Automobile Industry: Technology and Management at Nissan and Toyota.* Harvard University Press: Cambridge (Mass.).

Cypher, J. (1989). 'Strings Attached', *Dollars and Sense,* December.

Data Research Africa. (1992). 'A Study of Income and Expenditure and Other Socio-Economic Patterns in KwaZulu'. Report Prepared for the KwaZulu Finance Corporation, Durban.

Davies, R. (1990). 'Post-Apartheid Scenarios for the Southern African Region', *Transformation,* 11.

Dertouzos, M. *et al.* (1989). *Made in America: Regaining the Productive Edge.* MIT Press.

Destler, I.M. (1992). *American Trade Politics.* Institute for International Economics: Washington DC.

Dooley, Michael. (1993). 'A Retrospective on the Debt Crisis'. Prepared for conference on the international monetary system: What we know and need to know, Princeton, April 15–16.

Dornbusch, R. and Fischer, S. (1991). 'Moderate Inflation', *NBER Working Paper,* No. 3896. National Bureau for Economic Research.

Dornbusch, R. (1992). 'The Case for Trade Liberalization in Developing Countries', *Journal of Economic Perspectives,* 6(1), pp. 69–86.

Dornbusch, Rudiger. (1993). 'Mexico: How to Restore Competitiveness and Growth'. MIT mimeo.

Dosi, Giovanni. (1988). 'Sources, Procedures, and Microeconomic Effects of Innovation', *Journal of Economic Literature,* September.

Dunning, John H. (1992). 'International Direct Investment Patterns in the 1990's'. Background Paper for United Nations Symposium on Globalization and Developing Countries, The Hague.

Du Plooy, R. M. (1988). 'Productivity in South African Industry', *South African Journal of Economics,* 56(1), pp. 82–93.

Edwards, S. (1989). *Real Exchange Rates, Devaluation and Adjustment. Exchange Rate Policy in Developing Countries.* MIT Press.

Edwards, S. (1992). 'Openness, Trade Liberalisation, and Growth in Developing Countries'. Institute for Policy Reform, mimeo.

Enos, J. (1992). *The Creation of Technological Capabilities in Developing Countries.* Pinter: London.

Fallon, Peter R. (1992). 'An Analysis of Employment and Wage Behaviour in South Africa', *Informal Discussion Papers on Aspects of the Economy of South Africa,* No. 3. Southern Africa Department, World Bank: Washington DC.

Fallon, P., Askoy, A., Tsikata, Y., Belli, P. and Pereira da Silva, L. (1993). 'South Africa: Economic Performance and Policy Implications', *Informal Discussion Papers on Aspects of the Economy of South Africa,* No. 2. Southern Africa Department, World Bank.

Feldstein, Martin. (1986). 'International Debt and Economic Growth: Some Simple Analytics', *National Bureau for Economic Research Working Paper,* No. 2046, NBER: Washington DC.

Fishlow, Albert. (1990). 'The Latin American State', *Journal of Economic Perspectives,* Vol. 4(3), pp. 61–74.

Frankel, Jeffrey A. (1991). 'Is a Yen Bloc Forming in Asia?', in Richard O'Brien (ed.), *Finance and the International Economy: 5.* The Amex Bank Review Prize Essays, Oxford University Press.

Friedman D. (1988). *The Misunderstood Miracle*. Cornell University Press: Ithaca.

Fritsch, Winston and Franco, Gustavo. (1991). 'Brazil and the World Economy in the 1990s: Emerging Trade and Investment Issues'. (Mimeo).

Fukasaku, Kiichiro. (1992). 'Economic Regionalization and Intra-Industry Trade: Pacific–Asian Perspectives', *OECD Development Centre Technical Paper*, No. 53, February.

Garnaut, Ross. (1991). 'Australia Revolutionizes: The New Trade Commitments', *International Economic Insights*, July/August, pp. 2–5.

GATT. (1992). *International Trade 90–91*, Volumes I and II. General Agreement on Tariffs and Trade: Geneva.

Gerson, J. (1992). *The Determinants of Corporate Ownership and Control in South Africa*. University of California, Los Angeles.

Gisselquist, D. (1981). *The Political Economics of International Bank Lending*. Praeger: New York.

Goldin, I. (1992). 'External Financial Assistance and Post-Apartheid South Africa', *Economic Policy Research Series*, No. 9. University of the Western Cape.

Government of Malaysia. (1991). *The Second Outline Perspective Plan 1991–2000*. Kuala Lumpur.

Hart, Gill. (1992). 'A Malaysian Model for Post-Apartheid South Africa? The Uses and Abuses of Comparative Cases.' Unpublished paper, July.

Helleiner, G. K. (forthcoming). 'Introduction', in G. K. Helleiner (ed.), *Trade Policy and Industrialisation in Turbulent Times*.

Helpman, E. and Krugman, P. (1985). *Market Structure and Foreign Trade*. MIT Press: Cambridge (Mass.).

Holden, M. (1991). 'Real Exchange Rates and Their Measurement, *South African Journal of Economics*, 59(1).

Holden, M. (1992). 'Trade Reform: Finding the Right Road', *South African Journal of Economics*, 60(3), pp. 249–262.

Hoffman, K. and Kaplinsky, R. (1988). *Driving Force: The Global Restructuring of Technology, Labor and Investment in the Automobile and Components Industries*. Westview Press: Boulder, Colorado.

Hudson, D. J. (1981). 'Botswana's Membership of the Southern African Customs Union', in C. Harvey (ed.), *Papers on the Economy of Botswana*. Heinemann: London.

International Development Research Centre. (1992). *Towards a Science and Technology Policy for a Democratic South Africa*. December.

IDC. (1990). *Modification of the Application of Protection Policy*. Report of the Industrial Development Corporation, June.

International Monetary Fund. (1992). 'Issues and Developments in International Trade Policy', *World Economic and Financial Surveys*. International Monetary Fund: Washington DC.

Isaksen, J. (1993). 'Prospects for SACU after Apartheid', in Bertil Oden (ed.), *Southern Africa After Apartheid: Regional Integration and External Resources*. The Scandinavian Institute of African Studies: Uppsala.

Jacobsson, S. (1993). 'The Length of the Infant Industry Period: Evidence from the Engineering Industry in South Korea', *World Development*, 21(3), pp. 407–420.

Jacquemin, Alexis and Sapir, André. (1991). 'Europe Post-1992: Internal and External Liberalization', *American Economic Review*, pp. 166–170.

Joffe, A., Kaplan, D. E., Kaplinsky, R. and Lewis, D. (1993). 'Framework for Industrial Revival in South Africa', *Economic Trends Group Industrial Strategy Working Paper*. DPRU: University of Cape Town.

Kahn, B. (1991). 'The Crisis and South Africa's Balance of Payments', in S. Gelb (ed.), *South Africa's Economic Crisis*. David Philip: Cape Town.

Kahn, B. (1992). 'South African Exchange Rate Policy, 1979–1991', *Centre for the Study of the South African Economy and International Finance Research Paper*, No. 7. London School of Economics.

Kaplan, David. (1990). *The Crossed Line. The South African Telecommunications Industry in Transition*. Wits University Press: Johannesburg.

Kaplinsky, R. and Hoffman, K. (1992). *Transnational Corporations and the Transfer of New Management Practices to Developing Countries*. Report prepared for the United Nations Centre on Transnational Companies. Sussex Research Associates: Brighton.

Kaplinsky, R. (1992). 'The New Flexibility, Promoting Social and Economic Efficiency', in S. Holland (ed.), forthcoming.

Kaplinsky, R. and Posthuma, A. (1993). *Organisational Change in Zimbabwe's Manufacturing Sector*. Report prepared for United Nations University (Intech). Institute of Development Studies: Brighton.

Katseli, Louka T. (1992). 'Foreign Direct Investment and Trade Interlinkages in the 1990s: Experience and Prospects of Developing Countries. Background paper for United Nations Symposium on Globalization and Developing Countries.' The Hague. Reprinted as *Centre for Economic Policy Research Discussion Paper*, No. 687, July. London.

Knuper, R. (1983). 'The Conditioning of National Policymaking by International Law: the Standby Agreements of the International Monetary Fund', in *International Journal of the Sociology of Law*, 11.

Krugman, P. (ed.) (1986). *Strategic Trade Policy and the New International Economics*. MIT Press: Cambridge (Mass.).

Krugman, P. (1991). 'Has the Adjustment Process Worked?', *Policy Analyses in International Economics*, 34. Institute for International Economics: Washington DC.

Lall, S. (1990). *Building Industrial Competitiveness in Developing Countries*. OECD Development Centre: Paris.

Lall, S. (1991). 'Trade, Competitiveness and Foreign Investment in Manufacturing Industry'. Paper for Kenya–South Africa Trade and Investment Study. United Nations Development Programme: Oxford.

Lall, S. (1992a). 'Technological Capabilities and Industrialization', *World Development*, 20(2), pp. 165–186.

Lall, S. (1992b). 'Structural Problems of African Industry', in F. Stewart, S. Wangwe and S. Lall (eds.), *Alternative Development Strategies in Sub-Saharan Africa*. Macmillan: London.

Lall, S. (1992c). 'Technological Capabilities and the Role of Government in Developing Countries', *Greek Economic Review*, 14(1).

Lall, S. and associates (1992). *World Bank Support of Industrialization in Korea, India and Indonesia*. World Bank Operations Evaluation Department: Washington.

Lall, S. (1993). 'What Will Make South Africa Internationally Competitive?'. Paper presented at The Aspen Institute–Idasa conference, South Africa's International Economic Relations in the 1990s, April 27–30. South Africa.

Lawrence, Robert Z. (1987). 'Imports in Japan: Closed Markets or Minds?', *Brookings Papers on Economic Activity*, 1987(2).

Lawrence, Robert Z. (1990). 'U.S. Current Account Adjustment: An Appraisal', in *Brookings Papers on Economic Activity*, 2.

Lawrence, Robert Z. (1991). 'How Open is Japan?' in Paul Krugman (ed.), *Trade with Japan: Has the Door Opened Wider?* University of Chicago Press for the National Bureau of Economic Research: Chicago.

Lawrence, Robert Z. (1991). 'Emerging Regional Arrangements: Building Blocks or Stumbling Blocks?', in Richard O'Brien (ed.), *Finance and the International Economy: 5*. The Amex Bank Review Prize Essays: Oxford University Press.

Lawrence, Robert Z. and Litan, Robert E. (1990). 'The World Trading System after the Uruguay Round', in *Boston University International Law Journal*, Vol. 8(2).

Lawrence, Robert Z. and Schultze, Charles (eds.) (1987). *Barriers to European Growth: A Transatlantic View*. Brookings Institution: Washington DC.

Legassick, M. (1974). 'South Africa: Capital Accumulation and Violence', *Economy and Society*, Vol. 3(3), August.

Liebenstein, H. (1966). 'Allocative Efficiency vs. X- Efficiency', *American Economic Review*, 56, pp. 392–415.

Lipietz, A. (1987). *Mirages and Miracles*. London: Verso Publishers.

Lim, Linda Y.C. and Fong, Pang Eng. (1991). *Foreign Direct Investment and Industrialisation in Malaysia, Singapore, Taiwan and Thailand*. OECD Development Centre: Paris.

Lipton, M. (1989). 'The Challenge of Sanctions', *South African Journal of Economics*, 57(4), pp. 336–61.

Loxley, J. (1990). 'Structural Adjustment Programmes in Africa: Ghana and Zambia', *Review of African Political Economy*, No. 47, Spring.

Lucas, R. E. (1988). 'On the Mechanics of Economic Development', *Journal of Monetary Economics*, 22(1), pp. 3–42.

Lustig, N., Bosworth, B. and Lawrence, Robert Z. (eds.) (1992). *North American Free Trade: Assessing the Impact*. Brookings Institution: Washington DC.

McCarthy, C.L. (1986). *The Southern African Customs Union*. Report prepared for the Central Economic Advisory Services: Pretoria.

McCarthy, C. L. (1988). 'Structural Development of South African Manufacturing Industry – A Policy Perspective', *South African Journal of Economics*, 56(1), pp. 1–23.

McFarland, E.L. (1983). 'Benefits to RSA and her Exports to the BLS Countries', in M.A. Oommen, F.K. Ingonji, and L.D. Ngcongco (eds.), *Botswana's Economy Since Independence*. Tata McGraw-Hill: New Delhi.

Makgetla, N.S. (1993). 'Savings, Growth and Redistribution: A Statistical Approach.' Paper prepared for the Macro-Economic Research Group (MERG), and presented to MERG Workshop, 13–23 April. Johannesburg.

Malaysian Ministry of Finance. (1992/93). *Economic Report*. Kuala Lumpur.

Naudé, S. (1992). 'Economic Restructuring and Growth.' Paper presented at conference on Blueprint for Prosperity. Johannesburg.

Nelson, R. R. and Winter, S. J. (1982). *An Evolutionary Theory of Economic Change*. Harvard University Press: Cambridge (Mass.).

Nkuhlu, W. (1993). 'The South African Economy: Investment and Restructuring.' (Mimeo).

Noland, Marcus. (1990). *Pacific Basin Developing Countries: Prospects for the Future*. Institute for International Economics: Washington DC.

NPI. *Productivity Statistics*. National Productivity Institute: Pretoria.

ODI. (1983). *Does the IMF Really Help Developing Countries?* ODI Briefing Paper. Overseas Development Institute: London.

OECD. (1987). *Structural Adjustment and Economic Performance*. OECD: Paris.

Ovenden, K. and Cole, T. (1989). *Apartheid and International Finance*. Penguin: Australia.

Pack, H. and Westphal, L. E. (1986). 'Industrial Strategy and Technological Change: Theory versus Reality', *Journal of Development Economics*, 22(1), pp. 87–128.

Pack, H. (1988). 'Industrialization and Trade', in H. B. Chenery and T. N. Srinivasan (eds.), *Handbook of Development Economics*, Volume 1. North-Holland: Amsterdam.

Pack, H. (1993). 'Productivity and Industrial Development in Sub-Saharan Africa', *World Development*, p. 7.

Padayachee, V. (1988). 'The Politics of International Economic Relations: South Africa and the International Monetary Fund, 1975 and Beyond', in John Suckling and Landeg White (eds.), *After Apartheid: Renewal of the South African Economy*. James Currey: London.

Padayachee, Vishnu. (1992). 'The IMF and World Bank in Post-Apartheid South Africa: Prospects and Dangers', *ET Working Paper*, No. 6. Economic Trends Research Group: University of Cape Town.

Padayachee, V. and Goldin, I. (1992). 'External Financial Assistance and Post-Apartheid South Africa', *Economic Policy Research Series (EPRP)*, No. 9.

Parfitt, T. (1993). 'Which African Agenda for the Nineties? The ECA–World Bank Alternatives', *Journal of International Development*, Vol. 5(1), Jan/Feb.

Porter, Michael E. (1990). *The Competitive Advantage of Nations*. The Free Press: New York.

PTA. 1992. *PTA Trade and Development Strategy: Market Integration and Economic Transformation for Sustainable Growth*. Adopted by the PTA Heads of State and Governments, Lusaka, 30–31 January.

Pratt, C. (1983). 'The Global Impact of the World Bank', in Jill Torrie (ed.), *Banking on Poverty*. Toronto.

Prowse, M. (1993). 'In Search of the Secret of Asia's Economic Miracle', *Business Day*, April 30.

Ramos, M. (1991). 'The Development of the Forward Exchange Market in South Africa', *Centre for the Study of the South African Economy and International Finance Research Paper*, No. 3. London School of Economics.

Rodrik, D. (1992a). 'Closing the Productivity Gap: Does Trade Liberalization Really Help?', in G. K. Helleiner (ed.), *Trade Policy, Industrialization and Development*. Clarendon Press: Oxford.

Rodrik, D. (1992b). 'The Limits of Trade Policy Reform in Developing Countries', *Journal of Economic Perspectives*, 6(1), pp. 87–105.

R.S.A. (1987). *Report of the Commission of Inquiry into the Tax Structure of the Republic of South Africa*, RP 34/1187. Government Printer: Pretoria.

R.S.A. (1988). *White Paper on the Report of the Commission of Inquiry into the Tax Structure of the Republic of South Africa*. WP C-88. Government Printer: Pretoria.

Sachs, J. (1984). 'Theoretical Issues in International Borrowing', *Princeton Studies in International Finance*, No. 54. Princeton University.

Sacob. (1991a). *A Concept for the Development of a New Industrial Policy for South Africa*. South African Chamber of Business, May.

Sacob. (1991b). *Reaction of the South African Chamber of Business to the IDC Report on the Modification of the Application of Protection Policy*. South African Chamber of Business, August.

SADC. (1992). *Treaty of the Southern African Development Community*. Adopted at the SADC summit, Windhoek.

SADCC. (1992). *Towards Economic Integration*. Theme Document for 1992 Consultative Meeting, Maputo, January 29–31.

Sapir, André. (1992). 'Regional Integration in Europe', *Economic Journal*, November, pp. 1491–1506.

Scerri, M. (1988). 'Research and Development in South African Manufacturing Industries', *South African Journal of Economics*, 56(2/3), pp. 111–123.

Scerri, M. (1990). 'Research and Development and the International Competitiveness of the South African Manufacturing Sector', *South African Journal of Economics*, 58(3), pp. 341–56.

Schmitz, H. (1993). 'Little Shoemakers and Fordist Giants: Tale of a Supercluster?' Paper prepared for Workshop on Intra-firm and Inter-firm Reorganisation in Third World Manufacturing held at the Institute of Development Studies, April 14–16.

Shapiro, H. and Taylor, L. (1990). 'The State and Industrial Strategy', *World Development*, 18(6), pp. 861–878.

Stiglitz, J.E. (1987). 'Learning to Learn, Localized Learning and Technological Progress', in P. Dasgupta and P. Stoneman (eds.), *Economic Policy and Technological Development*. Cambridge University Press: Cambridge.

Stiglitz, J. E. (1989). 'Markets, Market Failures and Development', *American Economic Review Papers and Proceedings*, 79(2), pp. 197–202.

Stoneman, C. (1993). 'The World Bank, Income Distribution and Employment: Some Lessons for South Africa.' Paper delivered at the conference on Sustainable Development for Post-Apartheid South Africa, 25-26 March.

Strydom, P. D. F. (1987). 'South Africa in World Trade', *South African Journal of Economics*, 55(3), pp. 203–218.

Stuart, J. (1992). *The Economics of the Common Monetary Area in Southern Africa*. Economic Research Unit, University of Natal, Durban.

Tarp, Finn. (1993). 'South Africa: Background and Possibilities for Danish Traditional Assistance'. Danish Foreign Affairs Department. (Mimeo).

Thurow, Lester. (1992). *Head to Head: The Coming Economic Battle among Japan, Europe, and America*. Morrow: New York.

Tjonneland, E. (1992). *Southern Africa after Apartheid*. Chr. Michelsen Institute: Norway.

UNCTAD. (1991). *Handbook of International Trade and Development Statistics*. United Nations Conference on Trade and Development: Geneva.

UNCTC. (1991). *World Investment Report 1991: The Triad in Foreign Direct Investment*. United Nations Centre on Transnational Corporations: New York.

UNCTC. (1992). *World Investment Report 1992: Transnational Corporations as Engines of Growth*. United Nations Centre on Transnational Corporations: New York.

United Nations Economic Commission for Latin America. (1991). 'Latin American and Caribbean Trade and Investment Relations with the United States in the 1980s', *IDB–ECLAC Working Papers on Trade in the Western Hemisphere*, November.

Van der Merwe, E.J. (1990). 'Forward Exchange Cover Transactions of the South African Reserve Bank', *South African Reserve Bank Quarterly Bulletin,* March.

Van der Riet, D. and Hendy, I. M. (1986). 'Just in Time: An Analysis from the South African Perspective with Particular Reference to the Western Cape', *MBA Research Paper,* University of Cape Town Graduate School of Business.

Wade, R. (1990). *Governing the Market.* Princeton University Press: Princeton.

Wells, Louis T. (1992). 'Mobile Exporters: The New Foreign Investors in East Asia'. Paper presented at National Bureau of Economic Research conference on Foreign Direct Investment Today, May. Cambridge, (Mass.).

Westphal, L. E. (1990). 'Industrial Policy in an Export-Propelled Economy: Lessons from South Korea's Experience', *Journal of Economic Perspectives,* 4(3), pp. 41–59.

Williamson, J. (1982). 'A Survey of the Literature on the Optimal Peg', *Journal of Development Economics,* Vol. 11.

Williamson, J. (1993). 'Exchange Rate Policy in South Africa: Export-led Growth, Foreign Investment and Capital Flight'. Paper presented to The Aspen Institute–Idasa Conference on South Africa's International Economic Relations in the 1990s, April 27–30.

Wilson, F. and Ramphele, M. (1989). *Uprooting Poverty: The South African Challenge.* W. W. Norton and Co.: New York.

World Bank. (1987). *World Development Report 1987.* The World Bank: Washington, DC.

World Bank. (1989). *Sub-Saharan Africa: From Crisis to Sustainable Growth.* The World Bank: Washington DC.

World Bank (1991). *World Development Report 1991.* The World Bank: Washington DC.

World Bank. (1992a). *Global Economic Prospects and the Developing Countries.* The World Bank: Washington DC.

World Bank. (1992b). *World Development Report 1992.* The World Bank: Washington DC.

World Bank. (1992c). *World Bank Support for Industrialization in Korea, India and Indonesia.* Operations Evaluation Department, World Bank: Washington DC.

Index